6014   186774

AN INTRODUCTION TO THE PROCEDURE OF THE HOUSE OF COMMONS

AN INTRODUCTION TO THE PROCEDURE *of* THE HOUSE OF COMMONS

By

Francis Montriou

SIR GILBERT CAMPION, G.C.B.

Clerk of the House of Commons

LONDON

MACMILLAN & CO. LTD

1950

First Edition 1929
Second Edition 1947
Reprinted, with corrections, 1950

PRINTED IN GREAT BRITAIN BY
THE GARDEN CITY PRESS LTD., AT LETCHWORTH, HERTFORDSHIRE

FOREWORD

An Introduction to the Procedure of the House of Commons appeared originally in 1929. A second edition was already in print in 1937, but was held back to await the publication of the new edition of Erskine May's *Parliamentary Practice*, the standard work on parliamentary procedure, which must be continually referred to in any brief account of the subject. When, after a long delay consequent principally upon the war, May's *Parliamentary Practice* was published in the early summer of this year the publication of my *Introduction* was immediately taken in hand; and the necessary revision was made to incorporate the permanent changes in the rules, temporary changes of an emergency character being added in an Appendix.

This book is intended to serve as a practical guide to the procedure of the House of Commons. Apart from the first two chapters, the subject-matter is confined to a description of procedure in the strict sense. The arrangement adopted is to proceed from the general to the particular—from the opening of a new Parliament and the arrangement of the business of a whole session to the items which compose an individual sitting; and from an explanation of the rules which govern debate, generally, to the more specialized rules which apply to particular classes of business or forms of proceeding, such as motions, public bills, financial business, and private legislation. To this account of existing procedure I have prefixed a brief survey of parliamentary law and machinery in Chapter II, and in Chapter I a review of the development of procedure in relation to the main stages in the evolution of the House of Commons. In these two chapters I have attempted to provide, however briefly and imperfectly, the modern setting and the historical background for the rules and forms of procedure itself.

I am constantly reminded how easy it is to entangle oneself in the details of procedure, and how hard to reach a standpoint from which they can be seen in orderly arrangement. If there is a short cut to the mastery of technicalities, it consists in grasping the relationship between procedure and functions. The evolution of Parliament is largely a history of the procedural methods by which the House of Commons acquired its constitutional functions. In modern times it is the functions of the House which determine its procedure. The following is a summary sketch of this relationship.

The general function of the House of Commons is deliberation. So it requires rules for the conduct of debate, in general, and for the maintenance of order during debate. Such rules, in some form or other, are as essential for a debating society as for a parliamentary body. They comprise rules about the moving of motions, the proposing and putting of questions, rules of relevancy, etc. To these, in view of the chronic congestion of business from which it suffers, the House adds rules for the limitation or "closure" of debate. This part of procedure forms the subject of Chapter V of this book.

The House has also certain specific functions—the control of finance, the control of policy, legislation—each of which is served by one or more "forms of proceeding" (as the more complicated procedural constructions, built up out of the simple rules of the motion, with their own specialized rules are called). Thus, for the control of taxation, the House has evolved the Committee of Ways and Means, the "Budget" and Finance Bill: and, for expenditure, the group consisting of the Committee of Supply and Consolidated Fund and Appropriation Bills, and also the Committee of the Whole House on Financial Resolutions. This part of procedure is dealt with in Chapter VIII.

For the control of policy there is a whole group of forms of proceeding : the Address in reply to the King's speech; Motions on going into Committee of Supply; Substantive Motions; Motions for the adjournment of the House; Questions to Ministers, etc. These are mostly covered in Chapters III (Part II) and IV (Part II).

For legislation, there are the various readings and stages of Public Bills and Private Bills and also a new form of control —that for delegated legislation. See Chapters VI and IX and Appendix II.

In the course of their long period of evolution it may be that forms of proceeding invented for one function have come to serve the purposes of another function. There is much in the modern working of the Supply group of forms to show that they are consciously used for the control of policy instead of finance. A similar shift of function may be thought to have occurred, from the financial to the legislative function, in the case of the procedure on Financial Resolutions.

This is the substantive part of procedure. In addition there is a section which lays down the rules for the division of the time of the session between the various classes of business, and for the arrangement of the minor items of business in the programme of the sitting. See Chapter IV (Part II) and V.

From this point of view the different parts of procedure fall into position, and their arrangement can be described in a sentence. The functions of the House have created for their particular use a variety of forms of proceeding, governed by general and special rules, which require a proper allotment of the time of the House and suitable personal assistance and material equipment for their disposal.

It remains to offer my thanks for valuable assistance generously given to Sir Cecil Carr, K.C.B., Counsel to Mr. Speaker, who contributed new material in respect of Statutory Instruments; to Mr. E. A. Fellowes, C.B., Second Clerk Assistant, who re-wrote the section "Reform by Standing Order" in Chapter I; and to Mr. T. G. B. Cocks, who saved me much labour in bringing this edition up to date, and who also contributed the Appendix on Emergency Procedure.

G. F. M. C.

August 1946.

AUTHOR'S NOTE ON 1950 REPRINT

THE Second Edition of this book has been out of print for a year. A demand for an immediate reprint has presented me with something of a problem. Extensive changes in procedure, involving the revision and the reprinting of the Standing Orders, have been introduced since the publication of this edition. This fact would seem to call for a complete re-writing of the text. Such an undertaking would, however, require a considerable time, and it should in any case await the next (fifteenth) edition of May's *Parliamentary Practice*, references to which must inevitably abound in the more summary treatment of procedure followed in this *Introduction*.

In this reprint, therefore, a compromise has been attempted, which can only be made intelligible by taking account of the somewhat complicated process of revision which circumstances imposed on the action of the House of Commons. As the new Appendix IV (to which I shall refer) implies, this action was taken in two stages. (1) Between 1939 and 1945 a series of changes was made in the procedure of the House. As it was impossible to foresee which of these changes were solely due to the conditions of the emergency and which were likely to become permanent, they were not incorporated in the Standing Orders, but effected temporarily by sessional orders. (2) In the revision of procedure completed in 1948 a new set of Standing Orders was adopted, which incorporated some of the provisions of the emergency period, while rejecting others, and also added certain new provisions. In the Second Edition the text naturally reproduced the Standing Order position, and the provisions of the emergency period were relegated to an Appendix—Appendix IV, "Emergency Procedure."

What has been done in this reprint, then, is as follows : The text has been left almost as it stood, except for the citation of Standing Orders by their new numbers. But Appendix IV, "Emergency Procedure," has been replaced by a new Appendix which incorporates all the alterations in procedure since 1939 now made permanent. The reader's attention is directed to this Appendix by footnotes to the relevant portions of the text. All the post-war changes are thus clearly indicated by linking up the old procedure (in the text) with the new procedure (in the Appendix)—an arrangement which may be thought to give this reprint some temporary historical value for the student.

It should be noted that references to May's *Parliamentary Practice* are to the fourteenth edition.

My thanks are due to Mr. Charles Gordon, a senior clerk in the Journal Office, for his carefulness and dispatch in drafting the new Appendix IV and in " spotting " the places in the text where changes in procedure had to be indicated.

G. F. M. C.

March 1950.

CONTENTS

LIST OF AUTHORITIES xvii

Chapter I
HISTORICAL DEVELOPMENT OF PARLIAMENTARY PROCEDURE

PAGE

Scope of procedure of House of Commons 1
   Inseparable from procedure of whole Parliament . . . 2
   Historical approach necessary 2
      Constitutional importance of early procedure . . . 3
      Character of Parliament determined by pre-parliamentary constitutional framework 4

FOUR PERIODS OF PARLIAMENTARY PROCEDURE

FIRST PERIOD, 1300–1547

Early relations of King, Lords and Commons in Parliament . . 5
   Parliament a unitary body for decision 7
Functions of Commons 8
Procedure in legislation 9
   Statutes and ordinances 10
   Bills and Statutes 10
      'Common' Petitions 11
      Separate Petitions 11
      Petitions and Bills 11
      Individual Petitions—Private Bills 13
   Settlement of inter-parliamentary relations 14

SECOND PERIOD, 1547–1660

Development of Procedure 15
   1. Rules of Order in debate 15
   2. Motions 20
   3. Bills 22
   4. Committees 25

THIRD PERIOD, 1660–1832

Development of procedure 29
   Financial procedure 30
   Growth of Cabinet control 36
      Public money S.O.'s—King's Consent 36

FOURTH PERIOD, 1833–

New problem of parliamentary congestion 37
Control of parliamentary time 37
Reform by Standing Order 38
   First S.O. period 1833–1880 39
   Second S.O. Period 1880– 39
   Some results of S.O. reforms 40

Summary of development of procedure 41
   Corresponding development of parliamentary machinery . . 42
      The Speaker 42
      Committees 43

PAGE

Relations between legislature and executive main determinant of
    procedure 44
    Examples from foreign and Empire parliaments . . . 45
Principles and characteristics of House of Commons procedure . 47
    Reasons why many rules not universally applicable. . . 48
        Constitutional differences 49
        Special problems of congestion 49
        Survivals 49
    Principles generally applicable 50
        Moderation 51
        Fair Play 52
    Ceremonial element in procedure. 54

Chapter II
PARLIAMENTARY LAW AND MACHINERY
The Background to the Business of the House 57

DISQUALIFICATIONS FROM MEMBERSHIP

Miscellaneous disqualifications 57
Offices of Profit 59
    (1) which disqualify 59
    (2) which do not disqualify 60
Resignation of seat. Chiltern Hundreds, etc. . . . 62
Payment of Members 62

PRIVILEGES OF THE HOUSE OF COMMONS

Claimed by the Speaker at the beginning of a Parliament . . 63
    (1) formal, (2) freedom from arrest, (3) freedom of speech . 63
Not so claimed 66
    (1) right to provide for its proper constitution . . 66
    (2) power to commit for contempt 70
    (3) proceedings upon complaint of breach of privilege . . 72

THE SPEAKER AND OFFICERS OF THE HOUSE

Powers and duties of the Speaker 73
Development of the modern conception of the Speakership . . 75
The Chairman of Ways and Means, and Deputy-Chairman . . 78
Other Officers of the House 79

THE PALACE OF WESTMINSTER

The modern building and its administration 82
The Chamber 83
    Characteristics 83
    Members' seats 83
    Admission of Strangers, and the Press 85

PARLIAMENTARY PAPERS

Papers issued by the House in connexion with its business . . 86
    Papers issued daily 86
    Papers issued periodically 90
    The *Journal* 91
Papers presented to Parliament ('Accounts and Papers'). . . 92
    Presentation of Papers 93
        Returns, 'Command' Papers, 'Act' Papers . . . 93
    Printing and Publication of Papers 94
    Stationery Office Publications 96
Official Reports of Debates 97

Chapter III
A NEW PARLIAMENT AND THE WORK OF THE SESSION
I. MEETING OF PARLIAMENT

PAGE

A New Parliament 99
   Summoning and Dissolution 99
   Meeting 100
   Election of Speaker 100
   Swearing of Members 103
A New Session 104
   Prorogation of Parliament 104
   Effect of prorogation 105
   Alteration of date to which Parliament stands prorogued . 105
   Adjournment of the House 106
   Opening of New Session 107
   The King's Speech 107
   Debate upon the Address 108

II. TIME-TABLE OF THE SESSION

Main varieties of Business 109
   1. Bills: 'Public' and 'Private' Bills, 'Government' and 'Private
     Members'' Bills 109
   2. Motions: 'Substantive' Motions, Motions for the Adjourn-
     ment of the House 110
   3. Financial business 111
Control of the time of the House by the Government . . . 112
   Limitations upon Government control 113
   Share of Opposition in control of time and choice of Business . 114
Analysis of sessional business into groups 114
   1. First Group: Private Members' Business 115
   2. Second Group: 'Incidental' Business 116
   3. Third Group: 'Routine and Financial' Business . . . 118
   4. Fourth Group: Government 'Programme' of legislation . 122
     Average amount of time per session taken by each group . 122
Division of session into two parts 123
   1. First part: Beginning of session to Easter—Supplementary
     Estimates and Private Members' Business . . 124
   2. Second part: After Easter to Prorogation—Budget and
     Finance Bill, Main Estimates ('Allotted' days),
     Government Bills 125
Alternative use of autumn sittings 126
Plan of resuming Bills at stage reached in previous session . . 127
Methods adopted by the Government to secure more time . . 128
   1. 'Business' Motions 128
   2. 'Allocation of Time' ('Guillotine') Motions . . . 129

Chapter IV
A SITTING AND THE VARIOUS ITEMS OF BUSINESS
I. OPENING AND CLOSE OF SITTING

Normal hours of sitting 131
Close of the sitting 132
The Eleven o'Clock Rule 132
   1. Interruption 132
   2. Unopposed Business 132
   3. Adjournment of the House 133
   The 'projected' moment of interruption 133
   Adjournment on Friday 134
   Exempted business 134

PAGE

Methods of adjourning the House 136
Suspension of a sitting 136
The Quorum and counting the House 137

II. THE VARIOUS ITEMS OF BUSINESS
TIME-TABLE OF A SITTING . . . 138
1. Business taken immediately after Prayers 140
   Motions for New Writs 140
2. Unopposed Private Business 140
3. Presentation of Public Petitions 142
4. Motions for Unopposed Returns 144
5. Questions to Ministers 145
   Method of asking (a) oral questions, (b) questions for written
     answer, (c) 'private notice' questions 146-7
   Who may be questioned ? 148
   Rules relating to form and subject-matter of questions . 148
6. Introduction of New Members 152
7. Adjournment Motions on the Ground of Urgency . . . 152
   Procedure under S.O. No.9 152
   Rules relating to subject-matter of motions . . . 153
   Rules governing debate on motions 155
8. Business taken after any Adjournment Motion under S.O. No. 9 155
   (1) Motions for leave of absence 155
   (2) Oral notice of intention to move motion . . . 155
   (3) Personal explanations 158
   (4) Motions to set up 'money' committees 159
   (5) Lords' Amendments to a Public Bill 159
   (6) Privilege Motions 159
9. Business taken 'at the Commencement of Public Business' . 159
   (1) Presentation of Public Bills 160
   (2) 'Business' Motions moved by a Minister . . . 160
   (3) Motion to introduce Bill under 'ten minute' rule . . 161
   (4) Privilege motions (when notice has been given) . . 161
10. Public Business 162
    The Orders of the Day 162
    Procedure in dealing with Orders of the Day . . . 162
    Reading the Orders of the Day 163
    Dropped Orders 165
    Motions among Orders of the Day 165
11. Suspension of Business at 7.30 165
    Interruption at 7.30 on Private Members' Wednesdays . 166
12. Business regularly taken after 11 o'clock 166
    Proceedings in pursuance of Acts 166

Chapter V
FORMS AND RULES OF DEBATE
A. Motions

All forms of debate reducible to a single elementary type: Motion—
  Question—Decision 168
This process considered in relation to Substantive Motions . . 168
The Question—'proposing' the Question—'putting' the Question . 170
Motions other than substantive divided into
  (1) Ancillary Motions. 171
  (2) Superseding Motions, consisting of
        (a) 'Dilatory' Motions 172
        (b) The 'Previous' Question 172
  (3) Amendments 173
      Rules governing Amendments 173
      Amendments to Amendments 176

CONTENTS

Rule that the same Question may not be twice offered in the same session 177
Rule against anticipation 178

B. *Divisions*

Machinery for Divisions 178
Method of taking a Division 179
Points of Order arising in connexion with Divisions . . . 181
The casting Vote of the Chair 182
Personal pecuniary interest 183

C. *The Closure*

Closure divided into three kinds 184
  (1) 'Simple' 184
  (2) 'Contingent' 185
  (3) 'Special' 186
Closure at moment of interruption 186
Selection of Amendments 187

D. *Rules and Conventions of Behaviour in Debate*

Rules for addressing the House 188
Relevancy 190
Rule against speaking more than once 192
Breaches of Order in speaking 193
Rules of conduct for Members while not speaking . . . 195
  Powers of the Chair to maintain order 196

Chapter VI

PUBLIC BILLS

Main distinction between Public Bills 199
The Form of a Public Bill 199
Stages and Intervals between Stages 201

INTRODUCTION AND FIRST READING

(1) Bills introduced on Order of the House 202
With preliminaries
  (*a*) Resolutions of a Committee of the Whole House in case of 'Money' Bills 202
  (*b*) Resolution of a Committee of the Whole House in case of other Bills 202
Without preliminaries
  (*a*) As an ordinary Motion 202
  (*b*) As a Motion under S.O. No. 12 ('Ten Minutes Rule') . . 202
(2) Bills presented, without an Order, under S.O. 35 (1) . . 203
(3) Bills brought down from the Lords 203
Steps to be taken by a Member in introducing a Bill . . . 204

SECOND-READING STAGE

Preliminary Questions 205
Debate on Second Reading. Method of opposing
  (1) 'Six (Three) months' Amendment 207
  (2) 'Reasoned' Amendment 208

COMMITTEE STAGE

Committal 209
Functions of Committee 210
Powers of Committee over Bill 211

CONTENTS

	PAGE
Instructions	213
Purpose of a special Instruction	213
Rules for moving and debating Instructions	214
Proceedings in committee on a Bill	215
Bills committed *pro forma*	219
Report of Progress. Report of Bill	220

REPORT STAGE

Consideration of Bill, as amended	221
Proceedings on Report of Bill	222
Recommittal of Bill after Report	223

THIRD-READING STAGE

Debate on Third Reading	223
Communication of Bill to Lords. Messages to and from Lords	224

LORDS' AMENDMENTS

Bill considered	225
(1) on a subsequent day	225
(2) forthwith	225
Proceedings on consideration of Lords' Amendments	226
Stages in process of securing agreement between the two Houses	227
Indorsement of Bills	229
Royal Assent to Acts	229
Procedure under the Parliament Act, 1911	230

Chapter VII

COMMITTEES

Modern Committee system	232
Committees of the Whole House	233
Appointment	234
Procedure on going into Committee	235
Chairman	235
Procedure in Committee	236
Report of Progress, and on completion of Business	236
Procedure on consideration of Report	237
Standing Committees	238
Appointment and Constitution	238
Chairmen	240
Sittings	241
Procedure	241
Rules of Debate	242
Select Committees	243
Appointment and Order of Reference	243
Nominations	243
Special Powers	244
Sittings	245
Proceedings	246
Record of Proceedings	247
Procedure in considering Draft Report	247
Procedure on Bill	248
Presentation of Report	248
Joint Committees	249
Appointment	249
Procedure	250
Report	250
Sessional Committees	251

CONTENTS

Chapter VIII

FINANCE IN THE HOUSE OF COMMONS

	PAGE
The Financial System	253
Method of Control by the House of Commons	255
Plan of arrangement of chapter	258
Principles of financial procedure	259
Table of financial business	260

I. EXPENDITURE

Committee of Supply and of Ways and Means	261
Committee of Supply	262
Supply business	262
1. Ordinary annual ('Main') Estimates	263
2. Supplementary Estimates	264
3. Votes on Account	264
4. Excess Votes	265
5. Votes of Credit	266
6. Exceptional Grants (when presented as Estimates)	266
Allotted Days and conclusion of Supply	266
"Getting Speaker out of Chair"	267
Procedure in Committee of Supply	268
Form of Supply Resolutions	269
Amendments in Committee of Supply	270
Precedence among Amendments	270
Relevancy	271
Procedure on Report of Supply	272
Committee of Ways and Means (spending)	272
Consolidated Fund Bills	272
1. Consolidated Fund (No. 1) Bill	273
2. Consolidated Fund (Appropriation) Bill	274
Procedure	274
(Money) Committees of the Whole House	275
Kinds of business	275
1. Exceptional Grants (not presented as Estimates)	275
2. Demands by Message from the Crown	275
3. Addresses to the Crown	276
4. Incidental charges in connexion with Bills	276
Procedure in voting extraordinary grants	276
Scope of the Public Money Standing Orders	277
Procedure in a (Money) Committee of Whole House	278
Procedure on subsequent stages	279
Sessional Committees with financial functions	279
Public Accounts Committee	279
Estimates Committee	280

II. TAXATION

Annual and Permanent Taxes: Imposition, Repeal	280
Procedure in Committee of Ways and Means (taxing)	281
Procedure on Report of Ways and Means Resolutions	283
Finance Bill	284
The House of Lords and Finance	285
Restrictions based on Privilege	285
Relaxation of Privilege. Devices to save infringement of Privilege	286
Restrictions dependent on the Parliament Act	287

CONTENTS

Chapter IX

PRIVATE LEGISLATION

PAGE

Brief History 289

PRIVATE BILLS

General 291
Preliminaries to Presentation, Table of Dates 293
Stages before Committee 294
    Presentation and First Reading 295
    Second Reading 296
    Instructions and Resolutions 296
    Committal 297
Committee Stage 298
    Private Bill Committees 299
    Arrangement of business and sittings 299
    Proceedings in Committee 299
Stages after Committee 302
    Recommital 302
    Consideration of Bill reported from Committee . . . 303
    Third Reading 304
    Lords' Amendments 304
    Royal Assent 305
House of Lords' Bills 305
Late Bills, Late Deposits and Withdrawals 306
Suspension of Bills over Prorogation or Dissolution . . 307

PROVISIONAL ORDER BILLS

Procedure 308
    Presentation to Committal 308
    Committee Stage 309
    Proceedings in Committee 309

BILLS FOR CONFIRMING PROVISIONAL ORDERS UNDER THE PRIVATE
LEGISLATION PROCEDURE (SCOTLAND) ACT, 1936

General 310
Procedure under Section 7 of the Act 312
Procedure under Section 9 of the Act 312
Substituted Bills 313

SPECIAL ORDERS . . . 313

COMMITTEES AND OFFICERS FOR PRIVATE BUSINESS

Examiners of Petitions for Private Bills 314
Select Committee on Standing Orders 315
Court of Referees 316
Committee of Selection 317
Unopposed Bills Committee 318
Select Committee on a Private Bill 318
Joint Committees on Private Bills 319
    Proceedings 320

APPENDIX I :   Formal Communications between the Crown and the
House of Commons 322

APPENDIX II :   Statutes, Statutory Instruments and Measures . 324

APPENDIX III :   Sessional Time Tables 328

APPENDIX IV :   Alterations to Procedure since 1939 . . 330

APPENDIX V :   Special Procedure Orders . . . 335

INDEX 337

LIST OF AUTHORITIES

ABBREVIATED FORMS OF REFERENCE

ANSON.—*Law and Custom of the Constitution*, vol. i., Parliament, 5th ed., 1922.

BENTHAM.—*Essay on Political Tactics*, vol. ii. of Collected Works.

C.J.—*Commons' Journals*, 1547–

CARR.—*Delegated Legislation*, 1921.

DEB.—House of Commons Debates, Report of, 1803– (for various series, see p. 97).

GRAY.—*Influence of the Commons in Early Legislation*, 1932.

HAKEWEL.—*Modus Tenendi Parliamentum*, 1660.

HATSELL.—*Precedents*, 1785.

HOOKER.—Section in Mountmorres' *Irish Parliament*, vol. i., s. 3.

ILBERT.—*Legislative Methods and Forms*, 1901.

JEFFERSON.—*Manual of Parliamentary Practice*, 1797.

L.J.—*Lords' Journals*, 1509–

LOWELL.—*Government of England*, 1912.

MAITLAND.—*Constitutional History of England*, ed. 1926.

MANUAL.—*Manual of Procedure in the Public Business of the House of Commons*, 6th ed., 1934.

MARRIOTT.—*Mechanism of the Modern State*, 1927.

MAY.—*Parliamentary Practice*, 14th ed., 1946.

Modus Tenendi Parliamentum. Revised text in Clark's *Mediæval Representation and Consent*, 1936.

NOTESTEIN.—*The Winning of the Initiative by the House of Commons*. (Raleigh Lecture, 1924).

POLLARD.—*Evolution of Parliament*, 2nd ed., 1926.

PORRITT.—*Unreformed House of Commons*.

REDLICH.—*Procedure of the House of Commons*, 3 vols., tr. by A. E. Steinthal, 1908.

SCOBEL.—*Memorials of the Manner of Passing Bills* (in *Miscellanea Parliamentaria*, 1685).

SMITH.—*De Republica Anglorum*, 1583.

S.O. No. 1, etc.—Standing Orders of the House of Commons, Part I, Public Business.

S.O. 1, etc.—Standing Orders of the House of Commons, Part II., Private Business.

STUBBS.—*Constitutional History of England*, 5th ed.

TODD.—*Parliamentary Government in England* (ed. by Walpole, 1892).

USHER.—*The Institutional History of the House of Commons*, vol. xi of Washington University Studies.

THE PROCEDURE OF THE HOUSE OF COMMONS

Chapter I

HISTORICAL DEVELOPMENT OF PARLIAMENTARY PROCEDURE

Scope of Commons Procedure

The term 'parliamentary procedure' covers the relations of the House of Commons with the House of Lords and of both Houses with the Crown ; the mass of rules, practices and conventions by which either House regulates its own proceedings, and also the standing and temporary orders which it makes for this purpose ; and the machinery, such as presiding officers and other officials and committees, which it sets up for its assistance. Some of these matters are completely within the control of each House, but others are prescribed by the particular way in which Parliament is constituted. The study of the procedure of the House of Commons, therefore, cannot be confined to the House of Commons alone, but includes much of the procedure of the whole Parliament which directly or indirectly affects the House of Commons.

Further, the modern procedure of the House of Commons is quite unintelligible except in the light of its history. Though the development of procedure has been gradual and continuous, yet it is possible to distinguish certain periods (described in their main lines later in this chapter) the contribution of each of which to modern procedure is of a kind on the whole peculiar to that period. These periods, in chronological order, may be called the periods of (1) the settling of constitutional forms, (2) 'ancient usage', (3) parliamentary practice, (4) the House of Commons standing orders. The contributions of each of these periods to modern procedure are related like strata laid one above the other. Over some parts of the field the earlier layers are obliterated by the later ; in others they show through to the surface distinctly—but deceptively unless the conditions in which they were formed are borne in mind. This explains what the Standing Orders will show at a glance, namely that these orders are not in any sense a code, but everywhere assume a settled practice which they modify only in detail. A study of this practice leads back step by step to very early times. In some particulars it leads back, beyond the separate constitution of the House of Commons, to the origin of Parliament as a supreme court of justice. Nor are these points to be disregarded as matters of antiquity and curiosity. On the contrary, they are matters of everyday practice which recur each session, for example, when Parliament meets or is prorogued, or when it votes money or receives the royal assent to legislation. To misunderstand them is to be ignorant of the meaning of Parliament and of the position both of the House of Commons in Parliament, and of Parliament in the constitution.

It may be worth while considering this matter a little further with the help of an illustration drawn, for example, from the procedure of legislation. Among the Standing Orders will be found a rule (S.O. No. 37) which reads as follows:

> 'If on an amendment to the question that a bill be now read a second time or the third time it is decided that the word "now" or any words proposed to be left out stand part of the question, Mr. Speaker shall forthwith declare the bill to be read a second or the third time as the case may be'.

It may be explained that this rule refers to the parliamentary system of opposing a bill on a main stage not by directly voting against the question on the stage, but by moving either its postponement for six months or the substitution of a proposition explaining why it should be rejected. All the Standing Order does is to dispense with the further question consequent, under practice, on the rejection of either of these motions. Now the Standing Orders themselves do not anywhere lay down that a bill must be read three or any prescribed number of times. Nor do they lay down the curious practice which this Standing Order modifies. To understand its meaning one has to go back to the practice, common to both Houses, which existed at the end of the seventeenth century, when a more elaborate standard of courtesy forbade the opponents of a bill to dispose of it so roughly as by a direct negative vote. The rule that a bill should receive three considerations or 'readings' in each House was even then already old, and to find its origin one has to go back to the 'ancient usage' first recorded in the journals of the sixteenth century. But long before that period the principles of legislative procedure had already been settled —that both Houses should participate in it equally, that the bills of one House should be assented to by the other, and that amendments made by one House should be submitted to the other for approval. At this stage we approach a period when it cannot be said for certain that separate 'Houses' yet exist, and when perhaps a truer picture is that of a still undivided Parliament at which some Lords are always present but which the Commons attend only occasionally, transacting most of their business at unofficial or semi-official meetings outside Parliament. In fact at this stage the question has to be asked whether we are dealing with rules of procedure or constitutional principles. And the answer probably is, that at this stage rules of procedure are engaged in fashioning the constitution.

That this is the true answer will be suggested by other practices which will be mentioned later in this chapter. But the constitutional importance of parliamentary procedure is indicated by another consideration drawn not from English history only. In summoning parliaments of so-called estates, and even in securing the attendance of some of these estates through representatives, the English medieval kings were not doing anything very original. In Western Europe about the same time, and even earlier in some countries, in France and Spain, in Italy and Germany, bodies with very much the same constitution and similar functions were being assembled. What was original in England was not the invention of a parliament but the use that was made of this invention during the critical first century of its existence—particularly, as far as we can see, by one element, the knights of the shire. Of the many advantages which medieval England enjoyed over continental countries the possession of this class of influential men, trained in the business of local self-government, was perhaps the greatest. To this fact is mainly due the very different fate of parliamentary institutions in England and on the continent. It may well be asked by what means the knights of the shire, who were summoned in an inferior capacity compared with the Lords, who were members of the King's Council in Parliament, yet established by their fusion with the burgesses a co-ordinate 'house' of Commons, obtained for that House the right of being the sole grantors of taxes, and thus forged a weapon the skilful use of which in the course of time converted the humble right of petitioning the King into a control over legislation. The answer is, by inventing methods of procedure which (as developed by their successors, the common lawyers, in the seventeenth century) solved the difficult problem of how to get a large number of men really to co-operate in forming decisions, and by imposing those methods of procedure upon the other partners in Parliament and factors of the constitution.

Perhaps the foregoing remarks are enough to show that a satisfactory approach to the procedure of the House of Commons can only be made through a study of its long period of development; that the procedure of the House of Commons cannot be isolated from the procedure of Parliament as a whole; and that in the early stage of the long period of development rules of procedure are indistinguishable from what would now be called rules of the constitution. The English constitution was produced, not like modern constitutions by co-ordinating a number of different institutions with distinct functions and purposes, but by the gradual evolution of a single undifferentiated organ of government into specialised organs which never quite separated from the parent stem. The original central organ, the King in Council, became for certain purposes at the end of the thirteenth century, through the admission of elements not belonging to the council, the King in Parliament. But the King in Council still continued *in* Parliament as well as outside, and Parliament was from the first a body consisting of different elements distinguishable but not entirely separable, which may be most simply expressed as a central point—the King and his servants; an inner circle—the Peers; and an outer circle—the Commons. Much of the early history of Parliament, which was directed to settling the relations of the parts of Parliament to each other, consisted of steps in procedure taken chiefly by the Commons, which were entirely within the original conception of Parliament, but were such as to increase the influence of the Commons in what was coming to be the constitution. The most striking fact in the whole history of Parliament is the logical and consistent way in which the formal rules of its original legal framework were maintained, while procedure gradually evolved conventions which continually transferred the reality of power from the centre to the outer circle of Parliament.

ARRANGEMENT OF CHAPTER

In the following pages of this chapter an attempt is made to sketch the growth of the procedure of the House of Commons from the beginning. This will cover the following subjects: the relations of the Commons with the King and the Lords, the rules for the orderly conduct of debate, the special rules for dealing with the special forms of business—motions, bills, and financial business—the delegation of business to committees, and finally the changes made by the standing orders of the last hundred years in the developed practice of the House. A simple chronological arrangement by periods is chosen. This will not necessitate a description of the development of each subject in each period, because on the whole the contribution of each period is distinct from that of every other. There is a certain amount of overlapping in one subject—the development of financial procedure—and this will be treated as a whole in the third period, although its early stages belong to the first period.

The periods selected are:

1. From the establishment of Parliament to the beginning of the *Commons Journals*—about 1300 to 1547.
2. From 1547 to the Restoration, 1660.
3. From 1660 to the period of the modern standing orders, which commenced with the first reformed Parliament, 1832.
4. The period of the standing orders, 1833—.

This choice of periods is dictated on grounds of procedure primarily, and not of constitutional development. That is why the *Commons Journals* and the modern standing orders are used as landmarks to divide one period from another—a prominence which they would not possess for a survey which was primarily constitutional. Though there is an intimate connexion between the constitutional functions of a parliamentary body and its procedure, this connexion can only be dealt with here when it is strictly necessary for the purpose of explaining changes in procedure. For the reasons previously stated constitutional functions require fuller treatment in the first period than in any of the others.

FIRST PERIOD, 1300–1547

THE KING AND PARLIAMENT

The motive of Edward I and his successors in establishing Parliament and maintaining the representative elements as a permanent part of it has been variously interpreted by historians. It has been represented as a desire to weaken feudalism by substituting a national basis of government; a bid to win the support of the newer classes in the country districts and the towns against the barons; or a plan to keep in touch with local needs and difficulties by encouraging petitions and using local representatives as agents of the central government. Lately, however, there has been a reversion to the older view that the main motive was to obtain general assent to taxation. But, whatever his motive, it is generally agreed that the establishment of Parliament was due to the initiative of the King, freely taken and not in response to any demands from below. So far was Parliament from being a popular institution during most of the first period of its existence that attendance was regarded as a burden to be avoided, if possible; and fines and other punishments were required to enforce obedience to the royal summons, not only on members to attend, but even on constituencies to return members. Parliament was, and remained throughout the Middle Ages, 'the child of authority'.

In Parliament itself the power of the King was in law nearly absolute. He controlled the composition of Parliament, as it lay within his discretion to choose both the peers whom he would summon individually and the boroughs whom he would direct to send representatives. Parliament could not meet without his summons or continue after he had dismissed it. Everything done in Parliament was done not only in his own name, but, if he chose, by his own will, for he was not in theory bound to follow the advice given. He was the effective agent in adjudication and legislation, for it was the announcement of his decision which gave a judgment or made a law, and he might take his decision as well outside as inside Parliament. There were some legal limits to his powers, chiefly of feudal origin. He ought to act according to customary forms, consult his barons, not punish without recognized form of trial, or take more than the regular aids without consent. And there was a general obligation, recognized in his oath, to govern according to law and in the interest of his subjects. But the legal obligations were vague and hard to enforce. What was more important was that the barons since 1215 had shown the power to co-operate against him as national leaders, that it was hard to extract money from reluctant payers, and that in the last resort his subjects might rebel. It was in Parliament itself that effective limitations were ultimately imposed upon the royal power, and this was done less by any great constitutional statutes than by a gradual process of growth working through the procedure of Parliament.

References to Erskine May's
PARLIAMENTARY PRACTICE

This comparative table is intended for readers who possess the 15th edition of May. Opposite the page references to the 14th edition which appear in this reprint of the *Introduction to the Procedure of the House of Commons* will be found the corresponding references to the 15th edition.

Page in *Introduction*	Reference in text to May (14th Edition)	Corresponding reference to May (15th Edition)
33	770	786
58	194	192–3
	194–5	193–4
59	205	205
	207–210	206–7, 210
	214	214
60	203–4	202–3
61	207	206
	209–210	208–9
62	212	211
	213	213
63	49	48
64	73	74
65	57–9	57–8
	71	72
	75–6	76–7
	78	79
	130	131–2
66	56	55–6
	225–7	226–8
	815–17	321–2
67	179	178
	180	179
68	179	178
	180	179
	181	180–1
	183	182
69	182	181
70	189–190	188–9
72	53	53
	54	53–4
	96	97
	127	129
	134	135–6

Page in *Introduction*	Reference in text to May (14th Edition)	Corresponding reference to May (15th Edition)
73	94–5	95–6
78	238	238–9
79	240	240–1
81	240	241–2
84	222 n	222 n
86	253–260	256–262
91	250	252–3
	252	254
93	257	259
100	24	25
	262–3	264–5
103	270	272
104	271–2	273–4
	272	274
106	271	273
122	706	719
133	307 & 308	313 & 314
137	311	316
	312	316
139	354	362
	362	369
	547	557
	731	747
144	332	338
148	335	342
152	375	380
157	352	359
158	379	384
159	546	557
161	361	369
173	383	389
174	392–393	398
176	375	380–1
	376–7	381–2
177	377	383
	390	395–6
	491	499
	553–555	564–6

Page in *Introduction*	Reference in text to May (14th Edition)	Corresponding reference to May (15th Edition)
180	403	409
182	387	392–3
	408 ff	414 ff
191	423–5	430–3
	424	431
	426	433
193	422	429
	423	430
194	432	439
	433	440
	439	446–7
195	432	440
	433	441
196	435	443
	436	443
198	445	452
202	481	488
207	497	505
	498	506
208	498–500	507–8
	500	509
	502	510
212	506	515
214	510	519
	516	525
217	523	531, 533
218	510–11	520
	526	536
	739–42	755–8
219	530	540
	530–31	540
220	535	545
221	534	544
222	537	546–7
223	538	549
	540	551
224	544	554
	791	808
	792	808–9
226	546	557
	548	559
230	561	573

Page in *Introduction*	Reference in text to May (14th Edition)	Corresponding reference to May (15th Edition)
235	569	580
236	572	583
241	620	634
242	621	635
243	578 621	590 635–6
244	577	588
245	588 n	600 n
246	582 585	594 597
247	596	607
266	684	698
268	692	707
270	697 699	711 712–3
271	703	716–7
273	640	656
275	685	699
277	728–30	744–6
281	750	766–7
283	751	767
285	773	789
286	768	784
287	775	791
288	779	794–5
292	826 *et seq.* 843–44	837 *et seq.* 855–6
296	905 *et seq.*	918 *et seq.*
308	976 *et seq.*	991 *et seq.*
316	852 *et seq.*	863 *et seq.*
317	874 *et seq.*	886 *et seq.*
318	857 *et seq.*	869 *et seq.*
322	781	797
323	783 786 789	799 802 805–6

The Campfield Press, St. Albans

Organization of Parliament

How was the early Parliament organized ? The original conception of Parliament as a specially large and important meeting of the King with his council reinforced by persons not of the council, who were summoned to represent the shire-courts, cities and certain boroughs, was plainly set forth by what we know of the arrangements for the meeting of a Parliament which were followed throughout the Middle Ages. At the upper end of the Parliament chamber was the King's throne; below and in front of him were grouped his ministers and others forming his inner council; on each side of these were the seats of those summoned to his "great council", the Peers spiritual and temporal; while at the lower end of the chamber outside the bar were gathered the Commons with their Speaker at their head. This was the arrangement when business was *done* in Parliament, when the King's response was given to petitions or his demands announced, and when the answers of the various elements were made known by their spokesmen. Thus for the purpose of decision Parliament was a unitary body, as indeed it still is when the King's speech is read and his assent given to Bills.

Whether it was ever a unitary body for discussion is doubtful. It is possible that at an early stage discussion took place in the King's presence when the representative elements were in attendance. But, if so, it is probable that such discussion was confined to the council who had the right to offer advice, and unlikely that argument proceeded from beyond the bar where the Commons stood. If the description given in the *Modus Tenendi Parliamentum* of the proceedings of the early Parliament is to be trusted, discussion was carried on by each of the groups, of which Parliament was composed, meeting separately.

These groups or 'gradus' are there given as (1) The bishops and abbots, (2) the clerical proctors or representatives of the lower clergy, (3) the earls and barons, (4) the knights of the shire and, (5) the citizens and burgesses. They correspond fairly with the classes of medieval society. The chief matter to be discussed by these groups was the rate of tax which they were prepared to grant the King; and the fact that in very early days they sometimes granted different rates suggests that they may have reached their decisions separately. But if such an arrangement was ever tried its duration was short. The fact that the medieval Parliament exercised other functions—judicial, administrative, legislative, political—as well as the function of granting taxes, made the real line of demarcation one between those elements in Parliament which belonged to the body which had hitherto participated in these functions—the council whether in its royal or feudal aspect—and the newer elements which did not belong to the council and had not shared in these functions.

As counsellors of the King, the Lords spiritual and temporal remained in the council chamber to debate in the presence of the King or his Chancellor. The knights and burgesses withdrew elsewhere to debate. It was natural in these circumstances that they should coalesce in spite of the social superiority of the knights, who were of the same feudal status as the barons (including as they did the 'barones minores' or minor tenants-in-chief) and corresponded with the privileged class of *petite noblesse* in France. The fusion of knights and burgesses into the 'Commons' was helped by the withdrawal soon after 1330 of the representatives of the lower clergy who obstinately refused to grant taxes except in their convocations. For the eventual formation also of a 'House' of Lords the withdrawal of the lower clergy was important. It left the bishops and abbots with no reason for sitting apart from the Council in Parliament, of which they were members on much the same footing of baronial tenure as the earls and barons; and the eventual formation of a 'House' of Peers was assisted by these 'estates' combining to deprive the official elements of the Council such as the judges, who were not summoned on grounds of tenure and therefore were not Peers, first of vote and then of voice in Parliament.

The meetings of the knights and burgesses for discussion were at first unofficial and altogether outside Parliament. But they were not in any way frowned on by the King. On the contrary Edward III is said to have suggested such a fusion of the 'common' estates for discussion. It was probably the King who placed the refectory and afterwards the chapter house of the Abbey at their disposal, and deputed members of his council to advise them when they requested assistance. The under-clerk of the Parliaments was detailed to keep such minutes as they may have had and help to draw up their petitions. Of what passed at their meetings we have no official record until the *Commons' Journals* begin in 1547, but it is probable that they soon chose one of their number, who was no doubt a knight, to preside over their meetings, and he may well have been the same person as the prolocutor or 'Speaker' who announced their decisions in Parliament. There is no record, however, of a permanent officer of this sort before Thomas of Hungerford in 1377. The Rolls of Parliament only record proceedings in Parliament itself. From the Rolls we know that the session opened with a general review of the political situation from the King's point of view and a special demand for aid, generally delivered by the Chancellor; that the chief proceedings were on petitions and the trial of important suits; that the Commons tried to delay their grants until their petitions had been favourably answered, but were often unsuccessful; that the King chose the moment to dismiss all in attendance on Parliament who were not of his council; and that frequently after this had been done the Parliament continued in being and transacted business just as if the knights and burgesses and the barons not of the council had been present.

THE STATUS OF THE COMMONS

In the early Parliaments the position of the representative elements was humble and, for most of the reign of Edward II, precarious. They could make no constitutional claim to share in most of the functions of Parliament, which were in origin the functions of the council exercised in Parliament. In time some of these functions, such as a share in legislation and the right of giving counsel on matters of policy, were acquired by the Commons indirectly by the use which they made of their indispensability in the granting of supply. But they never became judges in the High Court of Parliament—a function which the Peers possessed as counsellors of the King. This fact explains the curious procedure known as 'impeachment' which was evolved in the latter half of the 14th century, and which may be described in modern language as a prosecution for a political offence (generally labelled 'treason') conducted by the Commons before the Peers. In this procedure the Commons were regarded as a jury of presentment, 'the grand jury of the nation', and the Peers as the highest national court of justice. Though this procedure has been imitated in modern constitutions, it is quite anomalous on the theory of two co-ordinate Houses, and would never have been invented but for the fact that the English 'upper' House inherited judicial powers from a pre-existing court, the King's Council, while the 'lower' House did not possess such powers because it had never formed part of that court.

In the matter of legislation the claim of the Commons to participate could not be based upon any pre-existing constitutional right. It was the King who 'made' new laws; and the council by whose advice the great statutes of Edward I were expressed to be made, was more often the council in its small official form than the council in the larger feudal form in which it appeared in Parliament. The relation of the Commons to legislation was in the capacity of petitioners, at first as individuals though soon as a body. The statute of York, 1322, although its meaning has been disputed, seems to lay down two principles: (1) that laws of general application should be made in Parliament, and (2) that the Commons' assent is necessary. These principles had never been definitely laid down before; and it is possible that their assertion was due to the need of a reason for the statute's repeal of the Ordinances of 1311 (which had been made by the barons alone though they had been submitted for the approval of the Commons in a subsequent Parliament). In any case the Commons had a long struggle before they succeeded in enforcing the general observance of these principles.

The Commons and Legislation

This struggle was conducted on two main fronts. In the first place the King's power to make laws outside Parliament had to be restricted. This was done, first, by appropriating the name of 'statute' to parliamentary legislation, and leaving the name of 'ordinance' for conciliar legislation, and, secondly, by restricting the sphere of ordinance. It gradually came to be admitted that laws of general application, especially if they were intended to be permanent, could only be enacted in statutes. But a wide field, for instance in the regulation of industry, continued to remain open to ordinance, and the Commons sometimes asserted the superiority of statute by securing that ordinances, the validity of which they did not contest, should be turned into statutes. Thus they made the ordinance of Labourers of 1349 a statute in 1351, and in 1353 the ordinance of the Staple and other ordinances made in a recent council were re-enacted in Parliament as statutes.

Procedure by Petition or Bill

The other main line of advance was the increasing part played by the Commons in making statutes. This was effected by a development of the procedure relating to petitions. The practice of petitioning the King goes back far beyond Parliament. Procedure on petitions was a large part of the business of

Parliament from the beginning. They were submitted in writing and were dealt with systematically by being sorted by Receivers and heard by committees of the council in Parliament called Triers. In the great Parliament of 1305, the records of which are unusually complete,[1] nearly five hundred Petitions were presented and they were heard by four bodies of Triers. Most of these petitions were from individuals, some from groups outside Parliament, and a few were parliamentary in the sense of being from groups within Parliament. Two of these, presented by *les pauvres hommes de la terre*, are supposed to have been from the Commons collectively. No distinction was made at this time in the treatment of petitions, whether individual or collective. From the individual and group petitions Private Bills are descended; from the collective Commons' petitions, Public Bills.

Origin of 'Public' Bills

The development of petitions can only be briefly indicated here. The following are the main stages. The first stage was that of the 'comprehensive' Commons' petition.[2] This was a single document presented by the Commons embodying a number of requests as articles. The first example of such a petition is one of eleven articles presented to the King *par la communaute de son Roialme* at Westminster in 1309. It is however not certain that at this period 'commonalty' meant the Commons to the exclusion of the Peers. But the similar petitions of 1325 and 1327 and throughout the reign of Edward III emanated from the Commons only. After 1422 the 'comprehensive' petition ceased and was replaced by separate petitions, which when they left the Commons were superscribed with the formula which is still employed, *soit baille as Seigneurs*.[3] The King's reply was entered on the back of the petition and also enrolled in the Rolls of Parliament. The function of turning such of the Commons' requests as were suitable into statutes was performed by the judges, and they drafted a statute by the simple process of combining a petition with its response. The proportion of statutes which originated as Commons' petitions rose continuously, until in the reigns of the first two Lancastrians it comprised almost all statutes, though it is true there was a

---

[1] The Rolls of this Parliament were edited by Maitland in the volume *Memoranda de Parliamento*.

[2] Gray, *Influence of the Commons in Early Legislation*, p. 203.

[3] The old spelling of the Norman French formulæ is retained in this section.

marked decline in the latter half of the 15th century. Commons' petitions ceased to be subjected to the process of examination by Triers and Auditors, like individual petitions, and were presented direct to the King in Council.

During the 15th century the Commons attempted to secure the enactment of their petitions as statutes in the form in which they were submitted to the King. In the famous petition of 1414 they claimed to be 'as well assenters as petitioners', and requested that their petitions should be enacted as statutes without any change of substance except with their assent. The King's reply does not read as a complete acceptance of the claim of the Commons, for he only granted 'that nothing be enacted to the petitions of the Commons that be *contrary* to their asking whereby they should be bound without their assent'. It appears that the difference between the King and the Commons was rather one of degree and that, apart from the statutes of 1413 which called forth the complaint of 1414, the changes made in petitions when they became statutes had not been of great substance and continued to be made to much the same extent after as before the petition of 1414.[1] There is evidence that in the reign of Henry VI amendments to Commons' Bills (to use the term which superseded 'petition') were sometimes submitted for their assent. Commons' Bills sometimes failed to receive the King's assent but not very frequently.

The well-known theory that the Commons towards the end of Henry VI's reign found a remedy for the King's propensity to whittle down their demands, when converting petitions into statutes, by inventing the new form of a bill drafted in the shape of a statute to replace the old form of petition,[2] seems to be dis-proved by Mr. Gray's researches. Apart from the discovery that the King's amendments were not very substantial and that, such as they were, they continued fairly constant throughout the Lancastrian reigns he shows that 'bill' and 'petition' were from early times interchangeable terms, and that, though about the middle of the 15th century a new type of bill drafted as a statute (*formam actus in se continens*) came into use, it was employed only for Private Bills and bills originating in the council, and not by the Commons for Public Bills until the next century.[3]

The part played by the Lords in relation to bills which became statutes is even more difficult to determine than that of

---

[1] Gray, pp. 261–85.   [2] Stubbs, ii, 608–9.   [3] Gray, pp. 46 and 47.

the Commons. The Lords were much slower in becoming a 'House' of Parliament than the Commons, and for the greater part of this period they remained in fact as well as theory the King's Council in Parliament. Bills introduced in the Commons appear not to have been superscribed with the assent of the Lords till the beginning of the 16th century. The assent of the King perhaps implied that of the Lords. Similarly it appears to be difficult to find examples of bills introduced in the Lords, and becoming statutes, which may be stated with certainty not to have emanated from the small council of officials and ministers who formed the inner circle of the enlarged council in Parliament. Lords' Bills were generally of an administrative character, affecting the King's household or government. They differ in form from Commons' Bills by not mentioning the Commons as petitioners but assenters, and surviving copies of the Bills themselves bear the superscription *A ceste bille les Communes sount assentuz*. As stated above, it was these Bills which were the first to be drafted in the form they would take as statutes. Lords' Bills were treated respectfully by the Commons, perhaps because of their real origin in the council. There seems to be no case before the end of the 15th century of failure on the part of the Commons to assent to a Lords' Bill, and only one certain case, in 1429, of their amendment of a Lords' Bill.

Private Bills

While the adoption of the procedure of collective petitions by the Commons in the 14th century gradually made the functions of Parliament predominantly legislative, the older individual petitions, which invoked the remedial jurisdiction of Parliament, followed a procedure which remained half judicial. They continued to be heard, generally by Triers, sometimes by the Lords as a body; and it was not till the 16th century that some Commons were added to the Triers. Only those which could not be referred to one of the courts were finally dealt with in Parliament. Some petitions were from groups, not individuals, but they were dealt with as individual petitions except that they were occasionally, as early as the 14th century, adopted for inclusion in the articles of the 'comprehensive' Commons' petitions, while individual petitions were not so included. In the 15th century, however, the practice became established of addressing petitions not only to the King and Lords, but also to the Commons, with the request that they should intercede with the King and Lords—a tribute to the growing importance of the Commons. Such petitions, if accepted by the Commons, were passed on to the Lords with the inscription *Soit baille as Seigneurs*, and were then presumably referred to the Triers. At the same time it became the practice for individual petitions addressed to the King and Lords to be submitted to the Commons for their assent, which was recorded by the inscription *A ceste bille les Communes sount assentuz*. The King's assent was endorsed in a form, different from that for Public Bills—*Soit fait come il est desire*.

POSITION OF COMMONS AT END OF PERIOD

In the reign of Henry VII the legislative activity of the Commons suffered a temporary eclipse. Fewer Commons' Bills reached the Statute Book and fewer Private Bills were introduced in the Commons. The policy of Henry VIII required a great deal of parliamentary legislation, but there was not much scope for the exercise of a real initiative by either House, especially the Commons. The policy associated with Cromwell, which was continued and developed in later reigns by the Cecils, necessitated a vigilant control of Parliament, involving the maintenance of a royal majority in the House of Commons and something like a regular programme of business for each session. Most Bills were presented to the Lords and put before the Commons with their authority as well as that of the King. Some Government Bills were however introduced in the Commons—one or two by Henry himself purporting to have been drawn up by his own hand. It suited the King on occasion that his measures should appear not only to be supported by the popular chamber, but to arise out of its spontaneous wishes. This was especially the case in the Reformation Parliament, when several Commons' Bills directed against the Church erred by an excess of zeal and had to be toned down before receiving the Royal Assent.

SUMMARY OF FIRST PERIOD

At the beginning of the first period of Parliament the House of Commons, forming itself by the amalgamation of knights and burgesses, had a position that was precarious and depended chiefly on the necessities of the King. At the end of the period their constitutional position was greatly strengthened, but politically, after an interlude of greater independence, they found themselves again under the control of the King. The important difference was that the control was now *indirect*. The

Commons retained in appearance their established rights, but great pains were taken that they should be exercised in the King's interest—a recognition of the importance of the Commons. The forms of procedure which they had been able to establish in their relations with the King and the Lords made them, in theory, equal partners in legislation. This theory it was the task of the next period to translate into fact.

SECOND PERIOD, 1547–1660

The second period of the development of the House of Commons falls into three portions: (1) the reigns of Elizabeth and her two predecessors, (2) the reigns of the first two Stuarts, (3) the civil war and Commonwealth. During the first portion of this period the Crown kept the Commons in leading strings with the help of the Speaker, and also of Privy Councillors whose election (together with many unofficial supporters) it took pains to secure. During the second portion the Commons passed out of the control of the Crown, produced leaders of their own, and went into open and permanent opposition to the royal government. During the third portion they prosecuted the civil war and tried, but failed, to exercise directly the functions of government.

It was during this period, especially the middle portion of it, that the Commons evolved a great deal of what is still the procedure of the House—the part that is referred to reverently as the 'ancient usage of the House'. This covers the following subjects:

1. the rules of order in debate, *i.e.* the discipline, which a large body has to impose upon itself to maintain order and regularity in the transaction of business, and the powers it gives its presiding officer for those purposes.
2. the forms of debate on motions, *i.e.* the rules for focusing a variety of opinions into decisions.
3. the forms of debate on Bills.
4. the development of the system of committees.

All this procedure will be found to bear clearly the mark of the period, during which it was developed. It is full of suspicion of the executive government, insistence upon the rights of the Commons, and determination to make the Speaker, a presiding officer only, the servant not the master of the House, and also to conduct its business in open House instead of in

C

small committees where official influence could make itself supreme.

1. RULES OF ORDER IN DEBATE

About the progress which the Commons had made in procedure before the *Journals* begin in 1547 only a few stray hints are available. All that the Rolls of Parliament enable us to see or hear of them is their recurrent appearance at the bar of the parliament chamber, which has now become the House of Lords, and the announcement of their decisions by the mouth of their Speaker. What discussions and divisions lay behind these apparently unanimous decisions it is generally impossible to guess. The *Journals* themselves until 1571 give little more than lists of Bills and readings. It is safe to infer, however, that the Commons would not have maintained themselves for two centuries as partners in legislation and useful allies of the despotic kings who followed the Lancastrian 'parliamentary regime', if they had not gone far to solve at any rate the elementary problems which confront, and have so often baffled, attempts to express the will of large assemblies. Behind the bills which the Commons transmitted to the Lords and the subsidies which they granted the King, there must have been a process of deliberation and a process of decision. In the first period the Commons are viewed only from the outside and nothing is seen but results. In the second period the curtain slowly rises on their domestic procedure, but the scene is already set by activities of which we know very little.

Let us place ourselves in the period soon after the *Journals* begin and see what progress the House has made in organizing the conduct of debate. We find that it has a president in the person of the Speaker, whose functions in this respect are still, and will be for another century, overshadowed by his duties as intermediary between the King and the House and as manager of the King's business there. The House is not without suspicion on this account, and makes orders that the Speaker "ought not to sway the House with argument and debate", and that he ought not to show Bills to the King until the House is possessed of them. It also invents a method of procedure which dispenses with his presence (see p. 27). On the other hand, it insists that Members and others shall accord him the respect due to his office. It prescribes rules, such as that when the Speaker stands up the Member standing up ought to sit down, and that no Member should leave the

House before him. The Speaker already has no ordinary vote, but only a casting vote. "If . . . the number of either side be alike, then the Speaker shall give his voice, and that only in this point, for otherwise he hath no voice" (Hooker, cited by Redlich, i. 31).

A little later we have an instance of the way in which the House resents in quite a modern fashion discourtesy on the part of one of its number to the Speaker. The *Journal* of 17th April, 1604, prints a letter received by the Speaker from a Member, Mr. John Tey, King's Alnager for London, in which the writer complains that he had made a Motion "for 2, 3 or 4 fit persons to be named for drawing up certain heads concerning drapery into a Bill" . . . but that it pleased the Speaker "to distaste my Motion, and without Question to the House of Allowance or Disallowance, to clip me off". The question of the propriety of this letter was submitted by the Speaker to the House and followed by apology and withdrawal.

The questions which first arise when a numerous body debates in common are: In what order are Members to speak? When are votes to be given, singly at the end of each speech, or all together at the end of the debate? How is the subject to be brought to a clear issue and the House to a definite decision? What are the 'parliamentary' limits to freedom of speech? All but one of these the House had solved when our reports begin. To see the originality of the solution let us glance at the procedure of another famous and successful body—the Roman Senate. There the subject of debate was fixed by an official request of the presiding magistrate for advice. Senators spoke in a fixed order of precedence, and each concluded his speech either by moving a motion or voting for a previous motion. (This practice was also adopted by the French pre-revolution Parliaments and provincial assemblies, misled, as Bentham acutely pointed out, by the analogy of a bench of judges.) At the end of the debate the president selected one of the motions—generally that of an ex-consul—and put it to the vote, but by that time the speeches of the prominent Senators and the votes already given or indicated generally made the result a foregone conclusion.

This was the procedure of an aristocratic body with official degrees of rank. The House of Commons early established the democratic principle that in the House all Members are equal. This is a fundamental principle on which a few words must be said. It is expressed in the rule of debate that no Member has a prior right of speaking over any other Member. It shows itself again in the method of voting, which allows no greater weight or prominence to attach to one Member's vote than another's, and in the old arrangement of business whereby no Bill or Motion received any precedence because it was brought in by one Member rather than another. Finally, as will appear later, it provided a motive for the invention of an original form of procedure, by which the House as a whole took over complicated and detailed business, such as the amendment of Bills, which it had previously left to small specially selected committees. This principle is characteristic of the period in which it originated, when the House of Commons was often, as a body, in opposition, and would allow the representatives of the Government, which it contained in its ranks, no more than the ordinary privileges of membership. As will be shown later, this attitude was stubbornly maintained long after the Government had become the leaders of the majority of the House and, except in respect of the precedence of business, still survives.

The way in which the House had settled the rules for conducting debate is thus described by Sir Thomas Smith:—

"He that standeth up bareheaded is to be understood that he will speak to the Bill. If more stand up who that is first judged to arise is first heard.[1] . . . Every man speaketh as to the Speaker not as one to another for that is against the order of the House. It is also taken against the order to name him who you do confute but by circumlocution, as he that speaketh with the bill, or he that spake against the bill or gave this or that reason. . . . To one bill in one day one may not in that House speak twice, for else one or two with altercation would spend all the time. The next day he may but then also but once.[2] No reviling or nipping words must be used, for then all the House will cry 'it is against the order', and if any speak irreverently or seditiously against the prince or the privy council, I have seen them not only interrupted, but it hath been moved after to the House, and they have sent them to the Tower."

The method of voting is described by Sir Thomas Smith as follows. He gives it in connexion with the discussion of a Bill: "(The Speaker) sayeth, as many as will have this bill goe forwarde, which is concerning such a matter, say yea. Then

---

[1] *Against* Bill first heard (rule laid down in *Journal*, 1604).
[2] No Member to speak twice on adjourned debate (23rd June, 1604).

they which allow the bill crie yea, and as many as will not say no: as the crie of yea or no is bigger, so the bill is allowed or dashed. If it be a doubt which crie is the bigger, they divide the house, the speaker saying, as many as doe allow the bill goe downe with the bill, and as many as do not sit still. So they divide themselves, and being so divided they are numbered who make the more part, and soe the bill doth speede."[1]

This account shows that the 16th-century method was in principle the same as at present, *i.e.* voting takes place at the conclusion of debate, all Members vote simultaneously, a division is only taken if the result of the cries of Aye and No is challenged. Some historical interest lies in the method of taking a division, which persisted until the destruction of the old Chamber, whereby one side went out of the Chamber to be counted, and the other sat still. This was a very inconvenient system for the side that went out, because their seats were liable to be taken by those who remained in, and they were thus likely to lose "all the indolent, the indifferent and inattentive" (Jefferson, 130). Consequently it became a matter of importance to have a general rule deciding on each occasion which side was to go forth and which remain in. The rule came to be, roughly, that those for the preservation of the orders of the House stayed in, and those for their alteration or for the introduction of any new business went out. But this rule was subject to numerous exceptions, and a great deal of space is given by Hatsell and the older authorities to an attempt to reduce them to some degree of consistency. All trace of what must have been a tiresome system of casuistry has vanished from procedure except in one point. There is evidence, which would require too much space to set out here, suggesting that the method, peculiar to English parliamentary procedure, of putting the question on an amendment to leave out words, *i.e.* "that the words proposed to be left out stand part", has something to do with this difficulty incidental to the old system of dividing, and that, while its origin is perhaps to be found in the method adopted by the House for dealing with amendments to a Bill offered by a committee (see p. 24), its retention was due to an unsuccessful attempt to find an

---

[1] The first division recorded in the *Journal* appears to be on 23rd March, 1553–4. A pre-*Journal* division in the Commons, held apparently at the suggestion of the King, is referred to in a letter dated 26th March, 1532 in *State Papers, Spanish*, 1531–3 p. 416 Notestein, p. 8).

automatic solution of the difficulty by framing the question in
such a way that the Ayes—the side which usually went out in a
division—should always go out.[1]

2. MOTIONS

'Motion' was—and is—the generic name given by the
House to any proposal submitted to it for formal decision.

The simplest form of debate is the procedure on the motion,
and all the more complicated forms are reducible to this
procedure. For instance, the procedure on a Bill is developed
out of the procedure on a motion by treating the Bill as a single
motion for the purpose of discussing its principle and as a
series of motions when discussing its clauses in detail. (Until
comparatively recently Bills were drawn with enacting words
prefixed to each clause.) In the developed procedure of the
House the debate on a motion involves three stages, the making
of the motion, the proposing of a question, and the vote on the
question; and, further, the question repeats the terms of the
motion, which should be so framed as to express a decision
of the House. It was not until the end of the 17th century that
the House consistently applied this rule. Before this time traces
are found of an alternative method of procedure by which the
duty of framing a question was placed on the Speaker, a
method which Hatsell refers to as the ancient rule of the
House, obsolete in his time. Scobel, in the middle of the 17th
century, expresses the rule thus: "After some time spent in
debate the Speaker, collecting the sense of the House upon
the debate, is to reduce the same to a question which he is to
propose, to the end that the House in their debate afterwards
may be kept to the Matter of the Question, if the same be
approved by the House to contain the substance of the former
Debate" (Scobel, 22). As late as 1697 we find the Speaker
"by the leave of the House declaring it to be their sense", etc.
(C.J., 27th January, 1697). Complaint was not lacking of the
use made of this power by the Chair in the direction of
"intricating" the question and "making plausible motions
abortive". Speaker Lenthall is criticized in Wood's *Athenae
Oxonienses* (quoted by Hatsell) as being "often much confused
in collecting the sense of the House and drawing the debates to
a fair question". Clarendon, in his *History of the Rebellion*,
boasts that in his capacity as Chairman of Committee of the

---

[1] For some time the question was put in the form "that the words proposed to be left out do *not* stand part."

Whole House he served the King by 'entangling' the committee in contradictory motions.

It is probable that this power of the Speaker to frame the question passed through two stages before it was finally abolished. At first it was openly employed as a censorship against motions displeasing to the Crown or the Privy Council. Perhaps in view of this an entry in the *Journal*, of 10th April, 1571, is significant, where a proposal of the Speaker is recorded "that from henceforward Men, making Motions, should bring them in writing". During the second stage it was employed by the Speaker ostensibly under the wishes of the House and merely to elicit its true opinion, *i.e.* as a method of procedure and not as a form of political control. Even in this form it was found to be open to abuses and misconception, and consequently fell into disuse.

The steps by which the House developed a form of procedure by which the true sense of the House should be expressed in every decision were:—

(1) It laid down the following rule: "Ordered that nothing to pass by order of the House without a question; and that no order without a question affirmative and negative" (1614, C.J. (1547–1628) 464).

(2) It took steps to see that the House should not be confronted with impromptu questions to be decided without due consideration. "When a motion hath been made the same may not be put to the question until it be debated, or at least have been seconded or prosecuted by one or more persons standing up in their places" (Scobel, 21). Later, previous notice of important questions came to be required.

(3) Not more than one question should be before the House at the same time. "When a Motion hath been made, that Matter must receive a determination by a Question, or be laid aside by the general sense of the House before another be entertained" (Scobel, 21). This is a restatement of an old rule of 28th June, 1604. It indicates the possibility of the withdrawal of a motion by leave of the House.

The method of superseding a question by moving the 'previous' question (*i.e.* "whether the question be now put") was invented in the 17th century—it is said by Sir Harry Vane in 1640 (Jefferson, 118).[1] There seem to be no references in our

[1] An earlier instance is found in 1604 in regard to a Bill. C.J.(1547-1628)226

authorities of this period to the method of moving amendments except 'provisos' (see p. 24), perhaps because amendment was a process which was still, and continued for some time to be, left to small committees.

3. BILLS

The respective shares of King, Lords and Commons in legislation through petition and bill in the 14th and 15th centuries has been traced in an earlier section (see pp. 10–14). When the *Journals* allow us to perceive the stages of the process by which the Commons performed their part of the joint function, we find that the procedure on Bills is not yet completely differentiated from the procedure on motions. The marks of Bill procedure—the three readings and reference to a committee —were not exclusively reserved for Bills. Motions were sometimes read more than once and were sometimes committed. The *Journal* of the 31st January, 1580, contains the following entry: "Motion made yesterday committed to the Privy Council being of this House." On the other hand, the Petition of Right (1628), although only once read, was sent to the Lords, received the Royal Assent and was held to be a statute.

In this early period it was already the usual practice of the House to read a Bill three times, but it was not the uniform practice. It is not until 1492 that the Rolls of Parliament mention more than a single reading. Bills were often read four times down to 1580, and they occasionally received even more than four readings—as many as six in 1554, and eight in 1549 (Usher, 199.)

Sir Thomas Smith's account of the procedure on a Public Bill at the beginning of Elizabeth's reign is as follows:—

"All bills be thrice, in three divers days, read and disputed upon, before they come to the question. . . . After the bill hath been twice reade, and then engrossed, and eftsoones reade and disputed upon enough as is thought; the speaker asketh if they will goe to the question. And if they agree he holdeth the bill up in his hand and sayeth, as many as will have this bill goe forwarde, which is concerning such a matter, say yea. Then they which allow the bill crie yea, and as many as will not say no: as the crie of yea or no is bigger, soe the bill is allowed or dashed. If it be a doubt which crie is the bigger, they divide the House. . . . It chanceth sometimes that some part of the bill is allowed, some other part hath much doubt and contrariety made of it: and it is thought if it were amended it would goe forwarde. Then they choose certain committees[1] of them who have spoken with the bill and against it to amende it, and bring it in againe soe amended, as they amongst them shall think meete: and this is before it is engrossed, yea and some time after. But the agreement of these committees is no prejudice to the House. For at the last question they will either accept it or dash it as it shall seeme good, notwithstanding that whatsoever the committees have done."

In this account it is easy to recognize the main features of Bill procedure as it exists at present—the three readings, the committal, etc. In order to see how the later procedure developed from this, it will be necessary to glance at two later accounts, first noting that the account given by Smith shows

(1) that the procedure was simple and informal. The three readings gave rise to debates, but only one question is expressly stated to have been put ("that this bill goe forwarde"), and committal was not necessary, but optional.

(2) The House abstained from making amendments itself, and contented itself with accepting or rejecting amendments made by a committee or referring the Bill back to the committee.

With the help of the far fuller accounts of Hakewel[2] (Member from 1601 to 1629) and Scobel (Clerk of the House 1649 to 1659) it is possible to fill in some details and note the direction in which procedure was developing. During the first half of the 17th century the House, as the frequent orders dealing with points of procedure recorded in the *Journals* show, was devoting considerable attention to its rules, especially during the first Parliament of James I and at the beginning of the Long Parliament. Hakewel's account includes the developments of the first period, and Scobel's covers both periods.

From these accounts it is clear that

(1) Procedure had become more formal. The three readings are still principally for the sake of information, and they are accompanied by an exposition of the substance of the Bill from the Speaker assisted by a brief or 'breviate' of its contents, which by Scobel's time had to be presented by a Member as an accompaniment to his Bill. But the readings are beginning to develop into stages, on which

---

[1] 'Committee' originally denoted an individual, not a body.
[2] Hakewel, according to Coke carried a library of precedents in his head.

a question is put for the sake of regularizing debate, although there was this difference from modern procedure, that debate *followed* the reading, and the question was, not that the Bill be *now* read a second (or third) time, but that it be read on a future day. Thus the first reading took place without any question, and debate on it was deprecated, though not without precedent when the Bill was 'generally disliked'. In addition to these questions on second and third reading, questions were put for the ingrossment of a Bill, for its passing, and (when it was desired to amend it, but not otherwise) for its committal. The number of possible questions had grown to three (or four, if the Bill was committed) in Hakewel's account, and four (or six) in Scobel's. It is just in this point of multiplying occasions for questions that the procedure of the next century was most ingenious. In 1848 Speaker Shaw-Lefevre, giving evidence before a Select Committee on Procedure, stated the number of possible questions on a Bill (excluding those on amendments) to be eighteen.

(2) In the process of amending a Bill it is clear from these accounts that the House still trusted almost entirely to a committee. The amendments came from a committee, according to Hakewel, in the form of interlinings and erasures of the Bill itself; according to Scobel, in something very like a modern amendment paper. But both accounts agree in showing that when the committee reported, not the Bill as a whole but the amendments offered by the committee were the subject of consideration, and that the House did no more than accept or reject the amendments, sometimes one by one but generally *en bloc*, unless to make verbal alterations, which could be conveniently written in at the Table.

The only kind of amendment habitually allowed to be done in the House was of a kind called the 'proviso'—a saving clause or reservation—which offered no difficulties, as it could be bodily attached to a Bill. It received as many readings as the Bill had received to which it was attached, and was treated as a belated portion of the Bill. Procedure had not yet developed the complicated forms and rules which must be observed by a large body in amending a Bill if it is to avoid confusion. The necessary experience had to be gained, and it is probable, as will be shown directly, that this experience was chiefly gained when the House made general use of the procedure (at that time only beginning) of itself sitting as a committee.

It may be noted in passing that it is possibly owing to the fact that the House first came to consider amendments in the form of interlinings and erasures of a Bill that it contracted the habit of verbal economy, of keeping as far as possible to the words of the Bill, which still marks its manner of dealing with amendments. What is meant may be made clearer by referring for a moment to the procedure of another Chamber. The French Chamber[1] proposes an amendment in the form of a complete alternative draft—an alternative motion, or article—or, to take an extreme case, treats as a single amendment a whole counter-project or alternative Bill. In contrast to this, the House of Commons exercises its ingenuity in contriving to effect the maximum amount of change by means of the fewest verbal alterations, transforming a clause by leaving out or altering a few governing words. It may be worth adding, as a further characteristic of our procedure, that, though having this humble origin in merely material convenience, this practice is retained for quite different reasons. Although it makes an amendment paper unintelligible unless carefully collated with the Bill, it has the advantage of focusing attention on essential points, of unmasking irrelevant amendments, and of relating the priority of amendments to the order of the pages and lines of a Bill, thus dispensing with the need, which the French system often entails, of debating and voting upon the order in which competing amendments are to be taken.

4. COMMITTEES

The next advance in procedure to be noticed—an advance which showed improved control by the House over the technique of debate, and tended still further to develop its control—was the taking over by the House itself, in the form of a Committee of the Whole House, of the whole process of considering and amending Bills, which it had hitherto left to small Select Committees. To appreciate this process it is necessary to glance at the development of the committee system.

[1] The French constitution of 1875-1940 rather than any more modern instance is chosen as a comparison because its history is fully documented and easily accessible.

The appointment of Select Committees is first recorded in the *Journals* in the 3rd Parliament of Elizabeth, 1571. Before that Parliament there are frequent entries recording the committal of a Bill to a single Member, generally a Secretary or Privy Councillor, as for instance, 2nd March, 1557/8, "Bill committed to be perused by Mr. Fitzchamberleyn" (probably "Vice-Chamberlain"). The term 'committee' originally signified an individual not a body, and committal in this sense had not a technical meaning, but was perhaps no more than a request for the opinion of a Member who, in virtue of his official position, could state the views of the Court. This was one of the methods by which the Privy Council exercised control over Bills.

At the same time there is no doubt that there had long been in existence a system of committees in the technical sense. From the fact that the *Journals* only begin to minute the committal of Bills to such bodies in 1571, probably no more is to be inferred than that a newly appointed clerk of the House introduced a fuller system of minuting. As stated more fully later (p. 46) the employment of small committees for the real work of a Chamber is a mark of a certain phase in the relations between a legislative body and the executive government—the phase which is called 'separation of powers'. Under the Tudors the relations between the Crown and the House of Commons were to a certain extent in theory at this stage, but in practice the Crown controlled the House of Commons not only through the Speaker, but also through Members who were Privy Councillors or had other official relations with the Court. The practice which had grown up of appointing such Members to all important committees resulted, as was intended, in their controlling the business of the House.

Such committees, which would now be called 'select' committees, were for long the chief machinery of the House. They were appointed by an informal method of nomination in the House which allowed the Speaker and 'those nearest the Chair' —the Privy Councillors and their friends—to control their composition. They first met in various places outside the House, generally in a place convenient for the lawyers, and later in the 'committee chamber' at Westminster. While small committees consisting of from 3 to 15 Members continued to be used, work of more than ordinary importance was devolved on larger committees, consisting of from 30 to 40 Members with the addition of specified classes of members (such as "gentlemen of the long robe" members who were of the Privy

Council, knights of the shire, etc.). The larger committees gradually developed into Standing Committees by being appointed for the consideration of all matters belonging to some specified class of business, such as "matters of religion", or "motions of griefs and Petitions". But Select Committees were at first the only committees to which Bills were referred.

The transition to Committees of the Whole House, which followed later, was partly due to the neglect of James I to maintain the Tudor method of controlling the House from within. Privy Councillors ceased to be returned in sufficient numbers to keep their hold on committees. At first there seems to have been nobody to take their place on these bodies. This is suggested by the practice which now grew up of allowing the larger Select Committees to be attended by other Members of the House, who had not been nominated of the committee, at first without, afterwards with, a vote. This was due to several causes, of which it is enough to mention that the quorum of a committee—eight—was relatively high and that they were apt to be "slenderly attended".

But the Committee of the Whole House seems also to have had a more deliberately intentional origin, which seems to indicate a desire on the part of the ordinary Member to deal in open House with the *arcana* which had hitherto been reserved for the 'Grandees'. Scobel (p. 49) says that "some Bills of great concernment, and chiefly [in] Bills to impose a tax", were committed to, and sometimes originated in, Committee of the Whole House "to the end that there may be opportunity for fuller debates, for that at a committee the Members have leave to speak as often as they see cause, and that such Bills, being of general concernment, should be most solemnly proceeded in and well weighed". A further reason may be found in the greater freedom of debate secured by the removal of the constraining presence of the Speaker, who was at this period expected to look after the interests of the King.

The first reference of a Bill to a Committee of the Whole House shows this pretty clearly. "Motion That the Bill touching 'hostile laws' should be committed. Affirmed that if Mr. Speaker were absent the whole House might be a committee, and thought fit to commit this Bill to the whole House, Mr. Speaker only excepted" (7th May, 1607). It was some time before the Speaker *necessarily* left the Chair for Committee of the Whole House. On 23rd March, 1609/10, Mr. Speaker, in a Committee of the Whole House, sits in the Clerk's chair, the

Clerk standing at his back, the 'Moderator' of the committee sitting on a stool beside him. But on 19th May, 1610, "Mr. Speaker retires to the Committee chamber", presumably to leave the House free to the Committee of the Whole House. By the time of the Long Parliament, at any rate, the Speaker regularly left the Chair on question put, and a chairman was chosen. (For the powers of the Committee, see Scobel, 36–9.)

While this process was going on at the beginning of the 17th century, Standing Committees were being turned into a complete system. There were five Standing Committees—for privileges and elections, religion, grievances, courts of justice, and trade (Scobel, 9). They were called 'standing' committees because they were "appointed at the beginning of the Parliament and remained during the session: other committees were made occasionally and dissolved after the business committed to them was reported". In the course of time these all, with the exception of the Committee of Privileges and Elections, became Committees of the Whole House—at first *de facto*, in 1628 in form as well. They were then given the name of 'Grand' Committees. Unlike Committees of the Whole House which had, as they do now, to ask leave to sit again, they were given power to adjourn themselves (C.J., 13th April, 1626). After the Restoration they began to take the committee stage of Bills, and soon became indistinguishable from Committees of the Whole House, although the formality of setting them up at the beginning of the session was continued until 1832.

One of these committees in particular, the Committee of Grievances, had a great history. Originating in the later Parliaments of James I it provided a sphere for the activities of the new class of leaders who were arising from within the House itself to take the place left vacant by the Privy Councillors. It developed a new form of small body for detailed and technical work—the sub-committee of the Committee of the Whole House. The same leaders were appointed to sub-committees of the Committee of Grievances and to sub-committees of other Committees of the Whole House. Through the Committee of Grievances they collected and sifted all the complaints of the kingdom, and through other committees they drafted relief Bills and took other suitable action. In this way they became a kind of Cabinet of the Commons which provided the organization for leading the struggle against Charles I. After the Restoration, though the system of sub-committees was dropped the Committee of Grievances continued as the very type of the Committee of the Whole House in its most important function.

The development, during the first half of the 17th century, of the Committee of the Whole House as an efficient method of discussing matters of detail provided the House with an instrument, which it employed in the latter half of the century, to establish its control over finance.

THIRD PERIOD, 1660–1832

During the third period, procedure in respect of the matters just described continued without any fresh developments. The main tendency, which was natural in a system based entirely on precedents, was in the direction of the elaboration of forms, the multiplication of questions and occasions for debate. In the matter of Bills, for instance, the number of possible questions (excluding those on amendments) was rising from the six mentioned by Scobel (see p. 24) to the number which Speaker Shaw-Lefevre, in his evidence before the Select Committee on Procedure of 1848, placed at the astonishing figure of eighteen. This was not altogether due to perverted ingenuity, as it seemed to a later age. Before the Reform Bill the number of silent Members was comparatively large, and opportunities had to be frequent to encourage the stream of oratory to flow. Also in the absence of well-organized parties and far-seeing Whips the chances of a Bill slipping through a stage were much greater. Stages were smaller obstacles than they are at present and had, consequently, to be multiplied in order to guard against surprise.

The formal character of the 'parliamentary practice' which reached its full development in this period is well expressed in a remark attributed to Speaker Onslow "that nothing tended more to throw power into the hands of the administration, and those who acted with the majority of the House of Commons, than a neglect of, or departure from, the rules of proceeding".

Perhaps it is surprising that, during a period when the great constitutional change occurred which transferred government to a Cabinet responsible to the House of Commons and drawn principally from its own Members, the House continued to maintain forms which were far more adapted to opposition than to the dispatch of business, and that it was left to the present period to redress the balance. Obstruction was not unknown. But its persistent use was unsuited to the impatient aristocratic temper of the 18th-century House. Besides it was not until after the Reform Bill that the increase in the volume of government business and the consequent congestion of the time of the House made obstruction an effective weapon. In other matters besides the control of time the House maintained much the same attitude towards the government as it had acquired in the reigns of the two Stuarts, an attitude of suspicion towards an external and none too friendly authority. This was due, no doubt, to the gradualness of the transition to Cabinet government, which went on almost unperceived, and also to the conservative attachment to old forms and precedents which tends to make the procedure of the House of Commons react slowly to changes in its functions.

This period did, however, make one important contribution, namely to the financial procedure of the House. It laid down the forms which converted the old somewhat blunt financial weapon of the Commons, the control of taxation, into effective detailed and exclusive control of expenditure and of administration. In order to describe this achievement it will be necessary to glance at the beginnings of this control in the first two periods of parliamentary development and also at the important finishing touches which were added in our own period.

FINANCIAL PROCEDURE

The financial procedure of the House of Commons remained almost unchanged from very early times until the latter part of the 17th century. This procedure was very simple, and consisted in passing a Bill of 'aids and supplies' for the Crown in return for the Royal Assent to Acts and a promise to relieve grievances. Such a Bill did not grant the King a definite sum of money but the right to levy taxes, and over the proceeds of these taxes the House had no control. In the 17th century the House made a new claim (which had the final result of transferring the control over the executive to itself). It began to require that the sums it voted should not be spent except on the purposes for which it had voted them. The power of appropriation, and the various methods adopted to enforce it over a greater area and with greater precision, are the chief factors which determine the development of financial procedure from the reign of William III. The stages by which this power was developed are a chapter of constitutional history, but it is necessary to glance at them in order to follow the corresponding developments of procedure.

The main stages in the establishment by the House of Commons of its predominant position in finance were:—

1. The progressive extension of the sphere of its authority until it included the whole range of national expenditure and revenue.
2. The exclusion of the House of Lords from participation in financial control.
3. The establishment of machinery to make the control of the House of Commons effective.

1. *The extension of the control of the House of Commons over finance.*

Before 1688 the King had been possessed of a large revenue (arising from Crown property, customary dues, and statutory duties granted for his life) which was independent of Parliament, and was supposed to be sufficient to cover the ordinary national expenditure. The King was therefore in theory under no necessity to demand supplies[1] except for extraordinary expenditure. In actual fact there had almost always been a margin of expenditure uncovered by non-parliamentary revenue, and the financial power of the House of Commons had begun as a control of that margin. The mode of extension of the control of the House of Commons in both these spheres was briefly as follows:—

(a) Revenue.—By 1688 the claim of the Crown to impose taxation on its own authority had been finally relinquished, and after the surrender by George III, on his accession, of the revenues from Crown lands the whole national revenue was provided by Parliament. Not long after, the national revenue became finally separated from the private income of the Sovereign.

(b) In expenditure the process is mainly that of bringing one branch of expenditure after another under the annual review of the House. The first step, taken soon after 1688, was to grant a fixed annual sum to the King, which was estimated to be sufficient with his non-parliamentary revenues to cover the ordinary peace-time expenditure, or 'Civil List'. The war expenditure of this and the

---

[1]The early meaning of 'supply' was 'make up a deficiency', 'supplement,' e.g. 'Nature is supplied in him by Art.'

following reigns was separately voted every year, upon Estimates in the case of the Army, as a lump sum in the case of the Navy (which escaped presenting Estimates until the 19th century). In course of time more and more of the peace expenditure was transferred from the Civil List to the Civil Service Estimates which were voted annually. The Estimates were next divided into separate votes for distinct services, and the appropriation of every vote was enforced. Even that portion of the expenditure which consisted of permanent charges withdrawn from automatic review every session was fixed by Act of Parliament, and remained completely under the control of the House of Commons.

2. *The exclusion of the Lords from a share in the control of finance.*

As the authority for a grant of supply to the Crown was from a very early period a legislative act, the advice and assent of the Lords was required. Consequently the method adopted by the Commons to exclude the Lords from participation in financial control was to draw a distinction between Bills of 'aids and supplies' and other Bills. As far back as the reign of Henry IV a formula was introduced for a grant which put the Commons in the foreground. The Commons made the grant with the assent of the Lords. But it was not until the 17th century that the Commons began to claim to make the grant alone. The steps by which the historical privilege of the Commons came to be defined in a form which lasted for the next two centuries were as follows:—

(1) In the first Parliament of Charles I, 1626, the enacting formula, which is still in use for Bills of aids and supplies, was introduced. It recites that the Commons have granted a tax, and then it is enacted by the King "by and with the advice and consent of the Lords", etc. (in the formula employed for other Acts) that the tax be imposed.

(2) The joint effect of the Resolutions passed in 1671 and 1678 is to deny the right of the Lords to *alter* aids and supplies, and to claim that the Bills for granting them "ought to begin with the Commons" (C.J. (1667–87) 235, 509).

This was the position reached in the 17th century. To complete the story:—

(3) In 1860, on the rejection by the Lords of the Paper Duties Repeal Bill, the Commons passed Resolutions

which restated their claims and, while admitting that the Lords had on occasion in the past exercised the right of *rejecting* such Bills, intimated that it was in the power of the Commons so to frame such Bills as to guard against an undue exercise of that power. In accordance with these Resolutions the whole financial scheme for the year, in which scheme the proposal for the repeal of the Paper Duties was included, was in 1861 embodied in a single Bill. This precedent has generally been followed since that date (May, 770).

(4) In 1911 the Parliament Act, which made the assent of the Lords to a 'money' Bill no longer essential, was passed (see p. 287).

3. *The establishment of financial machinery by the House of Commons to make its control over finance effective.*

During the first half of the 17th century the House evolved the procedure on Bills of 'aids and supplies', which in essentials has continued to be the procedure until the present time. These Bills were begun by the voting of 'heads' in Committee of the Whole House, and the Bill, drafted in accordance with these heads, was after second reading again committed to a Committee of the Whole House. Financial procedure was thus a combination of the Motion and the Bill—a Bill brought in on Resolutions previously discussed.

(1) *The preliminary stage of Resolutions.*—In dealing with this stage the Committee of the Whole House began about 1641 to develop two distinct functions, which became more differentiated later. In performing one function the Committee of the Whole House was called the Committee of Supply; in performing the other it was called the Committee of Ways and Means. This distinction did not at first correspond, as it came later to do, with the distinction between voting expenditure and imposing taxation, for, as stated above, until the 18th century, the granting of money to the Crown *was* the imposition of taxation. Both these committees therefore had the same function—to raise money. The difference seems to have been that the Committee of Supply raised money by the imposition of recognized taxes, long part of the fiscal system (which were indeed so assessed as to bring in roughly the same amount on each occasion), whereas the Committee of Ways and Means came into existence for

the purpose of devising new ways of raising money. An early mention in the *Journal* of such a committee is "The House resolved itself into a Committee to consider of some way of raising Monies" (1st December, 1641).[1] Monies were at first raised by borrowing, but during the Civil War the Committee of Ways and Means devised a number of new taxes, as, for instance, the excise duty. When, in the course of the next century, the authorization of expenditure became clearly distinguished from the imposition of taxation, the voting of the Estimates came to be the special function of the Committee of Supply, and, as more and more of the expenditure was transferred to the Estimates, the preliminary stage in this committee became the main stage in the control of expenditure. The function of the Committee of Ways and Means remained that of raising money by taxation to cover the amount annually voted in the Committee of Supply. After the Consolidated Fund was instituted in 1787, and the proceeds of taxes were no longer directly assigned to particular services but paid into a general pool, the Committee of Ways and Means met the votes of the Committee of Supply by authorizing the issue of money out of the Consolidated Fund, and thus acquired a spending as well as a taxing function.

(2) *The appropriation of grants by means of annual Bills.*—The appropriation of money means the control of expenditure and therefore of the executive. Appropriation might have been effected by a statute which declared once for all that the spending of money except for the purposes for which it had been granted by the House of Commons was illegal, just as statutes had declared that the levying of money for the use of the Crown without consent of Parliament was illegal. This would have based the principle of appropriation upon a constitutional law. The House preferred to attain this result *by a method of procedure, i.e.* by enacting every year that the sums voted *that year* shall be appropriated to stated purposes.

---

[1] See also C.J. (1640-42) 103, 138. Committee of Ways and Means at this time dealt with other matters besides the raising of money—for instance, with defence of the country and the state of the nation.

There may have been two reasons for this preference for a method of procedure: first, that the House still regarded the grant of supplies as an extraordinary and not a regular contribution; and secondly, that it preferred to represent the principle of appropriation, not as a new claim, but as the exercise of an old right—a view which was not without support from precedent.

Examples of appropriation are to be found in the reign of Edward III, but it began to be the regular practice in 1665, when the Commons inserted in a Bill granting a tax for the war with Holland, a clause appropriating the proceeds of the tax to that purpose. After 1688 appropriation became the invariable practice, and penalties were enacted against misappropriation. All taxes were specifically appropriated either to form a fund for a continuing service or to meet the annual supply, and this was effected either by a clause in the Bill imposing the tax or in some Act of the same session. After the system of national finance had been simplified by the substitution of a single consolidated fund for the previous aggregation of small separate funds, the whole of the money issued to meet the supply voted during a year came to be appropriated, as it is now except in abnormal circumstances, by a single Act, enforced by placing a check, independent of the Government, on the issue of money from the Exchequer.

Transition to Modern Procedure

The House thus applied to the control of finance the methods it had developed for the consideration of Motions and Bills, and attempted to exercise that control as a whole body. This method was adequate to the exercise of the power, to which the House was limited during the greater part of the 17th century, namely, that of granting to the Crown the proceeds of taxes to be levied under the control of the Crown. But when the House began to enforce the appropriation of grants to specific purposes—a practice which involved the need of machinery to control the administration—it was attempting a task too detailed and too expert to be performed by a large body collectively. Other bodies which, like the American Houses of Congress and the French Chambers,[1] have attempted to control finance directly, have found it necessary to supple-

[1] See p. 25n.

ment the action of the House by an elaborate system of committees, for the purpose of formulating a financial policy. The House of Commons would probably have been driven to the adoption of similar machinery (in spite of its having been employed by the Long Parliament). But before such a step was taken a variety of reasons, partly constitutional, partly political, had combined to introduce the system of Cabinet government, and in solving the political and constitutional problems the House eventually found the solution of the problem of procedure. The solution consisted in restricting the functions of the House to criticism of policy, reserving the power of initiating expenditure to the Crown through its Ministers, and entrusting the strictly financial supervision of expenditure partly to a reconstituted Treasury and partly to its own officials and select committees.

The Public Money Standing Orders

While Cabinet government was still in a rudimentary stage the House took a decisive step in the direction just indicated, by passing S.O. No. 78 (first passed as a Resolution in 1706 and made a Standing Order in 1713), which provided machinery for reserving to the Crown the right of initiating (and, by implication, of increasing) expenditure. This is a fundamental constitutional principle, but it is also a self-denying ordinance on the part of the House, which, by establishing the principle of appropriation, was for the first time in a position to profit by expenditure. It had been unnecessary to state this principle explicitly as long as the disposal of the supply granted by Parliament was at the unfettered discretion of the Crown. But when the House acquired the power to prevent money being spent except as it wished, it was only a step to transform this into a positive power of choosing the objects on which to spend money. This step was attempted in the early years of the 18th century, when the presence of unexpended balances in the exchequer proved a temptation to Members,[1] and, had it not been resisted, the right to initiate expenditure, which in most constitutions accompanies the right to direct its application, might, however contrary to the previously-established constitutional principle, have been acquired in practice by the House.

[1] Hatsell, iii, 166-77.

The other important Public Money Standing Order of this period (S.O. No. 79) lays down the already established principle that financial business must originate in a Committee of the Whole House.

FOURTH PERIOD, 1833–

The characteristics of this period are (1) the problem of how to make the best use of House of Commons time, and (2) a new method of regulating procedure by Standing Order.

The Problem of Time

Almost all the modern Standing Orders (that is to say, all with the exception of those relating to public money) deal with some aspect of the problem of the time of the House—who is to control it, how it should be divided between the Government and the rest of the House, how it is to be saved from dilatoriness and protected from unauthorized raids, and how it is to be increased by suitable delegation. If such matters and the kindred questions of securing the strict adherence to the pre-arranged programme of business of the daily sitting are excluded, few Standing Orders of any importance are left.

It is hardly necessary to explain how it was that the Government found the time at their disposal more and more inadequate with increasing intensity from the middle of last century. The revolution wrought in the scope of governmental functions by the social and economic changes which followed the Reform Bill is sufficiently evident. But before describing briefly the points to which the Standing Orders were successively directed, a word must be said about the position in which the Government found themselves with respect to the control of time at the beginning of this period.

The Control of Time

When the establishment of the Cabinet system made the Government the leaders of the majority of the House, it might have been expected that this would result in a privileged position being formally secured to the business of the Government. This result eventually took place, but it was deferred for nearly a century, owing to the tenacity with which the House clung to the principle of the equality of Members, and also because the House did in fact grant more by courtesy to the Government than it would accord as of right. Down to the beginning of the 18th century the practice had been maintained by which the arrangement of Bills and other orders was left to the discretion of the Speaker, subject to the overriding power of the House. Public Bills were preferred to Private, and precedence was given to certain Public Bills on the ground of their subject-matter (Hakewel, 134). The House also frequently made general orders for the arrangement of business and decided by vote between particular Bills. In the course of the 18th century the function of the Speaker in arranging business gradually ceased, and a new distinction was made of Order Days and Notice Days (*i.e.* of days on which business set down by order of the House and new business were respectively taken), two days a week being given to Order days. At the beginning of the 19th century one Order day a week was reserved to the Government, and this was increased to two in 1837, and to three in 1852.

The control of time by the Government, even on the days reserved for their use, was, however, by no means complete. Private Members had learnt to recoup themselves for the surrender of time to the Government by availing themselves of technicalities of procedure for the purpose of forestalling and interrupting Government business by motions raising debates on subjects selected by themselves.

Among devices used with this intention were:—

(1) Amendments to the question for reading an Order of the day proposing the reading of another Order.

(2) The Motion for the Adjournment of the House, which could at that time be moved by a Private Member before the Orders of the Day, between any two Orders of the Day, or (as now) in the course of debate on an Order.

(3) The exaggerated number of questions required in the course of a Bill, and the necessity of putting the question every time the Speaker left the Chair for committee, offered opportunities of delay, which were increased by the absence of any method of checking irrelevancy.

(4) The presentation of Petitions was permitted to take precedence of other business, and offered a convenient method of raising any subject desired. This was carried to great lengths, even before Reform, and after 1832 threatened to become the sole business of Parliament.

Reform by Standing Order

The previous paragraphs give an idea of the nature of the problem which the first reformed Parliament and its successors attempted to solve by a new use of Standing Orders. The process of reforming the practice of the House by Standing Orders may be divided into two periods. The first period (1833–80) was marked by the cautious nature of most of the proposals put forward and by the inquiries which usually preceded such proposals. Seven of the thirteen big committees on procedure[1] were set up during these 47 years as opposed to six in the 66 years that have elapsed since 1880.

To start with, the field for reform was large, but by 1880 a great deal of the dead wood had been cleared away. The elimination of a number of questions particularly on the various stages of a Bill; the reduction in the opportunities for spasmodic debates afforded by the presentation of Petitions and the reading of the Orders of the Day; the fixing of a time after which no "opposed" business could be taken; and the order enabling the House on one day a week to go into Committee of Supply without any preliminary motion—these were important contributions to the certainty of business and to its more rapid despatch.

The reform of Select Committee procedure, the inauguration of a new method of taking divisions, the appointment of a Deputy Speaker and various other reforms defining and regularising the machinery of the House, put a more business-like air on its procedure, while the reforms of the old financial Standing Orders and the cession of a third "order" day to the Government increased its efficiency. The most drastic innovation during the period was the order disciplining the disorderly Member. By 1880, however, evidence had been taken on every aspect of the problems of procedure, and further reform by agreement appeared to be impossible. The House was faced with the alternative of not fulfilling some of its functions or of devolving them on to committees. A balanced solution of the problem might have been reached in time, but after 1880 events moved rapidly to a crisis.

The second period of reform was prefaced by that threat of widespread obstruction which at one time appeared likely to break down completely the procedure of the House. Beginning in panic, the period is marked by the introduction of drastic measures, such as the closure and the restrictions upon both dilatory motions and substantive motions for the adjournment of the House. In 1902 the Government finally secured its hold

---

[1] These committees were those of the years 1837, 1848, 1854, 1861, 1869, 1871, 1878, 1886, 1890, 1906, 1913, 1932 and 1945-46.

upon the greater part of the time of the House, while the closure of Supply still further limited opportunities for criticism of the executive.

Devolution to Standing Committees was also a feature of the period. Beginning in 1882, made permanent in 1888, remodelled in 1906 and extended in 1919 and 1945[1], these bodies have never quite fulfilled the hopes entertained of them or given that relief which was expected of them. Recently the status of their Chairmen has been improved and larger powers conferred upon them. From time to time the House has shown itself irked by the predominance of the Government, but so far without result.

The Standing Order System

A word must be said about the general effect upon procedure of the Standing Orders. It is obvious that they have substituted a technical, strictly regulated system for the old easy-going methods of parliamentary practice. They are perhaps inevitable but they have made procedure far more difficult. It may be worth while to examine their effect in this respect. Parliamentary practice and the old usage depended, first, on a few rules resulting from a general agreement based on experience as to the right and natural—or, at any rate, the traditional—way of doing business. Some of these rules were explicitly laid down by the House chiefly in the 17th century in the form of Orders. Later there accumulated round these a considerable deposit of precedents and rulings made by the Chair, and so a body of parliamentary lore grew up, the knowledge of which was useful to a Member, as it gave opportunities, if he was ingenious, of scoring points in the parliamentary game. But ignorance did not positively penalize him. The system resulting from the Standing Orders is in complete contrast with all this. It is meant to, and does, definitely restrict the opportunities given by practice. Many Standing Orders are framed with great particularity to cover all possible contingencies without leaving any room for interpretation, while others leave a wide discretion to the Speaker or the Chairman. Both kinds, however, in fact constantly require interpretation, and a new kind of practice inevitably grows up through precedents and rulings based on the Standing Orders and on the old practice as amended by the Standing Orders. The resulting complexity is so great as to make procedure almost the life study of a few experts. The effect of this on the initiative of Members is discouraging. On

[1] And in 1947 and 1948; see Appendix IV.

the one hand modern practice by depriving ingenuity of its old opportunities has removed any incentive to the study of procedure. For, as a hole is found, it is systematically stopped up. On the other hand failure to conform with any one of a host of rules now frequently involves a Member in the penalty of being ruled out of order and not allowed to proceed.

Dependence of Procedure on Constitutional Functions

SUMMARY OF DEVELOPMENT OF PROCEDURE

The history of procedure during the four periods distinguished above shows a considerable measure of continuity and also a considerable amount of change, the latter consisting chiefly in the development of a different side of procedure during each period. For instance in the first period the proper share of each of the different factors in legislation—the King, Lords and Commons—was laid down. In the second period the rules of order in debate and the system of committees were established. In the third period, mainly, the House of Commons worked out its methods of controlling expenditure and taxation. While in the fourth period a system of Standing Orders, chiefly restrictive of debate, was imposed for the purpose of dealing with a rapidly increasing volume of public business.

These innovations in procedure correspond to changes in the functions of the House of Commons, which in their turn depend on changes in the position of the Commons in Parliament, particularly in their relations with the King and the machinery of government. These constitutional changes may be briefly indicated as follows.

In the first stage, the Commons, as newcomers to the national councils, were occupied in obtaining a recognized share in the business of Parliament and were often the minor partners in an alliance with the Lords against the King, or with the King against the Lords.

In the second stage, having firmly established themselves in Parliament, they gradually passed into the position of being the main opponents of the King.

In the third stage, the perennial antithesis between Government and Opposition ceased to be a struggle between King and Commons, and gradually became a contest between parties within the House of Commons itself, the issues being simple and mainly political.

In the fourth stage Government and Opposition became more completely internal to the House of Commons, while the matters at issue became highly complicated, economic and social questions predominating.

The correspondence between parliamentary procedure and constitutional functions may be made clearer if, instead of looking at the additions made to procedure in response to new demands, we look at the development that took place in the permanent machinery of the House of Commons. It will be enough to take two instances of such development, (1) in the position of the Speaker, (2) in the use of committees.

The position of its presiding officer and the nature of the subordinate bodies or committees through which it works are the two matters in which the nature and status of a deliberating body seem most clearly revealed. A body which is self-contained and competing for power, especially if it has no long experience behind it, is likely to put its ablest member in the chair and make him its leader in action as well as its president in debate. Such a body is also likely to find that it remains ineffective unless it delegates the initiative in work which is constructive and not merely critical to small committees of its leading members.

The Office of Speaker

As far back as can be seen, the office of Speaker had two quite distinct functions. On the one hand, he was regarded as the vindicator of the privileges of the Commons and their leader against any threat from outside. On the other hand, he was the moderator of their debates with the duty of eliciting true collective decisions. It may be said in passing that the history of the Speakership has been the transfer of emphasis from the former to the latter conception. In the first period of Parliament the former conception was completely predominant, and it led to the loss of the Speaker's independence, for, as the political value of an understanding with the Commons increased, the King found it useful to have a man whom he could trust in this position. For this reason the Speaker became, and remained well into the second period, a nominee of the King, and as a general rule used his position to manage the business of the Commons in the King's interest. In James I's reign the Commons reacted against this arrangement by dispensing with the Speaker's presence in the formative stages of important business, and when they began to challenge the Royal system of government the Speaker's dual allegiance became impossible, and he was forced out of dependence on the King without, however, retaining his leadership of the Commons.

After the Restoration the Speaker never recovered his old leadership and remained for a time in a somewhat false position, as, while he needed the King's approval of his election and while his remuneration during his tenure of office and his prospects on retirement depended on the King's favour, the chief importance of his office lay in his being regarded as the guardian of the rights and privileges of a body which was growing continually more assertive and truculent in its claims against the outside world and especially the King. With the ultimate predominance of the Commons, and the consequently increased importance of the domestic side of the Speaker's functions—those within the House itself—this difficulty subsided only to be replaced by the danger that the office might become subordinate to party, and the Speaker come to be regarded as the servant not of the whole House but of the party in power. Fortunately these two misconceptions, which were due to over-emphasis on the external and internal duties of the Speaker respectively, to some extent counteracted each other, and it was during this third period that the conception of the Speaker as an impartial presiding officer was formed, which was carried to its logical conclusion in the fourth period by his dissociation from every aspect of party politics both inside and outside Parliament (see pp. 74–76).

The Rôle of Committees

A somewhat similar course of development can be traced in the history of House of Commons' committees. When, early in the second period, the *Journals* begin to yield information on this point, a system of small 'select' committees is found to be in existence, and there seems to be no reason to doubt that this system was commenced some time in the first period. But once more the peculiar relation to the King, which has shaped so much of the procedure of the House of Commons, produced its result. It became the interest of the King to control these committees, and this he effected with the help of the Privy Councillors who during the Tudor period found their way into the House in numbers that were small indeed in relation to the size of the House but appear to have been adequate for the purpose. By means of these committees, which with their superior knowledge and influence they succeeded in running, the Privy Councillor Members kept their hands upon all important business of the House.

James I failed to maintain this essential connexion with the Commons, but, seemingly as a result of its previous history, the system of select committees had become suspect to the Commons when they went into open opposition, and they found in the Committee of the Whole House a method of open debate, immediately responsive to the general feeling of the House, for which in spite of its inherent difficulties they succeeded in evolving a workable procedure. When, however, during the civil war in Charles I's reign the Commons assumed the rôle of governing directly, they were driven back into a system of small specialist committees. After the Restoration the Committee of the Whole House seems to have become the sole type of committee, and, when the House of Commons became the master of governments, the principle that its rôle was indirect control not direct government was so fully accepted, that it resolutely refrained from setting up small specialist committees, which would have become rivals of the departments of the royal government, and contented itself with controlling those departments through Ministers responsible to itself. This made the rôle of the House of Commons essentially critical, and for criticism its own open Committee of the Whole House was not ill adapted. In time a new use was found for select committees, as quasi-judicial tribunals of inquiry and criticism, until various circumstances combined to transfer most controversial questions to extra-parliamentary commissions and committees of experts. When in recent years a system of standing committees was established, these bodies were framed on a non-specialist basis and were intended solely for the relief of the Committee of the Whole House through sub-division of labour, and their functions were limited to the consideration of Bills. Control of administration was still left to the whole House.

Briefly summarized, the course of development which it is attempted to indicate was as follows. In the first period the Commons had to use select committees because they had no other specializing machinery. In the second period they still needed the system, but dropped it as susceptible to control by the King. In the third and fourth periods they did not need it, because, through the concentration of political power in their House, they had the organization of the ministerial departments under their ultimate control.

COMPARISON WITH FOREIGN PROCEDURE
Position of Speaker

The inevitable correspondence between parliamentary procedure and constitutional functions may be observed in foreign legislative bodies. What is peculiar to English eyes in the position of the Speaker of the American House of Representatives can be traced back to the comparative independence of that body in relation to the executive government. The Speaker of the House of Representatives is at the stage of the Speaker of the House of Commons in an early period of parliamentary development. This is not meant to imply any criticism of American institutions, but merely that they have developed tendencies, which were prevalent and even predominant in the English Parliament of the 17th century, but which we have discarded in favour of other tendencies. The functions of the Speaker of the House of Representatives as the leader of the majority of the House overshadow his functions as its presiding officer, as was the case with the Speaker of the House of Commons before the Commons obtained control over the government. There is, however, this essential difference. He has never fallen under the control of the President as the Speaker of the House of Commons during the first and part of the second period fell under the control of the King. There has been nothing to undermine his position as leader. He has no rivals through the presence in the House of members of the administration. Within the House of Representatives he is a powerful political personage. It is true that he has lost control over the personnel and chairmanship of the numerous standing committees, where, rather than in the House itself, the most important business is done, and that recent changes are rather in the direction of the English conception of the Speakership. But on the whole his duties as presiding officer are secondary, and he is expected to use his wide discretionary powers in the interest of the party of which he is the leader.

The constitutional position of the Chamber of Deputies[1] is sufficiently like that of the House of Commons to have made the office of President approximate more closely to that of the modern Speaker. He is a presiding officer and not a political leader, though he is generally an ex-leader and may hope to be one again when he leaves the Chair. It may be merely a difference of temperament, rather than comparatively short experience of parliamentary government, which has prevented

[1] As it existed till 1940; see p. 25n.

the French Chamber from imitating the anxious care which the House of Commons has taken to dissociate the Speaker from even the appearance of political bias.

Committees

The doctrine of the separation of powers which is paramount in theory in the United States and (though it is inconsistent with parliamentary government) retains some sentimental allegiance in France, is responsible for quite as striking a procedural difference in the matter of committees. The House of Representatives thrown on its own resources, without the collaboration of ministerial Members or control of departments, has naturally had to improvise its own organization. This takes the shape of a system of permanent committees each corresponding to a province of government. These bodies entirely control legislation, each committee receiving all Bills connected with its particular province immediately on presentation, and having the power to re-draft Bills as it pleases or secure the presentation of Bills drafted to suit it. They draw up the estimates of expenditure without necessarily having regard to the views of the administration, and keep the activities of the departments under constant and meticulous investigation. Their functions being constructive as well as critical, there is little check on their initiative in expenditure. A similar system prevails in the French Chamber with less reason, as it controls the government and every department is represented there. But the reason why the implications of parliamentary government are not pushed to their logical conclusion as in the House of Commons is significant. It is that, owing partly to the existence of numerous " groups " instead of a few main parties, and partly to the fact that the Chamber can dismiss a ministry, but a ministry cannot in practice dissolve the Chamber, the Chamber is far more stable and durable than any ministry. Hence a certain lack of confidence which the Chamber shows in the transient ministries of its own creation. And hence the creation of its " permanent commissions" which last for the whole duration of a Chamber, and are thus enabled to develop a greater continuity of policy and a higher degree of authority than the more temporary ministries.

Conclusions

It seems that there are certain conditions, chiefly constitutional but also political, which are so decisive in their effect on procedure that any considerable difference in respect of them is enough to make the procedure of one parliament a closed book to another. The results just examined are such fundamental matters. This is particularly clear in the case of the position of the Speaker, if one considers for a moment the way in which the whole modern procedure of the House of Commons' standing orders, with their attempts to restrict obstructive debate without abusing the rights of the minority, and the many delicate duties of interpretation which they impose, are based upon a general faith in the Speaker's impartiality. Few of these provisions could be usefully borrowed by another Chamber, unless such a faith were established. And that takes time, as we have seen. Further, the fact that this is not a basis on which the American House of Representatives, for example, has chosen to build its own system, is due less to differences of national temperament than to a fundamental difference in the relation of the legislature to the executive government. The same point might be illustrated by the difference in the use of committees. But perhaps it is sufficiently clear that there is no real similarity between the English and American system of parliamentary procedure, in spite of the superficial similarity suggested by the common use of a great many parliamentary terms and even processes, such as the 'readings' of Bills, which were borrowed from the procedure of the 17th-century House of Commons by American State legislatures, and made current in Congress by Jefferson's *Manual*.

INFLUENCE OF ENGLISH PARLIAMENTARY PROCEDURE

There is thus a very definite limit to the extent to which the procedure of one Chamber can serve as a model for another. In the 19th century, when representative bodies were established all over the world, the procedure of the House of Commons was generally imitated, but it cannot be said to have worked efficiently except in countries, like France and Belgium, where very large adaptations were made to meet differences of a constitutional or political nature, and in the British dominions where common traditions made the system familiar or natural. Even in the Dominions constitutional differences, though comparatively insignificant, make a wholesale and indiscriminate application of our system out of the question. A comparative inquiry into the procedure of Dominion parliaments might reveal some surprising divergencies. Such an inquiry would require the pooling of a great deal of expert knowledge which

E

does not at present exist in an available form.[1] It would be a task worth undertaking. Democracy is a notoriously difficult system to work, and not the least difficult part of it is to get a large representative body to function efficiently. No system of procedure can be perfect. For one thing, it must always be adapting itself to new problems and is inevitably more or less out of date. Besides at best it cannot be more than a balance between advantages and disadvantages. For instance, if it tries to secure a maximum output the rights of minorities must suffer. If it aims at the greatest freedom of debate, the business of government, given modern conditions, must suffer. There is no absolute best. Even the House of Commons, with its unrivalled experience, could only gain by learning the methods by which other bodies of like traditions have coped with one or other of the difficult situations which constantly arise in a democratic assembly.

LIMITATIONS THROUGH CONSTITUTIONAL AND OTHER DIFFERENCES

There is no absolute best in parliamentary procedure. But there are certain principles which experience has taught the House of Commons to value, and it may be worth considering which of these principles are of more than local applicability, after making allowance for those differences in the Dominions which need to be taken into account. To work this out with any completeness would be too ambitious a project. Nothing more will be attempted here than a few obvious suggestions.

To begin with the limitations on interavailability. Constitutional differences exist, but they are perhaps not very important in respect of procedure, since the general relations between the legislature and the executive government, summed up in the term 'parliamentary government', which constitute the main determinant of parliamentary procedure, exist in common. The main constitutional differences are that Dominion parliaments are not sovereign bodies, but bound by constituent Acts, especially where the constitution is of a federal character, and that generally the second Chamber has greater power, especially in finance, than the House of Lords. This is particularly the case where the Senate is democratically elected. These constitutional differences might affect parliamentary procedure in unforeseen

[1] An opportunity now exists for the exchange of information about procedure between the officials of Empire parliaments through the recent establishment of a 'Society of Clerks at the Table' which publishes a valuable Journal.

ways. But they clearly do so in the matter of privilege. The privileges of the House of Commons—both privileges generally, *e.g.* in respect of its constitution and procedure, and privilege in respect of finance—could not be claimed wholesale as a matter of inherent right by the lower House of a Dominion Parliament.

Another limitation of a different kind is to be found in the greater numerical size and the greater volume of business of the House of Commons, which constantly threaten congestion, and have in the past threatened paralysis of its functions. This condition is not at any rate chronic in any of the Dominions, though some of them are occasionally faced with similar problems. This difference makes the greater part of the modern procedure of the House of Commons, embodied in its standing orders, of comparatively little interest as yet to the Dominions. Such matters as the elaborate time-tables of the House of Commons—the permanent time-tables for the daily sitting, for the session, and for supply, and the special time-tables for controversial Bills—may be placed in this category. Probably also certain elaborations of the rule of closure, such as the power possessed by the Chair to select amendments, are suited only to the peculiar conditions of the House of Commons.

In trying to bring out what is of general value in the procedure of the House of Commons one may leave on one side a certain number of rules the object of which is merely, for the sake of uniformity and regularity, to choose between several alternatives which are equally good or equally harmless. Hatsell's dictum: "And whether these forms be in all cases the most rational or not is really not of so great importance. It is much more material that there should be a rule to go by than what that rule is"[1]—explains a good deal of procedure. It is often rules of this kind which are most cherished and imitated in the mere letter of them. The most important rules of this type are those which, in some form or other, are necessary to enable a deliberative body, especially a large assembly, to work at all. An example may be given in the rules about proposing and putting questions. If it is not to waste time such a body must discuss something definite and know what it is discussing. It cannot afford time for general talk at the end of which the Chair or somebody else 'gathers up the sense of the discussion' and embodies it in a motion or question. In the House of Commons no one can speak except to move a definite motion, or amendment, or to the question proposed on such motion,

[1] Hatsell, ii, 149.

which question must reproduce the terms of the motion. Further, not more than one question can be before the House at the same time. The rules for putting the question on an amendment are peculiar, and more worthy of imitation in the spirit than in the letter. When an amendment is to leave out certain words of a motion and insert other words, the first question put is that the words proposed to be left out stand part of the question (see p. 174). This form is a perennial stumbling-block to the inexperienced (who, if they wish to vote against the amendment, find that they have to vote 'Aye') but the rule does contain something of value. If many amendments are offered, this method of putting the question, if the question is decided in the affirmative, not only rejects the amendment, but also decides something about the motion, *i.e.* that the words ordered to stand part cannot now be altered. This prevents discussion going back over the same ground indefinitely. Such a result is certainly worth retaining, but it might equally well be attained by other less confusing methods of framing the question on an amendment. There is nothing sacrosanct about this form. It grew up for definite historical reasons which no longer apply, but it is a form which is cherished in the House of Commons and faithfully imitated—to begin with at any rate—elsewhere.

PRINCIPLES OF GENERAL VALUE

These exclusions account for a good deal of the standing orders of the House of Commons. What is worthy of imitation in its procedure consists chiefly of the principles which it has worked out in an earlier period, and the rules which it has based on these principles, generally without enacting them in standing orders. To begin with the position of the Speaker: enough has been said to show that the prestige of his impartiality (the tradition of which has spread to all the occupants of the Chair both in the House and in any of its committees) is the key-stone of House of Commons procedure, and to indicate the steps taken by the House of Commons to place him as clearly as possible above all political attachments. The establishment of this convention, if it can be called a convention, cost the House of Commons such painful and long-continued efforts that it would be unreasonable to expect it to reproduce itself automatically anywhere else. With regard to the other point, selected as fundamental earlier in this chapter—the use made of committees—is there a place in a true parliamentary constitution for a system of permanent committees specializing in different branches of public service ? The conclusion hitherto accepted by the House of Commons on the basis of its earlier experience and that of some foreign Chambers seems to be that such bodies cannot be really important unless they are given control of policy, that to control policy they require to be able to initiate expenditure, and that, if they are given control of policy and the initiative in expenditure, they cannot fail more or less to duplicate the functions of ministerial departments, and thus produce an undesirable division of government responsibility. But if the experiments in any of the Dominions show that delegation of business to bodies of a similar kind, but consti-stituted on lines which avoid these disadvantages, offers the hope of relieving a Chamber of some part of its over-great burden, it would be of the greatest value to the House of Commons to profit by such knowledge.

Moderation

Among the other rules of practice two types may be selected, as they express something in the spirit of the House of Commons which has been a valuable contribution to the success of parliamentary institutions—a temper of moderation and the spirit of fair play. These are qualities which, though they under-lie a great deal of procedure, do not readily express themselves in rules; and when this rare feat has been accomplished it is not surprising that the resulting rule is so obviously acceptable and has such a look of hackneyed good sense that it is only by com-paring the procedure of other Chambers that one realizes that, after all, it required to be invented. Among such rules may be placed the rule that all speaking must be directed to the Chair, not to individual Members or the House as a whole; that another Member must not be referred to by name but by some circum-locutory phrase (to find which is itself a cooling process); and that language must be 'parliamentary'—a phrase which speaks volumes. It is true no doubt that the 'conversational' tone, which, except (in the past) on 'full dress' occasions, has usually been characteristic of debate in the House of Commons, has been helped by the small size of the Chamber and the lack of a special place to speak from. The vast expanse of the House of Representatives, and the 'tribune' provided for speakers in the Chamber of Deputies are said to encourage oratory at the expense of debate. But if the favourable conditions of the earlier House of Commons were accidental, they have been deliber-ately reproduced twice, when the Chamber has been rebuilt—in the 1840's and again to-day. In this connexion one more rule may be mentioned—the rule against the reading of speeches, without which the 'cut-and-thrust' of debate is impossible. This rule has a further virtue. It seems to make for argument rather than declamation, and for conciliation rather than violence. It is not of course such rules which created the 'atmosphere' of the House of Commons, but they help to preserve it and to make violence look and sound foolish.

Fair Play

The other great principle worked out by the practice of the House is that of fair play especially to the minority. Speaker Onslow's account of the tendency of the procedure of his day has been quoted above (p. 29). By way of illustration, reference may be made to the rules about the motion (which in the 17th century provided a guarantee against manipulation of the form of the question); the rule which forbids an attack upon a Member unless he is given an opportunity to reply, or any personal charge being made unless it is explicitly formulated; the rules about notice, which guard against surprise and the 'slipping through' of business and which cannot be suspended, unless the general agreement of the House shows that no one will suffer. The modern standing orders which have so greatly reduced the opportunities of opposition have not withdrawn these safeguards; and some of the most restrictive of them have given fresh occasion to show that the technique of fair play is still practised in the House of Commons. One or two instances may be given. The strictness of the rule which limits the discussion of supply to twenty[1] 'allotted' days is considerably mitigated by the convention, which very soon followed the rule, that the choice of subjects on these days is entirely in the power of the Opposition (see p. 120). This liberty of choice of subject is also given to the Opposition and to private Members on other occasions, such as periodical adjournment motions and Consolidated Fund Bills, when grievances can be discussed. The harshness of the closure rules is reduced by the provision that the Speaker must be satisfied that the rights of the minority are not infringed; and, before the power to select amendments is exercised, care is taken to find out the amendments to which the Opposition attach importance. Such rights of introducing legislation as are left to private Members are theirs without qualification and there is no power in any authority of the

[1] Now twenty-six ; see Appendix IV.

House to favour the progress of one private Member's Bill to the prejudice of another's. In addition to all this, in arranging the programme of each day's business the views of the Opposition are constantly consulted and, as far as the state of business permits, met. Indeed there is often some truth in the familiar complaint that facilities are given to the Opposition at the expense of the back-bench supporters of the Government.

Rights of Minorities

In comparing the position of private Members and the Opposition under the modern procedure of the House with their position under the old practice, it is safe to say that their principal loss is in the power to *initiate* business, and that their rights of criticism are reasonably well maintained. The loss of initiative is the natural result of the system of parliamentary government. With regard to criticism, opportunities for criticizing administrative policy are amply provided by the old forms of practice which are still retained, such as the various uses of the motion for the Adjournment and the various forms of financial procedure. These, together, occupy a proportion of the time of the House which is remarkably constant every session, and on the average amounts to about a third of the whole number of sitting days (see p. 122). Modern procedure has even added to opportunities of criticism by a development of the practice of questioning Ministers (see p. 145). Opportunities of criticizing the legislative proposals of the Government are also considerable; and, in the case of a Bill which is sufficiently important to be committed to a Committee of the Whole House there is a measure of co-operation between all parts of the House, in which every Member has an opportunity of contributing his quota to the improvement of the Bill. It is true that the greater strictness in the interpretation of rules, which is the natural result of applying a written code of standing orders, has had its effect upon the older parts of procedure. Examples may be drawn from the rule of relevancy, and the rules of financial procedure. The old latitude of debate which used to be allowed in the House has been replaced by a strictness which used to be applied only to committee proceedings. This is a gain in so far as it prevents the introduction of extraneous matter, as for instance when the motion for the second reading of a Reform Bill was met by an amendment for the production of papers on the state of Poland. But complaints are sometimes heard that advantage is taken of the strictness with which the rules of relevancy are applied to draft Bills with so precisely defined a scope as to make amendment very difficult. Similarly it is complained that the amendment of the financial provisions of Bills is increasingly fettered by the meticulous definition, extending sometimes to the enumeration, of the objects of expenditure specified in the preliminary resolutions to which the King's recommendation is given and which lay down the limits of expenditure that no amendment may exceed (see p. 277). These complaints raise very difficult questions which have only recently begun to be appreciated, as they involve divergent views about the extent to which, on the one hand, the Government should admit the House to a share of its initiative, and to which, on the other hand, the House has a right to exercise *constructive* criticism. It may be that the balance, which has been shifting for many years, is now definitely favourable to the Government's point of view. But it would be quite out of keeping with the spirit of the House of Commons, which tends to prevent parties in the time of their power from unduly pressing the advantages of their position, if a problem of this kind, once definitely posed, were not fairly examined and disposed of by a reasonable solution.

CEREMONIAL ELEMENT IN PROCEDURE

In concluding this sketch of the formal side of a process of such long and uninterrupted development, a word must be said about those elements of form and ceremony which the House of Commons, like most historical institutions, has preserved, largely out of respect for its own past, but not without appreciation of their present practical value. These elements may be briefly catalogued. At the beginning and end of a session and at intervals during its course the House is summoned to attend the King or his commissioners in the House of Lords (which represents the old parliament chamber) to hear the reading of the King's speech or the signification, in Norman French formulæ, of the royal assent which converts Acts agreed upon by both Houses into Acts of Parliament or statutes. At the beginning of every Parliament the Speaker-Elect submits himself for the King's approbation before presiding over the Commons. When occasion arises messages from the King are brought from the Bar to the Chair by a Minister of the Crown, and his answers to addresses are brought up by an officer of the Household in Court dress and read at the Table. A ceremonial quality also belongs to the various uses of the Mace which symbolize the authority of the House under the King, to the opening of the sitting with the Speaker's procession and the Prayers conducted by his Chaplain, to the Speaker's robes of office, the wigs and gowns of the Clerks, and the Court uniforms of the Serjeants and of the Members who move and second the address in reply to the King's Speech. This catalogue, which is nearly complete, shows that elements of ceremonial are sparingly used in the procedure of the House of Commons, but they are in one way or another constantly before the eyes of the House because they are attached to its permanent machinery, and because they mark those important moments when the House sees the results of its deliberations translated into the joint action of the whole Parliament.

The recurrent attendances of the Commons in the House of Lords may be examined for a moment as a typical instance of parliamentary ceremonial. As stated previously (see p. 7) the origin of this procedure is to be found in the original unity *for action* of the medieval Parliament—a unity which still exists, though it tends to be obscured by the greater emphasis which is now laid upon the separateness of the Chambers for deliberation. This ceremonial is therefore no artificial solemnity but an essential part of procedure—a part which retains its medieval setting but nevertheless expresses adequately what is still a vital aspect of Parliament. The characteristics of this instance of ceremonial will be found to belong generally to all the parliamentary ceremonial in which the House of Commons takes part. Stated briefly they are: (1) that it marks the proceedings which centre round decisions of Parliament rather than debates of the House, (2) that while it retains something which is of historical value it still has a real meaning, and (3) that this meaning generally expresses the relation of the House to the King and incidentally to the House of Lords.

The value of an established order of ceremonial forms for giving dignity to the corporate action of a body, for linking together the generations which compose its life, and for expressing the fundamental agreement in principle which underlies its much advertised surface divisions, should not be underestimated. That the need of such forms is felt by foreign legislatures of modern origin could be shown by many instances of not altogether successful imitation, revival and improvization. Unfortunately, appropriate ceremonial is difficult to invent—the art seems to have died with the Middle Ages—and it is difficult to transplant unless into a congenial soil. It is fortunate therefore for the newer parliaments of the Empire that they have ready at hand forms and ceremonies which are in no way strange or artificial for them, but arise naturally out of the constitution which they have in common with ourselves. It is doubly fortunate that these forms, the common practice of which is as potent to unify nations scattered in space as it is to link up generations divided in time, for the most part symbolize the relations of parliamentary bodies with the centre of imperial unity, the King. When, as in the occasional reunions of the Chambers in the whole Parliament, these forms represent vital constitutional facts, it can be realized that their value lies not so much in their preservation of the past as in the reminder which they give of the political wisdom which has kept the past alive by raising the fundamental principles of the constitution above the dust and heat of political changes and controversies.

CHAPTER II

PARLIAMENTARY LAW AND MACHINERY

THE contents of this chapter, which are inevitably somewhat miscellaneous, are intended to serve as an introduction to the detailed description of the business of the House by giving in outline an account of the system and organization, legal, personal and material, with which the House has equipped itself as the background or machinery for its activities. It will deal with such topics as the qualifications, or rather disqualifications (for the conditions are mostly negative), for membership of the House; the special powers or 'privileges' which the House claims as necessary to the maintenance of its dignity and authority; the powers and duties of the Speaker and the duties of the other officers who serve the parliamentary machine; the material conditions in which the House works and is observed at work; and the channels it has organized for the constant supply of information about the activities of the departments of state and public affairs generally.

In this account no space is available for a description of the parliamentary electoral system and this can be all the more easily dispensed with as it is not a subject which, like those about to be dealt with, can directly affect the procedure of the House. For an account of it the reader may be referred to May, *Parliamentary Practice*, c. 1; Anson, *Law and Custom of the Constitution*, vol. i. c. 4; Rogers, *Elections*, vols. 1. and ii.

DISQUALIFICATIONS FROM MEMBERSHIP

There are certain qualifications, once of historical importance, which are now *extinct*. Among these may be mentioned:—

Residence.—This was required by 1 Henry V, c. 1, but it gradually fell into disuse long before it was repealed in 1774.

Property.—The possession of landed property, worth £600 a year in the case of a knight of the shire, and £300 in the case of a burgess, was required by 9 Anne, c. 5, which was repealed in 1858.

Sex.—The disqualification of women was removed by the Parliament (Qualification of Women) Act, 1918.

The main disqualifications still in force are:—

Peerage.—An English Peer is disqualified, and also a Scottish Peer, whether representative or not; but not an Irish Peer, unless he is one of the representative Peers.

Clergy.—Clergy of the English Church and Ministers of the Church of Scotland are disqualified by the House of Commons (Clergy Disqualification) Act, 1801; Roman Catholic priests by the Roman Catholic Relief Act, 1829. Clergy of the Church of Wales are, since the Welsh Church Act, 1914, no longer disqualified.

Infancy.—The old common law disqualification of persons under twenty-one was made statutory by 7 and 8 Will. III, c. 25, s. 7, applied to Scotland by the Act of Union (May, 194; Anson, i. 80).

Aliens.—Under the Nationality and Status of Aliens Act, 1914, the old political incapacity of an alien is continued, but he can acquire political capacity (and so the right to sit in Parliament) by naturalization (May, 194).

Lunacy.—Under the Lunacy (Vacating of Seats) Act, 1886, the Speaker receives notice of the committal or reception of a Member as a lunatic. He must then obtain a report from the Commissioners of the Board of Control at once and a second report after six months. If lunacy then still continues, the two reports are laid before the House and the seat becomes vacated (Anson, i. 82; May, 194–5).

Bankruptcy.—Under the Bankruptcy Act, 1914, the disqualification comes into effect after six months from the date of adjudication, and continues in force unless removed by annulment of the adjudication or by a grant of discharge accompanied by a certificate that the bankruptcy was not due to misconduct.

Felony.—Under the Forfeiture Act, 1870, the disqualification of a convicted felon has been made statutory. It ceases when he has suffered the punishment to which he has been sentenced or has received a free pardon.

Corrupt Practices.—Under the Corrupt and Illegal Practices Act, 1883, (1) A candidate personally guilty of *corrupt* practices is permanently disqualified from sitting for the constituency in which the offence was committed, and for seven years for any other. (2) A candidate, guilty through his agent of *corrupt* practices, is disqualified for seven years from sitting for the place at which the offence was committed as also is a candidate personally guilty of *illegal* practices. (3) *Illegal* practices by an agent disqualify a candidate for that constituency during the Parliament for which the election was held. (4) Persons, not candidates, guilty of *corrupt* practices are disqualified for any constituency for seven years.

Government Contractors.—The disqualification was created by the House of Commons (Disqualification) Act, 1782, and was extended to Ireland by a similarly named Act of 1801. Reference must be made to the Act for the definition of what is meant by a Government contractor. Penalties for sitting or voting of £500 for every day are imposed. For the effect of the decision of the Judicial Committee of the Privy Council in the case of a contract made by a Member with the Secretary of State for India (H. C. Papers 406 and 452 of 1912–13) see May, 214, and Anson, i. 91. The disqualification was held by a Select Committee in 1855 not to apply to contractors for Government loans, but it has been thought necessary in recent Acts for raising loans to insert a clause allowing Members to subscribe.

Pension holders.—Certain pensions from the Crown, but not Civil Service or diplomatic pensions, disqualify the holders (6 Anne, c. 7, and 1 Geo. I, st. 2, c. 56).

Offices which disqualify

The holders of certain offices are excluded from the House of Commons.

(1) *A Sheriff* or *Returning Officer*—for the constituency in which he actually exercises his duties. But where the duties are performed by an acting Returning Officer the Returning Officer himself is eligible for election (Anson, i. 85; May, 207–210).

(2) *Judges.*—The English judges, by the law of Parliament declared by a Resolution of 1605 and by the Supreme Court of Judicature (Consolidation) Act, 1925; the Scottish and Irish judges, by statute. A Recorder only for the city to which he is appointed (May, 205).

(3) *Civil Servants.*—Commissioners of Stamps and Excise

were excluded by statute in 1694 and 1699, but the principle of the exclusion of what subsequently became the civil service was established by the Succession to the Crown Act, 1707. This Act excluded all the holders of new offices (created after 25th October, 1705) and certain specified holders of old offices, and its principle has been frequently restated by later Acts creating offices of this nature.

(4) *Colonial Governors.*—By sect. 24 of the Succession to the Crown Act, 1707.

Restriction on Number of Ministers in Commons

The law restricting the number of Ministers and their Parliamentary Secretaries entitled to sit in the Commons was simplified by the Ministers of the Crown Act, 1937 (Part II). Section 9 provides that the Prime Minister and a maximum of twenty of the principal Ministers, with twenty parliamentary secretaries and five Junior Lords of the Treasury (Government 'Whips') may sit in the Commons. Apart from the Ministers referred to in this Act, the three Members who hold office in the Royal Household and four law officers, three Ministers without portfolio (if Privy Councillors), and certain recently created Ministers and their parliamentary secretaries may sit. In normal times there is a permitted maximum of sixty-two paid ministerial offices whose holders may sit and vote in the Commons. These statutory limitations are important because large increases in the number of Members holding ministerial appointments would bring obvious dangers. Concern has recently been expressed by a Select Committee of inquiry, which in 1941 examined the holding of office by Members of the Commons, lest the number of Members owing allegiance to the Government should become too great a proportion of the whole House (May, 203–204).

Offices which do not disqualify

(1) *Ministers of the Crown.*—Apart from the restriction on the *number* of Ministers described above, the acceptance of 'political' office no longer entails any need to vacate a seat in order to seek re-election. This position was reached as the result of a long process beginning with the Succession to the Crown Act. Very briefly the steps in the process were these: The Act of Settlement, 1700, had

enacted that when the House of Hanover succeeded, the acceptance of *any* office of profit should make the holder incapable of serving as a Member of the House of Commons. From this rule, which, by concentrating Ministers in the House of Lords, would have condemned the Commons to insignificance, the House receded in time, and by sect. 25 of the Succession to the Crown Act replaced total exclusion in the case of old offices (created before 25th October, 1705) by the provision that acceptance 'of any office of profit from the Crown' should vacate a seat but not prevent re-election. This class of partially or provisionally excluded holders of office did not include the Secretary to the Treasury and, speaking generally, the other 'under-secretaries' who were expressly exempted by the House of Commons Disqualification Act, 1741.

The more important Ministers, however, remained subject to this requirement, and when a new post of this rank was created, as was frequently the case during the 19th century, the requirement was regularly reimposed by the creating Act. A small alleviation was provided by the Reform Acts of 1867 and 1868, which permitted transfer from one to another of certain offices without vacation of seat. By 1919 the political and administrative inconvenience of the rule was so far recognized as outweighing its constitutional propriety that an Act was passed (the Re-election of Ministers Act) which suspended its operation for nine months after the issue of a proclamation summoning a new Parliament, and in 1926 an amending Act (introduced by a Private Member), by removing the time limitation upon this suspension, finally placed Cabinet Ministers, like their under-secretaries, in the position of being spared the necessity of seeking re-election.

(2) *Commissions and commands.*—The receipt of a new or other commission in the Services does not vacate a seat in the Commons, but by Service regulations personnel serving in the Forces in normal times are prevented from becoming Members. (For details, see May, 209–210.)

(3) *Ambassadors.*—The office of Ambassador has been held not to disqualify (May, 207).

(4) *Offices without profit.*—Even where an office has no salary or profits attached, acceptance of it may vacate a

seat. Cases are mentioned by May (p. 213). There is, however, the case of Mr. Pringle, an Unemployment Insurance Umpire, whose election was reported by a Select Committee to be valid.[1] Where, however, the patent of an office includes a grant of 'fees, rewards,' etc., even though such fees, etc., do not actually accrue, a seat has been vacated. It is necessary to safeguard this principle in order to ensure that the House of Commons is a body acting without dependence on the executive or the Government.[2]

Resignation of Seat

A Member may not, according to a settled principle of Parliamentary law, directly resign his seat. By a useful fiction, originating about 1750 (Hatsell), he accepts an office which is nominally of profit, and thereby vacates his seat. The offices selected since 1750 are: (1) steward or bailiff of His Majesty's three Chiltern Hundreds of Stoke, Desborough and Burnham, and (2) steward of the Manor of Northstead. They count as offices of profit and vacate a seat because, though merely nominal, the warrants contain grants of 'wages, fees and allowances'. They are grantable during a recess, but it may be noted that the resulting vacancy is not one in respect of which the Speaker is empowered by statute (p. 68) to issue his warrant for a writ during a recess.

These offices have been granted where, owing to an election petition pending, it was doubtful whether the recipient was actually a Member and where a Member had failed to take the oath (May, 212).

Payment of Members

In the Middle Ages, Members were paid at the daily rate of 4s. for knights of the shire, and 2s. for burgesses. The modern payment system was introduced as the result of the carrying of a Private Member's Motion in 1911, and an Estimate providing a salary of £400 per annum was submitted to the Committee of Supply and included in the Appropriation Act, a procedure which has been continued since.[3] It was ruled by the Speaker in 1917 that the salary should be payable from the date on which a Member takes the oath. In 1924 the Speaker ruled that the salary should be payable with effect from the date (with certain

[1] H.C. 131 (1924-25). [2] See H.C. 3 (1945-46).

[3] In 1937 the salary was increased to £600 and in 1946 to £1,000, to keep pace with rises in the cost of living.

exceptions) on which the Clerk of the Crown certifies that all writs have been received by him, but the salary cannot be paid until a Member has taken the oath.

THE PRIVILEGES OF THE HOUSE

An account of the growth and development of privilege may be found in May (Chapters iii to x), Anson (Chapter iv), and Maitland (pp. 240-5, 320-4, and 374-80). Here nothing more can be attempted than a short sketch of the nature and extent of the various forms of privileges and the procedure of the House in the event of their breach.

At the beginning of a new Parliament the Speaker, when he goes up to the House of Lords to receive the royal approbation of his election, lays claim by humble petition to "the ancient and undoubted rights and privileges of the Commons", and particularly to four: freedom from arrest, liberty of speech, access to the royal person, and a favourable construction of all their proceedings. To this petition the Lord Chancellor replies that "His Majesty most readily confirms all the rights and privileges which have ever been granted to or conferred upon the Commons by His Majesty or any of his royal predecessors".[1] The House, however, does not base its claim to its privileges upon the confirmation of its petition. May points out that some have been confirmed by statute, and therefore are beyond the control of the Crown, while others, having been limited or even abolished by statute, cannot be granted or allowed by the Crown. The House has always claimed that its privileges are part of the unwritten law of the land, to be collected out of its own records and precedents, and only to be interpreted by itself. In this claim the courts may be said to have acquiesced except in so far as the legal rights of persons outside Parliament have been infringed, when conflicts of jurisdiction have arisen.

Privileges specified by the Speaker's Claim
(1) Formal Privileges

Two of these privileges may be dismissed briefly.

The request by the House for a favourable construction of its proceedings is generally held to be made merely by courtesy,

---

[1] These privileges were regularly claimed at the beginning of a Parliament after 1541 (Maitland, 242), The first Speaker to petition for freedom of speech appears to have been Sir Thomas More in 1523. Roper's *Life of More* contains the draft of the speech he made on this occasion. For the extent of this freedom in the reign of Elizabeth see May, p. 49.

although this privilege may have seemed of more importance to Members in the reigns of Elizabeth and several of her successors.

The claim of freedom of access to the royal person is not for the access of Members as individuals—a right which is possessed by individual Peers—but for the House as a body headed by the Speaker, and only for the purpose of presenting an Address. As the House can, and does commonly, communicate with the Crown through such of its Members as are Privy Councillors the privilege is (as Anson says) only important "as a mode of giving emphasis" to an Address.

(2) *Freedom from arrest*

"Freedom from arrest is now no very important matter, because this immunity does not extend to imprisonment on the charge of an indictable offence, and in 1869 imprisonment for debt was abolished" (Maitland, 377). Until comparatively recent times, in view of the free use of imprisonment which the law made in civil cases, the privilege was one of great importance and necessary to the discharge of its functions by the House. It is a right of great antiquity and has been traced back by some writers to pre-Norman times. It exists in many foreign legislatures—as, for instance, in the American Congress (United States Constitution, Article 1, Section 6), and the French Chambers, where, indeed, it seems far wider than here. Though a prescriptive right, it was recognized, extended and, in the 18th century, greatly restricted by statute. It no longer prevents the commencement of actions against Members or distraint of their goods, nor does it extend to the protection of their servants.

In its present form it protects Members from arrest in civil cases for the duration of the session and for a period of forty days before and after the session, the object being to protect them as well in going to, and returning from, Westminster, and forty days being the period of the notice of summons required in Magna Charta (Anson, i. 165). It may be mentioned in contrast that the immunity of Peers is perpetual, the person of a Peer being "for ever sacred and inviolable" (May, 73). The period of forty days holds good after a dissolution as well as after a prorogation. Since the immunity of Members is now a legal right based upon statute, the old process of securing their release by writ of privilege is unnecessary, and they are discharged immediately upon motion in court (May,

71). The doctrine that a Member's attendance in the House takes precedence of all other obligations once enabled him to resist a subpœna to attend as a witness, but this privilege is now regularly waived (May, 75–6; Anson, i. 166). The leave of the House is required for the attendance of one of its servants served with a subpœna to give evidence concerning any proceedings in Parliament. From service on juries Members, and officers of the House as well, are exempt under the Juries Act, 1870.

The privilege of freedom from arrest is not allowed to interfere with the course of criminal justice. Treason, felony and breach of the peace were always traditionally outside privilege. In the case of Wilkes in 1763 the House resolved that there was no privilege in the case of seditious libel, although the Court of Common Pleas had decided otherwise. The Committee of Privileges in 1831 reported that "it has been considered as established generally that privilege is not claimable for any indictable offence", and this doctrine has been held to cover criminal contempt of court. While the House refuses its privilege to Members arrested on criminal charges—in 1815 a Member, Lord Cochrane, was arrested for conspiracy while seated on the Government front bench, though not while the House was sitting—it expects to be informed of the cause of their arrest. In the case of several Acts suspending the Habeas Corpus Act it has been provided that the cause of arrest shall be *first* communicated to the House and its leave obtained, but generally communication is made after the arrest, by letter to the Speaker by the committing judge or magistrate (May, 78), and after conviction the Speaker is informed of the offence and the sentence.

It only remains to add that freedom from arrest and from molestation in coming, staying and returning is extended to witnesses summoned to attend before the House or a committee, and to others (including officers of the House) in personal attendance upon the service of Parliament. While this is not of importance in view of the nearly complete abolition of imprisonment in civil cases, the protection under privilege of witnesses, etc., from the consequences of statements made before the House or a committee may claim attention. May gives instances on pp. 57–9, 130. In these cases, however, the grounds on which the House acted seem to derive as much from a projection of the privilege of freedom of speech as from that of freedom from arrest or molestation.

(3) *Freedom of Speech*

The privilege of freedom of speech has been twice confirmed by statute—in 1512, following a decision of the Stannary Court in Strode's case, and in 1689 by the Bill of Rights (Art. 9).

Its original purpose was to protect Members against the King, and it is thus connected with the precautions taken by the House against the publication of debates and its control of the admission of strangers. The printing of anything said in the House without its leave was forbidden by the Long Parliament in 1641, and during the greater part of the 18th century the House treated reports of its debates as breaches of privilege. The House still holds these powers in reserve, and when it wishes to deliberate in secret, all that is necessary is for a Member to spy strangers.[1] Under Standing Order No. 105, the Question, " That strangers be ordered to withdraw" must be put forthwith by the Chair without debate or amendment (May, 225-7).

Since the end of the 17th century the importance of the privilege of freedom of speech has come to lie in the immunity it confers in respect of words spoken in Parliament from proceedings in the courts. The extent of this immunity has been defined by a series of decisions which it is not possible to trace here. The resulting position may be summarized roughly as follows: Not only are words spoken in Parliament privileged, but also, by the Parliamentary Papers Act (passed in consequence of the decision in Stockdale *v.* Hansard), all papers printed by order of either House and all faithful copies as well. This privilege would not, however, extend to the publication, apart from the rest of the debate, of an attack made in Parliament upon an individual (see May, 56, on Wason *v.* Walter).

A Member remains accountable to the House itself for words spoken in debate. In old days Members were punished by imprisonment and even expulsion. Now the milder penalties provided by the rules of the House (see p. 193) usually suffice, but these only protect other Members, the Chair and certain constituted authorities. For statements about private individuals a Member is free of any legal restraint.

[1] During the wars of 1914-18 and 1939-45, the additional safeguard of declaring a sitting to be a 'secret session' was adopted in order to give effect to the provisions of penal regulations made under emergency statutes. (For details of this procedure, see May, 815-17.)

PRIVILEGES NOT CLAIMED BY THE SPEAKER

1. *Right of the House to provide for its proper constitution.*

Within the framework of law governing elections the House exercises certain functions with a view to providing for its proper constitution. It declares by a Resolution passed at the beginning of each session that no Peer (other than a Peer of Ireland, who has been actually elected and not refused to serve) has a right to vote. This has always been treated as an authoritative declaration of the law, and in 1872 was upheld by a decision of the courts (Anson, 1. 130). By Resolutions similarly passed each session it lays down the procedure for persons elected for more than one constituency, for persons elected upon double returns, and against bribery and corrupt practices at elections.

This section of privilege may be further considered under the heads:—

(1) the filling of casual vacancies;
(2) the determination of disputed returns;
(3) the determination of legal disqualifications;
(4) the right of expulsion.

(1) The filling of casual vacancies

(a) During the Session

When a vacancy occurs during the session by death, elevation to the Peerage, acceptance of office, etc., the House on motion orders the Speaker to issue his warrant to the Clerk of the Crown to make out a new writ for the election of a Member. This is generally moved by the Chief Whip of the party to which the Member whose seat is vacated belonged. The motion, being a matter of privilege, does not require notice (see p. 140) and takes precedence of other business. When, however, a seat has been declared void on the grounds of bribery, or treating, the House resolves that a period of notice (generally two days) is required for the motion for a new writ, and then the motion is considered before the Orders of the Day (May, 180).

It is necessary to await the formal establishment of the vacancy before moving for the writ. In the case of a Member succeeding to a peerage, the seat is not vacant until the writ of summons to the House of Lords has been issued.[1] When a delay in applying for the writ of summons has occurred, the

---

[1] New writs have, however, been ordered by the House in the room of Members succeeding to peerages before the writ of summons to the House of Lords has been issued (May, 179; see also C.J. 22nd January, 1929).

House has inquired into the succession to the peerage, and, on finding it established, ordered a new writ. The seat of a Member *created* a Peer is not vacant until his patent has passed the great seal (May, 179), but in the interval he refrains from sitting in the House, and, in order to avoid a delay, frequently accepts the Chiltern Hundreds. If it is found later that a motion for a new writ has been agreed to by mistake, and that the seat is not vacant, the Speaker is ordered to issue his warrant to the Clerk of the Crown to make out a supersedeas to the writ (May, 180).

The Speaker's warrant for the issue of writs is directed, for constituencies in Great Britain to the Clerk of the Crown in Chancery, and for constituencies in Northern Ireland to the Governor of Northern Ireland. On the receipt of the warrant the writ is issued and transmitted through the post. The Clerk of the Crown is held responsible to the House, and has been examined in relation to an error in the writ and required to attend and amend errors in returns (May, 183), and Returning Officers have been summoned to explain delays in making returns in due course.

(b) *Issue of Warrants during the Recess*

In order to avoid the non-representation of a constituency for longer than necessary, the Speaker has the statutory duty of issuing his warrant for new writs during a recess (whether consequent upon adjournment or prorogation). A warrant cannot be issued in the recess for a seat vacated through acceptance of the Chiltern Hundreds (Anson, i. 178 n.) or on account of lunacy (May, 181). The authorizing statutes are: in case of vacancy by death or peerage, Recess Elections Act, 1784; by acceptance of office, Election of Members during Recess Act, 1858; by bankruptcy, Bankruptcy Act, 1883, s. 33. The formalities to be observed by the Speaker are laid down by the Elections in Recess Act, 1863, and in May (p. 181). They include: the receipt of a certificate from two Members specifying the cause of the vacancy; the insertion of a notice in the *London Gazette* by the Speaker; and an interval thereafter of five clear days before the issue of his warrant.

Under the Recess Elections Act, 1784, the Speaker is required at the beginning of each Parliament to appoint a certain number of Members—not more than seven nor less than three—to execute his duties in respect of the issue of writs in the event of his death, absence from the realm, etc.

This appointment holds good for the duration of the Parliament, and is ordered to be entered in the *Journals* and published in the *London Gazette* (May, 182).

(2) Determination of Disputed Returns

The right of the House to decide in cases where the returns of its Members are disputed was first established in the reign of James I. At first such cases were decided by a Committee of Privileges and Elections appointed by the House, but this became an open Committee of the Whole House in 1672, and was eventually replaced by the House itself. It seems inevitable that this method should result in the decision of election cases not on their merits but on strict party lines, and this was notoriously proved to be the case in the 18th century.

Some improvement was effected by the Grenville Act, 1770, which transferred these cases to a select committee, but a decision according to merits cannot be said to have been obtained until in 1868 a judicial was substituted for a political tribunal.

Under the Parliamentary Elections Act, 1868, and the Parliamentary Elections and Corrupt Practices Act, 1879, controverted elections are tried by two judges, and the petition is presented, not to the House, but to the High Court of Justice, within twenty-one days after the returns have been made to the Clerk of the Crown. The House has no cognisance of the proceedings until the decision of the judges, certified in writing, has reached the Speaker, together with any reports as to corrupt practices, etc., and any special reports on matters which should be submitted to the House. These are communicated to the House and entered in the *Journals*, and orders are made by the House for giving effect to the decisions of the judges. If, for instance, the decision is that another candidate, and not the sitting Member, is duly elected, the Clerk of the Crown is ordered to attend and amend the return accordingly; if it is that the election is void, a new writ is ordered unless the House sees fit to suspend its issue. When special reports are presented, the House usually orders copies of the judgments and the minutes of evidence to lie upon the Table. If bribery is reported to have occurred, the obligation of making inquiries and instituting proceedings now falls not directly upon the House but, under sect. 45 of the Corrupt and Illegal Practices Prevention Act, 1883, upon the Public Prosecutor. Where, however, general and notorious bribery and corruption have been proved, the House suspends the issue of writs with a view to further inquiry and the ultimate disfranchisement of the corrupt constituency. This inquiry takes the form of a Royal Commission appointed upon the joint address of both Houses, and in pursuance of its report a Disfranchisement Bill may be introduced (see May, 189-90, where a list of Royal Commissions and Disfranchisement Bills is given).

(3) Determination of legal disqualifications

Although the establishment of legal disqualifications upon an election petition has been transferred to the courts, the House retains its jurisdiction over these questions, if they do not arise out of controverted elections. In this way one of the questions which might be decided by a court is decided by the House itself (see Anson, vol. i. 182). In the case of sitting Members the House claims the right to decide any question of law or fact which arises as to their qualifications. Any doubtful question, whether of law or fact, which arises concerning the seat of a Member is habitually referred to a Select Committee, and the House awaits its report before taking a decision.

(4) Expulsion of Members

The House exercises the right of expelling Members who are, in its opinion, unfit to sit, and who would bring discredit upon it. The *legal* disqualification for crime does not, as defined by the Forfeiture Act, 1870, extend beyond felony. Misdemeanour, for example, is not a disqualification in law, though it may entail a disqualification in fact for a considerable period.[1] Expulsion vacates the seat of a Member, but it does not disqualify him from re-election. That one House cannot create a disability unknown to the law was the lesson of the Wilkes case.

On the same grounds of privilege the House exercises the power of suspending Members—a power the exercise of which in certain circumstances it has defined by Standing Order (see p. 198), but which is not, of course, created or exhausted in that definition.

2. *Power of punishing for breach of privilege*

Breach of privilege is contempt of the High Court of Parliament, and the power to punish the commission of it rests, as in the case of the courts, upon the inherent power of an authority to do all that is necessary to maintain its own dignity and efficiency. The courts do not check each other in committing

[1] Anson, i. 182.

for contempt, and on the whole the accepted doctrine is that they do not interfere with the action of either House in this matter.

Examples of breach of privilege are given by May (c. viii).

They are summarized by Anson (i. 187) as:—

(1) disrespect to any Member of the House, as such, by a non-Member;

(2) disrespect to the House collectively, whether committed by a Member or any other;

(3) disobedience to orders of the House, or interference with its procedure, with its officers in the execution of their duty, or with witnesses in respect of evidence given before the House or a Committee.

(1) Disrespect to a Member

Attempts to threaten or intimidate Members for their actions in the House have been declared to be breaches of privilege by the House and offenders have been punished in numerous instances by reprimand or imprisonment. Libels on Members have also been constantly punished, but they cannot be raised as breaches of privilege, if they concern a Member in any other respect than his conduct in the House. The offering of a bribe to a Member is a breach of privilege, and the acceptance of a bribe by a Member has been punished by committal to the Tower or by expulsion. Even the acceptance of fees by Members for professional services connected with any proceeding in Parliament is prohibited as "contrary to the usage and dignity of the House". Thus Members are incapable of practising as counsel before the House or any committee of the House.

(2) Disrespect to the House collectively

This is the original and fundamental form of breach of privilege, and almost all breaches can be reduced to it. Special instances of it are libels on the House at large, upon the Speaker, and upon select committees.

(3) Disobedience to the Orders of the House and interference with their execution

Among breaches of privilege of this class may be placed the publication of debates, which was frequently punished, especially during the 18th century, and which it still remains within the power of the House to treat as breach of privilege

(May, 53). When complaint is made of misrepresentation in the report of a speech, the Motion censuring the printer is still framed as though to publish debates at all were a breach of privilege (May, 54). To publish the evidence taken by a committee before it has reported to the House is a breach of privilege, whether committed by a Member or any other person. Other examples that may be mentioned are the misconduct of witnesses before the House or a committee, the forging of signatures to a petition, etc.

The molesting of witnesses has been mentioned already (p. 65), and the case of interference with officers of the House in the execution of their duty may be treated in connexion with the procedure of the House in punishing breaches of privilege (p. 65). As a final example of contempt may be mentioned the vexation of Members and officers of the House by proceeding against them in the courts for their conduct in obedience to the orders of Parliament, or in conformity with its practice (May, 127), and tampering with witnesses in regard to the evidence to be given before the House or a committee.

3. *Proceedings upon complaint of breach of privilege*

For offences committed in his presence, the Speaker, when accompanied by the mace, has the power to commit without previous order of the House (May, 96). Normally the House, in pursuance of resolutions of 31st January, 1694, and 3rd January, 1701, before ordering a person to be taken into custody refers the matter to the Committee of Privileges (see p. 252). The Committee of Privileges is appointed at the beginning of the session, and since 1904 has been regularly nominated in anticipation of matters to be referred to it (May, 134).

Complaint of breach of privilege should be raised as soon as possible after it has occurred. If it has occurred before the sitting of the House, it is raised before the commencement of public business (see p. 159). If it has occurred after the beginning of the sitting, it may be raised between the Orders of the Day; and if it arises out of the proceedings of the House it may be raised in connexion with those proceedings. If the complaint is made of an individual, he is ordered to attend at the Bar, or, if a Member, in his place, and examined and dealt with according to the seriousness of his offence, the adequacy of his explanation, or the fullness of his apology. When a newspaper is complained of, a copy must be produced in order that the paragraphs complained of may be read at the Table. Upon these preliminaries a motion is founded upon which debate may take place, and the House may resolve that the matter complained of is a breach of privilege, or order that it be referred to the Committee of Privileges.

Complaint of breach of privilege can only be considered by the House. If it is raised when the House is in committee, progress is reported.

The punishments inflicted by the House are:—

Admonition, addressed by the Speaker to the offender who, if a Member, stands uncovered in his place, and, if not a Member, stands uncovered at the Bar attended by the Serjeant bearing the mace.

Reprimand, addressed by the Speaker, in the same circumstances, in cases where the offence committed has been graver and the offender is in the custody of the Serjeant.

Imprisonment.—The offender is committed in the first instance to the custody of the Serjeant and transferred to one of His Majesty's prisons. If a Member, he is imprisoned in the Clock Tower. In the old *Journals* the Tower or Newgate are frequently referred to. The period of imprisonment is during the pleasure of the House, but cannot extend beyond the prorogation.

Fines.—The House of Commons has not imposed a fine since 1666, the doubt whether it is a court of record implying the further doubt whether it has power to impose fines. The House of Lords, on the other hand, is a court of record and does inflict fines.

Warrants for arrest are drawn up by the Speaker on the order of the House and are executed by the Serjeant, who is empowered to call upon the assistance of the civil power and to use such force as is necessary to effect the arrest. If the causes are merely stated to be contempt and breach of privilege, no court has power to inquire into the nature of the contempt. If, however, the warrant should state the nature of the contempt, and it appeared on the face of it that it went beyond the jurisdiction of the House, it would, according to opinions expressed by high judicial authority, be competent for the courts to inquire into its sufficiency (May, 94-5).

THE SPEAKER

The Speakership is an office of great antiquity and dignity. Since 1689, as 'first commoner' with precedence after Peers of the Realm, the Speaker was, by Order in Council of 1919, given precedence immediately after the Lord President of the Council. He resides in a great house in the north wing of the Palace of Westminster; holds (alone of subjects) levées, which are attended in Court dress; exercises ultimate control over all departments of the House; and has officers of his own appointment—a secretary, chaplain, librarian and others.

The Speaker is attended in the House, and in entering and leaving it at the beginning and close of the sitting, by traditional forms of ceremony. The most notable feature in such ceremony is the Mace, which may be regarded as the symbol of the authority of the House, and, through the House, of the Speaker.[1]

To show that, unless the Speaker is in the Chair, the House is not constituted, the mace is removed from the Table when the House is in committee. A similar distinction marks the proceedings in connexion with the election of the Speaker. The mace is kept under the Table until the new Speaker is elected. It is then placed upon the Table as a sign that the House is properly constituted for its own proceedings. Until, however, the royal approbation has been received, the Speaker elect is not fully in office, and this is symbolized by the fact that he is not preceded by the mace when leaving the House during the interval between his election and the receipt of the royal approval (see p. 102).

The Speaker presides over the House and represents it in all its external relations.

His *external* functions as spokesman or 'mouth' of the House and guardian of its privileges may be summarized as follows :—

(1) Only through the Speaker has the House direct communication with the Crown. With the Speaker at their head the Commons have right of access to the King as a body, according to the privilege claimed by the House at the beginning of a Parliament.

(2) He receives documents and messages addressed to the House from foreign countries and legislatures and communicates them to the House when he sees fit. Any document communicated by the Speaker is entered in the records of the House.

(3) He executes all the orders of the House—as, for instance,

[1] There is in the halo about the mace something, also, of the prerogative.

by issuing warrants for making out new writs, for the commitment of offenders and for the attendance of witnesses, and inflicts reprimand and censure in vindication of the privileges of the House.

The duties of the Speaker *in the House* are exercised partly by virtue of the practice of the House and partly under Standing Orders.

In virtue of practice he presides over the House, enforces the rules of debate and decides questions of order. He calls Members who wish to speak, proposes and puts the necessary questions and announces the decisions of the House. He exercises a general censorship over notices, particularly of Questions to Ministers (see p. 145), and satisfies himself that any Motion is in order before he puts a question upon it. He does not vote in the Chair except in the event of an equality of votes. The principle, as expressed by Speakers, on which in such a case he votes are stated on p. 182. It is no longer customary for a Speaker to speak or vote in committee (p. 27).

The various powers and duties of the Speaker, which are exercised under the Standing Orders, with regard, for instance, to checking irrelevance and repetition in debate, the refusal of dilatory motions and the avoidance of unnecessary divisions, the punishment of disorderly behaviour, the acceptance or refusal of motions to closure debate, and his power to exclude amendments which he has not selected, will be dealt with later in their appropriate places.

Mention must also be made in due course of the duties imposed by statute upon the Speaker—as, for example:—

Under the Parliament Act, 1911 (see pp. 230 and 287) and the Church of England Assembly (Powers) Act, 1919 (see p. 327).

Historical Development of the Speakership

The outstanding qualities of the Speakership, as we know it, its independence and impartiality, were developed slowly during a period of five hundred years. This development is fully traced in Porritt, chs. xxi and xxii, and Redlich, ii. 156–68. The subject is studied from the personal aspect in Dasent's *Lives of the Speakers*.

The roll of Speakers—from Sir Thomas Hungerford, 1377— is unbroken. At first his principal function was to serve as a link between the Crown and the House of Commons. In 1400 the Crown began the practice of directing the Commons to choose a Speaker, which came later to be regarded as an indispensable step in the appointment.

Stubbs, in *Lectures on Medieval and Modern History*, calls the Speaker of the Tudor period "the manager of business on the part of the Crown and probably the nominee either of the King himself or the Chancellor". In these reigns the custom grew up for the Speaker to declare himself unworthy of election and even to make a show of resistance against being led to the Chair—a custom which survived until Speaker Onslow broke it in 1727. Also it was the custom for the Speaker to receive an "allowance for his diet" of £100 from the Crown, and often, in addition, high office. For instance, Sir Edward Coke was both Speaker and Solicitor-General in 1593, and under Anne, Speaker Harley was at the same time Secretary of State. As "manager of the Crown's business" the Tudor Speaker used his powers in the House to arrange the order of business and to influence the fate of a Bill by his explanation of its effect.

The struggle between Charles I and the Commons established the principle that the Speaker's first duty is to the House, and his election began to be of more importance than the royal confirmation. It is a long step from Speaker Finch's "I am not less the King's servant for being yours" to Speaker Lenthall's "Sire, I have neither eyes to see nor tongue to speak in this place but as the House is pleased to direct me". In 1679 Charles II, who made difficulties about the election of Sir Edward Seymour and refused his confirmation, failed to obtain the election of his own nominee and had to compromise on a third candidate. This was the last case of refusal by the Crown to confirm a Speaker-elect, and by the end of the century the Speaker's independence of the Crown was an established principle.

In the 18th century dependence of the Speaker on the Crown threatened to be replaced by dependence on party. Onslow (1727 to 1761) was the first Speaker to throw off all suspicion of dependence on the Government by resigning the office of Treasurer of the Navy and contenting himself with the proceeds of fees for Private Bills. In his long career he was able to set a standard of impartiality which his immediate successors failed to maintain, and which it took nearly 100 years to recover. With his exception the Speakers of the 18th century took no pains to stand aside from politics. Addington, in 1801, stepped straight from the Chair to the

Premiership. Abbot (1802 to 1817) repeatedly spoke in debate, and even carried his partisanship to the Bar of the House of Lords.[1] This conduct was felt to be sufficiently improper to deserve the proposal of a vote of censure. It was some time, however, before the rule was established that a Speaker should not in committee take part in debate and division like any other Member. This was done with decreasing frequency by Manners-Sutton (in 1821, 1825, and 1834), by Shaw Lefevre (on a non-political subject, the management of the British Museum) in 1856, and—the last occasion—by Denison (on 9th June, 1870. Redlich, ii. 135).

During the 19th century the principle that the Speaker on his election ceased to belong to a party grew firmly established. Since Addington no ex-Speaker has continued to sit in the House. Further, the practice has grown up of re-electing the Speaker at the beginning of each new Parliament as long as he is willing to stand. On four out of the five occasions during the 19th century, when the majority passed from the party which had elected the Speaker, he was re-elected. For the exceptional case, when Speaker Manners-Sutton was opposed in 1835 by the Melbourne Government, allegations of interference in politics served as the ground. Finally, with the exception of Speaker Gully, who was opposed in 1895 in Carlisle (having just before the dissolution been elected by a small majority), it has become customary that the Speaker is not opposed in his constituency. Mr. Speaker FitzRoy and Mr. Speaker Clifton Brown were however opposed in 1935 and 1945 respectively.[2]

THE DEPUTY SPEAKER

Down to 1855 no provision existed for supplying the place of the Speaker during an enforced absence. The House had to adjourn or, if the absence were likely to be protracted, it went through the formality of electing another Speaker, who, when the real Speaker recovered, himself 'fell sick' and retired. This system, or lack of system, which was only possible because of the extraordinary healthiness of the Speaker,[3] was superseded by the provision made in 1855 for the Chairman of

[1] He took the opportunity of delivering a money Bill for the Royal Assent to make a speech against the relief of Roman Catholics.

[2] For further details see Report on Mr. Speaker's Seat, H.C. 98 (1938–39).

[3] He was only absent through sickness twenty-nine times during the three centuries 1547-1853 (see Report on the Office of the Speaker, H.C. 478 (1852–3), Evidence, p. 1).

Ways and Means, and in 1902 for the Deputy Chairman, to act when occasion arose as Deputy Speaker.

Either of these officers may take the Chair as Deputy Speaker in one of two ways:—

(1) After an announcement made by the Clerk immediately before prayers (or when the occasion arises) (S.O. No. 96 (1)).

(2) Informally at the request of the Speaker without any announcement (S.O. No. 96 (3)).

The formal method of appointment is required in order to confer certain powers upon the Deputy Speaker, the most important of which is the power to accept the moving of the Closure (S.O. No. 29 (5)), and any powers not actually exercised in the course of debate. The provisions of this Standing Order (No. 96) have received statutory authority by the Deputy Speaker Act, 1855.

OFFICERS OF THE HOUSE

The Chairman of Ways and Means

Committees of the Whole House are presided over by a Member of the House, specially appointed for the purpose, called the Chairman of Ways and Means, who has a deputy, the Deputy Chairman (see below). He is appointed for the duration of the Parliament—since 1910 by a motion made by the leader of the House after the sessional orders have been taken on the day of the delivery of the King's Speech. When a vacancy occurred during a Parliament in 1911, in 1931 and in 1945, the same course was adopted, but in 1921 (28th April) the older method was followed of calling a Member to the Chair as soon as the House had gone into committee. If in such a case disagreement arises in committee, the Speaker resumes the Chair and the House decides (May, p. 238).

The Chairman of Ways and Means has final authority over all points of order arising when he is in the Chair and there is no appeal from his ruling to the Speaker. He has power in committee to accept the closure and select amendments. He acts as Deputy Speaker (as described above) and also has various duties in connection with Private Bills (see p. 293). He has only a casting vote in committee.

The Chairman of Ways and Means follows the same tradition of abstention from party controversy as the Speaker. He no longer exercises the rights of the ordinary Member to participate in debates and divisions of the House. His independence has not the same formal guarantees as that of the Speaker, as he is appointed by the Government from its own supporters, and is unlikely to be reappointed on a change of government. His seat is liable to be contested, and his salary is placed on the estimates and not, like that of the Speaker, charged to the Consolidated Fund.

The Deputy Chairman

The Deputy Chairman (first appointed in 1902) is appointed, like the Chairman of Ways and Means, for the duration of a Parliament and, like him, now generally upon a motion made in the House. S.O. No. 96 (2), which authorizes his appointment, confers upon him in the absence of the Chairman of Ways and Means all the powers of the latter, including his powers as Deputy Speaker.

Temporary Chairmen

In the absence both of the Chairman of Ways and Means and of the Deputy Chairman, the Chair is taken at the request of the Chairman of Ways and Means by one of at least ten Members nominated by the Speaker at the beginning of the session to be the Chairmen's Panel (S.O. No. 96 (4)). From this Panel the Speaker nominates the Chairmen of Standing Committees (see p. 240).

Other Officers of the House

The Clerk of the House is styled in the letters patent (by which he is appointed for life by the Crown) "Under clerk of the Parliaments, to attend upon the Commons". He is mentioned in the earliest *Journals*, and the origin of the office is not later than the separation of the two Houses.

His duties in the House are to sign the Addresses, votes of thanks, and Orders of the House, to endorse Bills sent or returned to the Lords, and to read whatever is required to be read in the House. He sits at the Table until the House goes into committee, when his chair is taken by the Chairman. His experience and knowledge of the proceedings of the House and his advice upon questions of order are at the service of the Speaker, of Ministers and of other Members (May, 240). The growing interest which the self-governing Dominions take in the procedure of the imperial Parliament has added to the occasions and extended the range of the questions upon which he is consulted.

G

The Clerk of the House, also, as the head of the principal department of the House, the officers of which he appoints, is to a great extent responsible for the efficient working of the parliamentary machine.

The Clerk Assistant and Second Clerk Assistant sit at the Table at the left hand of the Clerk. The date of origin of the former office is 1640, of the latter that of the union with Ireland. These officers are appointed under the sign-manual, on the recommendation of the Speaker, and removable only on the Address of the House (19 and 20 Vict. c. 1). Their duties are to keep minutes of the proceedings of the House and of Committees of the Whole House, to receive notices of motions, amendments and questions handed in by Members at the Table, and to prepare the agenda of the future sittings for the Notice Paper and Order Book (see pp. 87-89).

The other officers of the House are organized in three departments under the direct control, respectively, of the Clerk of the House, the Speaker and the Serjeant-at-Arms.

The department of the Clerk of the House is composed of about thirty officers appointed by him. Candidates nominated by him are required to compete among themselves at the examination for the administrative posts in the Civil Service. The department is divided into four offices: the Public Bill Office, the Journal Office, the Committee and Private Bill Office, and the Table Office.

The Public Bill Office is responsible for the printing of Public Bills, after presentation and as amended, and for communications with the House of Lords regarding Bills after they have passed. It performs important functions in connexion with the control by the House of public money and is responsible for staffing all Standing Committees.

The Journal Office compiles the daily *Votes and Proceedings* and also the annual volumes of the *Journals*, together with the sessional and decennial indexes thereto. Among its other duties may be mentioned those in connexion with the presentation of papers.

The Committee and Private Bill Office is divided into the lesser departments of Financial Committees; of other select Committees; and of Private Bills. The Clerk or the head of the last is responsible for Private Bill Legislation in all its stages and also holds the position of Examiner of Petitions for Private Bills (see p. 294). The Table Office is principally concerned with the preparation of the Notice Paper and Order Book.

Each of these offices consists of a principal clerk, and senior and assistant clerks. The conditions of service of the Clerks of the House are regulated under the House of Commons (Offices) Act, 1812, by a Commission consisting of the Speaker together with certain Ministers, who are at the same time Members of the House of Commons.

In the department specifically called the 'Speaker's Department' are: his Secretary, who, in addition to dealing with the Speaker's official correspondence, assists him in his social and personal relations with Members; his Chaplain (an office instituted in 1659), who reads prayers at the beginning of every sitting; the Librarian, who, with the help of an assistant librarian and a staff, directs a large library, assists Members in their researches, and performs duties in connexion with the preservation, arrangement and indexing of Accounts and Papers (see pp. 92-95); two officers in charge of the 'Vote Office', who supervise the circulation and issue of Parliamentary Papers to Members; and accountants, who are responsible for the collection of fees on Private Bills, the payment of Members, and the issue of railway passes.

The Speaker's Counsel is a legal adviser to the Speaker and performs important duties in connexion with Private Bill Legislation. Curiously, though not a Member of the House, he regularly sits as Member of one of its committees[1]—the Committee on Unopposed Bills.

The Serjeant at Arms is the head of another department of the House. He is appointed by the Crown "to attend upon His Majesty's person when there is no Parliament, and at the time of every Parliament to attend upon the Speaker of the House of Commons". After his appointment he is the servant, removable by Address, of the House of Commons. His duties are stated by May (p. 240). Among them are, to attend upon the Speaker with the mace upon entering and leaving the House, going to the House of Lords, or attending His Majesty with an Address; to preserve order in the visitors' galleries and lobbies of the House; and to execute the Speaker's warrants for the commitments of persons ordered into the custody of the House. For the better execution of his duties in the House he has a chair close to the bar. He is assisted by a Deputy Serjeant and Assistant Serjeant, and his department includes the Messengers, Doorkeepers and Porters of the House. As Housekeeper of the House (by statute), he has

---

[1] He also assists the sessional Committee on Statutory Instruments.

charge of all its committee rooms, and the services of the police constables on duty at the House of Commons are under his direction.

The Comptroller and Auditor-General

The Comptroller and Auditor-General is appointed by letters patent and removable only by Address of both Houses of Parliament. His duties are:—

(1) to control the issue of money, granted by Parliament in a Consolidated Fund Bill, from the Exchequer Account on the demand of the Treasury;

(2) to ascertain by audit of the accounts of departments that no money has been spent except on the purposes for which it was voted by Parliament, and to report to the House of Commons thereupon. His Reports form the basis of the work of the Public Accounts Committee.

THE PALACE OF WESTMINSTER

The Lords and Commons sit in what is still a Royal Palace. The old Palace of Westminster was a congeries of buildings, most of which were destroyed by the fire of 1834. The great modern block of buildings, which replace those destroyed in the fire, runs north and south along the bank of the Thames. Beside the main floors, on which the two Chambers are situated, there is an upper floor, occupied chiefly by committee rooms, and a lower floor on the Terrace level, given up to the rooms of Ministers, dining-rooms for visitors, and so forth. On the main floor the range of rooms nearest the Thames consists of the Libraries and the dining- and smoking-rooms of the two Houses. Separated by these rooms from the river lie the Chambers themselves, so placed at either end of a long vista (through the inner lobbies of the Chambers and the great Central Lobby) that it would be possible, when the doors of the House of Lords and those of the House of Commons are folded back, to see the Woolsack from the Speaker's Chair. The Central Lobby below the lantern of the Central Tower is neutral ground. To the north of it the building was originally reserved for the Commons, to the south for the Lords. But the Commons' greater demands for space have resulted in their encroaching on the Lords, and since 1941 the latter have temporarily yielded their Chamber to the Commons.

The buildings of the Houses of Parliament fall within the sphere of administration of three separate authorities, whose functions may be roughly indicated as follows:—First, as forming part of a Royal Palace, they come under the control of the Lord Great Chamberlain in such matters as the admission of visitors when the House is not sitting. Secondly, in respect of the maintenance of the fabric, and the provision and upkeep of furniture, the responsible authority is the Ministry of Works. Thirdly, for the allotment of rooms and for the admission of visitors and of the Press, while the House is sitting, the Serjeant at Arms, acting under the Speaker, is responsible.

The Chamber

In the year 1547 the Commons moved from the Chapter House of Westminster Abbey to Westminster Palace, where they were given the use of St. Stephen's Chapel, and they continued to sit there until it was destroyed with the greater part of the Palace in 1834. For the next few years they sat in temporary quarters near the site of the present House of Lords, and in 1850 took over the then newly built Chamber, which was destroyed in its turn during an air-raid in 1941.[1]

The most striking characteristic of the Chamber is its small size.[2] This had been the characteristic of the old Chamber, and the House deliberately preserved it, altering Barry's plans to do so. The other characteristic is its rectangular shape, the benches not facing the Chair, as in most foreign Chambers, but running lengthwise and arranged in two main blocks on the right and left with a broad open space down the centre and a narrow gangway running across. The rebuilding plans of 1944 retain both these characteristics, and were approved by a large majority of the House.

Members' Seats

The seating on the floor of the Chamber accommodates only about half the total of Members. In addition two long side galleries find room for about a hundred more. A Member has, therefore, no seat of his own, still less the convenience

---

[1] Reference should be made to the Report on House of Commons (Rebuilding) H.C. 109 (1943–44).

[2] With about a hundred more Members to accommodate, it is only about a quarter the size of the American House of Representatives, which has a floor space approximately equal to that of Westminster Hall (Bryce, 1. 144). The dimensions of the House of Commons are 75 feet by 45 feet; those of the House of Representatives 139 feet by 93 feet.

of a desk to himself—advantages which are enjoyed by the members of most foreign Chambers. His only method of reserving a seat is to be present at prayers and occupy it (he can put a card on it in advance in order to signify his intention of being present at prayers) unless he is serving on a select or departmental committee, in which case, by the resolutions of the 23rd March, 1888, and 4th July, 1927, his card will secure him a seat without his attendance at prayers. Cards for the purpose are obtained by a Member personally from an attendant of the House who is on duty in the Chamber from 8 a.m. daily.

The exception to the rule that no seats are permanently reserved is in the case of the two front benches nearest the Speaker on each side of the House. That on the Speaker's right is the Government front bench, or Treasury Bench, that on his left the Opposition front bench. This arrangement is of great antiquity, as is shown by the quotation from the 16th-century Hooker given by Redlich (ii. 27): "Upon the lower row on both sides of the Speaker sit such personages as be of the King's privy council or of his chief officers." The distinction between the Government seats and those of the Opposition seems to have been established in Walpole's premiership. The effect of this arrangement is not only to distinguish one party from the other, but also to separate each front bench from the rest of its party—to draw a line between the official and the unofficial point of view—so that the more official back-bencher sits as near the front bench as possible, and a detached or critical attitude is expressed by a position on a back bench or below the gangway. The right to sit on the Treasury Bench was originally enjoyed by the Members for the cities of London and York, according to Hooker, and is still exercised by the Members for the City of London on the opening day of a new Parliament. Certain seats which are prominently placed from the point of view of the Chair generally tend to be appropriated by Members whose right on the score of long service or for some other reason is recognized as a matter of courtesy. Such seats are particularly those nearest the Chair on the benches below the gangway. These seats are occupied by leaders of third parties (when such exist) or of groups within the parties. The allocation of seats to a party is, if any question arises, decided by the Speaker (May, 222, n.). Members who have been thanked by the House retain their seats by courtesy (Hatsell, ii. 67).

At the north end of the Chamber, facing the inner lobby is the raised and canopied Chair of the Speaker. Below him are the seats of the three Clerks also somewhat raised, and below them, stretching between the two front benches, is the Table of the House, upon which every document presented to the House lies or is deemed to lie. At the lower end of the Table (resting on the Table when the House sits as a House, fixed beneath it when the House is in Committee) lies the mace (see p. 54), the symbol of the authority of the House.[1]

Admission of Strangers and the Press

In the Commons' Chamber now being rebuilt, the galleries for spectators and the Press are at the two ends of the Chamber. That opposite the Chair and above the bar is the main gallery, holding over 200 persons; the seat immediately facing the Chair is reserved for the Heir to the Throne. The front benches of this gallery are divided into sections for Peers, for Ambassadors of foreign countries, for High Commissioners of the Dominions and other distinguished strangers. The rest of the main gallery is open to the public and is called the 'Members' Gallery'. On the floor of the House opposite the Speaker and to his left, and divided by a barrier from the House, is another bench accommodating strangers. A bench in a corresponding position on the Speaker's right hand and behind the Chair is reserved for officials from the Government departments attending to advise Ministers in charge of the business before the House.

The Press Gallery is above and behind the Speaker's Chair. Since 1918 ladies have been admitted to the Members' Gallery. Admission to the Members' Gallery is by Orders which are allocated to Members in rotation, seven days in advance of the day required or, if there is room, by direct application after 4.15 p.m. (11.15 a.m. on Fridays) to the Admission Order Office. Admission to the Distinguished Strangers' Gallery is in the hands of the Speaker.

[1] The existing mace is that supplied to the order of the House of 21st May, 1660, or may even be the identical mace made during the Commonwealth with the substitution, for the original head, of one bearing royal emblems (Article 'Mace' in *Encyclopædia Britannica*). The American House of Representatives retains a mace, ornamented with the Eagle.

The gallery reserved for the Press contains over 160 places, some of which are reserved for the staff of the Official Report. Accommodation is also found for Members of the foreign, Dominion, and Indian Press in this Gallery. Admission to the Press Gallery is regulated by the Serjeant, under the direction of the Speaker.

PARLIAMENTARY PAPERS

Parliamentary Papers[1] may be divided into those connected with its own proceedings issued by the House itself, and those presented from outside. The latter are called, technically, 'Accounts and Papers'.

PAPERS DEALING WITH HOUSE OF COMMONS BUSINESS

The Papers issued *daily* consist of publications in the nature of minutes, agenda papers, and notice papers. Some of them come out in two 'editions', which are distinguished by the names 'Blue Paper' for the earlier edition and 'White Paper' for the later edition. The 'Blue Paper' is also called the ' Vote'.

The Blue Paper, or Vote

The Blue Paper is circulated to Members daily throughout the session. It is a composite mass of papers, which form part of a number of different serial issues. The order in which the various separate papers composing the Blue Paper are arranged is fixed by custom as follows:—

1. *Votes and Proceedings.*—This is a record of the proceedings of the House on the previous day—of *acta*, not *dicta*. It is published on the authority of a Sessional Order passed regularly on the first day of the session since 1680, and is prepared from the minute books of the clerks at the Table by the Journal Office.

A copy of *Votes and Proceedings* consists of a series of numbered entries each purporting to record a vote, or decision,

---

[1] See H. B. Lees-Smith, *Guide to Parliamentary and Official Papers*, and May, 253–260.

of the House. Certain proceedings, such as Questions to Ministers, which involve no decision of the House, are not recorded. On the other hand, a number of votes are recorded which are deemed to have been, but have not formally been, taken—as, *e.g.* orders upon the presentation of Public Petitions, Papers and Reports from Committees, which in the old procedure used to be brought up, considered and voted upon by the House, but are now for the most part dealt with informally. The method of recording debates in *Votes and Proceedings* is based on rules which are too detailed to be given here. Enough to say that, with certain exceptions, the results only are recorded.

The *Journal of the House*, a more elaborate and also more ancient record of the proceedings of the House, is published annually (see p. 91).

2. *Private Business.*—This Paper deals solely with matters relating to Private Bills. The first part of it consists of the agenda or Order Paper of Private Business (stages of Private Bills and motions relating to them) for the current day (see pp. 291–307). The second part contains notices with regard to Bills to be taken on future days, and memoranda of various kinds, given by the parliamentary agents acting on behalf of the promoters of, or petitioners against, Private Bills.

3. *Notice Paper of Public Business* (giving the agenda of the sitting for the current day). The items which this paper contains are arranged under the following headings:—

(1) Motions for Unopposed Returns (see p. 144).

(2) Questions for Oral answer ('Starred' Questions (see pp. 145–152).

(3) A heading—"at the commencement of Public Business"—which comprises:—

(a) notices of Public Bills which it is intended to present to the House under S.O. No 35 (1) (see p. 159), and

(b) notices of certain motions only to be moved at this time, such as motions moved by the Government relative to the business of the House (see p. 160), and motions for leave to bring in Bills under S.O. No. 12 (the 'Ten Minutes' Rule) (see p. 161).

(4) The 'Orders of the Day'—the heading which comprises all the items on which debate takes place, namely, stages of Public Bills, the business of the Committees of Supply and Ways and Means, and certain Motions (see p. 162). Government Orders are marked with a star.

(5) Notices of Motions relative to the Orders of the Day—such as amendments proposed to be moved on a stage of a Bill or other motions which are contingent on an Order of the Day. An Order to which there are such contingent motions is distinguished by a small italic '*a*' before it, and the contingent motion is marked with the number in brackets of the Order to which it relates (see 4 (1) below).

(6) Questions not for Oral answer, or 'Unstarred' Questions (see p. 147).

(7) Notices of sessional printed papers which have been received by the Vote Office the previous day (see p. 96, *Parliamentary Publications*).

(8) Notices of the various committees on public matters which are meeting that day—together with time and place of meeting.

(9) Notices given the previous day.—By far the greater number of these, as a rule, are of Questions. But there are also notices of amendments to Public Bills (in Committee of the Whole House or on Report). When amendments are offered to a Bill in considerable numbers, they are not printed here but as part of a different series called 'Supplement to the Votes' (which follows immediately).

4. *Supplement to the Votes.* It comprises:—

(1) Amendments to Public Bills set down for consideration on the current day in Committee of the Whole House or upon Report, if such amendments occupy more than (say) a couple of pages; also notices (in equal volume) given on the previous day of amendments to the above stages of Bills to be considered on a future day.

(2) The Amendment Paper of Public Bills under consideration on the current day in a Standing Committee,

also notices given on the previous day of amendments to Bills to be considered in Standing Committee on a future day. This paper is supplied to Members on application.

5. *Minutes of proceedings* on the previous day of a Standing Committee, *i.e.* the names of Members present, the fate of amendments moved, and the results of divisions with the names of the Members voting on each side.

6. *Division Lists* giving the names of Members voting in divisions of the House on the previous day.

The Blue Paper circulated on Saturday and on the day after the House has adjourned for a period differs from the one circulated on other days in containing, in addition to the items mentioned above, a complete programme, so far as known, of future business, or *Order Book* (see below). It does not contain a list of notices given the previous day, but such notices are inserted in their place in future business and are marked with an asterisk.

The White Paper

The White Paper contains those portions of the Blue Paper which relate to the current day's sitting, *i.e.* of the items enumerated above, Nos. 2. Private Business; 3. 'Notice Paper' (1) to (6), and 4. 'Supplement to the Votes' (1) (so far as it relates to Bills to be considered on the current day).

The White Paper is circulated only in the precincts of the House and is available about three-quarters of an hour before the House meets. It is strictly a second edition of those parts of the Blue Paper which it repeats and should not contain anything new, but advantage is taken of its later appearance to correct any verbal or formal errors that have been detected in the Blue Paper—as, *e.g.*, by rearranging in their right order amendments to Bills.

The Order Book

The Order Book, which is also coloured white, is issued each day before the meeting of the House. It serves as a programme, so far as notified, of the future business of the session, showing for each day any Questions, Motions and Orders (with their contingent motions) set down for that day, whether by order of the House or by notice given, and concluding with a list of

Notices of Motions for which no day has been fixed, or for an 'early day' (see p. 156). Such Notices are given with various objects, but seldom with a view to being ultimately discussed.

Periodical Papers

Under this (unofficial) heading may be grouped:—

(1) The Weekly list of Public Bills, circulated on Tuesday, which gives all the Public Bills introduced during the session together with the last stage passed by each from introduction up to the Royal Assent, and the name of the Member by whom it was brought in, distinguishing by an asterisk Government Bills from Private Members' Bills. It also gives a list of the Standing Committees showing the progress made with Bills referred to each committee.

(2) The Weekly List of Statutory Rules and Orders which are in process of 'lying upon the Table' (see p. 93).— This paper is not circulated but is available to Members who desire it. It gives a list of Rules and Orders, etc.— instances of exercise of subordinate law-making power by the Departments—which allow an opportunity for the expression of its disapproval by Parliament, together with the date on which each was presented to Parliament and the period of time during which it is open to a Member to move a Motion for the purpose of disapproving. The period of time is given in the Statute under which the Department has exercised the power to make the Rule or Order, and the method of calculating the length of the period varied widely, but has now been in most cases standardised at forty days by the Statutory Instruments Act, 1946 (see also p. 167).

(3) A list showing the Order of Questions, printed on yellow paper and circulated to Members at the beginning of a session and after every adjournment. Its purpose is twofold: first, it enables Members to see on which days questions to each Minister receive priority, and secondly, the order of precedence between the several departments which have priority on a particular day.

(4) The Private Bill List, issued about once in two months,

corresponds to the Public Bill List, but is drawn up on a somewhat different plan, as it gives for each Private Bill the date on which it passed each of its main stages.

Public Bills

Every Public Bill, after presentation, is printed by order of the House before being read a second time (see p. 203). Public Bills are numbered in a sessional series, the number—[Bill 1]—being printed on the back and at the foot of the first page. Every Bill is also distinguished by having printed on the back the short title, the long title, and also (if introduced in the House of Commons) the names of the Member introducing the Bill and of his supporters. Bills may be reprinted as amended.

The Journal

The *Journal* is a record of the proceedings of the House compiled from the daily *Votes and Proceedings* and the Minute Books kept at the Table. It is the most ancient record of the House, dating back to 1547, when the Commons left the Chapter House of the Abbey for St. Stephen's Chapel. From this date it is continuous, with the exception of a short period in the reign of Elizabeth.[1] The early *Journals* contain occasional short notes of speeches, but it is now, and has been since 1641, a record only of *res gestae* (May, p. 250). It is the permanent official record, a printed copy being accepted as evidence in a court of law as to what has been done in the House (Evidence Act, 1845, s. 3, and May, p. 252). It is published annually, and one volume usually contains the record of a session, though, if there should be two sessions comprised within one year (as in 1922), the second session is included in the same volume.

The *Journal* is not drawn up in the form of minutes like *Votes and Proceedings*, but is cast in a leisurely narrative style, which has not lost continuity with that of the 17th century. Committee proceedings, which were first included at a later date (in session 1829), are recorded in minute form.

The *Journals* are provided with a valuable set of indexes, one an annual index bound with each issue of the *Journal*, the other a General Index, published in separate volumes, and its first volume dates back to 1547. Since 1880 the volumes have

[1] From 1580 to 1604.

been published decennially. The plan of arrangement of the General Index is to provide so far as possible a complete collection of precedents as well as a guide to the proceedings of the House, and accordingly its contents are entered both under the title of every item of business and under general 'procedure' headings, such as 'Amendments', 'Bills', 'Committees', etc.

ACCOUNTS AND PAPERS

Under this heading is comprised all that great mass of official papers which is continually pouring into the House from the departments of state, either at the instance of the House or on the initiative of the departments themselves. Papers presented in response to the desire of the House are called *Returns* (see p. 144).

Returns

Returns are of two kinds, either to an Order of the House, or to an Address to the Crown. This distinction, which corresponds to the constitutional origin of the departments, is still rigorously observed. It amounts to this—that information which is wanted from a department which originally grew out of the Royal prerogative, such as a department of a Secretary of State, is prayed for by an humble Address to the Crown, whereas information required from a financial department or from a department constituted under statute is demanded by an order of the House.

Returns are not to be ordered from private associations such as Lloyd's, or for obtaining confidential documents, *e.g.* opinions of law officers.

Returns ordered in one session are presented in the next without a new order, as the order is held to have force over the prorogation.

Returns, the old method of extracting information, are growing relatively, if not absolutely, of less importance, owing to the constantly increasing stream of reports and other documents which flow spontaneously from the departments to the public, though many now by-pass Parliament (see p. 96).

The Papers which proceed from the department without being called for by the House are divided into two classes:—

(*a*) Command Papers, and (*b*) Act Papers.

Command Papers

Command Papers cover all the more important documents which the Government and the departments wish to publish on their own initiative.

Papers presented by Act

Papers presented by Act ('Act' Papers) comprise all the reports, returns, regulations, etc., which a great mass of recent legislation requires to be laid before Parliament. Like Command Papers, these are presented to both Houses simultaneously, unless the Act restricts the laying of the Paper to the Commons.

Other authorities for the presentation of Papers

(1) Pursuant to a Standing Order, *e.g.* the Attorney-General's Report on Private Bills.

(2) Pursuant to a Resolution of the House, *e.g.* Treasury Minutes on Surpluses and Deficits in the Navy and Army Estimates.

(3) Pursuant to the Report of a Select Committee, *e.g.* the Register of Expiring Laws.

(4) Pursuant to a Measure (see p. 167), *e.g.* a scheme under the Union of Benefices Measure, 1923.

In accordance with the Resolution of the House of 7th April, 1851, Papers are no longer presented formally in the House, but are deposited in one of the departments under the Clerk of the House, the Votes and Proceedings Office. Papers of special importance may still, though the process is exceptional, be presented in the House, the Minister, who must be a Privy Councillor, going down to the Bar and bringing them up when called by the Speaker. Upon the question "That they do lie upon the Table" debate may take place (May, 257), but objection to debate under such inconvenient conditions was raised in 1865, and modern procedure would appear to leave no opportunity for it.

Command Papers[1] are presented *during the Recess* (the period covered by a prorogation or adjournment of the House) by being delivered at the Library (S.O. No. 109), and are recorded in the *Votes and Proceedings* of the first day on which the House next sits.

[1] For an extension of this procedure to Statutory Instruments, see App. IV.

Annual volumes of Parliamentary Papers

Parliamentary Papers are bound together every year in the following order:—

(1) Public Bills. All Bills introduced into the House of Commons or brought from the Lords.

(2) Reports of Committees, *i.e.* of Standing and Select Committees of the House of Commons, and also of Joint Committees. The numbers borne by such Reports form part of the same series as that which includes Returns and Act Papers.

(3) Reports of Commissioners, *i.e.* of Royal Commissions, departmental committees, etc.

(4) Accounts and Papers. These include all Returns and Act Papers, and all Command Papers except those which fall under (3).

Index of Parliamentary Papers

The Index to Parliamentary Papers, which is compiled in the Library of the House of Commons, is brought out in two forms, annually and decennially. The last volume of the decennial index is for 1929-30 to 1943-44. In addition there is an index for the half-century 1852-99.

PRINTING AND PUBLICATION OF PAPERS

The question whether and under what authority Papers are printed depends upon the method of their presentation.

Returns to Orders and Addresses, and also Papers presented by Act ('Act' Papers) are printed, if at all, by order of the House and bear a number in a sessional series, which also includes Reports of Select and Standing Committees. The order for printing a Paper is given in practice by the Librarian of the House after consultation with the presenting department.

Command Papers are printed on the order of the departments from which they originate. At first they were printed as appendices to the *Journal*. In 1833 the system began of numbering them serially, at first with a plain number, afterwards with numbers preceded by letters indicative of 'Command'. There are in all four series:—

In 1833 began No. [1], which ran to No. [4222] of 1868-9.
In 1870 began [C. 1], which ran to [C. 9550] of 1899.
In 1900 began [Cd. 1], which ran to [Cd. 9239] of 1918.
In 1919 began [Cmd. 1], which still runs.

Estimates, though presented by Command of His Majesty, are printed by order of the House.

The extent to which Papers presented to the House are available to Members has been altered during recent years, and the steps necessary to obtain Papers are best explained by reference to these changes.

During the 19th century it seems to have been the ideal of the two Houses that all Papers which had any claim to public interest should, when presented, be printed, circulated free to all their Members, to certain persons and institutions outside, and finally sold to the public at the lowest possible price. Early in this century this expensive standard was being gradually reduced by the joint efforts of the departments, the Stationery Office and the Select Committee on Publications.

The first method adopted was to limit the class of papers automatically circulated to documents of special interest to Members, such as Estimates and other financial papers or papers indicated by the presenting Minister, and to issue the bulk of papers only to those Members who asked for them, a 'Pink List' of such papers when available at the Vote Office being circulated daily with the Vote. More recently a further economy was introduced. There had long been a class of Government publications called 'Stationery Office Publications', consisting of papers issued by departments but not considered of sufficient importance to be presented to Parliament. Such papers were not available to Members except on payment. The method adopted by the Stationery Office was to transfer to this category papers which had previously been in the class of parliamentary publications. Many 'Command' Papers were no longer presented to Parliament. Others were presented but not given a number in the Command series (which would have made them parliamentary publications). In the case of 'Act' Papers only those printed by order of the House were treated as parliamentary publications, the terms of the Act under which any particular paper was presented being deemed to have been complied with by the deposit of a copy in the Library of the House. A list of the papers then transferred from the class of parliamentary publications to that of Stationery Office Publications is given in an appendix to the Report of the Committee on

H

Parliamentary Publications, 1923, and has been enlarged by subsequent additions. Later, on the recommendation of this committee Members were permitted to requisition a single copy of a Stationery Office Publication of the current session needed for their parliamentary work.

That there should be a class of papers presented to Parliament and yet not parliamentary publications is a standing puzzle to many Members, especially as there is no distinction of substance between papers of one class and those of the other, and as papers occasionally fluctuate from year to year between the two classes. It may be as well to repeat the points of difference between the two classes.

Parliamentary Publications comprise:—

(1) Returns to Orders and Addresses.

(2) 'Act' Papers, which have been ordered by the House to be printed.

(3) 'Command' Papers which bear a 'Cmd.' number.
These are all:—

> (a) entered in the *Votes and Proceedings* and *Journal* of the House;

> (b) bound up in the 'Reports of Commissioners' and 'Accounts and Papers' sections of the annual volumes of Parliamentary Papers;

> (c) entered in the annual and decennial Library indexes of Papers.

> (d) available to Members on demand at the Vote Office.

Stationery Office Publications comprise:—

(1) 'Act' Papers not ordered by the House to be printed.

(2) 'Command' Papers printed without 'Cmd.' number.

(3) Papers issued by departments but not presented to the House (the great majority of Stationery Office Publications consist of these). These are all entered in the non-Parliamentary publications group in the Stationery Office Consolidated List, and are available only on requisition. Those presented to Parliament, (1) and (2), are also entered in the *Journal*, etc., but not in the printed Library indexes.

The Stationery Office issues two lists: (*a*) an annual 'Consolidated List of Parliamentary and Stationery Office Publications', and (*b*) a monthly circular containing lists of papers and reviews of their contents.

OFFICIAL REPORTS OF DEBATES

Reports of debates of the House of Commons began with the notes taken by Clerks in compiling the *Journals*. In 1628 and again in 1640 the House took objection to this practice and it was discontinued. The first continuous record of contemporary debates (D'Ewes *Journals* were records of debates in the Parliaments of Elizabeth compiled in the middle of the next century) is that of Anchitell Grey from 1667 to 1694 published as Grey's *Debates*. In the 18th century the House stiffened its resistance to the publication of its debates, and twice—in 1738 and 1762—declared such publication a breach of privilege. But it never succeeded in stopping the practice, and by the end of the century it was openly tolerated. Some of the records of debates for the whole of this period were collected by Cobbett in 1803 and published under the title *The Parliamentary History*. In 1803, when the Press obtained a reserved portion of the gallery for reporters, Hansard began the continuous series of reports known under his name.

Hansard's *Debates* was carried on under the original Hansard and his son, at first as a private venture, afterwards with a Government grant, from 1803 to 1892, when the contract, as it had now become, was transferred. From 1909 it has been an official publication carried on by a staff responsible to the House, speeches which had previously been summarised being reported in full and in the first person. This work is divided up by changes in management, etc., into the following series:—

1. *Hansard Debates*,	1st series, 1803 to 1820,	41 vols.
2. *Hansard Debates*,	2nd series, 1820 to 1830,	25 vols.
3. *Hansard Debates*,	3rd series, 1830 to 1891,	256 vols.
4. *Parliamentary Debates*,	4th series, 1892 to 1908,	199 vols.
5. *House of Commons Debates*,	5th series, 1909 to	

The usual method of referring to volumes of the Debates is by giving the numbers of the volume, the series, and the column referred to, in that order, *e.g.* 66 *Parl. Deb.*, 4s., 375; or 9 *H.C. Deb.*, 5s., 2094. In this book the House of Commons Debates are referred to as *Deb.*: and the date and column number are given. May gives the date of the session, or the year, as well as the number of the volume of Hansard, but not the serial number.

The Editor and staff of reporters of the *House of Commons Debates* are part of the Speaker's Department, and it is one of the functions of the Select Committee on Publications and Debates Reports to assist Mr. Speaker in the arrangements of the Official Reports of Debates.

CHAPTER III

A NEW PARLIAMENT AND THE WORK OF THE SESSION

THE main purpose of this chapter is to give an account of the manner in which a session of Parliament is opened and concluded and of the distribution of the work of the House of Commons over the session. It is necessary also to include a description of the method of summoning and dissolving Parliament.

I. MEETING OF PARLIAMENT

Summoning of New Parliament

The summoning and dissolution of Parliament are acts performed by the Crown, the statutory condition being the requirement that a new Parliament shall be summoned within three years after a dissolution (6 W. and M., c. 2). In fact, the sanction of annual sessions is primarily financial, but the principle of the continuous existence of Parliament is recognised by the form of the Royal Proclamation itself, which in the act of dissolving a Parliament summons its successor and appoints the day for its meeting.

Dissolution of Parliament

A Parliament is dissolved either by an exercise of the prerogative of the Crown or by the efflux of time.

The duration of a Parliament is limited by the Septennial Act, 1715, modified by the Parliament Act, 1911, to five years from the date of meeting announced in the Proclamation summoning it. Its duration is no longer affected by the demise of the Crown. The Reform Act of 1867, which made this change, omitted, however, to provide for the case of the demise of the Crown occurring in the interval between a dissolution and the meeting of the new Parliament. In this event, it seems that the situation would be governed by the Meeting of Parliament Act, 1797, which requires (a) the old Parliament to meet and sit for six months if the demise occurs before the date appointed by the Proclamation for the meeting of the new Parliament, or (*b*) the newly elected Parliament to sit and continue until a fresh dissolution, if the demise occurs after the appointed (even though before the actual) meeting of the new Parliament.

The dissolution of Parliament by the exercise of the royal prerogative is, as stated, effected by a Proclamation which at the same time summons the new Parliament. This is now regularly issued shortly after Parliament has been prorogued.

The prorogation of Parliament is the usual preliminary to its dissolution. In 1922, however, the Proclamation dissolving Parliament was issued at a time when both Houses stood adjourned.

Steps in summoning new Parliament

1. The Proclamation. This has three parts—the dissolution of the old Parliament, the order for the issue of writs for the election of members of a new Parliament, and the announcement of the date of meeting of the new Parliament.

2. The issue of writs, by the Lord Chancellor for constituencies in Great Britain, and also by the Governor of Northern Ireland for constituencies in Northern Ireland, to the Sheriffs and Returning Officers of Counties and Boroughs.

3. Nomination (or 'election') day, the eighth day after the Proclamation (Representation of the People Act, 1918, Schedule 2, Part I 2A).

4. Polling day, the ninth day after the nomination day (Rule 14A of the same schedule of the above Act).

5. Return of the writs, inscribed or endorsed with the names of the successful candidates, to the Clerk of the Crown in Chancery.

6. The meeting of the new Parliament on the day appointed by the Proclamation (unless prorogued by another Proclamation), which must not be less than twenty clear days after the date of the Proclamation (May, 262–3).

Sunday, Good Friday, etc., are not reckoned (May, 24).

Meeting of New Parliament, and Election of Speaker

The business peculiar to the first session of a new Parliament is the election of a Speaker and the swearing in of the House. This business accomplished, the session proceeds in all respects like any other session, with the King's Speech, debate on the Address, etc.—matters which will be discussed later.

The new Parliament meets on the day appointed by the Proclamation, usually a Tuesday (the first day of the week on which all Members can conveniently reach Westminster). On this Tuesday the House assembles generally at 2.45,[1] and on receiving Black Rod's message goes up to the House of Lords to attend the Lords Commissioners. After the letters patent constituting the Commission have been read the Lord Chancellor, in accordance with their tenour, directs the Commons at the Bar to repair to their own House, elect a Speaker, and present him the following day for the royal approbation. The direction of the Crown to appoint a Speaker has, since 1400, been regarded as an indispensable step in the appointment of a Speaker.

On their return, the Commons proceed according to the ancient forms to the election of the Speaker. The Clerk, rising, points with his finger to a Member who is understood to wish to propose a candidate, and, after that Member has moved, to another Member as seconder of the motion. If no other candidate is proposed, support is generally indicated by the leader of the House, and the proposed Speaker, having addressed the House, is called to the Chair by the general voice of the House without any question being put.

This is the usual method—a single candidate, no contest, no vote—arrived at by agreement reached beforehand between the parties.

On the other hand, if another Member is proposed for election, his proposer and seconder make speeches on his behalf, and then both candidates address the House. After a debate, in which the Clerk continues to indicate the speakers by pointing to them, he puts the question that the Member first proposed "do take the Chair of this House as Speaker", and, if a division follows, appoints tellers and directs the Ayes and the Noes to their lobbies. If the vote on the first Member is in the negative, the question is put on the second. It is customary in such divisions for the candidates to vote, and for each to give his vote for his rival.

The customary mode of election of the Speaker has been devised to show in every detail the independence and the non-partisan character of the office. Thus the Speaker is proposed by an unofficial Member, and not by a Minister. His proposer and seconder are generally a county and a borough Member, and

---

[1] For altered hours, see Appendix IV.

when a Speaker is elected without opposition the proposer and seconder usually come from different sides of the House.

On the following day (probably Wednesday) the House meets, with the Speaker-elect in the Chair, and once more, on receiving Black Rod's message, goes up to the House of Lords, where the Speaker acquaints the Lords Commissioners in a traditional formula that as the "object of the choice of the Commons he submits himself with all humility to His Majesty's gracious approval". On receiving the Lord Chancellor's assurance "that His Majesty most fully approves and confirms him as the Speaker", the Speaker proceeds to lay claim, on behalf of the Commons, "to all their ancient and undoubted rights and privileges", and, on these being confirmed, leads the Commons from the Bar of the House of Lords back to their own House.

Retirement of Speaker and Election of New Speaker

The election of a *new* Speaker generally takes place during the session. The steps in the process are best shown by reference to an actual case. On Monday, 18th June, 1928, the Speaker announced his intention of retiring[1] in an address to the House at the commencement of public business (all the Members being uncovered) and his announcement was followed by expressions of regret made on behalf of the Government by the Prime Minister and on behalf of the other parties by their leaders. On the following day the thanks of the House were tendered to the Speaker in a Resolution moved by the Prime Minister, supported by the leaders of the other parties, and agreed to by the House *nemine contradicente*, and after an expression of his sense of gratitude by the Speaker, a humble Address was voted *nemine contradicente* praying His Majesty to confer some signal mark of His Royal favour upon the retiring Speaker and concluding with the assurance that the House would make good whatever expense His Majesty should think fit to be incurred. At the end of the sitting the Members and senior officers of the House individually took leave of the Speaker. On the following day (Wednesday) the Prime Minister, addressing the Clerk of the House, acquainted the House that His Majesty had given leave to proceed forthwith to the choice of a new Speaker, and the election of the new Speaker was conducted in the same form as at the beginning of a new Parliament, after which the House immediately

[1] For procedure on death of the Speaker, see C.J. (1942–43), 57.

adjourned. On Thursday the Speaker-elect, on the receipt of
the Message by Black Rod, went up with the House to the
House of Peers to receive His Majesty's approbation, signified
by the Lord Chancellor, and on his return, after the receipt
of the royal approbation had been reported, the House resumed
its ordinary business.

Process of swearing Members

Going back to the proceedings of a new Parliament, it must
be noted that the first business after the Speaker has led the
Commons back to their own House and reported the royal
approbation, is for himself to set the example of taking and
subscribing the oath required by law (see below and May, 270).
This he does standing on the upper step of the Chair. Members
follow in a recognised order, those who await their turn remaining seated. The first sworn are the Members of the two front
benches, then the occupants of the several benches called by
the Speaker alternately from either side of the House and from
above and below the gangway. After taking the oath or making
his affirmation, every Member subscribes at the Table the
'test-roll' (a parchment folded bookwise and headed with the
oath) and is introduced by the Clerk to the Speaker. Evidence
of a Member's election is afforded by the 'Return Book' which
is presented to the Clerk of the House by the Clerk of the
Crown at the beginning of the new Parliament, and no further
evidence is required from a Member when he presents himself
to be sworn after a general election. A Member elected at a
bye-election, however, is required to bring with him to the
Table a certificate, which he obtains from the Public Bill Office,
that a certificate of his return has been received from the
Clerk of the Crown.

The process of swearing Members, begun on Wednesday
(assuming the House to have met on Tuesday), continues on
the following day, by the end of which the great majority of
the House have been sworn and the ordinary business of the
session can begin on a subsequent day. While the House is
being sworn the Speaker must be in the Chair, and a quorum
must be present (Parliamentary Oaths Act, 1866, s. 3.).

Form of Oath or Affirmation

The usual form and manner of taking the oath, as prescribed
by section 2 of the Oaths Act, 1909, are as follows. A Member
holds the New Testament, or, if he is a Jew, the Old Testament,
uplifted, and says or repeats after the officer administering

the oath: "I swear by Almighty God that I will be faithful and bear true allegiance to His Majesty King George, his heirs and successors according to law. So help me God." Or he may use the slightly different form prescribed by the Promissory Oaths Act, 1868, and kiss the book. A Member who objects to being sworn, either because he has no religious belief or because the taking of an oath is contrary to his religious belief, may make an affirmation under section 1 of the Oaths Act, 1888. Besides the two days set apart for this purpose at the beginning of a new Parliament the time for taking the oath or making an affirmation is during the sitting of the House and before the commencement of the Orders of the Day or after their conclusion (May, 271–2).

Failure to take the oath disables a Member from sitting or voting, but does not vacate his seat (Anson, i. 66). But a Member who sits or votes without having taken the oath, thereby (under the Parliamentary Oaths Act, 1866) vacates his seat and becomes subject for every such offence to a penalty of £500 (May, 272).

A New Session

After the election of the Speaker and the swearing of Members the further proceedings of the first session of a Parliament do not differ in any respect from those of any other session. The formal opening for business, the King's Speech, the debate on the Address, are common to all. Before describing these it will be best first to deal with the machinery by which a session is opened and closed, and to show the measure of control possessed over the times and seasons of its sitting by the House itself and by the Crown.

Prorogation of Parliament

It is the ancient right of the Crown to call both Houses of Parliament together when it needs their assistance and to put a temporary period to their labours when it pleases. Originally such meetings were of an emergency character and at irregular intervals. In time a settled practice grew up and the House of Commons took care that their advice should be required annually. Just as the Proclamation dissolving a Parliament orders the issue of writs for the election of its successor, so the act by which a session is terminated never fails to announce the date of the opening of the new session. This joint action of ending the old and providing for the new session is the "prorogation" of Parliament. Parliament is prorogued either by the Lord Chancellor, at the command of the King (in his presence or by his commission), or by proclamation. Under the Prorogation Act, 1867, the former method must be employed for concluding a session; the latter is permitted for the further prorogation of a Parliament already standing prorogued.

Effect of Prorogation

The effect of a prorogation is to pass a sponge over the parliamentary slate. All proceedings which have not been completed—as, *e.g.* all Bills which have failed to obtain the Royal Assent (although they may have passed the House of Commons itself)—lapse. In the new session they have to start from the beginning without profiting from the progress made upon them in the previous session. The fact that this rule does not apply to an impeachment is due to the judicial character of such proceedings. It was clearly laid down by the House of Lords in the case of the Earl of Danby (L.J. (1675–81), 496). Private Bills are sometimes permitted by a special provision to start in the new session at the stage reached in the previous session. Resolutions of the House generally apply only to the session in which they are passed (unless they are expressly passed as 'standing' Orders), and, if not so passed but intended to have continued force, are voted again every session. There are, however, some Resolutions, voted on a single occasion, but without any definite limitation of time, which the House continues to regard as being effective. For instance, the Resolution of 23rd March, 1888, by which a Member serving on a select committee is permitted to retain a seat without being present at prayers, still continues operative, and was in 1927 extended by an amendment.

Alteration of Date to which Parliament stands Prorogued

1. The date to which Parliament stands prorogued may be deferred to a later date by Proclamation (such later date to be not less than six days from the date of the Proclamation), in pursuance of the Prorogation Act, 1867. When the session ends in August and the new session is intended to begin in the following January, it is customary to prorogue Parliament to an intermediate date in the autumn and to prorogue it again from that date, perhaps more than once, until it is finally prorogued to the date at which the session is intended to begin. The inclusion in the Proclamation of a paragraph referring to " the dispatch of divers urgent and important affairs " is an indication that the date mentioned in that Proclamation is intended to be the beginning of the session.

2. The date to which Parliament stands prorogued may be accelerated in one of the following ways:—

(1) by Proclamation under the Meeting of Parliament Act, 1870, and the Parliament (Elections and Meeting) Act, 1943;

(2) in consequence of the demise of the Crown (when all Members again take the oath, see May, 271). The Succession to the Crown Act, 1707, requires Parliament, if prorogued, immediately to meet and sit. The further provision of this Act for the determination of Parliament six months after the demise of the Crown was repealed by the Representation of the People Act, 1867;

(3) pursuant to statute

(a) under various Acts for embodying or calling out the reserve forces of the Crown a Proclamation must be issued for a meeting of Parliament within ten days if it stands adjourned or prorogued beyond that period.

(b) under the Emergency Powers Act, 1920, if a Proclamation is issued declaring that a state of emergency exists, and if Parliament would not otherwise meet, a Proclamation is issued for its meeting within five days.

Adjournment of the House

Either House of Parliament may adjourn at its own discretion independently of the other or of the Crown. An adjournment leaves uncompleted business unaffected, *i.e.* capable of being carried on from the stage it had reached before the adjournment. On the day after an adjournment an Order Paper is issued of the business to be taken at the next meeting. An adjournment may be interrupted and the date of meeting accelerated in any of the ways mentioned in the preceding paragraph (see also p. 126).

The adjournment of the House for a recess is now secured by a Motion, moved after notice, "That this House at its rising this day do adjourn" to a certain date, and is agreed to at the commencement of public business. The general debate customary on such occasions (see p. 118) which until recently took place on this motion now takes place on the motion moved later in the sitting "That this House do *now* adjourn". This method, which has the incidental result of sparing the Government the necessity of keeping a quorum in the House, is a reversion to an earlier practice (Hatsell, ii. 82).

Opening of new Session

When the greater part of the House has been sworn, the preliminary business of the first session of a new Parliament is complete. What now follows is common to every session. Parliament has to be informed of the causes of its summons, in the King's Speech. In the case of a new Parliament the date for the King's Speech is usually fixed for the Tuesday a week later than the day on which it met.

The King's Speech

On this day the House of Commons meets shortly before twelve and after prayers the Speaker sits in the Clerk's chair (to symbolise the fact that business cannot be transacted until after the King's Speech has been delivered) awaiting Black Rod. On the announcement of his approach the Serjeant, according to the practice (which is employed on each occasion of the entry of Black Rod, and which recalls the 'storm and stress' period of the House's history), bars the door and keeps it closed until it has been rapped three times. On the entry of Black Rod the Speaker resumes his own Chair and, if the King is opening Parliament in person, Black Rod announces that "the King *commands* this honourable House to attend His Majesty immediately in the House of Peers". If Parliament is being opened by commission, the formula is varied as follows: "The Lords Commissioners *desire* the immediate attendance of this honourable House in the House of Peers to hear the commission read". As soon as Black Rod has retired in the ceremonious manner adopted in the Chamber by the bearers of Messages from the Crown, the Speaker, accompanied by the Clerk and Members of the House, goes up to the Bar of the Lords to hear the King's Speech read.

When the King opens Parliament in person it is customary for him to read the Speech himself, but there are many precedents, especially during the reigns of George I and Queen Victoria, for the Lord Chancellor reading the Speech in the royal presence. If Parliament is opened by commission, the Speech is read by the Lord Chancellor, but (since 1867) framed as the Speech of the Sovereign, not that of the Lords Commissioners.

The King's Speech is both an act of State and a Government pronouncement of great importance, the responsibility for which rests wholly with the Cabinet. It contains two parts, divided by a formal reference to the Estimates addressed to the Commons alone—first a statement about the foreign relations and policy of the country, and secondly a statement of the attitude of the Government towards matters of home policy, together with a summary of the proposed legislative programme of the session.

Debate upon the Address in answer to the King's Speech

On returning from the Lords the House does not immediately proceed with business, the sitting being by custom suspended until three o'clock. When it resumes, a certain amount of routine business is dispatched. The stereotyped form is gone through of reading a Bill which will never proceed any further[1] before the King's Speech is taken into consideration, to show that, although the House always begins work with the King's Speech, it is not bound to do so. Other incidental business, such as complaint of breach of privilege or the asking of private notice questions (p. 147), may also be taken now, but this is rare.

The Address in answer to the King's Speech is moved and seconded by two Members selected by the Prime Minister, one a representative of a borough, the other of a county, constituency. It is the custom for them to wear levée dress.

Formerly the Address was framed to follow the King's Speech paragraph by paragraph, but it is now moved in the form of a short expression of thanks. The debate, which follows, normally falls into two parts: (1) a general debate upon the policy of the Government as outlined in the Speech, and (2) debate on the amendments moved for the most part by the Opposition, advocating alternative policies, usually expressed in the form of regret for the omission from the Speech of the policies advocated. Some six days are by agreement usually devoted to this debate. At its conclusion the Address is voted and ordered to be presented to His Majesty "by such Members of the House as are of His Majesty's Privy Council, or of His Majesty's Household" (see p. 323).

During and immediately after the debate steps are taken to put the machinery for the business of the session into motion.

---

[1] The first day of sitting in every Parliament some one Bill and no more receiveth a first reading for form's sake (C.J., 22nd March 1603).

The various sessional committees are set up (see p. 251), and some of the standing committees are nominated (see p. 239). A ballot is held for Bills and Motions (see p. 157) (unless Private Members' time has been taken), and the Members who have secured precedence by the ballot present their Bills and give notice of their motions. Other Bills are also introduced and other motions notified. The business of the session is getting into swing, and an attempt must now be made to show what are the chief classes of business and how they are normally distributed over the different periods of the session.

II. TIME-TABLE OF THE SESSION

In order to get a view of the session as a whole it is necessary to consider in some detail:—

(1) What are the main varieties of the business of the House, what opportunities of debate are afforded by each, and in what order their claims on the time of the House may be ranged;

(2) the time of the House, who controls the disposal of it and under what rules and conditions;

(3) the divisions into which the session naturally falls, and how they differ from each other in respect of the distribution of business.

Main Varieties of Business

This term is intended to include the business, technically called 'public' business, upon which debate takes place. It does not cover the business of the first hour of a sitting—'Questions', etc.—which is described in the next chapter. As the purpose of this section is to give a general view of the 'lay out' of the session, and as the items with which it deals are the subjects of separate chapters, they will be sketched here only in broad outline and chiefly in order to show their relations to each other in the matter of time.

Public Business may be divided roughly into Bills, Motions and Financial business ('Money').

Bills

A Bill is a draft of a legislative proposal which, when it has been passed by both Houses and received the Royal Assent, will become an Act of Parliament or Statute. The first division

of Bills is into *Public Bills* and *Private Bills*, the former dealing
with public general interests and the latter with local or personal
interests (see Chapters VI and IX).

In the class of *Public Bills* the important distinction for our
present purpose is between a *Government Bill* and a *Private
Members' Bill*, the former being introduced and piloted through
the House by a Member of the Government and the latter by
a private or (more technically) unofficial Member.

A *Private Bill* (not to be confused with a Private Members'
Bill), besides the distinction in its scope, is distinguished from
a Public Bill in the manner of its introduction and other points
of procedure, and is governed by different Standing Orders.
The main point about a Private Bill for our present purpose is
that it normally passes without discussion on the floor of the
House, and only takes up time when, after persistent opposition,
it comes up for discussion during the latter half of a sitting.

Motions

Motions are defined on page 168. Only 'substantive' motions
are dealt with in this chapter, for the purposes of which they
may be classified, according to their origin, as *Government
Motions*, *Private Members' Motions* and *Opposition Motions*.

Government Motions are not of frequent occurrence, but
there are generally several every session. They provide a
natural form in which to submit some action or policy of the
Government to the House for its endorsement, *e.g.* a Treaty
concluded but not yet ratified. There is another class of Government Motion, which is much more frequent, the purpose of
which is to secure the approval of the House to Orders or
Regulations made by a Government Department under certain
Acts of Parliament, *e.g.* the Import Duties Act, Sunday
Entertainments Act. Such Motions are usually taken after
eleven o'clock.

Private Members' Motions are a regular feature of the business
of the session—particularly the early part, when certain days
are reserved for them. They are generally used to test the
feeling of the House with regard to proposals which are still
indefinite or ahead of public opinion. But in some cases they
have had direct results; *e.g.* the "Fair Wages Clause' in Government contracts originated in a Private Member's Motion.

Opposition Motions generally take the form of Votes of
Censure on the policy of the Government, but include other
motions moved from the Opposition Front Bench for the

purpose of criticism or to advocate alternative policies (see p. 114).

Motions for the Adjournment of the House (when moved independently, and not upon a question already proposed) are to be placed in the same class as 'substantive' motions. There are several distinguishable varieties of this motion, which, before it developed into a recognised technical form, seems to have been moved with two quite separate purposes: (1) for the purpose of voicing grievances before a contemplated adjournment, and (2) for the purpose of consultation outside the House before debating some sudden emergency. From (1) descends the use of the motion on the eve of the periodical holidays, and from (2) the technical forms (*a*) the *Adjournment of the House under S.O. No.* 9 (for the purpose of discussing a definite matter of urgent public importance (see p. 152), and (*b*) the use of the motion by the Government for the purpose of providing facilities for the discussion of a subject which, because of its indefiniteness or for some other reason, does not lend itself to being expressed as a specific motion. It is necessary to distinguish the technical from the non-technical use of the motion, especially as they serve rather different purposes.

Financial Business

Financial business is the subject of a separate chapter (Chapter VIII). All that need be said about it for the purpose of showing how it is distributed over the session is as follows:—
Expenditure is chiefly the business of the Committee of Supply, which votes the annual Estimates. The main Estimates are discussed for the most part in the early months of the financial year to which they refer and under a system of closure which ensures their being voted by August 5th. As they do not as a rule suffice for the needs of the year, Supplementary Estimates are regularly voted in the closing months of the financial year to which they apply and at the beginning of the session following that in which the main Estimates were voted. Expenditure receives provisional legislative sanction by the Consolidated Fund (No. 1) Bill, passed shortly before the beginning of the financial year, and final sanction by the Consolidated Fund (Appropriation) Bill, passed soon after the closure of the Estimates (pp. 255–258).

The imposition of *taxation* is a process with two main stages: *first* by Resolutions voted in Committee of Ways and Means

I

and afterwards agreed to by the House, and *secondly* by the Finance Bill, which is based on these Resolutions and is subjected to the regular procedure on Bills. The Ways and Means stage, in which the Budget is 'opened', is taken generally in April, soon after the Easter holidays, and the Finance Bill proceeds through its various stages in the summer and is passed towards the end of July (see pp. 280–285).

How are the various items of business which come under these general headings—Bills, Motions and Financial Business —distributed over the course of the session? In order to answer this question it is necessary to examine the rules under which the time of the House is controlled.

CONTROL OF THE TIME OF THE HOUSE[1]

The right to control its own time rests ultimately with the House, but the exercise of this right is, with minor exceptions, delegated under the Standing Orders to the Government. The use of certain days in the week is reserved to Private Members under S.O. No. 4.

(1) The completeness of the control which the Government exercises over the rest of the time of the House (with the exceptions set out below) depends upon two facts:—

    (*a*) The length of the sitting is normally fixed (see p. 131). If, as seldom happens, the amount of business set down by the Government is insufficient to fill the time of a sitting, the Government exercises the right, which it alone possesses, of moving the adjournment of the House. No practical possibility exists of Private Members' business being taken on a Government day except with the consent of the Government.

    (*b*) The length of the sitting is *not* fixed when it suits the Government to prolong it, for it possesses the exclusive right of suspending the rule terminating the sitting at a fixed hour. Thus when it chooses it can turn a sitting into the equivalent of two, and by this means it gains on an average the equivalent of eight sittings every session (see p. 129).

(2) The method by which the House is kept informed in advance of the business to be taken at a particular sitting depends partly on the Order Book and partly on a more

            [1] See Appendix III.

informal practice. In the case of Private Members' days precedence is unalterably fixed by the Ballot and registered in the Order Book. The Government, on the other hand, have the right to arrange their business on Government days in any order they please (S.O. No. 14), and as they have during the greater part of the session many more Orders than can be taken at a sitting, these are carried over from day to day (or for short intervals) and the state of the Order Book affords very little indication as to the business which is really going to be taken on a particular day. This information is provided by means of an announcement made in the House by the Leader of the House in answer to a question addressed to him on Thursdays by the leader of the Opposition as to the business for the following week.

(3) Limitations upon Government control of time.—In addition to the time reserved under the Standing Orders for Private Members' business the following deductions have to be made from the total amount of time available for the Government.

(a) By S.O. No. 7 (4) Opposed Private Business may be put down by the Chairman of Ways and Means for 7.30[1] on a Government day (see p. 142). By S.O. No. 9 a Motion for the adjournment of the House "for the purpose of discussing a definite matter of urgent public importance" (see p. 152) is, if it has satisfied the required conditions when offered, postponed for consideration until later in the day at 7.30.[1]

(b) Another liability is that the Government is bound by convention to 'find time' for certain business which is not its own. It has to give a day, when asked, for the discussion of a motion containing or implying censure upon its policy, and also finds itself once or twice every session under the necessity of giving a day for the discussion of some non-party or inter-party matter for the consideration of which there is a general desire in the House. Further there are various incidental matters which may occur (see below).

(c) Finally a very large proportion of the time of the House has to be surrendered by the Government for the consideration of business, which may be classed

[1] For altered hours, see Appendix IV.

as financial and routine. This is Government business but not part of the Government programme. The Government is responsible for it, but as part of the routine work of administration it recurs every session in much the same proportions, whatever Government is in power.

Opposition Time and Business

No complete idea of the control of House of Commons business and time could be formed without taking into account the effect of the two-party system, which is presupposed in many of the arrangements of the House, though it remains unrecognised by the Standing Orders. This makes the stock distinction between Government and Private Members' time, between official and unofficial business, not exhaustive. There is another kind of business—that of the Opposition—which makes use of both official and unofficial time. It will become apparent in taking a more detailed survey of the main varieties of business and their distribution over the session that the Opposition not only makes use of some portion of the time reserved for Private Members' Bills and Motions, but has secured certain advantages even in the sphere of Government business. For example, it has secured the initiative in the criticism of administration so far as that is exercised through discussion of the Estimates.

ANALYSIS OF SESSIONAL BUSINESS INTO GROUPS

It has been indicated that between Private Members' business on the one hand and what may be called the Government programme on the other there is a considerable range of subjects, which occur in what is nominally Government time, but which are more or less independent for their discussion of Government control. The plan on which they are arranged here is to start from Private Members' business, which is normally outside Government control, then to take a branch of subjects which may be called 'Incidental business', a branch which covers at one end matters which are obtruded into Government time by the Standing Orders, and at the other those for the discussion of which the Government 'finds time' in order to meet the wishes of the House. Between this group of subjects and the Government programme there is another group here called 'Routine and financial'—all technically Government business but to be distinguished, for reasons which will appear more clearly below, from the business which, like its own

programme of legislation, is completely within the control of
the Government. The various items, of which each of these
groups is composed, will be set out in order and, so as to enable
the relative importance of each to be gauged, the average amount
of time spent on each will be given, calculated on the basis of
two post-war periods, covering the years 1919 to 1926 and
1928 to 1936.

First Group: Private Members' Business

Private Members' business consists of Bills and Motions. A
limited portion of the earlier part of each session is reserved
for their discussion, and the ballot is used to determine the
precedence of Members on these days (see p. 157). (In the case
of Bills precedence relates to the second reading stage.) As
pointed out above, Private Members' time is sometimes used for
the purposes of Opposition business (and occasionally of
Government business), Members often balloting in effect for the
privilege of introducing a Bill or moving a Motion on behalf of
their party. But groups and combinations are also formed for
this purpose on a non-party basis. In strict theory, of course,
the individual Member ballots for himself. It is only the
successful *Member* who is entitled to precedence for his Motion
on the day chosen, not the *business* introduced by him, although
another Member may have given notice of such business on his
behalf.

(1) Private Members' Bills have precedence on Friday during
the earlier months of the session. In a session beginning
after Christmas Private Members' Bills have precedence
on Friday from the beginning of the session until Easter
together with the first, second, third and fourth Fridays
after Easter for the second-reading stages. They also have
precedence for their later stages, in the order of the most
advanced Bills, on the third, fourth, fifth and sixth Fridays
after Whitsuntide (S.O. No. 4 (1). In a session which
begins before Christmas, Private Members' Bills also have
precedence on Fridays until Christmas, but they lose as
much time after Christmas as they gain before it. The
later stages are taken on the second, third, fourth and fifth
Fridays after Easter Day, instead of after Whitsun. In
effect, the amount of time allotted to Private Members'
Bills is not increased, however early the session begins
(S.O. No. 4 (2). This amounts to 10 days (normally)

for the second readings, and 4 days for the later stages of Private Members' Bills—or 14 days in all.

The allotment of time to Private Members' Bills was changed, beginning with the session of 1928, as the result of the recommendations of a committee which sat in 1927. Before 1928 about 12 days on the average were allotted to the second readings of Private Members' Bills and only 2 to the later stages of the more advanced. The change recommended by the committee has widened somewhat the 'bottle-neck' which the majority of Private Members' Bills fail to pass.

It may be mentioned here that precedence between Private Members' Bills at the same stage and down for the same day is secured by the Bill which was first put down for that day over the Bill which first reached that stage, and by a Bill already standing on the Order Paper over a Bill the consideration of which was adjourned from an earlier day.

(2) Private Members' Motions have precedence on Wednesday until Easter, if the session begins after Christmas. Where a session begins before Christmas, Private Members' Motions also have precedence on Wednesdays until Christmas, but in return Government business takes precedence on an equal number of Wednesdays immediately before Easter (S.O. No. 4 (2)). The Motion first in order on a Private Members' Wednesday, if not concluded earlier, is interrupted[1] at half-past seven[2] (see p. 166). The normal amount of time spent on these Motions is 7 days. The total for the whole group of Private Members' business may average some 21 days.

Second Group: 'Incidental' Business

This is a very miscellaneous group of subjects, their chief common characteristic (for which they are here classed together) being that they all represent, to some extent but in a varying degree, inroads upon Government time.

(1) The item that may be disposed of first—Opposed Private Business (see p. 142)—represents not only an inroad upon Government time but also the intrusion into the time reserved for public business of a class of business normally dealt with at another time. The Chairman of Ways and Means in selecting the day on which this business is to be taken at half-past seven[2] is directed to

---

[1] This change was also made on the recommendation of the committee of 1927.

[2] For altered hours, see Appendix IV.

be impartial between Government time and Private Members' time (S.O. No. 7 (4)).[1]

(2) Adjournment Motions under Standing Order No. 9 (see pp. 152–4).—This form of Motion is generally used for the purpose of criticising the Government in connexion with some sudden and recent incident which can be laid to the blame of the administration. It is something like an emergency motion of censure, and is raised at the end of Questions, out of which it generally arises. If the terms and subject of the motion satisfy the conditions of S.O. No. 9 the motion stands over till 7.30 the same evening.[2] These motions are necessarily unforeseeable and mean the loss of Government time. As will appear later, the loss of even half a day at certain times of the year may be very awkward to the Government, and the possibility of time being taken under this heading must be reckoned with. In the period 1919 to 1926 the equivalent of one full day in each session was given over to Adjournment Motions, but in the period 1928 to 1936 an increasingly strict interpretation of the Standing Order has reduced the time to a negligible quantity.

(3) The next subdivision of this group consists of motions for which time is provided by the Government, but which can be distinguished from each other in respect of the nature and amount of pressure which they put upon the Government to find time for them.

(a) The first is the 'Vote of censure',—a motion generally moved by the leader of the Opposition and leading to a 'full-dress' debate. The challenge of a vote of censure is always accepted by the Government. Obviously many kinds of Opposition motion are possible which fall short of explicit censure, but yet indirectly reflect on the Government or advocate measures incompatible with its policy. Often it may be disputable whether the obligation upon a Government to give time for a motion of censure can or need be stretched to cover the case of a particular motion. The tendency seems to be for a Government to grant the time for such motions whenever there is any reasonable cause for them, deferring them, of course, till after the claims of their own proper business have been

---

[1] The average time taken by Opposed Private Business amounts to 2 days.
[2] For altered hours, see Appendix IV.

satisfied.   From 1919 to 1926 an average of 2 days a
session, and from 1928 to 1936, an average of 4 days
was taken by Opposition motions.

(*b*) There is another variety of such motions which may
be called "Private Members' motions in Government
time". For the discussion of these there is no obligation upon the Government to find time. In this
respect they afford no analogy to the vote of censure.
Coming, as they often do, from the Government side
of the House, they are dependent entirely upon the
good will of the Government (and upon the state
of business), and the only pressure that can be brought
to bear upon the leader of the House is evidence of
the wishes of a considerable section of the House.
As an example of the kind of motion described may
be mentioned the motion in favour of Parliamentary
Devolution, moved by a Private Member in 1919,
which led to a two days' debate.

(*c*) Very similar to the last group in object and differing
only in form are the occasional motions for the
adjournment of the House moved by the Government
in deference to the wishes of a section of the House
for the purpose of hearing a statement from a Minister
or discussing a matter which, because of its indefiniteness or for some other reason, it is not desired to
express in a motion. This is a use of the motion for
the adjournment of the House which is worth distinguishing separately. Being moved for the sake of an
independent discussion, and therefore either before
or between the Orders of the Day, it can only be moved
by the Government (see p. 163). This kind of adjournment motion accounts for 2 days a session.

(4) The last subdivision under the 'Incidental Business
group' must be made to include all the other items of
business for which the Government is not responsible, but
which make inroads into its time. As an example may be
taken motions complaining of breach of privilege, which
take precedence of other business (see p. 159).

The whole of this group, 'Incidental business', takes upon
an average some 8 or 9 days in a session. It tends to increase—
on the principle of compensation—when the Government have,
as regularly happens during war and times of emergency,
appropriated or cut down Private Members' time.

Third Group: Routine and Financial Business

The common character of all the items forming this third group is that, while technically Government business, they form part of the necessary routine of administration, not of what is called the 'Government programme', and take much the same amount of time whatever Government is in power. They represent the inherited habits, not the individual purpose, of the Government. In some cases, for example the main Estimates and the stages of the Consolidated Fund Bill, the Government allows the Opposition to decide the subject to be discussed.

(1) First in this group may be placed the debate on the Address, requiring an average of 6 days, which has been described above (p. 108).

(2) Next comes what may be called the 'non-technical' use of the motion for the adjournment of the House—that for the adjournment on the eve of one of the periodical holidays. The principle underlying this form may be expressed as 'grievances before adjournment'. It is specially intended for the purposes of the Opposition and the Private Member, though of course it is both moved by the Government and debated in Government time. The subjects to be raised on this motion—most subjects not involving legislation may be raised—are usually arranged in advance by consultation between the party Whips, or 'through the usual channels', as it is termed, and a certain portion of the time spent in debate on the motion is allotted to each subject.

(3) The *Main Estimates*.—The greater part of the Main Estimates are voted, as stated above, in the earlier portion of the financial year to which they apply, *i.e.* between 1st April and 5th August—on 'allotted' days (20, increasable to 23, in number[1]) under a system which provides for their being closured on the last two of such days (S.O. No. 16) (see p. 267). The practical effect of this arrangement on the development of procedure is important.

(a) It rids the Government of all anxiety about getting the Estimates voted. For it does not often matter which vote is taken on any particular allotted day, as immediate financial requirements are covered by the Consolidated Fund (No. 1) Bill (passed before the beginning of the financial year) until the middle or end of August, and all the votes will equally, under

[1] Now fixed at twenty-six ; see Appendix IV.

the Standing Order, be voted (with or without debate) by 5th August. In view of this it has become the practice for the Government gracefully to cede to the Opposition the right of choosing the particular vote to be taken on a day which has been allotted to Supply. This is arranged 'through the usual channels'.

(b) From the point of view of the Opposition a consequence of the transfer to themselves of this initiative in choosing the subject of debate has been to strengthen the pre-existing tendency to turn the attention away from the financial aspect of the Estimates, especially as whatever the Opposition does or says it cannot prevent the automatic voting of the Estimates by 5th August. Hence the tendency to select a vote rather as a peg on which to hang an attack on the policy of the Government, or an exposition of a rival policy (so far as that can be done without raising questions of legislation), than as a set of figures which require to be scrutinized, before passing. So clearly is this recognized that a demand from the Opposition for a day on which to raise a subject of policy is frequently countered by the Leader of the House with the reminder that the matter referred to is included in the Estimates, and that it is open to the Opposition to secure that the appropriate vote or votes are put down for an early allotted day. Similarly it has come to be habitual to avoid taking a decision at the end of discussion upon the more important votes so as to keep them available as pegs for discussion on later allotted days.

(c) Debate in Committee of Supply on the Main Estimates, in becoming a recognized method of criticizing the policy of the Government on broad lines, has tended to reduce direct front-bench motions, by which in the older procedure the function of criticism was mainly performed. It has also had the result of making less important the procedure of "getting the Speaker out of the Chair"[1] upon first going into Committee of Supply on each of the four main branches of Estimates, as the principle embodied in this procedure, that of raising grievances before granting Supply, is now expressed by the procedure in Committee of Supply itself. The amendments to

[1] For modification of this procedure, see Appendix IV.

the Motion for getting the Speaker out of the Chair, upon which the criticism of the Government was generally founded, and which are now granted priority by means of the ballot, are often used for the purpose of raising comparatively small points, and the debate on these has become short and rather perfunctory (see p. 263).

The Main Estimates occupy on an average 23 or 24 days of the session.

(4) *Supplementary Estimates, i.e.* supplementary to the Main Estimates (usually of the previous session) (see p. 264). Debate on the Supplementary Estimates is more strictly financial in character than on the Main Estimates owing to the narrow limits within which it is confined by the rule of relevancy, and often descends to the minutest detail. These Estimates occasionally raise large questions, but more often only present an opportunity for embarrassing the Government by protracted discussion, for not only have they to be voted without the benefit of the special closures such as those under which the Main Estimates are voted[1], but they have to be voted well before the end of the financial year during the busy weeks at the beginning of the session.

The average time spent on Supplementary Estimates from 1919 to 1926 was 10 days, but from 1928 to 1936 the average fell to 6 days.

(5) The *Consolidated Fund Bills.* The object these Bills have in common is to give legislative sanction to the issue of money to cover grants voted in Supply. Normally there are two at least every session: (*a*) the Consolidated Fund (No. 1) Bill, which has to be passed in time to receive the Royal Assent before the end of the financial year, and includes sums required to cover not only supplementary grants for the expiring year but also ordinary expenditure for the first five months or so of the coming year (see p. 272); (*b*) the Consolidated Fund (Appropriation) Bill, which issues money to cover expenditure for the rest of the year, and appropriates each sum voted during the session to the service for which it was voted, and is commonly passed soon after the conclusion of Supply (before 5th August). When passed, this Bill is called the *Appropriation Act* (see p. 273).

[1] This is no longer the case ; see Appendix IV.

The debate on these Bills serves the same function as debate on the Main Estimates, *i.e.* that of reviewing the policy of the Government; and the subjects to be raised (which include only subjects for which money is provided in the Bill under discussion) are selected by the Opposition and notified through the usual channels. If time suffices, Private Members raise subjects of which they have privately notified the Minister concerned.

The Consolidated Fund Bills take as a rule 4 or 5 days every session.

(6) The *Finance Bill* and the *Ways and Means Resolutions* on which it is based (see pp. 283-4).—This is the point at which 'routine and financial business' merges into the 'Government programme', but on the whole it is more conveniently treated as belonging to the former category. There is nothing with regard to the procedure on the Finance Bill which requires explanation here. Its treatment is left to Chapter VIII.

The Finance Bill and the Ways and Means Resolutions on which it is founded take together on an average some 12 to 15 days every session.

(7) Finally there are certain items of routine business such as the Army and Air Force (Annual) Bill (May, 706) and the Expiring Laws Continuance Bill which occasionally require the equivalent of half a sitting or more for their Committee stages. But the required time may be provided after 11 o'clock and need not be taken into calculation.

The time spent on these various groups of business works out at an average for each group as follows:—

	1919–26	1928–36
1st Group: Private Members' Business	16 days[1]	15 days[1]
2nd Group: Incidental Business ...	8 days	8 days
3rd Group: Routine and Financial Business—		
Address 5		6
Adjournment (Holidays) 3		4
Main Estimates 24		24
Supplementary Estimates 9		6
Consolidated Fund Bills 5		4
Finance Bill 12		15
	— 58 days	— 59 days
Total ...	82 days	82 days

[1] Allowing for days taken by the Government.

Out of a session which from 1919 to 1926 had an average of 138 effective days there was left a total of 56 days for the Government programme. From 1928 to 1936, longer sessions raised the number of effective days to 149. The whole of the extra time was available for the Government programme, because the demands made by the three groups of Private Members', incidental and routine business remain relatively fixed at about 82 days of each session.[1]

Two Periods of the Session

Having distinguished the main varieties of business and the time spent on them during the session, it remains to show in what relative order business is taken on the assumption that the session begins in the autumn.

The season of the year in which the session begins is of importance if the Government is to allow successfully for the conflicting claims of the various groups of parliamentary business, to dispose of its essential financial business at the necessary fixed dates, and to avoid an embarrassingly heavy programme in the closing weeks of the session.

Till 1928, it was considered that these objects were best attained by opening the session in the spring. Then, after concentration on the financial business till the beginning of August, a considerable number of days remained available in the autumn to permit the undisturbed completion of the Government programme.

A Joint Committee in 1924 considered the plan of beginning the session in the autumn, and reported unanimously against it.[2] Nevertheless it was adopted in 1928 and since it was found to afford a not inconvenient arrangement of time, the session has been opened in the autumn from 1928 onwards. Beginning in the autumn, then, the session falls into two clearly defined periods, of approximately equal length, each with a special character of its own and with a considerable preponderance of one or other of the main kinds of business. These periods are:—

1. *First period*, from some date in October or November to 31st March, the end of the financial year. This period, comprising some 74 or 75 days, or half the session, is

---

[1] A survey of the distribution of the time of the House during the first decade of the century is made in a striking article—" The Congestion of Business in the House of Commons"—contained in the *Round Table* for December 1911.

[2] See Report of Joint Committee on Sittings of Parliament (H.C. 112, 1924).

characterised first by Private Members' business, which normally takes up more than one-fourth of the total number of days available, and secondly by the urgency of financial business, especially the Supplementary Estimates for the closing financial year.

The Christmas adjournment cuts the period into two subdivisions of roughly equal length.

2. *Second period*, from the beginning of April to the beginning of August, together with a few days usually held in reserve till the autumn as a safeguard against some unforeseen delay or emergency business.

In the second period the Finance Bill and the Main Estimates take up nearly half the available time, with the remainder mainly devoted to the Government programme. The whole period is again of an average length of 75 days.

How is the programme of business arranged for each of these periods ?

First Period (*Autumn to end of March*)

(a) *Before Christmas.* Private Members' business, divided equally between Bills and Motions, takes 2 out of the 5 sitting days in each week before Christmas. After the debate on the Address, lasting 6 days, the remaining time at the disposal of the Government amounts to about 12 days, in which a limited number of Government Bills can pass their second-reading stage before Christmas.

(b) *After Christmas.* The governing date in this period is 31st March—or rather the 28th, by which date the Consolidated Fund Bill must have passed the House of Commons in order that it may receive the Royal Assent by the 31st. Immediately before Christmas, apart from Private Members' business on 2 fixed days each week, the Government could proceed with its legislative programme comparatively undisturbed. After Christmas, on the other hand, every group of business lays claim to a varying number of days and the progress of Government Bills is usually hindered by all the following factors:—

Private Members' business, which under the terms of S.O. No. 4 will continue to occupy some of the Wednesdays and Fridays before Easter, making an average of 12 days;

Routine and Financial business, which usually requires, for Main Estimates, 7 days (one day each for going into Committee of Supply on the three Service Estimates,[1] plus 2 days for the Vote on Account, plus 2 days on Service Votes); for Supplementary Estimates 3 or 4 days and for the Consolidated Fund Bill, 2 days;

Incidental business, such as Opposed Private business or Vote of Censure motions, which may account for a further 2 days.

Added together, these several items account for 25 out of a total of 40 to 45 days between Christmas and Easter, leaving a maximum of 20 days for the Government programme.

By 31st March, then, approximately half the session has passed, and the Government has used about half the total number of days available for its programme. The benefit to the Government of the days taken before Christmas now begins to be felt. Owing to the time devoted to it in the autumn Private Members' business has now been almost disposed of. Government Bills which passed the second-reading stage before Christmas will be coming back to the House from the Standing Committees and may be read the third time before Easter. At best, however, the amount of time available for Government Bills during this period of the session is often inadequate, and the Government is invariably obliged, when contemplating a heavy programme of legislation, to take special measures for gaining more time. The most frequent expedient is the taking of Private Members' days. This and other devices, the manner in which they are used, and the extent to which they are successful, will be discussed together in a later section (pp. 128–130).

Second Period (*Beginning of April to close of Session*)

The second half of the session finds its governing date early in August. By the 5th of August the 20 days[2] allotted by S.O. No. 16 for the consideration of Estimates must have been taken; and by common consent of all parties the House makes a practice of rising before August Bank Holiday. The business peculiar to this period is the Budget, which is 'opened' in Committee of Ways and Means generally in the first or second week after

---

[1] It is unnecessary, owing to the procedure of the Vote on Account, to go into Committee of Supply on the Civil Estimates before the beginning of the new Financial year.

[2] See p. 119*n*.

the Easter holiday, and when embodied in the Finance Bill makes its deliberate progress through the various stages of a Bill. The average amount of time spent on this business is 15 days. The largest item in the Financial Group—the Main Estimates—also takes up a good deal of time in this part of the session, for it is in this period, and with increasing frequency towards the end of it, that the bulk of the 'allotted' days fall. These account for 17 days in this period. Further, the Appropriation Bill usually takes another two days. This amounts to an average total for Financial Business of 34 days.

Private Members' business (at this part of the session only Bills) accounts for some 4 days; 'Incidental' business for 6 days.

This gives a total for these three groups of about 43 or 44 days, or rather more than half the total average length of this period of the session, which, as stated, amounts to about 75 days. The Government are thus left with about 32 'sitting' days for the completion of their programme of legislation.

Since 1931 it has been the practice not to bring the session to a close by prorogation early in August, but to hold in reserve a few days in October or November. This serves as an emergency period not only for uncompleted Government business, but also for the House as a whole to consider some urgent public question which has arisen during the summer adjournment; and S.O. No. 112 now empowers the Speaker to summon the House to meet at an earlier date[1] should such a question arise. If no situation demanding emergency measures has arisen, the House may meet only for the purpose of prorogation. Thus in 1936 Parliament was prorogued the day after it reassembled; but in 1931, when a second Finance Bill was introduced in the autumn, the House sat for over four weeks.

Effect of beginning the Session after Christmas

Prior to 1928 the practice of beginning the session after Christmas was generally considered more convenient for the Government programme than the present practice of beginning the session in the autumn.

The substantial advantage of the older system lay in the autumn sittings with which the session was brought to a close. When, at the beginning of August, the whole of the financial business has been disposed of, the Government could look forward to an autumn period of elastic length, from some date in

---

[1] E.g. 22nd October, 1935, instead of 29th October, on the occasion of the Italo-Abyssinian dispute.

October or November until Christmas, when its programme
could be brought to completion practically undisturbed by the
demands of other business. From 20 to 25 days might be
devoted almost continuously to Government Bills, and it was
held that the easiest method of completing the Government
programme was to give it a clear field at the end of the session.

The main drawback of the older system lay in the severe
congestion of business up to the end of March. The Address,
now disposed of in the autumn, then demanded 6 of the opening
days after Christmas. Practically the whole of the remaining
time was absorbed by Private Members' business, which under
the present system is also partly disposed of before Christmas,
and by the absolutely necessary financial business. As a result,
the amount of time available for Government Bills during the
first part of the session was so small that very few passed their
second-reading stage before Easter, and the standing committees
were practically unemployed during the whole of the period
from Christmas to Easter. This early delay led to the ultimate
congestion of work on the standing committees, a serious difficulty which the present system overcomes by a more even
distribution of Government days over the first part of the
session.

Plan of Resuming Bills at Stage reached in Previous Session

The analysis of the sessional time-table indicates that practically no margin of time is allowed for Parliamentary obstruction, delays, or other obstacles to the completion of Bills. In
consequence, the loss of Bills, upon which progress has been
made in one or both Houses without bringing proceedings on
them to completion, is a feature of the close of every session.
Since Lord Derby's Parliamentary Proceedings Adjournment
Bill, 1848, the possibility of avoiding such loss of time by sur-
mounting the gulf which the prorogation places between the
business of one session and the next, and by crediting Bills in a
new session with the progress they had made in the previous
session, has been examined and re-examined by Parliament.
For Private Bills arrangements having this effect have not in-
frequently been adopted (see p. 307). They have not hitherto
been applied to Public Bills for various reasons. In the case of
Government Bills the adoption of the plan would deprive the
Opposition of one of their strongest weapons. As regards
Private Members' Bills, either Bills which had been carried
over from the previous session would be given precedence over

K

Bills newly introduced, which does not seem very fair, or they would not be given precedence, in which case their chance of making any further progress would be very slight, or finally some rearrangement of Private Members' time would have to be made in their favour.

METHODS ADOPTED BY THE GOVERNMENT TO SECURE MORE TIME

It seems clear that the plan of suspending and resuming Bills will not in itself satisfy the needs of modern governments for additional time. It remains, therefore, to consider some of the measures taken by the Government for increasing the amount of time at its disposal. They fall under two general heads:—

(1) *Business Motions* are comparatively simple and proceed generally by suspending a Standing Order which happens to be inconvenient to the progress of Government business.

(2) '*Allocation of Time*' (or '*Guillotine*') *Motions* are more complicated and practically make a new set of rules for the business which they are designed to forward.

Business Motions

For other examples of such Motions and the procedure in moving them, reference may be made to p. 135. It is principally their effect on the time-table of the session that is considered here.

(1) Precedence is granted to Government business, sometimes for all Government business for a specified period, *or* for a particular item of business on a particular day, *or* for an intermediate combination.

Precedence is thus obtained over Private Members' Bills and Motions. This is the main expedient of the Government during the first period of the session, and its value is shown by the fact that, whereas in session 1935–6, when no inroad was made on Private Members' time the amount of time secured for Government Bills during the first period of the session was only 18 days out of 60, on the other hand, when Private Members' time was taken in the previous year, Government Bills secured as many as 45 days out of 69.

(2) A Saturday sitting may be held. This requires a motion made after notice (S.O. No. 3).

(3) Suspension of the 'Eleven o'Clock Rule'[1] (S.O. No. 1).—
This is an obvious and frequently employed method of
increasing the stock of available time. The average
number of House of Commons days gained every session
as an equivalent of the number of hours sat after eleven
o'clock[1] amount to 10 days, while in session 1929–30 it
amounted to as many as 23 extra days. When the necessary deductions are made, it may be estimated that by this
means some 8 days are gained in a normal session for the
benefit of the Government programme. The suspension
of the 'Eleven o'Clock Rule'[1] is generally moved for a day
at a time, but at certain periods of the session, such as
towards the end of the financial year or when a Prorogation
is approaching, it has been moved for a specified period,
and combined with the suspension of other standing
orders, and other special provisions, if necessary.

Allocation of Time ('Guillotine') Motions

'Guillotine' Motions are a form of closure by compartments
applied to the discussion of Bills. In 1920 such a motion was
proposed (but not proceeded with) for Supplementary Estimates. Their purpose is to ensure the completion of the debate
on a Bill in a certain number of days, and to distribute the days
allotted proportionately over the various stages of the Bill.
The need for such motions has been to a certain extend reduced
by the power given to the Chair in 1919 to select amendments
(see p. 187). They are sometimes not put down until a Bill has
been so long in committee with so little progress made as to
provide a case for the application by the Government of special
measures. The expedition of business secured by this method
has generally to be paid for by the loss of a day in the discussion
of the Motion itself. It is thus only for the purpose of securing
the passage of Bills, to which unusual importance is attached,
that a Government finds it worth while to resort to these
measures.

The chief features of a 'Guillotine' motion are:—

(a) the drawing up of a time-table which allots a certain number of days to each of the remaining stages of the Bill,
and in the case of the Committee and Report stages allots
a certain number of clauses to each day, or portion of a day.[2]

---

[1] For altered hours, see Appendix IV.
[2] See Appendix IV, " Business Committee."

(*b*) When the end of any allotted day or part day is reached, the Chair is directed to put forthwith the question under consideration and then to put the question upon clauses and Government amendments only (and this in the division-saving form "That the amendment be made").

(*c*) There are generally a number of other provisions—as, *e.g.*, the prohibition of 'dilatory' motions (see p. 172), and the prohibition or postponement, until after the conclusion of Government business on such an allotted day, of Opposed Private Business and of another disturbing form of Incidental business—Motions for the adjournment of the House under Standing Order No. 9. Reference should be made to the Motions themselves (*e.g.* for guillotining the Local Government Bill, 1928), which are very explicit. It will be seen that they have the effect on their allotted days of substituting a new set of rules for the Standing Orders dealing with the arrangement of time.

This drastic form of procedure is not popular in any part of the House. In 1935 a successful attempt was made to substitute for it a voluntary agreement, reached through representatives of the Government and of Opposition parties. The various stages of the Government of India Bill of that year were by this means allotted an agreed number of days, and its consideration was punctually completed in comformity with the schedule. It would be a triumph for the spirit of conciliation if this precedent comes in future to be generally adopted.

Chapter IV

A SITTING AND THE VARIOUS ITEMS OF BUSINESS

This chapter attempts to give in its main outlines a sketch of a sitting of the House of Commons, showing how it is opened and concluded, and describing the various items of business in the order in which they are taken.

I. OPENING AND CLOSE OF SITTING

Normal hours of sitting[1]

On Monday, Tuesday, Wednesday and Thursday the House meets at a quarter to three and adjourns normally between eleven and half-past (S.O. No. 1). On Friday the corresponding hours are eleven a.m. to four or half-past four p.m. (S.Os. Nos. 1 and 2). Before 1927 the hours laid down by Standing Order were noon to five or half-past five, but a Sessional Order, regularly passed since 1921 (and converted into a Standing Order in 1927) had prescribed the earlier hours of meeting and adjournment.

The House seldom sits on Saturday and only in case of grave emergency on Sunday. Unless otherwise fixed, the hour for meeting on Saturday has been twelve o'clock, but it might in future be expected to follow the rule for Friday. There is no prescribed hour for a Sunday sitting.

The normal adjournment of the House every week from Friday to Monday is settled by S.O. No. 3, under which the House at its rising on Friday stands adjourned to the following Monday without any question being put.

As the hours of meeting are fixed by the Standing Orders, the old practice of announcing to the House the hour of the next sitting survives only in the Memorandum to that effect now printed at the end of the daily issue of the *Votes and Proceedings* (and perhaps too in the order "Usual hour to-morrow", or "Eleven o'clock to-morrow", given by the Serjeant to the attendants of the House at the close of the

[1] For altered hours, see Appendix IV.

sitting). When it is intended to sit at an hour other than that fixed by the Standing Orders a Resolution, of which notice is required, is moved at the commencement of public business.

Close of the Sitting

A fixed hour for the interruption of business was not introduced until 1888. Originally fixed at twelve o'clock, it was changed in 1906 to the hour still in force—eleven o'clock.[1] The 'Eleven o'Clock Rule', as it is generally called, is laid down in S.O. No. 1, and contains three main provisions: (1) the interruption of business at eleven o'clock, (2) an allowance of half an hour during which unopposed business may be taken, and (3) the adjournment of the House by the Speaker without question put at half-past eleven[1]. After describing these provisions in that order it will be necessary to consider some points that arise in applying them, then the close of the Friday sitting, and lastly the case of business which is *exempted* from the operation of the rule.

THE 'ELEVEN O'CLOCK RULE'[1]

(1) *The moment of interruption of business.*—At eleven o'clock[1] on Monday to Thursday the Speaker interrupts the business under discussion (by rising in his Chair and calling "Order, Order") and directs the Member in charge of that business to name a day for its resumption. If the House is in committee, the Chairman similarly interrupts business and leaves the Chair to make his report to the House (see p. 236). If the Committee "reports progress" (see p. 237), a day is fixed for the resumption of its proceedings.

All 'dilatory motions' (see p. 172) lapse at the moment of interruption without question put.

(2) *Unopposed business after eleven o'clock*[1].—The Order of the Day, upon which proceedings were interrupted, having been disposed of, the Clerk proceeds to read the other Orders one by one. As each is read it is either appointed for a future day or, if no objection is raised, it may be proceeded with at once. Such proceedings may involve several stages of a Bill or the transition into Committee of the Whole House. Anything, in fact, which could be done before eleven[1] may be done now so long as there is no objection raised. If objection is raised, the matter under consideration becomes opposed business and cannot be proceeded with, but must be set down for another

---

[1] For altered hours, see Appendix IV.

day. Opposition is signified by saying "I object" or by challenging a division, but not necessarily by rising to speak, unless it is then expressly indicated.

When all the Orders of the Day have been thus disposed of, as usually happens in about five minutes, some twenty minutes may remain before half-past eleven and the automatic adjournment of the House under S.O. No. 1 (10) are reached. This gap is bridged by the Speaker, on a motion made by a Member of the Government, proposing the Question: "That this House do now adjourn". This question may be immediately agreed to or debated until half-past eleven.[1] Advantage is frequently taken of this opportunity to raise a debate for the purpose of obtaining from the Government statements of a fuller and more detailed character than could be made at Question time.

(3) *Automatic adjournment of the House.*—If debate on the Question for the adjournment of the House or any other proceedings (except a division in progress) continue until half-past eleven[1], the Speaker pursuant to the Standing Order adjourns the House without Question put.

The 'projected' moment of interruption

A problem arises in applying the rule about interrupting proceedings at eleven to the case of business upon which a division is in progress at that hour. When in this case does the 'moment of interruption' occur? Practice has interpreted the rule in the direction of facilitating the progress of business in cases where the division (having occurred upon an amendment, for example) has not completely disposed of the business under consideration. In such cases the Chair, after the announcement of the division figures, puts any further questions necessary to dispose of such business. If no one rises to speak, such question or questions may be decided by division, if necessary, even though these proceedings occupy the time reserved for unopposed business, and even if they are protracted beyond the time for the adjournment of the House under the Standing Order. May (pp. 307 and 308) gives examples showing the cases in which more questions than one have been put from the Chair in such circumstances. It must be noted, however, that a decision on such further question or questions is prevented by a Member rising to speak. This constitutes the

[1] A full half-hour is now invariably allowed, under an arrangement described in Appendix IV.

'projected' moment of interruption, and everything follows as if, through the exclusion from reckoning of the time spent in division, this moment coincided with eleven o'clock[1]. It is not quite clear whether what provokes the interruption of business is the mere rising to speak of a Member or the fact that his rising is taken to signify opposition. But it seems probable that merely rising to speak is sufficient, because:—

(1) speaking without intention to oppose is sufficient to bring about interruption at eleven o'clock[1]—and this is a 'projected' eleven o'clock;

(2) the time during which opposition is a bar to proceeding does not begin until the business under consideration at eleven[1] is disposed of (S.O. No. 1 (6));

(3) opposition cannot be signified more emphatically than by challenging a division—and this, as we have seen, is not a bar to proceeding.

Adjournment on Friday

With the substitution of four for eleven o'clock[1] and half-past four for half-past eleven, the rules for the adjournment of the House on the four earlier days of the week apply also to Friday, *except for the fact* that no opportunity for raising a debate on the adjournment is provided between four and half-past (unless moved by a Member of the Government before the conclusion of the Orders of the Day), S.O. No. 2 directing the Speaker, in effect, to adjourn the House at the conclusion of the business on the Paper or at 4.30, whichever is the earlier.[2]

Exempted Business

Certain business is exempted (except on Friday)[2] from the provisions of the Standing Order, with regard to interruption, *i.e.* it is not interrupted at eleven o'clock[1]; it may be entered upon, or resumed, or proceeded with after eleven, though opposed; and the House may be called upon to sit after 11.30 to deal with it. Such business falls into two categories:—

(1) business exempted by Standing Order;
(2) business specifically exempted by vote of the House.

(1) *Business exempted by Standing Order* (S.O. No. 1 (4)) This may be divided into:—

(a) certain classes of financial business, *i.e.* Bills originating in Committee of Ways and Means,

---

[1] For altered hours, see Appendix IV.
[2] But see alteration in this rule, Appendix IV

and Reports of the Committee of Ways and Means and of Committees of the Whole House authorizing expenditure, but not of the Committee of Supply;

(b) proceedings made in pursuance of an Act of Parliament or Standing Order.—The most usual variety of such business is a motion for an Address to the Crown against an Order in Council (or Departmental Rules and Orders) made in pursuance of an Act which specifically provides Parliament with such an opportunity for reviewing departmental legislation. As such motions are, of course, made by Private Members, and Private Members have no control of the time of the House, their exemption from the eleven o'clock[1] rule is an essential condition of their being discussed at all. Another type of such motions is moved on behalf of the Government for the purpose of *approving* Rules and Orders in pursuance of Statutes which prescribe the need of such approval (see p. 166).

(2) *Business specifically exempted by vote of the House.*— Standing Order No. 1 (8) prescribes a form of motion to be moved by a Minister at the commencement of public business for the purpose of exempting certain specified business from interruption under the Eleven o'Clock Rule, *i.e.* "That the proceedings on (*specified business*) be exempted at this day's sitting from the provisions of the Standing Order (Sittings of the House)."[2] Sometimes *all* Government business is thus exempted at a particular sitting. These motions must be decided without amendment or debate. Such motions are also made and agreed to in respect of all Government business for a specified period, *e.g.* the closing weeks of a session, but in this case they are open to amendment and debate. Further, provision for the exemption from interruption of certain items of business may form an incidental part of the timetable contained in a 'Guillotine' Resolution (see p. 129).

When any exempted business, proceedings on which have been protracted beyond eleven o'clock[1], has been disposed of,

---

[1] For altered hours, see Appendix IV.

[2] For an extension of this procedure, see Appendix IV.

the Eleven o'Clock Rule[1] reasserts itself against any subsequent business. Such business is proceeded with as though it were being taken after the moment of interruption and must be deferred if opposed.

If exempted business is concluded before 11.30[1], the Speaker adjourns the House without Question put at 11.30, even though the Orders of the Day are being read. But if exempted business is not concluded until after 11.30, the Speaker does not adjourn the House until all the Orders of the Day have been read.

Again, if unexempted business is under consideration at 11.30[1], the Speaker adjourns the House, although exempted business stands later on the Paper.

Methods of adjourning the House

As we have seen, the normal ways of adjourning are:—

(1) *By Motion*, at any time until just before the stroke of half-past eleven[1] (or later if the Eleven o'Clock Rule has been suspended). (It must be remembered that only a Member of the Government may move the adjournment of the House between any two Orders of the Day.)

(2) *Without Question put*, at half-past eleven[1] (on Fridays at half-past four, or at the conclusion of the business on the Paper whichever be the earlier), or (when that hour has been passed owing to exempted business) at the conclusion of the business on the Paper.

The Standing Orders also provide for:—

(3) the adjournment of the House at the Speaker's discretion in the case of grave disorder (p. 198) (S.O. No. 24); and

(4) adjournment through absence of a quorum (p. 137).

When it is proposed to adjourn beyond the next sitting day, a Motion to that effect, of which notice is normally required, is moved at the commencement of public business.

Suspension of a Sitting

Suspension of a sitting may take place for various reasons set out below. When a sitting is suspended, the Speaker (having, as a rule, named an hour for resuming) goes out without the mace, which remains on the Table as the House is technically sitting. A sitting is suspended:—

(1) regularly, on the first day of the session between the return of the House from hearing the King's Speech in the House of Lords and the commencement of proceedings preliminary to the debate on the Address;

[1] For altered hours and procedure, see Appendix IV.

(2) casually, while waiting unoccupied for the return of a Bill from the Lords, or for a Message to attend the Lords Commissioners;

(3) also when business is concluded before 7.30[1] on a day on which that hour is secured for a Motion for the adjournment of the House under S.O. No. 9, or reserved by the Chairman for Opposed Private Business; and

(4) when the absence of a quorum has been ascertained before 4 o'clock (1 o'clock on Friday) (May, 312).

QUORUM AND COUNT OF THE HOUSE

The Quorum of the House is formed by forty Members, including the Speaker—a number which has remained unchanged since a quorum was established in 1641. Once the Speaker has taken the Chair, the initiative in ascertaining whether a quorum is present rests with the House, but it is incumbent on the Speaker to satisfy himself that a quorum exists before taking the Chair (May, 311).

Between 8.15 and 9.15[1] no notice may be taken of the absence of a quorum,[2] but if the figures of a division taken during that period disclose the absence of a quorum, the business on which the division was taken stands over until the next day, and the next item on the Paper is called.

Before 4 o'clock (1 o'clock on Friday) the House cannot be counted out. If a count reveals the absence of a quorum, the sitting is suspended. If a sitting is thus suspended, the arrival of a Message for the attendance of the House in the House of Lords makes a House, regardless of the numbers present, as obviously a rule made by one House for its domestic business cannot affect the business common to Parliament as a whole.

Proceedings in counting the House

Subject to the qualifications mentioned above the procedure in counting the House is as follows: A Member calls the attention of the Speaker to the fact that there are not forty Members present. Whereupon the Speaker, announcing that "notice has been taken that forty Members are not present", orders strangers to withdraw (an order which has no effect on the Galleries, but applies to the Members' Lobby and the seats for Strangers below the Bar). The division bells ring, and at

---

[1] For altered hours, see Appendix IV.
[2] For similar provision affecting Friday, see Appendix IV.

the expiration of two minutes the Speaker proceeds to count the House. If less than forty Members prove to be present, and it is later than 4 o'clock, the Speaker adjourns the House until the next sitting day. If, however, it is earlier than 4 o'clock, he suspends the sitting and leaves the Chair until four, unless in the meantime the presence of a quorum is reported to him. If the suspension lasts until 4 o'clock, the Speaker on resuming the Chair again counts the House, and, if less than forty Members are present, adjourns it as above. On Friday, 1 is substituted for 4 o'clock. Since the passage of S.O. No. 27 in 1927, which permits the House to be counted out at 1 o'clock on Fridays, the suspension of a sitting owing to absence of a quorum is unlikely.

In Committee of the Whole House, when a count is claimed, the Chairman follows the procedure in force in the House to ascertain the presence of a quorum. If less than forty are present, he retires from the Chair, and on its resumption by the Speaker reports to him. The Speaker counts the House again and, if a quorum is now present, leaves the Chair for the resumption of the Committee; but, if a quorum is not present, he proceeds as if the original count had been in the House.

If a division discloses the absence of a quorum at any time except between 8.15 and 9.15[1] (see p. 137), the same results follow as if it had been disclosed by a count of the House.

Finally it may be added that by present practice the Chair, before accepting a claim for a count of the House, waits for a reasonable period (at least an hour) after the previous ascertainment of a quorum, whether by a count or by the figures of a division.

II. THE VARIOUS ITEMS OF BUSINESS

An attempt must now be made to describe the various items of business which make up the programme of a sitting. Many of these items are formal and take up little time. Some of them are infrequent, and it is most unlikely that they would all occur at the same sitting. Nor is the relative order of all the items rigidly fixed (particularly those composing heading 8), but an order which is most common or most convenient is adopted or suggested.

[1] For altered hours, see Appendix IV.

Time-Table of a Sitting

(showing the order and the approximate time of taking the various items of business which may be taken at an ordinary sitting.)

2.45 *till* 2.50[1], Prayers.

1. *Business taken immediately after Prayers.* Motions for New Writs (p. 140).
2. 2.50 until not later than 3.0[1], *Unopposed Private Business* (p. 140).
3. *Presentation of Public Petitions* (p. 142).
4. *Motions for Unopposed Returns* (p. 144).
5. 3.0 (not later) until 3.45 (not later)[1], *Questions to Ministers*, of which printed notice has been given (p. 145) and 3.45 (not later) until 3.50 (about)[1], *'Private Notice' Questions* of an urgent character (p. 147).
6. *Introduction of New Members.*
7. *Motions for the adjournment of the House under S.O. No. 9* (p. 152).
8. *Business taken after any Motion for Adjournment under S.O. No. 9:*—
   (1) Motions for leave of absence (now practically obsolete).
   (2) Giving of oral notice of intention to move a Motion (p. 155).
   (3) Ministerial Statements and personal explanations (p. 158).
   (4) Motions to 'set up' a 'Money' Committee (p. 159), *Manual* 40; May, 731).
   (5) Lords' Amendments (if not material) to a Public Bill (p. 159; May, 354 and 547; *Manual*, 40).
   (6) Privilege Motions (this is the most convenient moment, but they may be moved at other times as well) (see p. 159).
9. *"At the commencement of Public Business":*—
   (1) Presentation of Public Bills (see p. 160).
   (2) "Business" Motions moved by the Government (p. 160).
   (3) Motions for leave to bring in Bills and to nominate Select Committees (under S.O. No. 12) (p. 161).
   (4) Privilege Motions (where notice has been possible) (May, 362).

---

[1] For altered hours, see Appendix IV.

10. *Public Business.*

    4 *o'clock (about)*[1], Orders of the Day and Notices of Motions (p. 162).

11. 7.30 *until* 11.0[1] (unless disposed of earlier), Following Business (when granted precedence):—

    (1) Adjournment Motions under S.O. No. 9.

    (2) Opposed Private Business under S.O. No. 7 (p. 165), and

    (3) (unless begun earlier), The second Private Members' Motion under S.O. No. 4 (p. 166).

    11.0[1] Interruption of Business (p. 166).

    11.30 (not later)[2] Adjournment of the House (p. 133).

12. Business regularly taken after 11 o'clock[1]. Proceedings in pursuance of Acts (p. 166).

Friday Sittings

The main differences in the case of Friday sittings are that:—

(1) The House meets at 11.0 and adjourns not later than 4.30[2];

(2) Ministers are not bound to, and as a rule do not, answer oral questions;

(3) Motions for the adjournment of the House under S.O. No. 9, and for bringing in Bills, etc., under S.O. No. 12, are not in order.

1. BUSINESS TAKEN IMMEDIATELY AFTER PRAYERS

Motions for New Writs

A writ for the filling of a vacant seat is a matter of privilege, and motions for new writs are therefore made without notice (see p. 67). The regular time for moving them is immediately after Prayers.

2. UNOPPOSED PRIVATE BUSINESS

Private Business in the House is normally unopposed, and as such is taken at the time of Private business, *i.e.* after Prayers and before 3 o'clock[1] on Mondays, Tuesdays, Wednesdays, and Thursdays, and at 11 o'clock on Fridays.

'Private Business' includes any business before the House in regard to Private Bills (see p. 291).

Private Business consists of:—

(1) Private Bills, with any notices of motions relating thereto;

---

[1] For altered hours, see Appendix IV.

[2] But see alteration in this rule, Appendix IV.

(2) Notices of Motions at the time of Private Business;
(3) Provisional Order Bills;
and appears in that order upon the Order Paper.

(1) Private Bills are set down in the first instance on instructions given by the Parliamentary Agents with due notice according to the Standing Orders. They are placed on the Order Paper in the following order:—

> Lords' Amendments.
> Third Readings.
> Consideration of Bills ordered to lie upon the Table.
> Second Readings.

In conformity with the order of the House giving Unopposed Private Business precedence of Opposed Private Business, Bills opposed on first being set down and set down again by order of the House, then follow in the same order. These Bills are distinguished by the words 'By Order', which are to be found in brackets after every such Bill.

If the promoters propose to move amendments on consideration or verbal amendments on Third Reading, a notification to this effect appears in brackets after the title of the Bill. In the same way the necessity for obtaining the King's or the Prince of Wales's Consent on Third Reading is indicated (see p. 304).

Then follow 'Notices of Motions' relating to the Bills set down, each Motion being marked with the same number (in brackets) as the Bill to which it refers. These notices most commonly deal with the following subjects:—

> (a) Motions to put off any stage of a Bill for three or six months.
> (b) Motions to suspend Standing Orders by the Chairman of Ways and Means.
> (c) Instructions to Private Bill Committees.
> (d) Motions to commit Bills to Joint or Select Committees.
> (e) Recommittal motions on consideration.
> (f) Amendments on consideration.

(2) Notices of Motions, at the time of Private Business, are notices relevant to Private Business but not referring to the business actually set down for that particular day. They include, amongst others, the following subjects:—

(a) Motions such as (b) (c) (d) (e) above, but not relating to any Bills appearing on the Order Paper for that day.

(b) Amendments to Standing Orders [Private Business] moved by the Chairman of Ways and Means.

(c) The nomination or setting up of the Committee of Selection.

(d) Motions involving communications with the Lords relating to Private Business.

(3) Bills for confirming Provisional Orders or Orders under the Private Legislation Procedure (Scotland) Act, 1936, appear in the same order as Private Bills. In addition, such Bills are presented at the time of Private Business by the Minister concerned. Notices of such presentations appear on the Order Paper after second readings.

Opposed Private Business

Any item of Private Business becomes opposed when, on its being called, any member says "I object". Any such business that has become opposed, or has not been reached by three o'clock, is postponed without question put until such time as the Chairman of Ways and Means shall determine. In practice, however, business which is not completed or reached is put down automatically for the following day.

When it becomes clear that the opposition to any Private Bill is not likely to be withdrawn, it is necessary to dispose of it as 'Opposed Private Business'. Such business is taken at half-past seven o'clock[1] on Mondays, Tuesdays, Wednesdays or Thursdays (not Fridays) or as soon as any motion for the adjournment of the House under Standing Order No. 9 has been disposed of and may be discussed until eleven o'clock[1], provided that no opposed private business other than that then under discussion is taken after half-past nine o'clock[1].

The Chairman of Ways and Means is given discretion under Standing Order No. 7 as to the day when such business may be set down; but he is directed to distribute it as equally as possible between days when Government business has precedence and other sittings; he also directs the order in which the business is to be taken.

3. Presentation of Public Petitions

Petitions may be presented either (a) orally, or (b) informally.

(a) A Member who has signified his intention of orally presenting a Petition by entering his name on the

[1] For altered hours, see Appendix IV.

list (which is placed day by day on the Opposition side of the Table for the purpose), or by giving notice privately to the Speaker, is called by the Speaker immediately after Private Business, and, after reciting the 'prayer' and stating the description of Petitioners and the number of signatures, deposits it by placing it in a bag kept for the purpose at the back of the Chair (S.O. No. 91). If the Petition is very bulky, assistance may be rendered by the messengers of the House on notice given to the Serjeant.

(b) Informal presentation of a Petition is effected by simply placing it in the receptacle referred to above at any time during the sitting of the House.

Orally presented Petitions, and those presented informally, which are deposited before four o'clock, are, if in order, acknowledged by an entry in the *Votes and Proceedings* of the current day.

Petitions which refer to a Motion on the Order Paper or to an Order of the Day may also be presented at the commencement of proceedings on such Motion or Order. This opportunity is not often utilized.

Practice with regard to Petitions

A Paper containing the rules with regard to Petitions, drawn up on the authority of the House, is circulated to Members at the beginning of each Session and copies can be obtained at any time from the Vote Office. Reference should be made to this Paper and also to the many detailed applications of the rules contained in May, Chap. XXIX. The practice may be summarized as follows:—

A Member who has received a Petition for presentation, after satisfying himself that it is in order, as regards both form and contents, and affixing his name at its head, presents it either orally or informally, as stated above. If it is not obviously out of order, it is acknowledged by an entry in the *Votes and Proceedings* and ordered to lie upon the Table, and referred to the Committee of Public Petitions, in one of whose reports its subject and the number of its signatures, which are in order, will be stated along with other petitions on the subject, and, if of peculiar importance, it may be printed at length. If irregularities are detected in a petition after its acceptance has been notified in *Votes and Proceedings*, an order may be made for its withdrawal or rejection.

L

Who may present Petitions ?

The only outside bodies privileged to present petitions to the
House at the Bar are the Corporation of London by its sheriffs,
and (if the right still exists) the Corporation of Dublin by the
Lord Mayor. In all other cases petitions are presented by a
Member who, in virtue of his representative character, is
precluded from presenting a petition from himself, although
his petition may be presented for him by another Member.

Form of Petition

A petition consists of the following parts:—A formal superscription to the House, the designation of the petitioners,
general allegations, and a prayer. Of these the most important is
the prayer, which states the particular objects of the petitioners,
and may be said to constitute the petition. The rules require
the prayer to be placed at the head of each separate sheet,
if there are more than one to which signatures are attached,
and to be written by hand on the first signed sheet, though it
may be mechanically reproduced on the others. The other
rules as to the form of petitions, which are contained in the
Paper referred to above, are so framed as to ensure that
(1) the wording of the petition as presented to the House
is identical with the wording submitted to the signatories,
and (2) the signatures represent real and not mythical persons.

Contents of Petitions

The language of a petition must be decorous and temperate,
and respectful towards the Sovereign and towards Parliament,
the courts of justice and other constituted authorities. Nor
may it allude to debates in either House of Parliament or to a
motion which has not been printed on the Notice Paper.

4. MOTIONS FOR UNOPPOSED RETURNS

After the presentation of petitions (if any), and provided it
is not yet three o'clock[1], a motion may be moved (notice having
been given) for an Unopposed Return, *i.e.* for a Paper compiled by a department for the information of the House (see
p. 92). Such a motion requires the assent of the Minister in
charge of the department concerned, and unless this is signified
to the Speaker in advance, he will pass over the motion (May,
332). If, in spite of official consent having been notified, such
a motion is opposed, it stands over until a day allotted to private
Members' motions, but the Speaker has overruled unofficial

[1] For altered hours, see Appendix IV.

opposition to such a motion when it has been officially 'granted'. It should be added that another Member, if duly authorized, may move such a motion in the absence of the Member in whose name it stands.

5. QUESTIONS TO MINISTERS (S.O. No. 8)

Not later than three o'clock[1] the Question 'hour' begins. This is a more important item of business than any yet described. It is expected to provide lively moments and seems to be of unfailing interest to Members and the public. It is modern and affords a useful method of supervising the administration of the Government. Its effectiveness is generally recognized. Questions "turn a searchlight upon every corner of the public service" (Lowell, i. 332). Their chief object is "the explanation to the public of the meaning of political events", and "they are often arranged by the Government itself so as to give them an opportunity of making announcements in a somewhat informal way" (Redlich, ii. 241 and 242). They are "serviceable as obviating the necessity in many instances of more extended debate and of motions for papers" (Todd, 1892, ii. 85). And finally "Questions afford to the Private Member under modern conditions almost his only opportunity" (Marriott, i. 571).

Most of these authorities agree also that the privilege of asking Questions is liable to abuse and that the number of Questions has increased inordinately. We shall come in a moment to the rules of order governing the form and subject-matter of Questions, which have grown almost as rapidly as Questions themselves (p. 149). How rapidly Questions have grown is shown by the following facts and figures. The first recorded Question was asked in 1721 by Lord Cowper in the House of Lords: "whether there was any ground for a certain rumour" (a form of Question which would now be out of order). For more than a century Questions were infrequent and looked at somewhat askance as an irregular form of debate. In 1835 a notice of a Question was first printed. In 1849 a special position was assigned to them on the Order Paper. In the session of 1847 there were 129 Questions, or an average of 1 a day. In 1880 there were 1,546, or 13 a day. In 1900 there were 5,106, or 41 a day. After 1902, when the system of answering certain Questions non-orally was introduced, and although the principle was adopted of restricting Members at first to 8, then to 4, and finally in 1920 to 3 daily, the numbers still

[1] For altered hours, see Appendix IV.

continued to rise until in 1923 the daily average was 109. Since then, after a period of decline, the average has risen to about 130, amounting roughly to 30,000 in session 1945–46.

Before stating the rules which govern the framing of Questions the practice of the House in asking Questions may be stated. Questions are divided into (1) Oral or 'Starred' Questions, (2) Questions for printed answer ('Unstarred'), and (3) Private Notice Questions. Of these Oral Questions are by far the most numerous. To them is allotted the whole of 'Question time' proper, *i.e.* from not later than three o'clock to not later than a quarter to four[1].

Method of asking Oral Questions

Questions for oral answer are handed in at the Table during a sitting in writing,[2] marked with an asterisk and with the day on which they are to be answered (which must be at least one clear day[1] ahead). Suppose a Question to have been handed in on Monday. On Tuesday it is printed in the Notice Paper, and on Wednesday, at earliest, it appears on the Order Paper for answer. A Member is limited to three 'starred' Questions on any one day, and, although he may put down such a Question for Friday, the Standing Order (No. 8) does not give him the right to have it answered on that day. When Question time begins, the Speaker calls the name of the first Member printed in the list of Questions in the Order Paper, and the Member rises and states the number of his Question. (The correct formula is "Question No. 1, Sir, to the [Secretary of State for India].") The Minister addressed reads out his reply or, if it is of unusual length, asks permission to circulate it with the *Official Report*. The Member asking the original Question, or any other Member, is entitled to ask a supplementary Question or Questions arising out of the original Question or reply, but the Speaker keeps a careful watch on this practice so as to safeguard the rights of Members later on the list. After all the Questions on the list have been called, if there is still time before a quarter to four, the Speaker goes through the list a second time,[3] calling the names of Members who were absent on the first round, and if any of these are still absent, their Questions may be asked by other Members authorized by them.

---

[1] For altered times and procedure, see Appendix IV.

[2] Questions may be sent by post and are accepted, provided they bear the signature of the Member sending them, as having been handed in on the day in which they were received, or (if the House is not sitting when they are received) on the next sitting day. For alterations, see Appendix IV.

[3] This practice is now discontinued (May, 820).

Any Question which there has not been time to reach, and also any Question which a Member may happen to have on the list beyond the three to which he is entitled, receive a printed answer in the *Official Report* unless a Member notifies the Table before 3.45[1] of his desire to postpone a Question. A Minister has entire discretion, on grounds of public interest, either to refuse an answer to a Question asked or to give an answer to a Question standing on the Paper but not asked. He has also been allowed to answer a Question not reached. After 3.45[1] only such oral Questions may be asked as have not been answered owing to the absence of a Minister.

Questions are arranged on the Paper in an order of precedence, according to the Ministers questioned, which varies for each day of the week. A list showing the order of precedence of Ministers for every day of the week is prepared as occasion requires, and a copy is posted in the 'No' lobby at either end of the Chamber.

Method of asking 'Unstarred' Questions

These are handed in at the Table in writing, with the day for reply specified, but without an asterisk. They do not require a clear day's notice, and can be put down for answer on the day following that on which they are handed in. The replies are circulated, together with the replies to any Questions on the 'Oral' list which were not reached by a quarter to four[1], and a typewritten copy of the reply is in both cases sent by the department to the Member asking the Question. A department is not bound to supply the answer to an 'unstarred' Question punctually on the day on which it is down.

Questions on purely local matters or dealing with individual cases should, as a rule, be put down for written answer.

Method of asking Private Notice Questions

Private Notice Questions are of two kinds: (*a*) those of an urgent character, and (*b*) non-urgent. The latter may only be asked if there happens still to be time before a quarter to four[1] after the conclusion of Questions upon the Paper. Those of an urgent character must be submitted to the Speaker in time to permit of their due consideration before the House meets, and he is the sole judge of their urgency. A copy of the Question should at the same time be sent to the Minister to whom it is directed. At a quarter to four[1] the Speaker calls the name of the first Member on this list, and the Member so called asks

---

[1] For altered hours, see Appendix IV.

his Question as follows. "I desire to ask the Minister of . . . the following Question, of which I have given him private notice: Whether", etc. (reading the terms of his Question). On the reply supplementary Questions may be asked. A special form of Private Notice Questions, contemplated by the Standing Orders, are those referring to the business of the House. These are regularly asked by the leader of the Opposition. Questions addressed to the Speaker may only be asked by private notice and not as oral Questions on the Paper.

Who may be Questioned ?

At one time Questions were allowed to be addressed to Private Members, who were officially connected with the Metropolitan Board of Works, the British Museum or a Royal Commission, about the business of such bodies. Now, however, they may only be addressed (*a*) to Ministers and such Private Members as are commissioned by the Government to answer for departments (such as the Charity or Ecclesiastical Commissioners), who have no Minister generally responsible in the House, and (*b*) to Private Members about a "Bill, Motion or other matter connected with the business of the House in which such Members are concerned" (May, 335). As an example of the latter may be mentioned the Chairman of the Kitchen Committee. A Question to an ex-Minister with regard to transactions during his term of office is out of order.

Rules relating to the form and subject-matter of Questions

It was mentioned just now that the rules which govern the framing of Questions have grown *pari passu* with the increase of the number of Questions themselves. They are based on a considerable number of Speakers' Rulings, given on individual cases as they occurred during the last sixty or seventy years, and collected and applied as precedents so as to form a small body of case law, which is continually being enriched in detail and still awaits consideration as a whole. A Ruling, once given, continues to be applied until it is revoked by a subsequent Ruling.

The Rules, in the form in which they at present exist, are set out below, arranged under three main headings so as to be more easily understood and remembered. It may be noted that they apply equally to all types of Questions—oral, unstarred, private notice, and supplementary.

The first requirement is that a Question shall be of a genuinely interrogative character, and the rules under this heading set out a number of points characteristic of the 'Question' which presumes too much upon the fact that it is introduced by the word 'whether'.

The second heading, dealing with the subject-matter of Questions, lays down the indispensable requirement that some degree of ministerial responsibility must be involved, and gives a list of matters for which experience shows that ministerial responsibility is erroneously supposed to exist.

The third heading groups together the points, most frequently recurring in Questions, which involve a breach of constitutional usage or parliamentary etiquette.

Putting these together, it may be said that, to be in order, a Question should be genuinely directed to seeking information or pressing for action, addressed to a Minister[1] who is officially responsible for the matter with which it deals, and framed in accordance with the rules of constitutional usage and parliamentary etiquette.

The following are examples of these Rules:—

A. *Information or Action*

(The object of a Question is to obtain information or press for action)

(1) A Question should not be in effect a short speech, or an argument, or limited to giving information, or framed so as to suggest its own answer or convey a particular point of view.

(2) The facts on which a Question is based may be set out briefly, provided the Member makes himself responsible for their accuracy, but extracts from newspapers, quotations from speeches, etc., are not admissible. (Where the facts alleged are of sufficient moment, the Speaker requires *prima facie* proof of their authenticity.)

    Besides these general rules the following types of Question may be enumerated as being *out of order*, viz.:—

(3) Questions seeking an expression of opinion;

(4) raising questions of policy too large to be dealt with in the limits of an answer to a Question;

(5) repeating in substance Questions already answered or to which an answer has been refused;

(6) multiplied with slight variations on the same point;

(7) containing epithets or rhetorical expressions, controversial or ironical statements, innuendo, satire or ridicule;

---

[1] Or other Member.

(8) being trivial, vague or meaningless;

(9) being hypothetical in form;

(10) requiring information set forth in accessible documents (such as Statutes, Treaties, etc.) or in ordinary works of reference;

(11) seeking, *for purposes of argument*, information on matters of past history.

B. *Responsibility of Minister*

(12) A Question should be directed to a Minister officially responsible for the subject-matter with which it deals. (This rule is held to cover not only Questions requiring action, but also those seeking for information.)

Without detracting from the generality of this rule, the following types of Question are *out of order* on this ground, viz.:—

(13) Questions seeking information about the internal affairs of foreign countries or the Dominions;

(14) dealing with matters transferred to the Government of Northern Ireland;

(15) raising matters under the control of local authorities (*e.g.* provincial police, certain aspects of education, public health, and other matters);

(16) seeking an expression of opinion on a question of law, such as the interpretation of a statute, or of an international document, a Minister's own powers, etc.;

(17) raising matters under the control of bodies or persons not responsible to the Government, such as Banks, the money market, the Stock Exchange, joint stock companies, railways, employers' organizations, trade unions, etc.;

(18) dealing with matters referred to a Royal Commission, or (but more doubtfully) a departmental committee;

(19) asking whether statements in the Press, or of private individuals, or unofficial bodies are accurate;

(20) referring to speeches made outside the House (except those of Cabinet Ministers, when it is permissible to ask the Prime Minister whether they represent the policy of the Government);

(21) dealing with the action of a Minister for which he is not responsible to Parliament[1];

[1] In 1924 a Question asking the Attorney-General whether he had communicated with certain Members before deciding to withdraw a prosecution was on this ground disallowed privately by the Speaker.

(22) putting to a Minister a Question for which another Minister is more directly responsible, or asking one Minister to influence the action of another;

(23) dealing with matters within the jurisdiction of the Speaker. (Questions on such matters should be addressed to the Speaker by private notice.)

C. *Constitutional propriety and the Rules of Order*

1. The following types of Questions are *out of order* as infringing constitutional propriety, viz.:—

(24) Questions introducing the name of, or containing reflections on, the Sovereign, or the Royal Family, or referring to the influence of the Crown;

(25) referring to the grant of honours, the prerogative of mercy, or the ecclesiastical patronage of the Crown;

(26) asking what advice a Minister proposes to give the Crown (but it is in order to ask what advice he *has* given);

(27) addressed to a court official or referring to the action of a court official (*e.g.* the action of the Lord Chamberlain with regard to the licensing of plays);

(28) containing discourteous references to the House of Lords. (The Speaker has deprecated *any* references to their debates);

(29) criticizing decisions of the House of Commons;

(30) seeking information about matters which are in their nature secret, such as decisions or proceedings of the Cabinet (including the Committee of Imperial Defence and other committees of the Cabinet), advice given to the Crown by Law Officers, etc.;

(31) reflecting on the decision of a Court of Law, or being likely to prejudice a case which is under trial.

2. The following types of Question are *out of order* as infringing some general rule of order, viz.:—

(32) Questions containing personal charges or reflecting on persons otherwise than in a public capacity;

(33) introducing the names of persons or bodies invidiously or for the purposes of advertisement;

(34) referring discourteously to a friendly foreign country;

(35) anticipating a Question already on the Paper, or a motion (notice of which has already been given) which must be decided without debate.

3. The following are *out of order* as raising matters for dealing with which the rules provide a more convenient method, viz.:—

(36) Questions reflecting on the conduct of certain persons whose conduct may only be challenged on a substantive motion (May, 375);

(37) suggesting amendments to Bills, or asking for information which should be moved for as a Return, or dealing with matters before a parliamentary committee;

(38) referring to debates or answers to Questions of the *current* session.

6. INTRODUCTION OF NEW MEMBERS

The first business after all Questions have been disposed of is the introduction of Members returned at by-elections. Such 'new' Member, having obtained from the Public Bill Office a paper certifying that the certificate of his return sent by the Crown Office has been received, enters the House during Question time and remains below the Bar until he receives the signal from the Speaker—"Members desiring to take their seats will please come to the Table". In obedience to the Resolution of the 23rd February, 1688, declaring "the ancient order and custom of the House", he must be 'introduced', or accompanied to the Table, by two Members of the House. At the Table he is sworn by the Clerk, signs the Test Roll, and is introduced to the Speaker in the same way as a Member returned at a general election (p. 103).

7. ADJOURNMENT MOTIONS ON THE GROUND OF URGENCY
Procedure under S.O. No. 9

A Member who desires to move the adjournment of the House under this Standing Order must submit to the Speaker in advance the terms in writing of the matter to which he desires to call attention. On consideration of these terms the Speaker decides whether the proposed matter is one which falls within the definition contained in the Standing Order or whether it must be ruled out of order. The point at which the Member rises to obtain the leave of the House is after Questions and before the business taken "at the commencement of Public Business" (see p. 159). The formula is: "Mr. Speaker, I beg leave to move the adjournment of the House in order to call the attention of the House to a definite matter of urgent public importance, namely," etc. If he considers the terms of the motion in order, the Speaker inquires whether the Member has the leave of the House, and, if it is not unanimously given, calls on those Members who support the motion to rise in their places. If at least forty Members rise, the required leave is granted and the motion stands over till half-past seven[1], when it takes precedence of all business (see p. 165). The same result is achieved if, less than forty Members but not less than ten having risen, the mover exercises his right to challenge a division on the question whether the motion shall be made and obtains a majority in its favour. Not more than one such motion can be made during the same sitting. If the leave of the House is refused, the same matter cannot be raised again under the Standing Order during the same session.

Rules relating to the Subject-Matter of Urgency Adjournment Motions

The matter of such a Motion must by Standing Order be (1) definite, (2) urgent, and (3) of public importance. Each of these terms of the definition has been elucidated by Rulings from the Chair, the effect of which may be summarized as follows:—

(1) *A definite matter.*

    (*a*) Not more than one such motion can be made at the same sitting.

    (*b*) The motion must not deal with more than one subject.

    (*c*) It must not be framed in general terms, but must deal with a particular case.

    (*d*) It must not deal with a hypothetical case, or be based on uncorroborated report.

    (*e*) Official information must be available.

(2) *Urgent.* The matter upon which the motion is based:—

    (*a*) must have happened recently and be raised at the first opportunity;

    (*b*) must require the immediate attention of the House and the Government, and not be postponable until an opportunity is provided by Supply, etc.;

    (*c*) must not be a matter upon which notice has been given. (Postponement of such a motion is accordingly not permitted, as ruled on 3rd May, 1922, though exception was made on 13th March, 1922 (*Deb.*, 1762) and 24th February, 1921 (*Deb.*, 1132).)

[1] For altered hours, see Appendix IV.

(3) *Of public importance.*

> The motion must raise a larger issue than a merely individual grievance (26th June, 1913. *Deb.*, 1246).

In addition, examples of the grounds upon which the Speaker has ruled such motions out of order may be given under the following heads:—

(4) The responsibility of the Government must be clearly involved. It is not involved in the case of:—

   (*a*) the refusal of the Government, in the exercise of its statutory discretion, to intervene in trade disputes;

   (*b*) an attack by newspapers upon certain Members (8th December, 1920. *Deb.*, 2226);

   (*c*) the refusal of the Government to prevent the holding of a political meeting (13th June, 1922. *Deb.*, 191);

   (*d*) the action of County Councils or other local authorities,

   and, generally, in circumstances similar to those referred to in the section "Rules relating to the subject-matter of Questions" under the heading 'B' (p. 150);

(5) The matter upon which the motion is based must involve official action beyond the ordinary administration of the law.

   E.g. It has been ruled that the advice given by the Home Secretary as to the exercise of the prerogative of mercy cannot be raised by such a motion (29th Nov., 1920. *Deb.*, 930).

(6) The following matters cannot be raised by such motions because the procedure of the House provides other means of raising them:—

   (*a*) grievances which can only be remedied by legislation;

   (*b*) matters involving privilege;

   (*c*) the conduct of those bearers of high office whose conduct may only be challenged upon a substantive motion (see p. 169).

(7) The following matters cannot be raised by such motions in accordance with the general rules of debate:—

   (*a*) a matter identical with one already decided in the same session (see p. 176), and

   (*b*) a matter the discussion of which would anticipate a motion of which notice has already been given (see p. 178).

Rules governing Debate upon Urgency Adjournment Motions

Debate must be strictly relevant to the matter with regard to which leave to move the adjournment was granted.[1] Nor can matters be introduced which would be out of order if submitted as part of the terms upon which such leave was granted. The ordinary rules of debate must be observed which exclude, besides, matters referred to above, matters under adjudication by a court of law, the terms of a Bill before the House of Lords, etc.

8. Business taken after any Motion for Adjournment under S.O. No. 9
8 (1) *Motions for Leave of Absence*

This moment or after the conclusion of public business is the time for moving such motions, and they require notice. They have, however, fallen into disuse together with the attempts which occasioned them to enforce the attendance of Members by the direct action of the House.

8 (2) *Oral Notice of Intention to move Motion*

Another and more important item of business which may be taken at this time is the giving notice orally of intention to move a motion on a future day. The kind of motion covered by this practice is (with the exception of amendments on first going into Committee of Supply on each of the main branches of the Estimates) the 'substantive' motion, *i.e.* a motion which is not incidental to any other proceedings (see p. 168). As a general rule all substantive motions require notice, but this requirement may be waived by general consent of the House.

At first sight it is rather puzzling to find that the practice of the House treats the notice of motion as having an existence distinct from the motion itself. But it is a logical distinction. They exist in quite different connexions. The notice, *i.e.* the promise or permission to move a motion on a certain day, is an item of business like an Order of the Day and affects the time-table of the House. It is accordingly dealt with in this chapter. The motion itself is a stage, the first stage, in the process of debate, and is reserved for the next chapter. It is not possible to make an absolute separation between notices and motions, but to do so as far as possible will involve less repetition than to take them out of their proper context.

---

[1] For the forms of adjournment motion which admit of general debate, see pp. 117 and 118.

A Member gives oral notice by rising in his place and stating his motion at length or in general terms. If he adopts the latter course, he must hand in the full terms at the Table at the latest on the day before the motion is to be moved. Anything, however, in the nature of a personal charge must be stated at length and not in general terms. In order to ensure his notice being printed in the Notice Paper a Member giving oral notice must in the course of the same sitting hand it in at the Table in writing. Written presentation has, since the beginning of the 19th century, become the essential part of the process of giving notice, and the earlier method of giving oral notice has fallen into disuse except for three purposes:—

(1) In the case of motions moved on ceremonious occasions (the retirement of the Speaker, etc.).

(2) In the case of Ministers who give, if they like, oral notice of their Bills on the first day of the session with the object of 'blocking' the raising of the subject-matter of such Bills by way of amendment to the Address (see p. 108). These are given for 'an early day' (see p. 90).

(3) In the case of Private Members who draw places in the periodical ballots for motions (see p. 158).

The rules of the House with regard to notice are governed by the very limited time which is allotted for the discussion of motions. To this fact are due the limitation of the *extent* of notice, and the determination of precedence among motions by the ballot.

Extent of Notice

A notice of motion cannot be given for any day more distant than the second day (from the date of giving notice) on which motions have precedence over Orders of the Day (S.O. No. 6).

The original purpose of a limitation of time (made in 1853 as the result of a recommendation of a Committee of 1837) was to revive an interest in notice of motion days, which had flagged owing to the fact that motions were put down months in advance and were stale when they came to be discussed. In session 1839 there were 15 counts out in a session of 83 days (Redlich, i. 80), mostly on 'motion' days.

As to the minimum period of notice there is no rule requiring more than that notice shall be given in at the Table the day before, and appear on the Paper the same day as, the motion itself is taken. It is considered more courteous, however, to give a rather longer notice where possible.

The day for which notice has been given may be changed by a fresh notice, but only so as to postpone it. If time permits, however, there does not seem to be anything to prevent a notice being taken off the Paper and put down afresh for an earlier day, though this must be regarded as against the spirit of the rules.

Ballot for Bills and Notices of Motions

These ballots are of two kinds: (*a*) the ballot for Private Members' Bills which takes place outside the House on the first Thursday[1] of the session (unless the Government takes Private Members' time), and (*b*) the periodical ballots for notices of motions, or for amendments on going into Committee of Supply (either alone or in combination), which, as long as there are days to ballot for, take place in the House immediately after Questions. It will be convenient to describe here the procedure for both kinds of ballot.

(*a*) *The ballot for Bills.*—The House makes an order (partially retrospective) on the second day of the session (generally a Wednesday) that all Members who have entered their names on the list placed for the purpose in the 'No' lobby on the first and second days of the session shall be entitled to ballot, and about half the House usually avail themselves of the opportunity. The ballot takes place the next day in a committee-room, generally at twelve o'clock, with the Chairman of Ways and Means in the Chair, and any Members, who wish, in attendance. The days to be balloted for are all the Fridays which are allotted to the second readings of Private Members' Bills. The method of holding the ballot is as follows:—The Chairman has a list of the Members balloting, with a number against each name. A Clerk draws from the ballot-box folded slips of paper containing numbers. As he draws, he calls the number, and the Chairman calls the name of the Member corresponding to that number on his list. During the sitting of the House that day, successful Members (about fifty or sixty places, of which some sixteen are certainties, are balloted for) hand in at the Table the titles of their Bills. On the fourth day of the session (normally Friday) the Bills are presented by Members in the order of the ballot and a day named by the Member presenting it for the second reading of each Bill (May, 352).

[1] If, as is usually the case, the session begins on Tuesday.

(b) *The periodical ballots for notices of motions.*—These are held in the House immediately after Questions (with the Speaker in the Chair, but otherwise in the manner described above). The ballot for the first two Wednesdays usually takes place on the first Thursday pursuant to an Order of the House and the ballot for subsequent Wednesdays a fortnight in advance, that is on the second, third, etc., Wednesdays of the session for the fourth, fifth, etc., Wednesdays. The successful Members, when their names are called, state their motion in general terms, *e.g.* as follows: "I desire to give notice that this day fortnight I will call attention to (Rural Housing) and move a Resolution." A Member must at the same sitting hand in at the Table a copy of the notice given in the House.

A ballot is held in the same manner for notices of amendments on first going into Committee of Supply on each of the four branches of the Estimates (see p. 268). If necessary, such a ballot is combined with one of the periodical ballots for motions.

The ballot, it should be remembered, gives precedence to a Member, not to business, and another Member can only give notice in place of a Member who has been successful in the ballot, but cannot himself move a motion, or present a Bill.

Terms of Notice

The Speaker, and the Clerks at the Table acting under his authority, exercise a certain degree of censorship over the terms of a notice (May, 379). Irregularities are amended and notices which are obviously out of order, such as a reflection on a vote of the House, may be withheld from the Notice Paper. The Speaker has also intervened when a notice orally given is of such a character, and directed it not to be accepted. The House has also directed that a notice which has been printed should be removed from the Paper.

A change in the terms of a notice after it has been printed in the Notice Paper is permitted, provided the alteration has not the effect of enlarging the scope of the original terms.

8 (3) *Personal Explanations*

Explanations of the circumstances in which office was resigned, made by ex-Ministers, may be included under this heading. They cannot lead to debate and ought not to contain controversial matter. If the occasion requires, the Speaker permits, not a reply, but a relevant statement, on behalf of the Government. Personal statements are also made by unofficial Members on behalf of themselves, occasionally on behalf of other Members unable through illness or absence to speak for themselves, and even (though permission has been refused) on behalf of persons not Members, whose conduct has been reflected upon in debate. The Speaker carefully limits such personal explanations to the circumstances which are the subject of explanation, and no other speech is, as a rule, permitted.

Ministerial statements of policy may also be made at this time, though they are now more usually made in response to a Question at Question time.

8 (4) *Motions to set up 'Money' Committees* (see p. 274)

Such motions do not require notice and may be moved before Questions, or at the end of the sitting after the conclusion of Public Business.

8 (5) *Lords' Amendments to a Public Bill*

When they raise no question of principle, Lords' Amendments are taken at this time. Otherwise they are ordered under S.O. No. 54 to be taken on a future day. But when the state of business requires it they can be taken as soon as the Message containing them is received from the Lords, even though doing so involves the interruption of the business under discussion (see p. 224) (May, 546).

8 (6) *Privilege Motions*

A Privilege Motion, of which notice has not been given, and which does not refer to a breach of privilege occurring in the precincts of the House itself (in which case it is taken immediately upon its occurrence) is usually taken at this point, so that if a debate arises the inconvenience of a curtailment of Question time or of the interruption of the Orders of the Day may be avoided.

For the general question of Privilege, see pp. 70–71 and for procedure in making complaint of breach of privilege, p. 72.

9 " AT THE COMMENCEMENT OF PUBLIC BUSINESS "

The commencement of public business is the moment when the Speaker calls the name of the first Member whose name stands upon the Order Paper for presenting a Bill or making

M

a motion "at the commencement of public business", or, if
there are none of these, when he calls upon the name of the
Member in charge of the first motion standing at the head of
the Orders of the Day, or directs the Clerk to read the Orders
of the Day. It is important to fix the moment of this transition,
for none of the business which we have hitherto been describing
can properly be taken after the commencement of public
business.

On the Order Paper, under the heading "At the commencement of public business", any one of four items of business
may be set down, which are here taken in the order of their
priority.

9 (1) *Presentation of Public Bills*

S.O. No. 35 (1) of 1902 gives a Member the right to present
a Bill without obtaining the leave of the House, and such
presentation carries with it the first reading of the Bill. Most
Bills, whether Government or unofficial, are now presented
in this way (see p. 203).

9. (2) *'Business' Motions moved by a Minister* (see p. 128)

Such motions include those moved for the purpose of:—

(*a*) exempting certain business "from the provisions of the
Standing Order (Sittings of the House)", *i.e.* from the
operation of the 'Eleven o'Clock[1] Rule' (see p. 132);

(*b*) permitting other business, including Estimates supplementary to those of a previous session, to be taken before
eleven o'clock[1], or the business of Supply to be taken
after eleven o'clock[1] on an allotted Supply day (S.O.
No. 16 (2)) (p. 267).

The foregoing motions may be divided upon but do not
admit of amendment or debate. Other motions moved at this
time, such as a motion to permit an opposed Private Bill to be
entered upon after half-past nine[1], may be debated (S.O. No. 7 (5)),
(and see p. 142). The same motion may combine more than
one of such objects, but in that case it will on the demand of
a Member be separated into its component parts, each being
put from the Chair as a separate Question, in accordance with
the rule that complex Questions which are not open to amendment may be divided.

[1] For altered hours, see Appendix IV.

Motions for votes of thanks set down by a Minister may be moved either at the commencement of public business or at the head of the Orders of the Day (May, 361).

9. (3) *Motions for leave to bring in Bills and to nominate Select Committees under S.O. No. 12*

S.O. No. 12 of 1888 (the so-called 'Ten Minutes Rule') is now generally employed by Members for the purpose of obtaining leave to bring in Bills which they hope by a judicious explanation to turn into unopposed Bills, or upon which they intend to make a demonstration knowing that further progress is unlikely. The facilities provided by this rule for the nomination of select committees are seldom employed.

By the procedure under this rule, after a speech (which should not exceed the conventional limit of ten minutes) from the Member making the motion and a speech of like duration from a Member who opposes it, the Speaker may put the Question on the motion, or, if he prefers, "that the debate be now adjourned". If the former question is put and decided in the affirmative, the Member, who has thus obtained leave to bring in a Bill, answers the inquiry of the Speaker: "Who will prepare and bring in the Bill ? ", proceeds to the Bar and thence advances to the Table with the customary three bows, where he presents a 'dummy' Bill to the Clerk and, after its title has been read, announces through him a day for the second reading (see p. 203).

In order, presumably, to prevent the House deciding on such a motion without due consideration of its possible importance, the Speaker has the discretion under the Standing Order of putting the Question for the adjournment of the debate instead of the Question upon the motion itself. This discretion was last exercised on 11th February, 1930. It must be remembered that Bills of the first importance are habitually introduced under Standing Order No. 35 (1) without discussion at all, and the nomination of Select Committees, now generally done by agreement between the Whips of the parties, is seldom opposed.

9. (4) *'Privilege' Motions of which notice has been given*

At the end of motions put down for this time, there may stand upon the Order Paper a motion respecting a breach of privilege in the event of there having been time to give notice. An Order of the Day for a debate on a privilege motion which has been adjourned stands at the head of the Orders of the Day.

10. Public Business

We now reach the main business of a sitting, which normally occupies the time from four o'clock[1] to the moment of interruption. Public Business consists of Orders of the Day and Notices of Motions (*i.e.* motions of which notice has been given, dealing with matters of public business). The important effect of the old distinction between these two classes of business upon fixing the agenda of the House and giving control of its time to the Government is referred to above (p. 37).

The Orders of the Day

The term 'Orders of the Day' is used in two different senses: (1) the narrower sense in which it is distinguished from Notices of Motions, and (2) a wider sense in which it includes such motions. The latter sense is the more important in modern practice. It is in this sense that the term is used in the Order Paper, and the important result follows that a motion on the Order Paper cannot, any more than an Order of the Day, be passed over, postponed in favour of other business, or anticipated by a motion for the adjournment of the House (unless moved by the Government).

Orders of the Day (in the narrower sense) consist of:—

(1) a stage of a Bill (other than the first reading);
(2) the committee stage of Supply, Ways and Means (p. 261) or a Money Resolution (unless under the urgency procedure of S.O. No. 84) (see p. 274) or a Bill;
(3) the Report stage of any of (2);
(4) an adjourned debate on any question, including that proposed on a motion.

Procedure in dealing with the Orders of the Day

In view of the monotonous regularity with which the programme of business arranged by the Government is carried out from day to day and from week to week, it is hard to realize that for the greater part of the 19th century the Government, while theoretically in control, was never secure from having its programme either delayed by amendments to the reading of an Order proposing the discussion of totally irrelevant subjects, or disturbed by proposals to alter the order in which they had arranged their various items, or interrupted by motions for the adjournment of the House moved between one Order and the next, or delayed by prolonged debate on opposed

[1] For altered hours, see Appendix IV.

private business or on motions for the adjournment of the
House moved before the commencement of public business
(see p. 38). It is important to grasp why, exactly, this can no
longer be done, especially as the Standing Orders are not very
explicit on the subject.

S.O. No. 13 (which gives the Speaker the power to direct
the Clerk to read the Orders of the Day without a Question
being put) removes the opportunity for a general debate,
which used to arise when it was necessary to put a Question
for that purpose. As is shown by a Speaker's Ruling of 7th
August, 1872, this Standing Order had by then been extended
to include the rule that immediately on the disposal of one
Order of the Day the next must be called. No gap remained
between two successive Orders during which a motion, such
as that for the adjournment of the House, could be entertained
(although this disability was, somehow, not extended to the
Government).[1] Further, S.O. No. 14, by directing that "the
Orders of the Day shall be disposed of in the order in which
they stand upon the Paper", rendered an amendment, moved
on the reading of an Order, to take a later Order in its place, no
longer admissible. Finally S.Os. Nos. 7 and 9 removed the
two opportunities for raising debates with the effect of post-
poning the hour for reaching the Orders of the Day. By this
means the Orders of the Day have become secure from postponement, interruption or interference against the wishes of the
Government.

Reading the Orders of the Day

To recapitulate, the effect of S.Os. Nos. 13 and 14 is that:—

(1) No question is required for reading an Order of the Day.
(2) Immediately after one Order is disposed of the next
Order standing on the Paper must be proceeded with
(unless a motion for the adjournment of the House is
moved by a Minister of the Crown).

When an Order of the Day is read, the Speaker calls upon the
Member in charge of it, or, in the case of an adjourned debate,
upon the Member who was speaking when it was adjourned,
or who moved the adjournment of the debate. No other Member may intervene except to raise a point of order, or, if the
Member in charge gives way, to ask a question relating to the
Order of the Day. As an Order of the Day is a matter set

---

[1] The only exception to this rule is provided by urgent matters such as
matters of Privilege and (in certain circumstances) Lords Amendments.

down for consideration by the House itself, the right to deal
with it is vested in theory in the House at large. This means
in practice that one Member may act for another (preference,
of course, being given to a Member selected by the Member
in charge of the Order), and also that an Order of the Day may
not be passed over but must be (a) proceeded with, or (b)
deferred to another day, or (c) discharged.

(a) *The Order proceeded with.*—When the Order is read, the
Member in charge indicates to the Speaker that he
wishes it taken 'now'. Then, if it is a stage of a Bill, the
Speaker calls upon the Member in charge to make
the requisite motion. If the Order is for Committee of the
Whole House, the Speaker leaves the Chair (under S.O.
No. 17); if it is for receiving a Resolution reported from
a Committee of the Whole House, the Clerk reads the
Resolution, and so on.

(b) *The Order deferred to another day.* (It may be worth
repeating that it cannot be postponed after subsequent
Orders on the same day.)—On the Order being read, a
day is proposed by the Member in charge of the Bill, or
by another Member acting on his behalf, or by a Clerk
at the Table on instructions received from the Member
in charge, and the Order is announced by the Speaker
as deferred to that day. The proposal of a day was originally and still is technically a motion, and the announcement of the Speaker a putting of the Question. But as no
opposition can arise on this point, the Member in charge
of an Order has in practice the right of deferring it to any
date he pleases. When a day is thus fixed, the Order
appears in the *Order Book* for that day. Before that day is
reached, a later day may be substituted on instructions
being given at the Table, but not an earlier day, even
though an error was made in naming the day, unless
the error is corrected before the reading of the Orders is
concluded.

(c) *The Order discharged.*—When the Order of the Day is
read, a motion may be made that the Order be discharged.
This method is employed for the withdrawal of a Bill.

An Order which has been deferred may be discharged, before
the day to which it is deferred is reached, by instructions given
at the Table and subsequently notified by an entry in *Votes
and Proceedings*.

Orders of the Day not reached owing to an adjournment of the House are set down for the next sitting after the Orders already appointed for that day, subject, of course, to the rules giving precedence to Government business, and permitting the Government to arrange its business in what order it pleases.

Dropped Orders

When proceedings upon an Order of the Day are cut short at the moment of interruption without another day being appointed, or by the House being counted out, or by a sudden adjournment of the House, such an Order becomes 'dropped', *i.e.* it disappears from the Notice Paper. A 'dropped' Order may be restored to the Paper for a specified day upon instructions being given at the Table, and if progress has been made upon it the stage at which it is entered is that reached by the last vote taken upon it in the House or Committee.

If it is essential that proceedings on a dropped Order shall be resumed at the next sitting, a motion to that effect is placed upon the Paper at the commencement of Public Business, the Order itself being printed in italics at the place among the Orders of the Day at which it is proposed to proceed with it.

Notices of Motions among the Orders of the Day

When a motion, notice of which stands among the Orders of the Day, is reached, the Speaker calls the Member in whose name it stands. Several names are, as a rule, attached to motions except motions which have secured precedence by ballot, for, unlike Orders of the Day, motions may only be moved by Members in whose names they stand (except in the case of a Member of the Government, who can always be represented by a colleague). A motion not moved for want of a mover, or not reached, drops from the Paper unless directions are given at the Table for its revival.

11. Suspension of Business at half-past Seven[1]

The business under consideration at 7.30[1] must be postponed without Question put in the two following cases:—

(1) if a motion for the adjournment of the House has (under the procedure of S.O. No. 9) been arranged for that time, or

(2) if Opposed Private Business set down by the Chairman of Ways and Means stands on the Paper for that time.

[1] For altered hours, see Appendix IV.

If both classes of business are appointed for 7.30[1] on the same evening, the motion for the adjournment of the House has precedence. The rules relating to the interruption of business do not apply to the suspension of business. The Speaker, or in committee the Chairman, leaves the Chair without putting any Question, and the business under discussion is postponed until the conclusion of the business thus taking precedence over it, when it is resumed at the point it had reached, the Question under consideration at 7.30[1] being again proposed from the Chair.

Interruption of business at 7.30[1] on Private Members' Wednesdays

On the Wednesdays before Easter which are devoted to Private Members' motions the motion standing first on the Paper, *if not concluded before*, is interrupted at 7.30[1] in precisely the same way as business interrupted at 11 o'clock[1] (S.O. No. 1 (10)) (see p. 132), and the Member whose motion stands next is called.

12. BUSINESS REGULARLY TAKEN AFTER 11 O'CLOCK [1]
Proceedings in pursuance of Acts of Parliament

Apart from various kinds of financial business taken at this hour, which are described elsewhere, the business most usually taken is motions for addresses or resolutions in connexion with Orders and Rules made by His Majesty in Council or public departments in pursuance of power given by Statute (see App. II. pp. 324–7).

Rules and regulations generally require to be laid before Parliament as soon as made, where they lie on the Table for a specified period, during which time they may be annulled by the presentation of an address by either House but without prejudice to the validity of any action taken under them. This is the most usual procedure with regard to laying rules, the chief points about it being that the rules are valid when laid and continue so unless either House intervenes within the prescribed period. But there are other ways in which Parliamentary supervision is exercised, the main varieties being the following:—

(*a*) Rules are sometimes laid in draft with the proviso that they shall not be brought into operation if either House passes a negative resolution (Rules under Prison Acts).

(*b*) Orders and regulations laid in draft sometimes require to

[1] For altered hours, see Appendix IV.

be vitalized (generally without any power of amendment) by addresses or resolutions of both Houses before they come into operation (Government of India Orders in Council under the Government of India Act, 1935, and Special Orders under the Gas Undertakings Acts, etc., see p. 313. These orders may be amended in either House, and it has been found difficult to devise a satisfactory procedure for ensuring that amendments made in one House are identical with those made in the other).

(*c*) Orders made under the Import Duties Act, 1932, which impose duties, are laid before the House of Commons when made, and cease to have effect after twenty-eight days unless approved by a resolution of that House (22 Geo. V., c. 8, s. 19 (2)). Orders under the same Act which do not impose duties cease only if the House within forty days resolves that they be annulled (ib. s. 19 (3) as amended by the Statutory Instruments Act, 1946, s. 5 (2)).

In the case of Church of England Measures (which are not, of course, statutory rules) the procedure requires a resolution in each House for their presentation to His Majesty for the Royal Assent.

Great divergences formerly existed in the periods during which rules, etc., were required to lie before Parliament, the time varying from 8 to 100 days, and also in the method of calculating these days. In every case the statute under which the rule or order was laid required to be consulted. The period of laying for most classes is now standardized at 40 days by the Statutory Instruments Act, 1946. The method of reckoning is also made uniform, no account being taken of time during which Parliament is dissolved or prorogued or during which both Houses are adjourned for more than four days. A list of Rules and Orders, giving the date on which each was laid and the number of days it requires to lie on the Table, is published weekly (see p. 90).

The date from which the period is calculated is the date on which a complete copy of the document is available to Members (*Deb.* 15th June, 1910, c. 1315).

Chapter V

FORMS AND RULES OF DEBATE

This chapter deals with the procedure by which a debate is conducted, describing all the successive steps—the moving of a motion, the proposing and putting of a question, and the process of voting—which are necessary to the attainment of a decision of the House. It also deals with the various forms of closure, and the rules of order governing speaking and behaviour in the House. The intention is to put together in one chapter all the rules which, miscellaneous as they appear, affect the conduct of a debate, irrespective of the nature of the business debated.

A. MOTIONS

A description of the procedure of debate must start with the *Motion*, which is the form in which debate on any subject must originate. When a motion has been moved (and seconded) the Speaker *proposes* the Question (in the same terms as the motion), as the subject of debate, and at the conclusion of the debate *puts* the Question for the purpose of eliciting the immediate decision of the House. Motion, Question, Decision are all parts of a process which may be called the elementary form of debate (see p. 20). This simple form of debate is capable of being made involved by the introduction after the Question has been proposed of a new motion, involving a new subordinate process of debate of the same form (Motion, Question, Decision) which has to be disposed of before the House can return to the Question on the original motion. These new motions are sometimes called 'Subsidiary' motions, to distinguish them from the Substantive motions, on which they depend, and they are themselves divided into various types, as will be shown later.

Rules Relating to Substantive Motions

A substantive motion is a self-contained proposal submitted

168

for the approval of the House, and drafted in such a way as to be capable of expressing a decision of the House.

The rules relating to the manner of giving notice of a motion are stated in the previous chapter (pp. 155–8).

The rules with regard to the motion itself are:—

(1) A motion which requires notice can only be moved by the Member in whose name the notice stands. This does not apply to motions for unopposed returns or for leave of absence. A motion standing in the name of a Member of the Government may also be moved by a colleague, for one Minister can always represent another.

(2) The moving of a motion in a form different from the terms of the notice is out of order if the effect of such alteration is in any way to go beyond the scope of the notice.

(3) A seconder is required to a motion moved in the House except in the case of
  (a) an Order of the Day,
  (b) a formal motion,
  (c) a motion moved by a Member of the Government or a Privy Councillor.
  A seconder is not required in committee.

(4) A substantive motion is the only admissible method of raising a question on the conduct of the holders of certain high offices, a list of whom is given below. The purpose of this rule is to ensure that the House will have an opportunity to record an opinion upon the allegations contained in such a motion—an opportunity which would not be provided by the motion for the adjournment of the House under S.O. No. 9, or by an amendment to the Question on going into Committee of Supply, or by a question to a Minister. The persons referred to are: the Sovereign, the Heir to the Throne, the Viceroy of India[1], the Governors-General of the Dominions, the Lord Chancellor, the Speaker, the Chairman of Ways and Means, Members of either House of Parliament, and Judges of the superior courts in the United Kingdom (including a judge in a court of bankruptcy and of a county court).

(5) Finally, certain matters by their very nature are inadmissible in debate, whether upon a motion or otherwise.

[1] Now no longer applicable.

Such are matters anticipating an Order of the Day
(p. 178), and matters which have already been decided
during the current session.

Proposing the Question

The moment at which the Question is proposed is at the
conclusion of the speech of the mover (or of the seconder,
when a seconder is required). The Question, as already stated,
repeats the terms of the motion, and that has to be framed in
such a form as to be capable of expressing a decision of the
House.

Putting the Question

At the conclusion of debate the Speaker rises to *put* the
Question, repeating once more (with the preface " The Question
is that") the terms of the motion which have already been
proposed as a Question. He then proceeds to 'take the sense'
of the House by saying, "As many as are of that opinion say
'Aye'", and "As many as are of the contrary opinion say
'No'", and decides whether in his judgment the Ayes or the
Noes have it. It may be assumed for the present that the House
agrees to the Question without a division, thus concluding the
process. If the Speaker's judgment is challenged, a division
follows (see p. 179).

The decision, which the putting of the Question has thus
elicited from the House, turns the motion into a Resolution
or an Order. 'Resolutions' declare the opinions and embody
the purposes of the House. By 'Orders' the House directs
subordinate bodies and persons (such as its committees and
its officers), and also regulates the progress of its own business
(when action by itself is not explicity mentioned).

Orders and Resolutions are sometimes declared by the
Speaker, at the request of a Member of the Government, to
have been passed *nemine contradicente*. This is usually done
on occasions of ceremonial, such as addresses of congratulation or condolence to the Sovereign, or on occasions such as
cases of breach of privilege, when the House wishes to express
its corporate spirit.

Withdrawal of Motion

To withdraw a motion the Member who moved it must
signify his desire in the House. The Speaker then 'takes the
pleasure' of the House by saying, "Is it your pleasure that the

motion be withdrawn?" Provided no one objects, he declares the motion withdrawn. It must be borne in mind that, when an amendment has been moved to a motion, the motion cannot be withdrawn until the amendment has been disposed of.

Motions are similarly withdrawn in committee.

MOTIONS (OTHER THAN SUBSTANTIVE)

These may be divided into three classes:—

(1) *Ancillary* motions are motions (made most frequently in connexion with an Order of the Day), which are recognized by the practice of the House as the regular way of proceeding with the various kinds of business— as, *e.g.* the various stages of Bills.

(2) *Superseding* motions are motions which, though independent in form, are moved in the course of debate on another Question and seek to supersede that Question.

(3) *Amendments* are motions which are in form dependent upon a Question proposed from the Chair and merely seek to modify it.

In proceedings in connexion with class (2) the Question already proposed from the Chair is called (to distinguish it from the new Question) the 'original' Question. In the case of class (3) it is called the 'main' Question.

(1) *Ancillary Motions*

Examples of Ancillary motions are: upon a Bill, "That the Bill be now read a second time"; on consideration of Lords' Amendments, "That this House doth agree with the Lords in the said Amendment"; upon consideration in the House of a Resolution of a Committee of the Whole House, "That this House doth agree with the Committee in the said Resolution". These motions are so intimately connected with the procedure on Bills and Money that they are best left to be dealt with in the chapters on those subjects (VI and VIII). They differ from Substantive motions in not requiring notice or seconder. In some cases (as, *e.g.*, upon the consideration by the House of Resolutions of a Committee of the Whole House) the Question is put upon them without their having been actually moved, while in other cases (as "That a Paper (or Report) do lie upon the Table") they have become so merely formal that they are recorded as a matter of course without having actually come before the House (see p. 86).

(2) *Superseding Motions*

This class is composed of the so-called 'Dilatory' motions, and the 'Previous Question'.

(*a*) ' Dilatory' Motions

During a debate in the House any Member having risen to speak to the Question before the House may offer to move "That this House do now adjourn" or "That the debate be now adjourned". If such motion is accepted by the Speaker[1] (see p. 75), he proposes this motion as a new Question, which supersedes the original Question and must be disposed of before the debate upon the original Question can be resumed. Debate upon such a motion must be strictly relevant to the reasons why it is desirable to adjourn the House, or the debate (S.O. No. 25). In Committee the corresponding motion is "That the Chairman do report Progress and ask leave to sit again", or "That the Chairman do leave the Chair".

To apply the term 'dilatory' to these motions upon every occasion is perhaps somewhat sweeping. They still sometimes serve their original purpose of affording a peg upon which to hang a request to the Government for an explanation of its intentions when a new situation suddenly arises, and with that object are in such circumstances even moved by Ministers. But they are so readily available for another purpose that the name is not inappropriate.

The effect, if carried, of the motion "That this House do now adjourn" is, of course, the indefinite supersession, through the immediate adjournment of the House, of the matter during the discussion of which it was moved. The effect of carrying the motion "That the debate be now adjourned" is to supersede the Question *temporarily*, because before passing to the next business the House normally appoints a day for the resumption of the debate adjourned. Neither of these motions, being stock parliamentary forms, can be amended (see p. 175), nor can they be moved with any addition or modification. If either motion is defeated, it cannot be moved again without some intermediate proceeding. Hence the practice of moving the adjournment of the House and of the debate alternately. But this is a game that can only be played in partnership, as each occasion

---

[1] If, in the opinion of the Chair, the moving of a motion of this kind is an abuse of the Rules of the House, the Chair empowered by S.O. No. 26 to put the Question upon it forthwith without allowing it to be debated, or to decline to receive the motion.

of moving or seconding such a motion exhausts the right of the mover to speak to the original Question (see p. 189).

The motion "That this House do now adjourn", besides being moved in the course of debate upon another Question, may be moved at the commencement of public business or between Orders of the Day by the Government, and (under the restrictions of S.O. No. 9) by any Member. When so moved it is more a substantive than a subsidiary motion, especially in the latter case, where, being intended to afford an opportunity for criticizing the Government, its purpose is clearly defined by the statement upon the strength of which leave to move the adjournment was obtained (see p. 155).

For the lapsing of dilatory motions at the moment of interruption of business, see p. 132, and for further restrictions on their discussion, see May, 383.

(b) The 'Previous Question'

This once popular method of evading a decision has become infrequent owing to its inherent disadvantages and the restrictions which have been placed upon it. It was last moved in 1943 (20th Jan.). The form in which it is now moved is "That the Question be *not* now put". If it is carried, the House passes to the next business, but the effect upon the Question which it supersedes is merely to prevent it being *now* put. There is nothing to prevent its being put another day. If, on the other hand, the motion is negatived, the unexpected consequence follows that the Question has to be put immediately. The result is the same as if the closure had been carried. The Previous Question may also be moved in the form "That this House do now proceed to the Orders of the Day".

The restrictions to which this motion is subject are that it cannot be moved in committee, or upon an amendment, or upon a motion relating to the transaction of public business or the meeting of the House.

(3) *Amendments*

An amendment is a subsidiary motion which interposes a new process of Question and decision between the main Question and its decision, not, like the Previous Question, for the purpose of getting rid of the main Question, but for the purpose of altering its terms. A seconder is required for an amendment in the House. Notice is not required for an amendment except in certain cases—as *e.g.* amendments on going

into Committee of Supply, proposing new clauses on consideration of a Bill, etc. (May, 392-393), but it is generally given where
the amendment is to an important motion or a Bill. A Member
who is in possession of the House at any moment after the
(main) Question has been proposed, and before it is put, is
entitled to move an amendment.

From the point of view of their form amendments are
divided into:—

(1) Those which propose to leave out words.—The Question
which is put on an amendment of this form is "That the
words proposed to be left out stand part of the Question
(or Clause or Bill)" (see p. 19). The effect of negativing
this amendment is to prevent any other amendment
being moved to these words, as the House has ordered
them 'to stand part', and the main question, if no further
amendment is offered to a later part of the text, may then
be put. If the amendment is agreed to, the main Question
is put with those words omitted.

(2) Amendments which propose to leave out certain words in
order to insert or add certain other words.—Two Questions are necessary to dispose of this type of amendment.
The proceedings begin as in the last case. If the House
resolves "That the words proposed to be left out stand
part of the Question", the main Question may be put.
If, however, the House negatives the Question "That the
words proposed to be left out stand part of the Question",
the Speaker proceeds to put the further Question:
"That those words (*i.e.* the words proposed to be substituted) be there inserted (or added)", when the words
of the proposed amendment may themselves be amended.
If this further Question is agreed to, the main Question
as amended is put. If it is negatived, an amendment
proposing a new form of words may be moved. The
House may disagree to these words even at the risk of
leaving the main Question in a mutilated form.

(3) Amendments which propose merely to add or insert
words.—These present little difficulty. The Question
put upon them is "That those words be there added
or inserted". If this Question is agreed to, the main
Question, so amended, is put. If it is disagreed to,
the main Question is put unamended.

Amendments are out of order

(1) If they are irrelevant to the Question to which they are moved, or would, if carried, produce a defective, meaningless, or ungrammatical form of words.

(2) If they are inconsistent with any words already agreed to or seek to reinsert in a different form words which the House has agreed to leave out.

(3) If they are 'too late', *i.e.*
    (*a*) when offered to words which have been ordered to 'stand part';
    (*b*) when offered to a part of the Question prior to a part which has been amended;
    (*c*) when offered to words which have been added or inserted.

(4) If they propose to leave out words in order to re-insert them as part of substituted words. (This difficulty can be generally adjusted by turning the amendment into two or more amendments.)

(5) If they are offered to certain motions which are established forms of procedure, unless they are of a form recognized by practice. (*E.g.* to a motion "That a particular Bill be now read a second time" no amendment is in order except a 'six months' or a 'reasoned' amendment (see p. 207); to the Question "That this House do now adjourn to a [specified] date", no amendment is in order except one substituting another date: to 'dilatory' or 'closure' motions no amendment whatever is in order.)

The practice with regard to the 'saving' of amendments (see p. 216) is only adopted in the case of the committee and report stages of Bills and in the case of 'Business of the House'[1] and 'guillotine' motions. It was also adopted in 1934 and 1936 in the case of a Government Motion to approve Regulations made under the Unemployment Assistance Act, 1934.

The rule against speaking more than once to the same question (see p. 192), which prevents a Member moving an amendment if he has already spoken to the main Question or moved an amendment thereto, is relaxed when the House is considering the amendment of its Standing Orders and also 'Business of the House'[1] and 'guillotine' motions.

---

[1] Unless they are required by standing order to be decided without amendment or debate.

N

Amendments to Amendments

An Amendment to an Amendment stands in the same relation to an amendment as an amendment itself does to a motion. It may be called a 'sub-subsidiary motion', and it interposes a new process of Question and decision between the main amendment and *its* decision. In theory there is nothing to prevent further degrees of involution—amendments being moved to Amendments to Amendments, and so on like boxes fitting inside each other in a Chinese puzzle. And indeed something like this occurs, as will be seen, in proceedings between the House of Lords and the House of Commons on amendments made by one House to a Bill of the other House (p. 227).

The rules applicable to amendments apply *mutatis mutandis* to Amendments to Amendments. But it should be stated that:—

(1) Where the main amendment is to leave out words, obviously the only amendment that can be proposed to it is to leave out some of the words which *it* proposes to leave out (and so in effect restore them to the main Question).

(2) Where the main amendment is to leave out words in order to insert other words, the moment at which the amendment to this amendment may be moved is when, the Question to leave out the original words having been agreed to, the Question for inserting the new words has been proposed.

Rule that the same question may not be twice offered in the same session

The rule is stated in May as follows: "No Question or Bill shall be offered in either House that is substantially the same as one on which its judgment has already been expressed in the current session" (May, 375).

The important points in connexion with this rule are:—

(1) Judgment must have been expressed. Consequently a motion which has been withdrawn, or has not been seconded, or has been superseded, may be repeated (May, 376–7).

(2) The rule does not apply as between the various stages of Bills. The different stages are intended as so many

opportunities of reconsideration. Hence decisions taken in committee may be reversed upon the Report stage, and these again on consideration of Lords' amendments.

The rule does, however, apply *within* each stage of a Bill, and an amendment cannot therefore be moved during progress upon a stage of a Bill which is inconsistent with a decision already taken upon an earlier clause or amendment (see p. 217).

(3) In deciding whether a Question is 'substantially the same' as a Question already decided, the Chair is sometimes helped by a consideration of the matter developed in the earlier debate. Where the second Question is entirely covered by the earlier decision, it is out of order. But where by a reasoned amendment on second reading certain provisions only of a Bill have been objected to, a second Bill containing the other provisions has been held not to be out of order (May, 491).

(4) An amendment repeating the same question which the House had decided upon a motion has been ruled out of order (May, 377).

(5) An affirmative decision of the House may be modified or rescinded in the same session. Technically, the Question for this purpose is not 'substantially the same' as the earlier decision. A rescinding motion has certain inherent limitations. It cannot be employed to rescind a *negative* vote of the House. Nor is it permissible to rescind an amendment, as is shown by the proceedings in connexion with an amendment (to a Resolution reported from a Committee of the Whole House) made against the wishes of the Government (11th November, 1912), when a rescinding motion was proposed on a subsequent day, but abandoned in favour of withdrawing the amended Resolution and introducing another of a somewhat different form (May, 390).

(6) The decision of the House against an amendment to a Bill or Motion prevents a substantially similar question being raised later by a second Bill or Motion (May, 491).

(7) The practice governing the relations between the two Houses has the effect of introducing certain modifications into the rule in the case of a Bill rejected by the second House (May, 553–555).

Anticipation in Debate

The Anticipation rule, which forbids discussion on a matter standing on the Paper being forestalled, is dependent on the same principle as that which forbids the same question being twice raised in the same session. In applying the Anticipation rule preference is given to the discussion which leads to the most effective result, and this has established a descending scale of values for discussions—Bills, Motions, Amendments, etc. Thus a Bill or other Order of the Day *must not be anticipated by* (or more shortly '*blocks*') discussion of a motion, amendment, or subject raised on another motion, such as that for the adjournment of the House. A motion standing on the Paper for leave to bring in a Bill blocks discussion of a motion (except for the presentation of a Bill), amendments, etc. Any substantive motion standing on the Paper blocks the discussion of an amendment, etc. An amendment on the Paper blocks the raising of its subject in debate (as *e.g.* on a Consolidated Fund Bill, or on a motion for the adjournment of the House). The abuse of blocking motions is obviated by the direction given to the Speaker to have regard to the probability of the matter anticipated being brought before the House within a reasonable time (S.O. No. 11).

B. DIVISIONS

When, as described above, the close of a debate is reached with the putting of the Question by the Speaker, the decision of the House is ascertained in the last resort by voting. The process of taking and counting the votes is called a 'Division' because Members actually leave their seats and divide into two separate bodies.

Machinery of a Division[1]

Before describing the procedure in the House upon a division it may be useful to explain the conditions, topographical and other, in which the process takes place. The debating chamber (or 'House') is bordered on all sides by corridors. Out of these, two 'Lobbies' are formed, each comprising one long side of the rectangle and a small portion of both short sides, and each capable of being isolated by the locking of two main doors, one at each end of each lobby (in the short sides of the rectangle) and of two other doors communicating directly between the long side of each lobby and the House. The 'Aye'

[1] Slight adjustments pending return of the Commons to the Chamber now being rebuilt (see p. 83) are omitted.

lobby is on the Speaker's right, having its main entrance behind the Chair, the 'No' lobby is on his left, its main entrance facing the Chair. Members voting 'Aye' pass out of the House behind the Chair, turn to their left and, passing through the folding doors into the 'Aye' lobby, walk down its length, file out past the Tellers, and re-enter the House opposite the Chair. The 'Noes' leave the House at the end facing the Chair, turn to the left into their lobby, walk down its length, file out past the Tellers and re-enter the House behind the Chair. The numbers in each lobby are counted by the Tellers and the names are taken by officers of the House called 'Division Clerks'. The arrangement for recording names is as follows: Just before reaching the exit from the lobby where the Tellers are stationed a Member finds the lobby blocked by two desks labelled 'A to J' and 'K to Z' respectively, controlling two narrow gangways, down one of which, according to the position of his name in the alphabet, he files for the purpose of giving his name to be recorded.

Before each division clerk is a list containing in alphabetical order the names of one half of the Members of the House. The name of each Member, as he passes through, is marked on the division sheet in duplicate, and one set of the sheets, after being examined by officials, is sent to the Printers and appears in the issue of the 'Vote' of the next day (see p. 89). The other set is sent to the Official Reporter. Any errors in the printed list, due to the wrong name having been marked or printed, are corrected by means of a Memorandum added to a subsequent issue of the division lists on a request being made at the Public Bill Office.

Method of Taking a Division

Now to return to the proceedings in the House itself. In order not to break the continuity of the account only the main features will be dealt with here, incidental points of order being referred to as they arise, but fuller treatment being left to a later section.

As stated, the Speaker, after putting the Question, says, "As many as are of that opinion say 'Aye'", and "As many as are of the contrary opinion say 'No'". From the strength of the answering cries of 'Aye' and 'No' (and from consideration of the probabilities of the case), he suggests, "I think the 'Ayes' (or the 'Noes') have it". To this opinion the House may agree, but on questions of any importance the House prefers a division, and the Speaker's opinion is challenged by continuing cries of 'No' or 'Aye', as the case may be. Accordingly he indicates that a division is to be held by giving the order "Clear the Lobby", which sets the whole process in motion.

On receipt of this order:—

(1) the exit doors of both lobbies are locked,
(2) division bells start ringing and the cry 'Division' is repeated by the policemen throughout the precincts of the House.

This is the point at which a division has started. Members go to their lobbies.

At the end of two minutes the Speaker again puts the Question (see May, p. 403), and his opinion that the 'Ayes' (or the 'Noes') have it is sometimes accepted at this point by the House, in which case the division is 'called off'. If it is not accepted, and the Speaker does not choose to exercise his powers under S.O. No. 34 (Division unnecessarily claimed) (see (a) below), the process continues as follows:—

(1) Tellers are appointed—two for the 'Ayes' and two for the 'Noes'. A Teller for the 'Ayes' and a Teller for the 'Noes' take up their positions at the exit of either lobby. It may happen that the Tellers, or a Teller, for the 'Ayes' (or the 'Noes') are not forthcoming. In this case the 'Noes' (or the 'Ayes' as the case may be) are declared to 'have it'.

(2) The exit doors of the lobbies are unlocked and Members start filing out, having given their names to the Clerks, and are counted as they emerge by one Teller, the other checking the figures. If the Government Whips are acting as Tellers, a Government Teller always counts.

Members who are incapacitated by some physical infirmity from passing through the lobbies are counted in the House.

At the end of six minutes from the giving of the order to clear the lobby all the doors leading into the lobbies (not, of course, the exit door from each lobby) are locked upon the order from the Chair "Lock the doors", and they remain locked until the numbers of the division are announced.

When all the Members dividing have been counted and the Tellers in each lobby have agreed upon the numbers, a Teller for the 'Ayes' and a Teller for the 'Noes' successively state their respective figures to a Clerk at the Table, who enters them upon a 'division slip' and hands the slip to the Teller

for the majority (an action which, as it discloses the result of
the division, is anxiously observed by the House on important
occasions). The Tellers then form up a pace or two below
the Table facing the Speaker in the following order: the
senior Teller and the junior Teller for the majority and the
senior Teller and the junior Teller for the minority. When
the Speaker says "Order, Order", they bow, advance a step
forward together, and the senior Teller for the majority
reads out the figures on the slip " 'Ayes' to the right—'Noes'
to the left—". They then bow once more and return to their
seats. Meanwhile the division slip is presented to the Speaker,
who once more announces the figures of the division. This
concludes the process and the House returns to the business
before it.

If the Tellers disagree, a second division must take place.
But if they agree, after the figures have been announced, that
an error has taken place, the correct procedure is for both to
report it to the Chair so that the corrected figures may be
recorded.

Members sometimes, through inadvertence, remain in a
lobby out of sight of the Tellers until after the latter have left
the doors, although it is the duty of the latter to satisfy themselves that the lobby is empty before they leave. A Member
uncounted for such a reason may, if he can substantiate the
fact that he was present, and succeeds in raising the matter
immediately after the announcement of the numbers, obtain
an order from the Chair for the addition of his name and vote
to the list and total number of the lobby in which he claims
to have voted.

It also occasionally happens that a Member in the course of
a division finds himself voting in the wrong lobby. If he defers
raising the matter until after the division, the inference from
the precedents is that his request for the correction of his
error will be refused. If, on the other hand, he proceeds to vote
in the other lobby as well, there are precedents in favour of the
rectification of the division list at his request, made at a later
opportunity on the same day or even on a subsequent day.

Points of order in connexion with divisions

(*a*) Division unnecessarily claimed.—The Speaker has the
power (under S.O. No. 34), if he thinks a division
unnecessarily claimed, to call the Members who support
and who challenge his decision to rise successively in

their places, and either to declare the determination of the House or to name Tellers. The point at which a division can be thus cut short is, as indicated in the Standing Order, immediately after the Question has been put for the second time, not, as is sometimes thought, when the division is first challenged.

(b) Members are now allowed to vote without having heard the Question, and also, having heard it, to abstain from voting. This change from the old practice of the House was made in 1906 in connexion with the reform in the method of taking divisions then introduced.

(c) It must be remembered that a Member's vote must agree with his 'voice'. Objection may be taken to a Member's vote on the ground that he had, when the Question was put, called out for the opposite side to that for which he had proceeded to vote (May, 387). Objection on such grounds may only be taken before the figures are announced.

(d) Method of raising a point of order during a division.— The rules of the House permit a point of order, which requires to be immediately dealt with, to be raised even while a division is in progress, but require the Member raising it to address the Chair seated and covered.[1] Lady Members are not required to be covered (*Deb.*, 4th February, 1929, c. 1407).

The casting vote of the Chair

The Speaker has no vote as Member, but, as Speaker, he has a 'casting' vote when the numbers are equal. It has become the practice when giving a casting vote for the Speaker to assign his reasons, and a consideration of some of these statements indicates the principles which guide the Speaker in this matter (May, 408 ff.).

Speaker Addington, who led the way in 1795 in laying down the principles on which he proposed to exercise the right of giving a casting vote, did not take the matter very far. Apart from forming a judgment upon the merits of each case (which is what every Member is presumed to do) he laid down his intention of voting for an opportunity for the further discussion of a matter when that was the Question before the House.

---

[1] This practice seems to have originated in the 18th century. The form in which it is stated by Hatsell (ii. 143) does not quite agree with the modern practice.

Subsequent Speakers have made the matter more definite, and it seems that the guiding principle is that a Speaker does not on his sole responsibility make a change in the *status quo*, and in particular that he takes the course which is best calculated to avoid change in the law, to uphold previous decisions of the House or a committee, or to maintain constitutional usage.

The Chairman in a Committee of the Whole House has, like the Speaker, only a casting vote, and he gives it on the same principle. But his position is easier because generally an opportunity for reconsideration of a point raised in Committee will be provided in the House itself.

Personal pecuniary interest

The rule that a Member whose 'pocket' will be affected by the result of a division should abstain from voting is well established. It is also so well observed that there is in debate upon matters of public policy only a single instance on record of the vote of a Member being disallowed on this ground—namely, in the matter of a grant in aid in connexion with a projected railway from the coast to the Victoria Nyanza, 1892.

In the case of Private Bills the disallowance of Members' votes on the ground of direct pecuniary interest has been more frequent, and here there is a special aspect of the question which has never been decided, *i.e.* whether a Member personally interested in a Bill is entitled to vote against a competing Bill.

The 'basic' ruling on the general question is that of Mr. Speaker Abbot on the 17th July, 1811: "This interest must be a direct pecuniary interest, and separately belonging to the persons . . . , and not in common with the rest of His Majesty's subjects, or on a matter of state policy". Reference must also be made to the Report of the Select Committee on Members of Parliament (Personal Interest) (No. 274 of 1896).

Objection to a vote on the ground of personal interest must be raised immediately after the division, and (*a*) in the House, in the form of a substantive motion, affecting as it does the conduct of a Member of Parliament, and not as a point of order, and (*b*) in Committee in the form of a motion made in the committee, not upon a motion to report Progress (*Deb.* 11th February, 1913, c. 1085).

The Member whose vote is impugned, having been heard in his defence, withdraws before the Question is proposed.

The point should be stressed that the rule is limited to the vote of a Member, and does not prevent his speaking to, or moving, a motion.

C. THE CLOSURE

The 'Closure' rule, which is simple enough in intention, has developed some subtleties in its application to the varying details of debate. It may prevent confusion to distinguish three kinds of closure:—

(1) 'simple' closure,

(2) 'contingent' closure, and

(3) 'special' closure applicable to the committee and report stages of Bills.

A fourth paragraph will deal with the further complications which arise when the closure is moved at the moment of interruption of business.

To begin with, the points which are common to all forms of the closure may be mentioned.

The motion for closure is put in the form "That the Question be now put", and is decided without amendment or debate.

(1) The closure may be moved not only at the end, but also in the course of a speech.

(2) It is moved *in the House* with the Speaker in the Chair, and *in Committee* with the Chairman of Ways and Means or the Deputy Chairman in the Chair. It cannot be moved in the House with the Deputy Speaker in the Chair unless the Speaker's absence has been formally announced.

(3) It lies in the discretion of the Chair to "refuse the closure if in his opinion the motion is an abuse of the rules of the House or an infringement of the rights of the minority". He is not obliged to assign any reason for his refusal.

(5) To carry a closure motion not less than a hundred must vote in its support.

1. *The 'Simple' Closure* (S.O. No. 29 (1))

The procedure is best explained by an example.

During debate upon the Question "That Mr. Speaker do now leave the Chair" (for Committee of Supply on a branch of the Estimates) a Member moves "That the Question be now put". Two steps follow: (*a*) The Speaker (we will suppose) accepts the motion and puts the Question "That the Question be now put", which is agreed to by the requisite number of votes. Then (b) he accordingly proceeds to put the Question "That I do now leave the Chair".

It will be noted that in its simplest form the closure requires two Questions to dispose of the business upon which it is moved, each of which may, of course, entail a division.

2. 'Contingent' Closure (S.O. No. 29 (2))

This is an extension of the 'simple' closure, but is best considered separately, because it gives a new power.

The 'simple' closure asks the House to decide that a Question be now put.

The 'contingent' closure only comes into operation after the process of the 'simple' closure has been concluded without disposing of all the Questions already proposed from the Chair. A Member may then claim "that such further Question be put" (or claim successively that each such further Question be put). The Chair, unless it withholds assent, proceeds immediately to put such further Question (or Questions).

Example.—To the Question "That Mr. Speaker do now leave the Chair" an amendment has been moved to leave out all the words after "That" and add other words, and upon this the Question has been put "That the words proposed to be left out stand part of the Question". The two steps of the 'simple' closure have been gone through, (1) the Question "That the Question be now put" has been agreed to, and (2) the Question "That the words proposed to be left out stand part of the Question" has also been agreed to. But the main Question, "That Mr. Speaker do now leave the Chair", remain undisposed of. This is the Question that can now be 'claimed', and the Speaker, if he approves, immediately proceeds to put this Question.

It will be noted that the 'contingent' closure has only one stage. The Member does not claim *to move* "That the Question 'That Mr. Speaker do now leave the Chair' be now put". Upon that motion the Speaker could only put the Question: "That the Question be now put", and a second step as in the 'simple' closure process would have to be gone through. The Member does not *move*, he *claims*, "That the Question 'That Mr. Speaker do now leave the Chair' be now put", and accordingly the Speaker, if he approves, proceeds to put the Question "That I do now leave the Chair".

3. 'Special' Closure (for Clauses on Committee and Report Stages of Bills) (S.O. No. 29 (3))

The 'special' closure for clauses differs from the 'contingent' closure in that it does not necessarily follow a previous application of the closure. It differs further in requiring two steps like the 'simple' closure.

In explaining this form of the closure some knowledge of the procedure on Bills must be assumed. But it is not necessary to go through all the possible ways in which this form of closure can be applied. With the preliminary warning that it is not moved when an amendment is under consideration, the following examples may be given:—

(a) *in Committee on a Bill.* The closure motion may be moved in the form "That the Question 'That (certain specified words) stand part of the Clause (or Schedule)' be now put", or "That the Question 'That a clause stand part of (or be added to) the Bill' be now put".

(b) *on the Report stage of a Bill* the motion might be "That the Question 'That (a specified) Clause (or Schedule) be added to the Bill' be now put", or "That the Question 'That (certain specified) words of a Clause (or Schedule) stand part of the Bill' be now put", or "That (certain specified) words stand part of a proposed Clause (or Schedule)."

When such closure motion has been carried, and the further motion consequential upon it has been agreed to, any amendments standing to the words of the Bill affected by the motion fall without discussion.

4. Closure at moment of interruption of business

There is a natural tendency for the mover to defer a closure motion until the last possible moment. Hence frequent use is made of the facilities which S.O. No. 1 (3), read in conjunction with S.O. No. 29, gives for moving and obtaining a decision on closured business at the moment of interruption under the 'Eleven o'Clock'[1] Rule. It will be remembered that under that rule the moment of interruption which falls normally at eleven o'clock[1], is 'projected' beyond the conclusion of any division which may be in progress at that hour (see p. 133). In the following examples closure is moved at the 'projected' moment of interruption.

[1] For altered hours, see Appendix IV.

(*a*) The 'simple' closure at the moment of interruption.—The division on a motion to reduce a vote in Committee of Supply has been carried on beyond eleven o'clock[1] and resulted in the proposed reduction being negatived. The Chairman proceeds to propose the Question necessary for the conclusion of the business before the House, *i.e.* that the sum specified in the vote be granted. If anyone now rises to speak or objects to further proceedings, he interrupts the business. This being the moment of interruption, a Member moves that the Question that the sum be granted be now put (the first of the two stages of the 'simple' closure process).

(*b*) The 'contingent' closure at the moment of interruption.— Debate has taken place upon an amendment to a Private Member's motion, the Question on the amendment being "That the words proposed to be left out stand part of the Question". Closure has been moved on this Question at eleven o'clock[1] and carried, and the closured Question agreed to on division. A Member may now claim that the main Question be now put (the single stage of the 'contingent' closure).

(*c*) The 'special' closure at the moment of interruption.— The Question has been put on an amendment to a Bill in committee, and this question has been disposed of by a division carried beyond eleven o'clock[1] without the closure having been moved. At the conclusion of the division the Chairman's "Order, Order", preparatory to leaving the Chair, constitutes the moment of interruption, and a Member moves "That the Question 'That the clause stand part of the Bill' be now put" (the first of the two stages of the 'special' closure process).

Selection of Amendments (S.O. No. 31)

The Standing Order (Selection of Amendments) of 1919 includes among the permanent powers of the Chair (in the House or in Committee of the Whole House) a duty which the Standing Order of 1909 had allowed the House to impose upon it only by a special decision and in respect only of certain words of a Bill or motion to be specified on each occasion. The object of this drastic provision is, of course, to make sure as far as possible that the limited amount of time available for discussion shall be spent on those amendments which the

---

[1] For altered hours, see Appendix IV.

House wishes to consider. It gives the Chair the power of passing over any amendment, however perfectly in order. In exercising this discretion the Chair sometimes announces, when entering upon the business in question, which amendments it will be permissible to move during that day's consideration, or it may give the reason why a particular amendment is not called. Sometimes also, as the Standing Order provides, the Chair invites a Member to give an explanation of the objects of his amendment before deciding whether or not to allow it to be moved. A reason often given by the Speaker for not 'calling' an amendment to a Bill on report is that it has been fully discussed in committee.

As in the case of the closure, the power of selecting amendments can only be exercised in the House by the Speaker, and in committee by the Chairman of Ways and Means or the Deputy Chairman. In 1934 Chairmen of Standing Committees were given similar powers (S.O. No. 57 (5)).

D. RULES AND CONVENTIONS OF DEBATE

1. Rules for addressing the House

A Member wishing to speak rises in his place uncovered and addresses the Chair. He may rise to speak at any time between the proposing of the Question and the moment when it has been fully put (*i.e.* the voices of both Ayes and Noes have been collected). Or, if there is no Question before the House, he may rise with the intention of making a motion. When several Members rise together, it is the duty of the Chair to select one, calling him by name. The Member so called addresses the House by formally directing his remarks to the Chair. He must not read his speech or speak in any language but English. If he wishes to refer to another Member, he must not do so by name, but employ a descriptive periphrasis. He has a right to finish his speech uninterrupted, unless another Member rises to raise a point of order, but he may give way out of courtesy to a Member who wishes to correct a misapprehension, or elicit an explanation, or who wishes to move an amendment which would otherwise be passed over.

(1) *Rising uncovered.*—It is a long-standing convention of the House that a Member may only wear a hat when seated.[1] If through illness or infirmity a Member is

---

[1] This rule does not apply to Lady Members.

unable to rise, he is permitted to address the House seated. During the progress of a division a Member wishing to address the Chair for the purpose of raising a point of order is required to do so seated and covered (see p. 182).

(2) A Member speaks from his seat, which must be 'within the House'. The side-galleries, though seldom spoken from, are technically within the House, but not the cross-benches below the Bar.

(3) A Member may only speak when there is a Question before the House. The exceptions to this rule are when he is speaking in order to move or second a motion, and also when a ministerial or personal explanation is made.

(4) The practice of 'catching the Speaker's eye' is thus expressed by May: "When two or more Members rise to speak, the Speaker calls on the Member who, on rising in his place, is first observed by him." The older method of deciding between several Members wishing to speak was by a motion that one of the aspirants "be now heard" or "do now speak", and there are examples of such motions recorded during the earlier years of the 19th century. The substitution, for this decision by a party majority with the waste of time it involved, of the unfettered discretion of the Chair is a great improvement. In 'seeing' a Member the Chair looks alternately to either side of the House, and calls representatives of smaller bodies within the big groups. By a natural extension the views of the members of the parties and groups are ascertained as to the persons whom they select to voice their opinions on important occasions. So limited is the time available and so great the number of 'representative' speakers that there is often little opportunity for Members who are not thus provided for in advance. Account must also be taken of the very different value of the various hours of the sitting. The first and last hour (used elastically) of a debate are the most important, but the hour before dinner is becoming more appreciated. The 'dead' hours are, *par excellence*, the dinner-hour between 8 and 9.30, and a shorter more movable period in the neighbourhood of 5 o'clock.

By a rather graceful practice a Member rising to make a 'maiden' speech is allowed priority by other speakers.

He must not, however, have deferred claiming this right beyond the Parliament in which he was first elected.

Precedence is also granted on the resumption of a debate to a Member who had not concluded his speech at the moment of interruption, or who moved its adjournment when it was last before the House. The adjournment, with this object in view, is moved formally without a speech, and in order to secure precedence on resumption a Member must rise immediately and not wait to be called. This is a convention which belongs rather to an earlier conception of the Speaker's rôle, as it seems to seek to fetter his choice. It survives as a convenient means of notifying to the House in a formal manner the name of the Member who will open the debate on its resumption. In an important debate the adjournment is sometimes moved by a party Whip in order to secure precedence on its resumption for one of his leaders.

(5) The enforcement of the rule of addressing the Chair prevents a debate degenerating into personal attacks, recrimination between Members, or desultory conversation. The same purpose is served by the rule against referring to another Member by name and requiring the substitution of a formal description such as "the honourable Member for . . . . .".[1] The Speaker and Chairman use the same method for referring to Members except when 'calling' to speak. A Privy Councillor is referred to as 'right honourable', a commissioned officer of one of the three services as the 'honourable and gallant', and a Member of the Bar as the 'honourable and learned'.

(6) The prohibition of the reading of speeches, like the absence of an orator's tribune, discourages rhetoric and puts a premium on the debater's talent of finding his points in the earlier speeches.

2. RELEVANCY IN DEBATE ON MOTIONS

The duty of calling to order Members whose speeches wander from the Question before the House imposes a difficult task upon the Chair. Some general principles can be derived from rulings on the subject which are referred to in May,

---

[1] A similar convention is retained in the American House of Representatives.

p. 423–5. In complicated matters, such as Bills and financial
business, relevancy depends so much on the subject-matter
that no rules of general application can be laid down, and its
detailed application is best left to be considered in the appropriate chapters. In other kinds of business it is necessary to
consider each case upon its merits. Several rulings, however,
indicate that:—

(1) Where the business before the House is a motion to
provide machinery, it is not in order to discuss the merits
of the policy which it is sought to put into operation.
For instance, on a motion to make a sessional order a
Standing Order it has been held that the order itself is
not open to debate (May, 424). On a motion to continue
statutory regulations it is not in order to discuss the
merits of the Act under which they are made. The policy
of a Bill cannot be discussed on an 'Allocation of Time'
motion (see p. 129).

(2) Matters are irrelevant which obviously go beyond the
jurisdiction of the House or the Government, *e.g.*
matters under the consideration of the House of Lords,
or the proceedings of a Committee which has not
reported.

(3) Matters otherwise relevant are out of order if their
consideration would conflict with the rules against
reconsidering matters already decided by the House
(p. 176), or against anticipation (p. 178).

(4) The debate on 'dilatory' motions (see p. 172) (which
were originally intended to permit the House to consider
any subject not covered by the question before it at the
time of the moving of the motion) is now restricted by
S.O. No. 25 (of 1882) to the reason why the adjournment
of the matter under consideration is desirable.

(5) Motions for the adjournment of the House which are
substantive (see p. 169) are in a different category from
dilatory motions, although they have the same form.
The ordinary occasion on which they are moved is the
eve of an adjournment of the House beyond the next
sitting day, and their purpose on such an occasion is to
afford the House a last-minute opportunity of bringing
grievances to the notice of the Government. Any matter
of administration is accordingly in order, but not matters
which would require legislation (May, 426). They are,

O

of course, subject to the rule against anticipation, and cannot deal with matters which require to be raised by a substantive motion (p. 169).

The Chair enforces relevancy by calling a Member to order, and is empowered by S.O. No. 20 to order a Member who persists in irrelevancy to discontinue his speech.

3. THE RULE AGAINST SPEAKING MORE THAN ONCE

This rule is only applicable in the House, not in committee.

Except when he has the right of reply (see (a) below), a Member may not speak more than once *to the same Question*, even if the debate on that Question is adjourned and resumed days or weeks later.

Accordingly:—

(1) A Member, who has spoken to the main Question, may not move or second an amendment, a 'dilatory' motion, the Previous Question, or an instruction to a Committee, for in doing so he would technically be speaking twice to the main Question.

(2) A Member, who has moved or seconded an amendment ('dilatory' motion, etc.), may not, after such amendment (or motion) has been disposed of, speak to the main Question, or move or second another amendment ('dilatory' motion, etc.).

But:—

(3) A Member, who has spoken to the main Question, or moved or seconded an amendment ('dilatory' motion, etc.), *may* speak to an amendment ('dilatory' motion, etc.), subsequently moved by another Member, as in doing so he is speaking to a new Question.

Exceptions to and relaxations of the rule against speaking more than once

(a) A right of reply is granted to the mover of a substantive motion (including a substantive motion for the adjournment of the House (p. 173)).

The rule is relaxed:—

(b) in the case of a Bill under consideration as amended by a standing committee, in favour of the Member in charge and also of the mover of an amendment in respect of that amendment;

(c) in favour of a Member who complains that his meaning
has been misinterpreted by another speaker, so long as
he deals only with the misconception and does not
attempt to develop his arguments;

(d) to allow a Member, whose conduct or character has been
impugned in the debate, to make a personal explanation;

(e) to allow a Member to raise a point of order;

(f) by indulgence of the House (especially where a reply is
desired from a Minister).

Reservation of Speech

The mover of an Order of the Day or *seconder* of a substantive
motion is permitted to reserve his speech until a later period
of the debate if, instead of rising to speak, he signifies that he
is moving or seconding by raising his hat while remaining
seated. This useful convention, now recognized, was contrary
to the older practice of the House presumably because it was
held that in employing it a Member had *tacitly* exercised his
right to speak. The privilege is not accorded to the mover of
a motion or the mover or seconder of an amendment or of
a motion other than substantive (May, 422).

4. Breaches of Order in Speaking

The following list is given by May (p. 423):—

A Member, while speaking, may not (1) allude to a debate of
the same session upon any question or Bill not then under
discussion; (2) speak against or reflect upon any determination
of the House, unless he intends to conclude with a motion for
rescinding it; (3) allude to debates in the other House of
Parliament; (4) utter treasonable or seditious words, or use
the King's name irreverently or to influence debate; (5) speak
offensive or insulting words against the character or proceedings
of either House; (6) refer to matters pending a judicial decision;
7) reflect, unless upon a substantive motion for that purpose,
upon the conduct of persons in authority; (8) make personal
allusions to Members of Parliament, or (9) obstruct public
business.

(1) The rule against this breach of order is not always strictly
enforced and it is not applied to debates on different stages
of a Bill. What is valuable in the rule can generally
be obtained by an application of the relevancy rule.

(2) This rule is strictly enforced. It covers any decision of the House, and also any action taken by the Chair in carrying out the discretionary powers imposed upon it by the House, such as the acceptance of the closure motion.

(3) This rule is relaxed to permit reference to Government statements in the other House.

(4) Treasonable or seditious language has been punished by committal to the custody of the Serjeant at Arms or to the Tower (*Deb.*, 3s. 259, c. 168). Such a gross offence needs no discussion, but a word must be said about another mode of reference to the King—the use of his name in order to influence the decision of the House—which is also out of order. This does not, of course, apply to the views of the Crown when acting on the advice of Ministers, but to an attempt to attribute to the Sovereign personal views.

(5) This rule applies also to insulting language against a statute as the work of Parliament.

(6) It is very difficult to see in advance whether reference to a matter may prejudice the conduct of judicial proceedings, but if there appears to be any likelihood of its doing so, the Speaker intervenes.

(7) This refers to the holders of certain high offices (a list of which is given on page 169) whose conduct may not be raised except by means of a substantive motion.

(8) If language of a character covered by the term 'unparliamentary' is used, the Chair intervenes and causes it to be withdrawn. May (p. 432) gives a list of expressions which have been taken exception to at various times. Precedents of the action taken in the case of challenges and quarrels, and also in the case of the ancient procedure of 'taking down' words objected to, are given by May on pages 433, 439. Imputation of motives to the action or language of a Member comes under this prohibition.

(9) Obstruction by speech is very difficult to define. Under S.O. No. 20 the Chair may direct a Member who 'persists in irrelevance or tedious repetition either of his own arguments or the arguments used by other Members in debate' to discontinue his speech. Obstruction of a less definite kind is restrained by the various forms of closure, and has at different times figured more or less

prominently in the tactics of opposition. To accuse
another Member of obstruction is not out of order
(May, 432).

Citing documents not before the House

The rule as laid down by May (p. 433) is, "A Minister is not
at liberty to read or quote from a dispatch or other state paper
not before the House, unless he is prepared to lay it upon the
Table."

The rule is akin to the rule of evidence in courts of law, and
is a recognized standard for ministerial practice. It only
applies to direct quotation from a paper, not to a mere summary
of arguments contained. Nor is it always enforceable in the case
of actual quotation. In the first place it may be overriden by
considerations affecting the public interest. Nor does it apply
to private memoranda or correspondence or generally to any
papers the production of which would, but for it, be refused to
the House as being beyond its jurisdiction. The conclusion
from these divergent considerations is that papers which cannot
be laid *in toto* should not be read or quoted in extracts.

Law Officers' Opinions

These opinions being confidential, are usually not laid on
the table, or cited in debate, and their production cannot be
demanded as of right, but a Minister is not debarred from
citing them if he chooses.

5. RULES OF CONDUCT FOR MEMBERS NOT SPEAKING

The rules of conduct to be observed by Members present in
the House during a debate may be laid down as follows: (1)
to keep their places; (2) to enter or leave the House with
decorum; (3) not to cross the House irregularly; (4) not to
read books, newspapers, or letters; (5) to maintain silence;
(6) not to hiss, clap or interrupt; (7) to abstain from obstructive
behaviour.

(1) The Resolutions of 10th February, 1698, and 16th February, 1720, ordering Members to keep their places and
not walk about the House, or stand at the Bar or in the
passages, cannot be carried out in the letter. The present
House affords seats for little more than half its Members,
and during debates which attract a full House the space
at the Bar often remains crowded for the greater part of
the sitting without objection being raised. On other

occasions, too, Members are permitted to stand at the Bar for longer or shorter intervals so long as they do not interrupt. Walking about the House is not a relaxation towards which Members appear to feel any temptation.

(2) Members enter or leave the House uncovered, and in doing so, or in passing near the Chair, make a bow towards it (whether to its occupant or to the Mace, or because in the old House that was the direction of the altar, is uncertain).

(3) It is disorderly to cross between the Chair and a Member speaking from one of the two lower benches, or between the Chair and the Table, or between the Chair and the Mace, when it is taken off the Table by the Serjeant (May, 435).

(4) Reading books and letters, and even newspapers, is now often overlooked on the assumption that it is in preparation for a debate and not for amusement.

(5) and (6) The obligation to be silent while present during debate imposed by the Resolution of 5th May, 1641 (see May, p. 436), which forbids even whispering, has become an obligation not to interrupt, and that depends to a certain extent upon times and seasons. A Member who persists in speaking while a full House is impatiently waiting for a division, learns by experience that he cannot expect an orderly hearing.

Certain cries are disorderly in themselves, such as hissing, crowing, clapping, cries of 'Shame', and, of course, the use of any words which would be disorderly if used in the course of a speech. Other 'parliamentary' cries, such as 'Hear, hear', or 'Divide', are disorderly if persisted in for so long and in such volume as seriously to impede or even to prevent debate. In either case the Chair intervenes to restore order, employing, if necessary the powers conferred by the Standing Orders (see below).

(7) Obstruction is an elastic term. Persistent and wilful obstruction of the business of the House may amount to an abuse of the rules and be dealt with under S.O. No. 22. A case of intentional delay in leaving a division lobby was thus dealt with on 14th April, 1926 (*Deb.*, 423).

Maintenance of Order

The ultimate authority in matters of order is the House itself, and all doubtful points are referred to it. But practice and the Standing Orders have defined the powers of the Speaker and other occupants of the Chair with considerable detail, and in such matters there is no appeal from the decision of the Chair. Without the intervention of the House no penalty more serious than withdrawal from the House for the remainder of a sitting can be inflicted.

The powers exercised by the Chair in maintaining order may be taken in the following sequence: Powers in respect of (1) minor breaches of order; (2) 'grossly disorderly' conduct; (3) 'disregard of the authority of the Chair' (after disorderly conduct), and (4) 'grave' disorder.

(1) Minor breaches of order are checked by the Chair as soon as they occur. Members also call each other to order, and bring points of order before the Chair. Such incidents are generally concluded simply and briefly by the Member desisting from the conduct, or withdrawing the words, objected to. When the Speaker or Chairman rises to deal with a point of order, it is highly disorderly for Members to remain standing or to interrupt him.

(2) Grossly disorderly conduct comprises refusal to withdraw offensive language, insulting behaviour, obstruction and disregard of the authority of the Chair. It is punished by the Chair by a direction to withdraw for the remainder of the sitting (S.O. No. 21). It is often a preliminary to (3).

(3) The punishment of the offence of (persistent) disregard of the authority of the Chair or abuse of the rules of the House, is left to the House. The procedure is laid down in S.O. No. 22. It generally, but not necessarily, pre-supposes the previous intervention of the Chair (under S.O. No. 21) culminating in the refusal of the offending Member to obey the direction to withdraw from the House for the rest of the sitting. When this point is reached, the Speaker refers the matter to the House by 'naming' the Member, and (usually) the Minister leading the House for the time being moves that the Member be suspended from the service of the House. This motion must be put to the question "without amendment, adjournment, or debate". If the House agrees to the suspension, the Speaker again directs the Member to withdraw, and if he still persists in refusing to do so, even when summoned under the Speaker's orders by

the Serjeant, force is resorted to, the attention of the House being called by the Speaker to the fact that it is necessary. In such a case the suspension of the Member is for the remainder of the session (see below).

If the Member is 'named' in Committee of the Whole House by the Chairman, the latter immediately suspends the proceedings and reports the circumstances to the House when the Speaker has resumed the Chair. From this point matters proceed as above.

The period of suspension, which remained undefined from 1902 to 1926 (S.O. No. 22) is now fixed at five 'sitting' days for the first offence and twenty for the second, the uncompleted portion of the sitting on which the offence was committed counting as one day. The 'first' offence is taken to mean the first during that session. A Member serving on a Private Bill Committee is not exempted from such service by reason of his suspension under this rule. Apart from this, suspension means exclusion from the precincts of the House (*i.e.* the area within the walls of the Palace of Westminster) (H.C. 411, p. 64 (1888), Qn. 1164, referred to by May (p. 445).

Members must be 'named' and their suspension voted on by the House separately unless the offence of disregarding the authority of the Chair has been committed jointly.

(4) 'Grave' disorder means disregard of the authority of the Chair on the part of a considerable portion of the House. The power conferred on the Chair (under S.O. No. 24) to deal with it is to adjourn the House, or to suspend the sitting until a specified hour.

Chapter VI

PUBLIC BILLS

The origin of legislation by Bill and the history of the procedure upon it have been traced in Chapter I (pp. 22–25). The distinction between Public Bills and Private Bills is stated in Chapter III (p. 109), and is dealt with more fully in Chapter IX (p. 291). The distinction between Government Bills and Private Members' Bills, as regards their relative precedence in the allocation of the time of the session, is explained in Chapter III (pp. 109 and 115). In this chapter the procedure on Public Bills will be set out in detail.

For the purposes of procedure the principal distinction drawn between Public Bills is between Money Bills and Other Bills. 'Money' Bills are Bills whose *main* object is to authorize expenditure or to impose taxation (or, technically 'to impose a charge upon the public revenue, or upon the people'). They are introduced upon Resolutions of the Committee of Ways and Means or of a (Money) Committee of the Whole House with the recommendation of the Crown.[1] The range of Bills here called 'Money Bills' is not precisely, though nearly, identical with the range of those covered by the definition of Money Bills contained in the Parliament Act, which latter are called in this book 'Parliament Act Money Bills' (see pp. 287–8).

Some Bills contain, as a subordinate part of their proposals, the imposition of a charge. These Bills do not originate in a Committee of the Whole House, but include a clause (or clauses) which require, before they are taken in committee on the Bill, to be authorized by a resolution, recommended by the Crown and agreed to by a (Money) Committee of the Whole House.

They are colloquially called 'Bills with Money Clauses'.

The Form of a Public Bill

The form of a Public Bill is that of a draft statute. It contains the following parts, not all of which, as will appear, are essential:—

[1] An alternative practice, now generally employed, is laid down by S.O. No. 80, of 1938.

Short title, given for convenience of citation.—The short title is printed at the head of the Bill or Act, and is also set out in the last clause—"This Act may be cited as the Act, 19 ". Occasionally the title at the head of a Bill, under which it is introduced, and the title set out in the title clause are not identical, as in the case of the Consolidated Fund (Appropriation) Bill, which is enacted as the Appropriation Act. By the Short Titles Act, 1896, the public general Acts passed between 1707 and 1896, which did not already possess them, were given short titles, and groups of Acts were given collective titles (Ilbert, 272).

Long title.—The long title sets out in general terms the purposes of a Bill, and is usually meant when the 'title' is referred to without qualification. It should cover the contents of the Bill (see p. 204) and is amended if amendment of the Bill makes this necessary (see p. 210).

Preamble.—A Public Bill now generally dispenses with a preamble, unless it resembles in character a Private Bill.[1] The purposes for which preambles were once framed—namely, for stating the reasons and intended effects of proposed legislation —are now generally served by an explanatory memorandum (see below).

Enacting formula.—A Bill is preceded by a short paragraph which is called the 'enacting formula'. This formula, which was developed in the 15th century, runs as follows:—"Be it enacted by the King's Most Excellent Majesty, by and with the advice of the Lords Spiritual and Temporal, and Commons, in this present Parliament assembled, and by the authority of the same, as follows:—" In the case of Consolidated Fund Bills and Finance Bills the enacting formula is preceded by words:—"Most gracious Sovereign, We, Your Majesty's most dutiful and loyal subjects the Commons," etc.—in which the Commons claim the sole responsibility for the grant of money or duties (see pp. 31–34; Maitland, 185; and Anson, i. 298).

Clauses.—The body of a Bill consists of a series of numbered clauses, each with a descriptive title printed in the margin. Long clauses are divided up into sub-sections "(1), (2)," etc., sub-sections into paragraphs "(a), (b)," etc., paragraphs into sub-paragraphs "(i), (ii)," etc. Long and complicated Bills have their clauses grouped in 'Parts' distinguished by Roman

---

[1] A preamble has been employed, as in the Parliament Act, 1911, to place solemnly on record the intentions of the framers of a Bill, which might have been, but were not, included in the Bill itself.

numerals and titles in capitals, and these Parts are often broken up into smaller groups of clauses with their titles in italics. Prefixed to Bills is a Table of Clauses, showing the numbers and titles of clauses and also any grouping into Parts. The clauses of a Bill are arranged in such a way that the leading principles are embodied in its opening clause or clauses, "so that, when the first fence is cleared, the remainder of the course may be comparatively easy" (Ilbert, 241). For "Bills are made to pass as razors are made to sell" (Thring, *Practical Legislation*, quoted by Ilbert). (But razors are also meant to cut, and Bills to make law.) At the end of a Bill are placed the formal clauses (definition clauses, 'saving' clauses, and clauses indicating the geographical 'extent' of a Bill). If it is a temporary measure, a clause stating its precise duration is required (S.O. No. 56).

Schedules.—At the end of most Bills is found a set of provisions called 'Schedules'. These contain matters of detail dependent on the provisions of the Bill. A Schedule is as much a part of a Bill as the preceding clauses, upon one of which it is dependent, and by means of which its provisions are enacted.

Memorandum.—An explanatory Memorandum, though it is not technically part of it, is often printed attached to a Bill. Its contents are governed by certain rules of order (see p. 204).

STAGES IN THE DISCUSSION OF BILLS AND INTERVALS BETWEEN STAGES

The principal stages in the discussion of Bills are:—

> Introduction
> Second Reading
> Committee Stage
> Report Stage
> Third Reading, and
> Consideration of Lords' Amendments.

These stages are discussed in this chapter in that order. Intervals between these stages are prescribed in the case of Bills originating in a Committee of the Whole House,[1] which may not pass through more than one stage on the same day. An exception is permitted in the case of Consolidated Fund Bills (p. 274). Other Bills are permitted to pass through more than one stage—in cases of urgency all their stages—on the

---

[1] Including the Committee of Ways and Means.

same day, but normally intervals, which in the case of important Bills are necessary to allow them to be reprinted after being amended, are observed between each stage.

INTRODUCTION AND FIRST READING

There are three ways in which a Bill may be introduced:—
(1) It may be presented upon an Order of the House.
(2) It may be presented without an Order under the procedure laid down by S.O. No. 35 (1).
(3) It may be brought down from the Lords.

(1) *Bills brought in on an Order of the House*

This is the old procedure, which has been practically superseded except in the case of 'Money' Bills and Bills introduced under S.O. No. 12. Bills introduced on an Order may be preceded by certain preliminary business.

With Preliminaries.

(a) A certain class of Bills, whose main object is the expenditure of money or the imposition of taxation, generally called 'Money' Bills (see p. 199), are still required to be preceded by Resolutions passed in Committee of the Whole House and agreed to by the House on Report. In this case the Bill is ordered to be brought in immediately after the Resolutions are agreed to.

(b) Occasionally Bills, other than Money Bills, are founded upon Resolutions of a Committee of the Whole House— as, *e.g.*, the Parliament Bill, 1910. Objection has been taken to this course on the ground that it involves a double discussion of the same questions in committee, and also the discussion of details before the discussion of principles (May, 481).

Without Preliminaries.

(a) In the absence of these preliminaries a motion is made that leave be given to bring in a Bill. This question has often led to protracted debate, which serves no useful purpose, as it cannot fail to anticipate the discussion of the principle of the Bill proper to the second reading.

(b) The old method is frequently used, however, in a modified form under S.O. No. 12 (the 'Ten Minutes Rule'), which authorizes the Speaker to put the Question after "a brief explanatory statement" from the mover and an opponent (see p. 161).

When, whether with or without any of the preliminaries mentioned above, and with or without restricted debate, the Order for leave to bring in a Bill has been granted, or a Bill has been ordered upon a Resolution, the procedure is as follows: The Speaker asks, " Who will prepare and bring in the Bill ?" The Member who has been granted leave reads the list of his backers (not more than 11), concluding with his own name, and goes from his place to the Bar, whence, on his name being called by the Speaker, he proceeds to the Table, with the customary three bows, and hands his Bill in 'dummy' (see p. 161) to the Clerk of the House. The Clerk reads the short title of the Bill and announces the day named by the Member for the second reading of his Bill.

(2) *Bills presented without an Order under S.O. No. 35 (1)*

The great majority of Bills, whether introduced by the Government or by Private Members, are brought in by being presented under this Standing Order. When the name of the Member, who has notified his intention of presenting a Bill, is called by the Speaker, he brings his 'dummy' Bill to the Clerk of the House from behind the Chair. The Clerk reads the title, etc., as above.

(3) *Bills brought down from the Lords*

A Bill brought down from the Lords is not necessarily proceeded with in the Commons unless a Member wishes to 'take it up'. The process of taking it up is as follows: The Member who proposes to do so signifies his intention at the Table, and names a date on which he wishes the Bill to be put down as an Order of the Day for second reading. This transaction is deemed to be an Order of the House for the first reading and printing of the Bill, and is recorded accordingly.

Notice is required of intention to present a Bill, except a Bill founded upon preliminary proceedings. Notice of a Bill to be presented under S.O. No. 12 or 35 (1) is placed "at the commencement of public business" (see p. 159), while notice of a motion for leave to bring in a Bill according to the old procedure is placed among the Orders of the Day. All Bills are now, as a matter of course, after introduction deemed to have been read the first time and ordered to be printed. In the case of Bills presented under S.O. No. 35 (1) the need for putting questions on these points is expressly waived. In the case of Bills brought in on an Order of leave and of Bills brought from the Lords[1], the first part of S.O. No. 35 requires the question to be put on these two points, but provides that they shall be decided without amendment or debate. In practice the provisions of S.O. No. 35 with regard to these questions have come to be applied to all Bills, however introduced.

Steps to be taken by a Member in introducing a Bill:—

First, notice must be given at the Table of intention to introduce a Bill on a specified date, whether by presenting it under S.O. No. 35 (1), or by moving for leave, and this notice must be accompanied by notice in writing of the short title and long title of the Bill (see p. 200). In drafting a Bill technical knowledge is generally necessary, even if the purpose of the Bill is apparently simple. No expert advice is officially available to the Private Member, as the duties of the Parliamentary Counsel's Office ('The Government Draftsman') are limited to Government Bills. Special care should be taken to see that the Bill contains nothing which is not covered by the 'long' title, and also that its main object is not to incur expenditure or impose taxation (in technical language, "to impose a charge upon public funds or upon the people"). Subsidiary provisions involving expenditure make a Bill dependent on the good will of the Government, as they require the recommendation of the Crown (see pp. 274–5). The document handed to the Clerk of the House as part of the ceremony of presenting a Bill is known as the 'dummy' Bill, and is obtainable from the Public Bill Office.[2] To this office must be given the text of the Bill itself for transmission to the printer, together with the memorandum, if any, explanatory of the objects of the Bill. These memoranda descend from the briefs or 'breviats' which used to be drawn up to assist the Speaker in 'opening the substance' of the Bill to the House at the first reading (see p. 23). They should be restricted to explaining the objects of the Bill in non-technical language, without *ex parte* statements or arguments, and the Public Bill Office is responsible for their censorship.

---

[1] The remainder of this paragraph has been superseded by amendments to S.O. No. 35.

[2] The names of Members backing a Bill should be written on the 'dummy' Bill. Names can be added afterwards to Bills presented under S.O. No. 35 1), but not to Bills brought in by leave of the House.

SECOND-READING STAGE

Preliminary Questions

During the interval before it is printed a Bill is examined by the authorities of the House whose duty it is to scrutinize Bills. For this reason and also the fact that Members have had no opportunity of forming an opinion on its objects, though it is not contrary to the letter, it is felt to be contrary to the spirit of the rules to take the second reading of a Bill which has not been printed. In 1920 the Speaker on this ground prevented the second reading of a Private Member's Bill being proceeded with, and it is sometimes put forward as an objection to the reading a second time of a Bill, to the merits of which there is no opposition. No change can be made in the text of a Bill after it has been printed by order of the House except to correct an error.

The chief questions with regard to which a Bill is examined before second reading are:—

(1) *Is its main object to impose a charge?* If so, unless introduced by the Government under S.O. No. 80, it must be founded upon Resolutions of a Committee of the Whole House (see pp. 199 and 202).

(2) *Does it affect private rights?* If it appears that it does, notice is sent by the Public Bill Office to the Member in charge, and the Examiners are ordered by the House to examine the Bill in respect of its compliance or non-compliance with the Standing Orders for Private Bills. Meanwhile the Bill still stands for second reading, but a memorandum "to be reported upon by the Examiners" appears in brackets after the title of the Bill in the Order Book, and the Bill cannot be proceeded with until the Examiners' Report has been received. The Examiners' Report presents three possibilities:—

(a) If they report non-compliance with the Standing Orders and the Standing Orders Committee thereupon reports that compliance ought not to be dispensed with, the order for the second reading is read and discharged and the Bill usually withdrawn.

(b) If they report that no Standing Orders are applicable, the Bill proceeds as an ordinary Public Bill.

(c) If they report that the Standing Orders have been complied with, or if, not being complied with, the

Standing Orders Committee reports that they ought
to be dispensed with, the Bill proceeds as a 'hybrid'
or 'semi-private' Bill.[1] After being read a second
time it is committed to a Select Committee, nominated
partly by the House and partly by the Committee of
Selection, and is proceeded with in Committee as
though it were a Private Bill (see p. 318). After report
it is recommitted to a Committee of the Whole
House, and its further progress is as a Public Bill.
Hybrid Bills are regularly introduced by Government
Departments, such as the Post Office. They are also
introduced by Private Members, who are liable for
the fees payable in respect of them.

(3) *Are the contents of the Bill covered by the long title?*
If it appears that they are not, the Bill must be withdrawn,
as the Speaker would refuse to propose the question for
its second reading. On this question being raised after
the second reading the Speaker has ruled that it is then
too late to take exception to a Bill on this ground, as it
must be assumed that the House, in reading a Bill a
second time, has approved of its contents (28th November,
1911, *Deb.*, 215).

(4) *Is the Bill substantially similar to a Bill of the same session
upon which a decision of the House has already been
taken?* This is a particular instance of the rule that the
same question may not be twice offered in the same
session (see p. 176). Under this rule a motion for leave
to bring in a Bill has been ruled out of order because a
Bill for the same purpose had been refused a second
reading earlier in the session (21st May, 1912, *Deb.*, 1754).
It is not out of order, however, to present a Bill merely
because another of the same substance has previously
been *presented*. But if one of the Bills is given or refused
a second reading, the other is not proceeded with. Bills
having the same (short) title are distinguished by a
number, according to priority in date of introduction,
printed in brackets after the title.

(5) A rule was at one time in force that a second Bill at
variance with a Bill passed during the same session
could not be introduced. In 1721, indeed, the session
was terminated by a prorogation of two days in order to

[1] Reports have been made that the Bill should proceed as a Private Bill.

allow clauses of an Act passed in that session to be repealed. But this rule has been annulled by section 1 of 'Brougham's' Act, now embodied in the Interpretation Act, 1889, s. 10.

DEBATE ON SECOND READING

On the day ordered for second reading, the short title of the Bill is printed as one of the Orders of the Day, and when it is called the Member in charge rises to explain and recommend the provisions of his Bill, and concludes his speech by moving that it "be now read a second time"; or he may say "Now" without rising and reserve his speech for a later moment in the debate (see p. 193). It is not necessary, though usual, for such an Order of the Day to be seconded. After the second reading has been moved (and seconded) the Speaker proposes the Question, and debate proceeds. Debate is, of course, governed by the rule of relevancy, though the rule in this case admits of a wide interpretation, as the whole principle of the Bill is under consideration. Reference to alternative methods of achieving the objects of the Bill, and even, in some cases, reference to other Bills, is permitted (May, 497). But anticipation of the Committee stage by discussion of the details of the Bill is not in order.

Opposition may be effected by voting against the Question, but as the Question is only that the Bill be now read a second time, the result of negativing it would not be to prevent the Bill being put down for second reading on a subsequent day, although, in the case of a Private Member's Bill at all events, such a result would be for all practical purposes fatal. By custom, and also by courtesy,[1] one of the traditional methods of defeating a Bill is almost always employed.

(a) An amendment may be moved to read the Bill "*upon this day six months*" (after Whitsuntide "three months"), and the question on the amendment is proposed in the form "to leave out the word 'now' and at the end of the Question to add the words upon this day six (three) months". The carrying of this amendment is accepted as definite rejection of the Bill, even if, as might very well be the case, the session extended beyond the period of six or three months.

---

[1] After all, the House has ordered it to be read a second time. In old days Bills have been ordered 'to be rejected,' 'to be rejected and torn,' and one was 'tossed over the Table' by the Speaker (May, 498).

P

(b) What is called a *reasoned* amendment may be moved, setting out the grounds on which the Bill should be refused a second reading, or laying down some principle inconsistent with its purpose. May (pp. 498–500) gives examples of such amendments. The Question on such an amendment is to leave out from the word "That" to the end and add the words expressing disapproval. The amendment must not attach a condition to the second reading (which might be equivalent to a mandatory instruction, see p. 213) or anticipate the committee stage, and must be relevant. The effect of carrying such an amendment is not technically conclusive. May says: "The House refuses, on that particular day, to read the Bill a second time, and gives its reasons for such refusal: but the Bill is not otherwise disposed of" (May, 500). In practice, however, the intention of this form is so well recognized, and the reasons for rejection usually so uncompromisingly expressed, that the replacement of the second reading on the Order Paper would be inconceivable. But if the language of the amendment substituted for the second reading motion were non-committal, it is possible that the question whether the Bill were really dead would have to be raised.

These amendments may also be moved to the third readings of Bills. If either of them is moved and rejected, the Speaker is directed by Standing Order No. 37 to declare forthwith that the Bill is read a second (or third) time.

Further points on the second reading that may be mentioned are : —

The Previous Question (see p. 173) may be moved, but it does not have the effect of killing a Bill, merely that of stopping it on a particular day. When the Order of the Day for a Bill is read, and it is not moved or postponed, it becomes a dropped Order (see p. 165). Counsel, and individuals not represented by Counsel, may be heard at this stage at the Bar of the House, if the Bill is of such a nature as peculiarly to affect their interests. The last occasion on which leave for this purpose was granted was on the Newfoundland Fisheries Bill, 1891 (May, 502).

When it has been read a second time, and not before, amendments to the text of the Bill for consideration in committee are received at the Table.

COMMITTEE STAGE
COMMITTAL OF BILLS

Under the system of standing committees introduced in 1907, the presumption is that all Public Bills, with certain exceptions, will be referred to a standing committee. S.O. No. 38 lays down (in effect) that, on being read a second time, a Bill stands committed to a standing committee unless

(a) it is a Bill for imposing taxes, or a Consolidated Fund Bill (in which case it stands committed to a Committee of the Whole House under the practice of the House relating to charges, see pp. 33–34);

(b) it is a Provisional Order Bill (see p. 308);

(c) or unless, immediately after the Bill has been read a second time, a Member moves that it be committed to a Committee of the Whole House or to a select committee, or that it is expedient that the Bill be committed to a joint committee. Such a motion does not require notice, must be made immediately after the Bill has been read a second time, does not admit of amendment or debate, and may be decided, though opposed, after the time for opposed business. Only one of the alternative committees may be proposed, and if the motion for it is negatived the Bill *eo ipso* stands committed to a standing committee;

(d) or unless the Member in charge of the Bill move that it be committed in respect of some of its provisions to a standing committee and in respect of other provisions to a Committee of the Whole House. This motion may receive the modicum of debate allowed to Bills introduced under the 'Ten Minutes Rule' (*i.e.* a short statement for and against) if the Speaker thinks fit. The question is then put. If it is negatived, the whole Bill stands committed to a standing committee.

If for the reason under (a) or (c) the Bill is committed to a Committee of the Whole House, the Member in charge of the Bill names a day for the Committee.

The rules relating to the distribution of Bills among the various standing committees, and also the constitution, etc., of these bodies, are dealt with in Chapter VII (pp. 238–40). If it is desired to transfer a Bill from a standing committee to a Committee of the Whole House, or a select committee, a motion is made for discharging the former committal and for committing the Bill to the desired committee. Such a motion does not get the benefit of being decided without debate, or of being taken after the time of opposed business, which it would have obtained under S.O. No. 38, if it had been moved immediately after the Bill was read a second time. Debate on it is limited to the expediency of the transfer.

FUNCTIONS OF A COMMITTEE ON A BILL

The function of a committee on a Bill is to go through the text of the Bill clause by clause, and word by word, if necessary, with a view to making such amendments in it as may seem likely to render it more generally acceptable. In doing so it has a fairly free hand, but is limited in various ways.

(1) In the first place it is bound by the decision of the House, given on second reading, in favour of the principle of the Bill. It should not, therefore, amend the Bill in a manner destructive of its principle.[1] It should be stated that the effect of this rule is now only to disallow *amendments* which are contrary to the principle of the Bill. It does not prevent a committee negativing a clause, even though the omission of that clause nullifies the Bill (see p. 218).

(2) It should not admit amendments which are irrelevant to the Bill. It was formerly the rule that no amendment could be moved in committee which was outside the long title in which the objects of the Bill are stated. This was found to be too rigid a rule, and the House in 1854 opened the door of a committee to amendments "relevant to the subject-matter of a Bill," though beyond its title, provided the committee proceeded to extend the title so as to cover them. (This power is given by the important General Instruction to committees in S.O. No. 40.)

(3) There is another means by which the powers of a committee over a Bill may be extended, *i.e.* by the House passing a Special Instruction (see p. 213). This is the utmost extension of its powers which a committee can receive.

Examples of the application of these rules to proceedings in committee are given below (p. 217). As here generally stated, they constitute the limits within which a committee is free to

[1] In the old procedure an opponent of the principle of a Bill was not allowed to serve on the committee appointed to consider it (Scobel, 47).

act. The duty of keeping within these bounds is enforced in the committee itself, for there is no authority who can overrule it in respect of its own proceedings, or to whom an appeal from the decision of its Chairman can be made.

On the other hand, the powers of a committee cannot extend beyond its own stage to bind the House. When a Bill is reported from the committee, the Speaker can rule upon the manner in which the committee has exercised its powers, not indeed with a view to invalidating its proceedings, but in order that the House may decide upon its own future action with regard to the Bill.

A standing committee, guilty of a technical irregularity, such as that of inserting in a Bill a provision imposing a charge without the previous sanction of a Committee of the Whole House, has had the Bill recommitted to it for the purpose of striking out such provision (see p. 243).

Control of House over Bill committed

The control of the House over a Bill, once it is committed, is thus very small. It does not intervene in the proceedings of the committee, nor does it (except in the case of a select committee or a technical irregularity) recommit a Bill, even if it appears that a committee has exercised its powers of amendment so as to transform a Bill. The responsibility of the Chairman is normally a sufficient safeguard against such a risk, but it may happen that the cumulative effect of amendments which, taken singly, were not beyond the subject-matter of the Bill may be so great as to raise the question whether the principle of the Bill, as amended by a committee, remains the same as that to which the House agreed on second reading. In 1856 the Partnership Amendment Bill was withdrawn on objection being taken in the House that the amendments made by the committee had transformed the original Bill. In the case of two Bills—the Tithe Rentcharge Recovery Bill, 1889, and the Franchise and Registration Bill, 1913—the Speaker was appealed to when the Bills were in committee as to the effect of certain proposed amendments. In giving his opinion on the former Bill that the effect of the amendments, if carried, would be to transform the Bill, the Speaker was careful to safeguard the jurisdiction of the Chairman, and to leave any action with regard to the Bill to the discretion of the House and the Government. In the case of the latter Bill the Speaker advised the

House that it should be withdrawn. Both Bills were, in deference to the Speaker, withdrawn.

Destructive Power of Committee

The power of a committee to destroy a Bill is more limited
in form than in fact. This is well put in a sentence in More's
Notes of Debates in the Long Parliament, 14th April, 1641,
quoted by May (p. 506): "No committee can destroy a Bill,
but they can lay it down." A Bill cannot be withdrawn in
committee, for this requires the leave of the House. Nor can a
committee 'defeat' a Bill. But it can take action which indirectly achieves either of these results.

Committee of the Whole House.—The first object can be
effected as follows: The committee reports progress without
asking leave to sit again, thus putting an end to its own
existence. This is equivalent to refusing to proceed with a
Bill, which is accordingly withdrawn. If it wishes to destroy
a Bill, it leaves out an essential clause, by negativing the
question "That the Clause stand part of the Bill", and reports
the Bill, as amended, to the House.

Standing Committees.—There is nothing to prevent a Standing Committee destroying a Bill by negativing the essential
clause in the same way as a Committee of the Whole House.
It has, in fact, disagreed to all the clauses of a Bill and made a
special report to that effect (C.J. (1919) 363). A result similar to
that which a Committee of the Whole House secures by omit-
ting to ask leave to sit again can be secured in a Standing Committee by passing a motion "That the Committee do not proceed further with the consideration of the Bill", and reporting
the Bill, without amendment or so far as amended, back to the
House with a Special Report explaining the circumstances
which, in the opinion of the Committee, render it inexpedient
to proceed any further with the consideration of the Bill.
According to present practice, such a motion will, as a general
rule, only be accepted from the member in charge of the Bill.
Where, however, a committee has negatived the sole effective
clause of a Bill and the Member in charge of the Bill declines
to enable the committee to dispose of the Bill without unnecessary waste of time by moving "That the Committee do not
proceed further with the consideration of the Bill," some other
Member has been allowed to make a motion to that effect. In
three cases a motion "That the Committee do not proceed

with the consideration of the Bill" has been accepted from the Member in charge of the Bill before the committee has made any progress with it.

In *a Select Committee* the right of moving that the committee should not proceed further with the consideration of the Bill is not restricted to the Member in charge of the Bill. The House normally accepts a special report from a Select Committee that, in their judgment, the Bill ought not to pass into law. But as a Select Committee is only a preliminary committee on the Bill, such a report may be less effectual in arresting the progress of the Bill in the case of a Select than in the case of a Standing Committee. If a Committee failed to report a Bill, it might be instructed to report it forthwith or by a day named; and if it attempted to get rid of the Bill by adjourning *sine die*, it might be revived, and instructed to proceed with the Bill. In 1868 a Select Committee, after consultation with the Speaker, negatived all the clauses of a Bill, making a special report to the House.

Special Instructions to Committees

The object of a special instruction to a committee is either to give it power to do something which it could not otherwise do, or to direct it to do something which it might otherwise not do. The first type of instruction is called 'permissive', the second 'mandatory'. A mandatory instruction may be given to a Select Committee or to a Private Bill Committee, and with the concurrence of both Houses to a Joint Committee but not to a Committee of the Whole House or to a Standing Committee.

Purpose of an Instruction to a Committee of the Whole House or Standing Committee

The first point, then, about a special instruction to a committee on a Public Bill (of which a Committee of the Whole House is the type which has regulated modern procedure) is that it is given for the purpose of extending the powers of the committee. What can be done by it which could not equally be done under the General Instruction given by S.O. No. 40? As far as the rules go, very little, for a Special Instruction must itself be 'relevant to the subject-matter of the Bill'. It would seem, then, that of most Special Instructions it might be said in advance that they are either unnecessary or else out of order, either covered by the general instruction of S.O. No. 40, or else not relevant to the subject-matter of the Bill. Still they are used, and will continue to be used, for the questions how far a committee can go under S.O. No. 40, and how much farther it can go with a Special Instruction, are just those questions of degree which resist general rules, but yield to practice and precedent.[1] May, in Chapter XX, gives valuable lists of decisions with regard to the three classes of Special Instruction, namely, those which are unnecessary, those which are too remote from the Bill, and those which are in order, being neither too remote to be relevant nor yet too obviously relevant to be needed.

It should be remembered, too, that the mere moving of an instruction provides valuable guidance to the committee. Whether it is accepted by the House, or ruled out of order, whether as unnecessary or foreign to the Bill, in any event, doubts that might have arisen in the breasts of the committee will be set at rest. Hence instructions will continue to be moved, and some, which are not very obviously necessary, may be accepted, *ex majori cautela*.

Besides, there are certain functions of a committee not open to such doubts. They always require an instruction. These are —to divide a Bill into two or more Bills,[2] to consolidate two Bills into one Bill, to give priority to part of a Bill with power to report such part separately to the House, and lastly to extend the operation of a Bill geographically (*i.e.* to extend a Bill which is by its title limited to part of the United Kingdom to another part, or the whole, of the United Kingdom. Examples of this last type of instruction are given in May, 510.

It should be mentioned that the powers conferred by an instruction moved upon the committal of a Bill continue operative if it is recommended (May, 516).

Rules for Moving and Debating Instructions

An instruction requires notice, as also does an amendment to it which in any way enlarges its scope. An instruction to

---

[1] An important ruling on the principles limiting instructions was given by the Speaker in the case of the Government of Ireland Bill, 5th May, 1893 (*Deb.*, 205).

[2] This is confined by Speakers' rulings to the case of a Bill which, as drafted, is divided into parts, or which, comprising more than one subject-matter, lends itself to such division into parts (*Deb.*, 6th June 1917, 162; 10th July, 1917, 1757).

make such provision in a Bill as would entail a charge requires the recommendation of the Crown (see p. 259).

The time for moving an instruction is:—

(*a*) to a Committee of the Whole House—when the order for the committee is first read, except instructions authorizing charges which are given when the Resolutions, on which they are founded, have been agreed to by the House.

(*b*) to a Standing, or Select, Committee—immediately after the committal of the Bill, or subsequently as an independent motion.

Debate on an instruction is governed by the ordinary rules with regard to relevancy (p. 190) and anticipation. An instruction is regarded as a subsidiary, rather than a substantive, motion (see p. 168). Consequently the mover of an instruction has no right of reply, nor can he move a further instruction to the same committee. An amendment would be out of order which, if carried, would have the effect of destroying the form of the instruction. Thus it would be out of order to seek to defeat an instruction by turning it into a declaratory resolution.

PROCEEDINGS IN COMMITTEE ON A BILL

The procedure to be described is that of a Committee of the Whole House. The description applies generally to proceedings in a standing or select committee, which are modelled on those in Committee of the Whole House, except that in a select committee the Chair has neither the power to select amendments, nor the other restrictive powers given by Standing Order to the Chairman of a Committee of the Whole House.

The order in which the text of a Bill is considered in committee is (1) Clauses, (2) New Clauses, (3) Schedules, (4) New Schedules, (5) Preamble (if any), (6) Title (if an amendment of it is required).

(1) *Clauses*

The Chairman calls each clause by its number and, if no amendment is offered, immediately proceeds to propose the Question "That this clause stand part of the Bill". On this Question a debate on the provisions of the clause may take place. After it has been proposed it is no longer in order to move an amendment. As soon as the first clause is disposed of the Chairman calls the next clause and so on. Strictly, a separate Question is necessary on each clause, but on uncontentious Bills it is not unusual to save time by putting the Question on groups of clauses.

When amendments are moved to a clause the Chairman calls them—or rather those which he *selects* under S.O. No. 31 (p. 187)—in turn according to the order by line and word of the place in the clause at which they are offered. Those of which notice has been given have already been arranged in this order on the amendment paper by directions given to the printer. When several amendments are offered at the same place, precedence is given to an amendment to leave out words in order to insert other words over an amendment merely to leave out words, but where there is no such distinction, the Chairman decides which amendment he will receive. He also decides, where necessary, that an amendment offered at one place shall be moved at another place of the same clause, or of another clause, or even that it shall be moved as a new clause. He takes care to propose the Question on each amendment in such a way as to 'save' subsequent amendments, *i.e.* if the amendment is to leave out words to some of which subsequent amendments are offered, he proposes that only the words down to the first word touched by a subsequent amendment stand part of the clause. When the Question thus put on part of the amendment is negatived, no further Question is put on the remaining words proposed to be left out by the Amendment, but the Chairman announces that these words are left out.

When the Question is proposed on an amendment, debate should, strictly, be relevant to that amendment and not refer to other amendments, but the Chairman sometimes, for the convenience and with the assent of the Committee, allows debate to range over several amendments, which raise different aspects of the question raised by the amendment actually under consideration, on the understanding usually that, when these later amendments are called, they may be divided on, if desired, but not discussed. In this matter, and the regulation of debate generally, the Chairman is assisted by his power under S.O. No 31 to select amendments. He has also power to accept the closure (see p. 184).

Rules of Order respecting Amendments

Amendments to Bills in committee are governed by the same general rules of order as amendments to motions, and they are divisible into the same three types (see p. 173). Any part of a Bill may be amended except what may be called the 'framework,' *i.e.* the enacting words at the commencement of a Bill, the marginal titles of clauses, or the figures and letters which distinguish parts, clauses, sub-sections, and paragraphs of a Bill.

There are also certain special rules of order respecting amendments in committee which will be given chiefly as relating to amendments to clauses, although they mostly apply to amendments to schedules, etc. These special rules are:—

(*a*) If an amendment refers to, or is not intelligible without, a subsequent amendment or schedule, notice of such amendment or schedule ought to have been given before the related amendment is moved.

(*b*) An amendment should be relevant to the subject-matter of the clause to which it is moved and not constitute a direct negative of the Bill or clause. In the case of Bills the scope of which is very restricted it is not easy to grasp at once the full effect of this rule. May (p. 523) gives the following examples of amendments ruled out on this ground:—

    (i) to a Bill the scope of which was restricted to the repeal of a section in a statute—an amendment proposing the continuance and extension of the section;

    (ii) to a Bill for extending a statute to London with certain modifications—amendments proposing modifications of the statute not relating to such extension;

    (iii) to an Expiring Laws Continuance Bill—amendments proposing amendment of the Acts to be continued, or proposing to make them permanent;

    (iv) to a Statute Law Revision Bill (which deals solely with Acts no longer in force)—an amendment proposing to deal with an Act still in force.

(*c*) An amendment should not be inconsistent with the Bill as so far agreed to, or with a decision already taken on a previous amendment.

(*d*) An amendment to leave out a clause is not in order in committee, as the proper course is to vote against the clause standing part of the Bill. Consequently it is out of order to propose to leave out the only effective words of a clause, or the words upon which the rest of the

clause is dependent, as this is equivalent to destroying
the clause.

(e) Amendments have been ruled out of order as vague,
trifling, or tendered in a spirit of mockery.

(f) They have been ruled out of order for proposing to
introduce sweeping constitutional changes as part of
the incidental machinery of a Bill—as, for instance, that
the Address of one House alone should effect the repeal
of a Bill, or a Referendum held on its provisions.

(g) For the disallowance of amendments imposing or increasing money 'charges,' see May, 739-42.

When the amendments to a clause have been disposed of,
the question is proposed "That the Clause (as amended) stand
part of the Bill". Debate on this Question must be confined
to the Clause as amended (or not amended). It is open to a
committee to negative this Question, even though the clause
is the sole effective clause of the Bill, and the effect of negativing
it is to destroy the Bill. The Question having been once proposed, the motion cannot be withdrawn, with a view, for
instance, to proposing further amendments, as the motion
automatically follows the consideration of the amendments,
and needs no mover.[1]

Motions to postpone a clause are in order so long as the
clause has not been amended or the question for its standing
part proposed. Postponement of a clause is normally until after
the clauses have been disposed of and before the new clauses
are brought up, but a clause may be postponed until after the
new clauses or after a certain new clause, or other point specified,
and postponed clauses, when reached, may be again postponed.

For the procedure, pursuant to an instruction, of consolidating two Bills into one or dividing one Bill into two or more
Bills, see May, 510-11.

At one time a question was necessary for the filling up of the
portions of a Bill left in blank (now printed in italics), which
are concerned with the imposition of charges. Under S.O. No. 44
this is no longer necessary (see May, 526).

(2) *New Clauses*

New Clauses are considered after the clauses of the Bill have
been disposed of, and the insertion of any that are passed in
their proper place in the Bill is not fixed by the House but left
to be settled between the Member in charge of the Bill and the

[1] For new procedure, see Appendix IV.

Public Bill Office, which is responsible for reprinting it as amended. The order in which new clauses are considered is that in which they stand on the Paper (and that is the order in which they have been handed in, with the exception that clauses offered by the Minister in charge of the Bill are placed first).

The procedure on a new clause gives an opportunity for a debate on its principle and then for the proposal of amendments before the Question for its adoption is put. The Member in whose name it stands, on being called by the Chairman, 'brings up' his clause in a speech stating the reasons for its adoption. Its title (printed in the margin) is read by the Clerk, and the Question is proposed "That it be read a second time". If this Question is agreed to, amendments may be moved, and after they have been disposed of the Question is put "That the Clause (or Clause as amended) be added to the Bill".

New clauses must be relevant to the subject-matter of the Bill and not inconsistent with a previous decision of the Committee on the Bill.

(3) *Schedules and* (4) *New Schedules*

The procedure on schedules and new schedules is similar to that on clauses and new clauses. The final Question on a schedule is put in the form "That this schedule (as amended) be the 'first' schedule of the Bill".

(5) *Preamble*

By S.O. No. 43 the preamble "stands postponed without question put until after the consideration of the clauses and schedules if any". Clauses and schedules include proposed new clauses and proposed new schedules. A preamble may be amended. It is not in order to move a preamble to a Bill introduced without one (May, 530).

(6) *Title*

No Question is put on the title, unless it is required to amend it in consequence of amendments made in the Bill, and, when so amended, no Question is put on the title as amended (May, 530–31).

Bills committed pro forma

The object of committing a Bill *pro forma* is to enable the Member in charge, by leave of the House, to amend it extensively before the real committee stage begins. By this means the time spent on second reading is not wasted, and the time to be spent in committee probably shortened. The proceedings on a Bill committed *pro forma* are dependent on general agreement. The amendments are deemed to have been made, and the Chairman reports the Bill, as so amended, to the House, when it is ordered to be reprinted and is referred again to a committee for real discussion.

Report of Progress

If consideration of a Bill is still unfinished at the conclusion of a sitting of a Committee of the Whole House, the Chairman, on the motion of a Member, puts the Question "That I do report progress and ask leave to sit again". A motion directing the Chairman to leave the Chair (without the additional words about asking leave to sit again) has the effect, temporarily at any rate, of disposing of the Bill as a dropped Order (see p. 165).

REPORT OF BILL

When proceedings in Committee of the Whole House on a Bill are finished, the Chairman puts the Question "That I do report the Bill as amended (or without amendment) to the House", and leaves the Chair under S.O. No. 18 without putting another question for that purpose. The Speaker immediately resumes the Chair, and the Chairman, approaching him, makes his report from the committee. The formula is:—

(1) If the Bill has been amended, "I beg to report that the committee have gone through the Bill and made amendments thereunto". Whereupon, on being referred to by the Speaker, the Member in charge of the Bill names a day for the Bill as amended to be taken into consideration and the Bill, if materially amended, is ordered to be printed as amended in the committee. In the case of an important Bill undergoing heavy amendment in committee it is not unusual at one or more stages in its progress to order the amended clauses to be printed, and this has also been done to show the effect of proposed Government amendments (May, 535).

(2) If the Bill has not been amended in Committee of the Whole House, the formula is, "I beg to report that the committee have gone through the Bill and directed me to report the same without amendment". The Bill, not

having been amended, escapes the Report stage. It may be read the third time immediately, or ordered to be read a third time upon a future day. It should be remembered that (with one exception to be stated immediately) a 'Money' Bill may not go through more than one stage on the same day. In the case of a Consolidated Fund Bill, however, the third reading may be taken immediately after the Bill has been reported from committee (S.O. No. 85) (see p. 274).

Bills reported from Standing and Select Committees

A Bill reported from a Standing Committee, whether with or without amendment, always has to undergo a Report stage (S.O. No. 49).

A Bill reported from a Select, or Joint, Committee is, on the receipt of the Report, ordered to be recommitted to a Committee of the Whole House (May, 534) (see p. 249).

THE REPORT STAGE (CONSIDERATION OF BILL, AS AMENDED)

The Report stage of a Bill has become a more formal repetition of the committee stage with the rules of debate, which are proper when the Speaker is in the Chair, applied. For example, a Member can only speak once to the same question, except when the Bill has been reported from a standing committee (see p. 192, and S.O. No. 52). Amendments require a seconder, new clauses notice as well. Amendments which were rejected in committee may be moved again, and attempts may be made by amendment to restore the original text of the Bill. The power of the Speaker to select amendments may, however, be relied upon to check excessive repetition of debates which have already taken place in committee. The development of the Report stage into a second committee stage seems to have occurred within the last 100 years. Previously the procedure on the Report stage seems to have been more akin to the present procedure on Lords' amendments. It is not probable that debate was confined exclusively to the amendments proposed by the committee, but it seems that they were the main business, that a motion was required to insert each of them in the Bill, and that fresh amendments, though not out of order (they were even permitted on third reading at that time) were not numerous (see p. 24).

The Report stage opens when the Order of the Day is called, without any Question being proposed. No opportunity is provided for a motion to postpone consideration, such as exists on second or third reading. It may, however, be deferred to another day at the desire of the Member in charge, or any Member may move that the Bill be recommitted. If the motion for recommittal is opposed, the Speaker, after allowing a brief explanatory statement for and against, puts the Question without further debate (S.O. No. 50). On a Motion to recommit the Unemployment Insurance (No. 2) Bill in respect of a proposed new clause, the Speaker allowed debate unrestricted by Standing Order No. 50 (*Deb.*, 12th December, 1929, c. 714). If no such motion is made, and no amendment is offered to the Bill, on being referred to by the Speaker the Member in charge either names a day for third reading or moves "That the Bill be now read the third time".

Proceedings on Report

The order in which the Bill is discussed differs on Report from the order in committee, and is as follows: (1) New Clauses, (2) the Bill as amended, (3) New Schedules, (4) Schedules of the Bill.

New clauses require notice on Report (S.O. No. 46).[1] In view of this rule it has been held that a new clause standing in the name of one Member cannot be moved by another Member, that a Member who has not been present to move his clause when called by the Speaker may not move it at the end of the new clauses on the Paper, and also that any material difference between the clause as proposed to be moved and the clause as given notice of is out of order (May, 537). In other respects, except that it requires a seconder, the procedure on a new clause moved on Report is the same as in committee.

When the new clauses are disposed of, the Bill as a whole comes under consideration, and the Speaker calls upon the Member, in whose name the first amendment which he has selected stands on the Paper, to move his amendment. On Report, unlike committee, no question is put on each clause that it stand part of the Bill. Amendments are moved to the Bill, not to a particular clause, and amendments to leave out a clause, series of clauses, or the preamble, are moved as amendments to the Bill. A motion to postpone a clause is not in order.

[1] The temporary relaxation of this rule has been withdrawn.

The admissibility of amendments is governed by S.O. No. 51: "No amendment may be proposed which could not have been proposed in committee without an instruction from the House." Even where an instruction has given power to a committee to make certain provision in a Bill, an amendment on Report to make similar provisions, though apparently covered by the same instruction, would not be in order, for an instruction exhausts its virtue in committee.

Other amendments out of order are: Amendments inconsistent with the provisions of the Bill as so far agreed to, or an amendment to leave out the only effective clause of a Bill, or an amendment the effect of which would be to negative the Bill (May, 538), or an amendment which would increase the charge above that authorized by the Committee on the Bill, although within the terms of the Financial Resolution.

The proceedings on new schedules follow those on new clauses. After any amendments to the schedules have been disposed of, the title of the Bill may be amended.

Recommittal of Bill after Consideration on Report

As no amendment imposing a charge, whether upon the public revenue or upon local rates, or which increases taxation, may be moved on Report, it is necessary to recommit a Bill for the purpose of making such an amendment. A Bill recommitted in respect of a charge upon local rates may be considered in committee forthwith. But if it is recommitted in respect of a charge upon the public revenue, it cannot be considered in committee until a resolution sanctioning such a proposal has been recommended by the Crown, passed by a Committee of the whole House and agreed to by the House. A Bill may be recommitted as a whole, or as to certain clauses or as to amendments of which notice has been given.[1] Recommittal may be moved at the beginning or end of the Report stage, or when the order for the third reading of the Bill has been read, when it can be moved as an amendment to the motion that the Bill be read the third time. It is only when moved at the beginning of the Report stage that the provisions for restricting debate under S.O. No. 50 apply (May, 540).

THIRD READING

The third reading of a Bill is taken, as a rule, immediately after the Report stage has been concluded. As mentioned

---

[1] And on Report is again considered so far as recommitted.

above (p. 201), except in the case of 'Money' Bills, there is nothing to prevent the second reading and all subsequent stages of a Bill being taken at the same sitting. To the Question "That the Bill be now read the third time", the same amendments which are in order on the second reading may be moved (see pp. 207–8). At one time it was allowable at this stage to move amendments to the text of the Bill, now S.O. No. 53 prevents other than verbal amendments being made. An amendment has been made to the title (May 544). Consequently, if there is a desire to amend the Bill at this stage, the Order for third reading is discharged and the Bill recommitted. This can also be done by an amendment to the Question for reading a Bill the third time.

The debate on third reading is more restricted than on second reading, and is limited to the contents of the Bill.

When the Bill has been read the third time, it is communicated in due course to the Lords, without further Question, The Question "That the Bill do pass" which was once put, has been tacitly dropped.

COMMUNICATION BETWEEN THE TWO HOUSES

When a Bill has been passed by the Commons it is immediately communicated to the Lords. Messages are employed for other purposes as well as communicating Bills—for example, in connexion with Joint Committees—but, as the communication of Bills is their principal object, it may not be out of place to describe them here.

The modern fashion of *Messages* dates from 1855. Before that date the Lords sent messages by their attendants, the Masters in Chancery, or their assistants, the judges; the Commons by one of their own Members (generally the Chairman of Ways and Means or the Member in charge of the Bill), who was generally accompanied by 30 or 40 Members (May, 791). In 1855 the present method was arranged between the two Houses. A message sent by either House is now carried by one of its Clerks, and is delivered informally without necessarily interrupting the proceedings of the other House. If, however, occasion arises, the Speaker interrupts the reading of the Orders of the Day, or even the business under discussion, in order to inform the House of the receipt of a Lords' Message and to give the opportunity of moving any motion consequent upon it (May, 792).

The old procedure of *Conferences* between the two Houses has fallen into disuse. For its principal function—that of communicating reasons for disagreement upon Bills—messages were substituted in 1837 for conferences, unless the latter were preferred. Since 1837 only one conference on such a matter has been held, in 1858. Conferences were exceedingly ceremonious affairs and no discussion was permitted. There was another type of conference—the Free Conference—at which discussion was permitted. The Free Conference fell into disuse in 1740, was revived as an experiment in 1836, and has not been employed since.

CONSIDERATION OF LORDS' AMENDMENTS

"Lords' Amendments to public Bills shall be appointed to be considered on a future day, unless the House shall order them to be considered forthwith" (S.O. No. 54). This Standing Order dates from the time when the receipt of a Lords' Message was a real proceeding, which interrupted the business of the House. It has been adapted to the modern practice whereby a Lords' Message is received without any communication to the House being ordinarily made.

(1) The appointment of a future day for the consideration of a Lords' Message is made nominally by Order of the House, but this is one of the numerous formal Orders referred to on p. 87. In practice the Member in charge of a Bill can have the Lords' Amendments to it put down as an Order for any day he selects by giving a notification to the Table. In the ordinary way the Amendments are at the same time ordered to be printed.

(2) The consideration *forthwith* of Lords' Amendments now means, not merely their consideration following the communication of the Message containing them to the House, but their consideration *without a previous Order of the House*, whether on the day on which the Message is received or on a subsequent day. A motion that the Lords' Amendments be considered forthwith is moved by the Member in charge of a Bill, after notifying the Speaker, either before the commencement or at the end of the Orders of the Day. As this practice involves the consideration of Lords' Amendments without notice and without their having been printed, it is generally reserved

for Amendments which are not material. When they are
material, if there is any need for urgency owing to the
state of business, the Lords' Message is communicated to
the House and the motion for the Lords' Amendments
to be considered forthwith may be made between any
two Orders of the Day, or even by interrupting the
business under discussion (May, 546).

PROCEEDINGS ON CONSIDERATION OF LORDS' AMENDMENTS

When the Order of the Day is read for the consideration of
the Lords' Amendments to a Bill, the Speaker proposes the
Question "That the Lords' Amendments be now considered".
To this Question an amendment may be moved to consider
the Lords' Amendments "on this day three months", or to
"lay them aside". But generally the House agrees to the
Question, and the process of consideration begins with the
reading by the Clerk of the first Lords' Amendment. This is
technically the 'second reading'. If it is desired to move an
amendment to the Lords' Amendment, or to postpone or divide
it, now is the time to do so. It must be remembered that the
Lords' Amendments, not the Bill itself, are under consideration, and that the Bill itself may only be amended by the
Commons if such amendment is consequential on agreement
or disagreement to a Lords' Amendment, or on waiving a
Commons' Amendment disagreed to by the Lords. The rule
was expressed by the Commons at a Conference in 1678 as
follows: "It is contrary to the constant method and proceedings
in Parliament to strike out anything in a Bill which hath been
fully agreed and passed by both Houses" (May, 548).

If no amendment is proposed, the Member in charge of the
Bill moves "That this House agrees (or disagrees) with the
Lords in the said Amendment". The debate which may take
place on this motion must be confined to the Amendment
under consideration, and not extend to other Amendments or
the merits of the Bill. When the first Amendment has been disposed of, the same process is repeated with the other Amendments till all are disposed of. If an Amendment infringes
Privilege (see p. 285) the Speaker calls the attention of the
House to the fact when the Amendment is read. If the Member
in charge of the Bill wishes Privilege to be waived, he moves to
agree with the Lords, and when this motion has been agreed
to by the House, the Speaker announces that a Special Entry

will be made in the Journals. If the Member wishes Privilege to be insisted upon, he moves to disagree with the Lords (see p. 286). If any Amendment has been disagreed to by the House, it is then necessary to appoint a committee to draw up reasons for such disagreement. The committee withdraw immediately and report their reasons at the same sitting, and these are taken as agreed to by the House and communicated by message to the Lords.

If the House agrees to the Lords' Amendments, the proceedings on the Bill are complete and the Bill returns to the Lords to await the Royal Assent. If, however, it has amended a Lords' Amendment or disagreed to a Lords' Amendment, then in respect of such Amendment further exchanges take place between the two Houses, and this process continues until every amendment made by one House is agreed to by the other (when the Bill is ready for Royal Assent), or until one House insists upon its disagreement to an amendment made by the other House. In this latter case the Bill is lost for the session.

Stages in Process of Securing Agreement between the Two Houses

The process of securing agreement between the two Houses may lead to complications too long to set out in detail. It may be worth while, however, to follow it a little way, stating the proceedings in both Houses and remembering that the rôles of the two Houses, as about to be given, will be reversed when the Bill at issue between them is a Lords' Bill, not, as here supposed, a Commons' Bill. The following account gives the principal possibilities but is not exhaustive, even as far as it goes.

First stage (*in Lords*).
Commons' Bill amended.

Second stage, Lords' Amendments (*in Commons*).
A. The Commons amend a Lords' Amendment, or
B. The Commons disagree to a Lords' Amendment and communicate reasons.

Third stage (*in Lords*).
A. becomes "Commons' Amendment to Lords' Amendment".
   (1) The Lords amend the Commons' Amendment to the Lords' Amendment, or
   (2) The Lords disagree to it, and communicate reasons.

B. becomes "Commons' Reason for disagreeing to Lords Amendment".

In reply to it

(1) The Lords amend the Bill in lieu of their Amendment disagreed to by the Commons, or

(2) The Lords insist upon their Amendment with reasons. (This may be fatal.)

(3) The Lords do not insist upon their Amendment. (This ends the process by producing agreement.)

Fourth stage (in Commons).

A. (1) becomes "Lords' Amendment to Commons' Amendment to Lords' Amendment".

(a) The Commons amend the Lords' Amendment to Commons' Amendment to the Lords' Amendment, or

(b) The Commons disagree to it, and communicate reasons.

A. (2) becomes " Lords' Reason for disagreeing to Commons' Amendment to Lords' Amendment". In reply to this

(a) The Commons (possibly) amend the Bill in lieu of their Amendment to the Lords' Amendment disagreed to by the Lords, or

(b) Insist upon their Amendment to the Lords' Amendment. (This may be fatal.)

B. (1) becomes "Lords' Amendment to the Bill in lieu of Lords' Amendment disagreed to by the Commons". Upon this

(a) The Commons may amend the Lords' Amendment to the Bill in lieu of Lords' Amendment disagreed to by the Commons, or

(b) The Commons may disagree to it, giving their reasons.

B. (2) becomes "Lords' Reason for insisting upon their Amendment disagreed to by the Commons". Upon this

(a) The Commons do not insist upon their disagreement to the Lords' Amendment, or

(b) They insist upon their disagreement. (This is necessarily fatal.)

It would be tiresome and confusing to carry this series any further. In theory it may continue *ad infinitum*. In practice a way is usually found of ending it one way or the other before then. Not many Bills go beyond the fourth stage, at which, as stated above, positions necessarily fatal to the Bill begin to be reached.

INDORSEMENT OF BILLS

When a Bill is communicated from one House to the other, an 'indorsement' is written at the top of the first page, indicating the proceedings that have taken place on it. For instance, a Bill passed by the Commons is indorsed "Soit baillé aux Seigneurs". When the Bill is returned with amendments from the Lords, the indorsement is "A ceste bille avecque des amendemens les Seigneurs sont assentus". If the Lords' amendments are agreed to, the Bill is indorsed "A ces amendemens les Communes sont assentus", and, if they are disagreed to, the indorsement is "Ceste bille est remise aux Seigneurs avecque des raisons". These indorsements are made by the Clerk of the House and the Clerk of the Parliaments respectively.

ROYAL ASSENT TO ACTS

Bills awaiting the Royal Assent remain in the custody of the Clerk of the Parliaments, except Bills granting supplies and imposing taxation, which are returned to the Clerk of the House for the Speaker to carry up to the House of Lords when the Commons attend for the Royal Assent. In order to satisfy the rule that a Bill, which has passed both Houses, cannot be withheld from the Royal Assent, no Bills are allowed to reach their final stage after a commission has been issued, as otherwise the commission would have to be altered so as to include them.

The Royal Assent is generally given by commission and not in person. The validity of this method is certified by the statute of 33 Henry VIII, c. 21, which requires the commission to be issued under the great seal and the sign-manual. The only commission issued without the sign-manual was for giving assent to the Regency Bill, 1811, when George III was incapable of signing, and the great seal alone was affixed. The manner of signifying the Royal Assent is as follows:—On receiving the message by Black Rod that their attendance is desired by the Lords Commissioners, the Commons, headed by the Speaker, go up to the Bar of the House of Lords. There they find three of the Commissioners seated on a form between the Woolsack and the Throne. The Lord Chancellor announces the purpose of the Commission, and it is read at length, and then, as the title of each Act is read by the Clerk of the Crown, the Royal Assent is signified by the Clerk of the Parliaments in the customary formula, which dates from the time when legislation was by petition to the Crown.

The formula for the Royal Assent to an Act granting supply or imposing taxation, which always stands at the head of the list, is "Le roy remercie ses bons sujets, accepte leur benevolence, et ainsi le veult". For other public and most private Bills the formula is "Le roy le veult"; for a personal Bill "Soit fait comme il est désiré".

The formula for refusing the Royal Assent is "Le roy s'avisera". The character of this formula is said to be due to the need of the 14th-century kings to temporize with the Commons, and to leave the fate of their petitions for legislation open until supplies had been voted—which was not till the end of the session. In time, however, it came to mean final dissent.

The Royal Assent has been seldom refused by a sovereign since legislation by Bill superseded legislation by petition, except by Elizabeth and more frequently by William III, and never since the establishment of cabinet government, the last occasion when it was refused being in 1707, when Anne refused the Royal Assent to the Scotch Militia Bill.

PROVISIONS FOR THE PASSAGE INTO LAW OF BILLS REJECTED BY THE HOUSE OF LORDS (PARLIAMENT ACT, 1911) (May, 561)

The Parliament Act provides machinery for overriding the rejection[1] by the Lords both of Money Bills (as defined by it) and other Bills. The provisions in respect of Money Bills are stated in Chapter VIII (p. 287). In the case of 'Other' Bills the main provisions are as follows:—

(1) A Bill rejected by the Lords in three successive sessions (whether of the same Parliament or not) is, provided that two years have elapsed between its second reading in the first session and its passing by the Commons in the third session, presented for Royal Assent, unless the House of Commons directs to the contrary.

---

[1] 'Rejection' means not only failure of the Lords to pass the Bill, but their passing it with Amendments to which the Commons do not agree.

(2) A Bill remains the same Bill as that presented in the first session if it contains only amendments certified by the Speaker to be necessary owing to the lapse of time, or to represent amendments made by the Lords.

(3) The House of Commons may suggest amendments to the Bill in the second or third session, and these, if agreed to by the Lords, are treated as Lords' Amendments and inserted in the Bill.

(4) To obtain the benefits of the Act a Bill must have been sent up to the Lords at least a month before the end of each of the three sessions.

Chapter VII

COMMITTEES

THE origin and development of the Committee system have been described in Chapter I (pp. 25-9).

In this chapter the method of appointing committees and the manner in which they conduct their business will be dealt with.

The various types of committee are:—

The Committee of the Whole House.

The Standing Committee.

The Select Committee.

The Joint Committee (which is a Select Committee of the Commons sitting with a Select Committee of the Lords).

The Private Bill Committee or 'Group' (which together with certain Select Committees appointed to consider business relating to Private Bills, is described in Chapter IX on Private Business).

MODERN COMMITTEE SYSTEM

The course of historical development has given the House of Commons a somewhat varied and complicated system of committees very different from that of purely modern legislatures such as the French Chamber[1] or the American House of Representatives. The basis of the committee system in these chambers is the division of the whole field of legislation into distinct categories and the allocation of a separate category to each Standing Committee. The House of Representatives has some fifty or sixty Standing Committees, each with its separate and special subject. In France these correspond with the provinces of the various departments of state, and their object seems to be the control not only of the legislation, but of the administration, of the departments by the development of bodies of parliamentary experts, who may be helped, in putting Bills into shape and criticizing Estimates, by their continuous experience and specialized knowledge of the work of a department.

[1] Under the constitution of 1875-1940.

Whether such a system, which has the inevitable result of a certain division of responsibility between the Minister and a Parliamentary Committee, is good or bad, its principle is entirely foreign to the House of Commons. Until recent times, for two hundred years the typical House of Commons Committee has been the Committee of the Whole House. In setting up Standing Committees its object has been almost solely to relieve its burdens by a division of labour, and it has aimed at making them miniature Committees of the Whole House, with a shifting rather than a permanent personnel, who are not likely to develop a specialist point of view, but rather to judge the matters that come before them much as the House itself would. The one exception—the Scottish Standing Committee —is a concession to an altogether different principle, which is not capable of being generally applied.

In its third type of committee—the Select Committee—the House has an instrument, not for relieving itself of work which, could it but find the time, it might do equally well itself, but for performing work for which it is unsuited. Careful and detailed inquiry, the examination and weighing of evidence, especially in matters which, though of public, are of little political, interest, are functions which a numerous assembly has neither the capacity nor the inclination to perform. In these matters Select Committees of one of the Houses, and particularly of the House of Commons, were for long the only bodies which could be entrusted with the necessary powers to conduct inquiries, and they have a long record of valuable service. Such duties they will no doubt continue to perform, but their scope has been to a certain extent restricted by the increasing employment of Royal Commissions and of departmental committees, which have a wider field of choice, especially in matters where technical qualifications are needed, and are not under the disadvantage of having their labours prematurely cut short by a prorogation of Parliament.

COMMITTEES OF THE WHOLE HOUSE

A Committee of the Whole House is the House itself sitting with a Chairman instead of the Speaker in the Chair, and conducting its business in a more informal manner. It is technically regarded as an *ad hoc* body, appointed by the House for the consideration of a particular business, sitting and resuming its sittings by the direction of the House, and ceasing to exist when it has completed its business. Each Committee of the Whole House is treated as a separate body, distinguished from every other by a title taken from the business it is appointed to consider. Even the Committees of Supply and of Ways and Means which, because of the extent of their subject-matter, continue in existence for the greater part of the session, live, so to speak, from day to day by having a day for their next sitting appointed by the House.[1]

Committees of the Whole House are divided into:—

> Committees on (Public) Bills.
> Committees on Matters, *i.e.* on business, now almost exclusively financial, which is brought before them in the form of motions.

The functions of these committees in dealing with their business are described in the chapters devoted to Public Bills and Finance, respectively. Here only the formal procedure connected with their appointment, rules of debate and reports, need be considered.

APPOINTMENT OF COMMITTEE OF THE WHOLE HOUSE

The normal method of appointing a Committee of the Whole House on a *matter* is by a resolution that the House will on a future day resolve itself into committee to consider a particular matter. The committee designated by a short title taken from its subject-matter becomes an Order for the day specified.

The Committee of Supply and the Committee of Ways and Means are set up according to this method.

A 'Money' Committee (see p. 274) is either set up by an Order of the House for a future day, or entered upon immediately without an Order in the manner authorized by S.O. No. 84 (see p. 276).

A Committee of the Whole House on a *Bill* is appointed:—

(*a*) in the case of Bills for imposing taxes or Consolidated Fund Bills, by the automatic committal of the Bill immediately after it has been read a second time under S.O. No. 38 (see p. 209).

(*b*) in the case of other Bills, by an Order made immediately after second reading, that the Bill be committed to a Committee of the Whole House for a future day, or that the House will immediately resolve itself into a committee on the Bill.

[1] These committees are now appointed for the duration of the session. (See App. IV.)

PROCEDURE ON GOING INTO COMMITTEE OF THE WHOLE HOUSE

When the Order of the Day is read for a Committee of the Whole House, the Speaker immediately leaves the Chair without question put, and the House thereupon resolves itself into committee (S.Os. Nos. 17 and 42).

This is the normal procedure, but there are exceptions:—

(1) for a committee on a Bill (May, 569).—On *first going* into committee on a Bill, if an instruction, which stands on the Paper and is in order, is moved, it must be disposed of before the Speaker leaves the Chair (see S.O. No. 42).

(2) for the Committee of Supply (see S.O. No. 17);

As soon as the Speaker leaves the Chair the Serjeant places the mace under the Table, and the Chairman of the committee takes the chair which is ordinarily occupied by the Clerk of the House.

CHAIRMAN OF A COMMITTEE OF THE WHOLE HOUSE

The Chairman of Ways and Means and the Deputy Chairman ordinarily in turn take the chair of a Committee of the Whole House.

In their absence the chair is ordinarily taken by one of the Temporary Chairmen (see p. 240), or by some other Member at the request of the Chairman of Ways and Means or the Deputy Chairman, or on the suggestion of the Government.

The chairman of a Committee of the Whole House has a casting vote only, *i.e.* only votes when the voices are equal as in the House itself and in any committee, except a Private Bill 'Group' (see p. 298).

The powers of a chairman of a Committee of the Whole House are similar to those of the Speaker in the Chair of the House. He exercises the powers under S.O. No. 20 (irrelevance or repetition), and S.O. No. 34 (division unnecessarily claimed). The powers under S.O. No. 29 (closure of debate) and S.O. No. 31 (selection of amendments) can only be exercised by the Chairman of Ways and Means and the Deputy Chairman, not by temporary chairmen. There is no appeal from a chairman to the Speaker, or from one chairman to another.

PROCEDURE IN COMMITTEE OF THE WHOLE HOUSE

The rules governing procedure in debate are those which apply when the Speaker is in the Chair, except that

(1) Members may speak more than once to the same Question.

This right is adapted to the thorough discussion of detail, but in practice it is sparingly employed unless for the purpose of obstruction.

(2) A motion does not require a seconder.

(3) A motion for the Previous Question is out of order.

For the procedure in dealing with disorderly conduct in committee, see p. 197.

For interruption by Black Rod with a message to attend in the House of Lords, see App. I, p. 322.

For complaint made of breach of privilege in committee, see p. 73.

Motions in Committee of the Whole House

A motion containing several distinct propositions cannot be required to be divided in committee (May, 572). Resolutions, of which notice has been given, may be moved in any order that the mover chooses. Once a motion has been proposed, it must be proceeded with until progress is reported unless it is agreed to, with or without amendment, negatived or withdrawn.

With regard to amendments the rules are dictated by the subject-matter and vary for the different types of committee (see under 'Public Bills', 'Financial Business', etc.).

REPORT OF PROGRESS AND REPORT ON COMPLETION OF BUSINESS
In Committee.

A Committee of the Whole House has no power to decide when to sit again, but must await the direction of the House.

(1) If it has not completed its business, it reports progress. This may occur—

(*a*) through the interruption of business at 11[1] or 4 o'clock (see p. 132). In that case the Chairman leaves the chair without question put;

(*b*) through the committee agreeing to a motion that the Chairman do report progress and ask leave to sit again. (If the committee agrees to a motion that the Chairman do leave the chair, no report is made and the Order for the committee becomes a 'dropped'

[1] For altered hours, see Appendix IV.

Order. For the use of these motions as 'dilatory' motions, see p. 172.)

(2) When a committee has concluded its business, the Chairman puts a question for reporting to the House and leaves the chair on this question being agreed to (S.O. No. 18).

In the House.

As soon as the Chairman has left his chair the mace is put upon the Table and the Speaker resumes the Chair of the House. The Chairman then approaches the Speaker and makes his report, using one of the following formulæ:—

(1) If the business of the committee is not completed, he reports "that the committee have made progress in the matter referred to them and ask leave to sit again". Whereupon the Member in charge of the business, on being referred to by the Speaker, names a day for the next sitting of the committee, and this is treated as an Order of the House for the committee to sit again that day.

(2) If the business of the committee (*e.g.* resolutions) is completed, the Chairman reports "that the committee have come to certain resolutions". Whereupon the Member in charge names a day for receiving the Report of the resolutions.

(3) If the committee has agreed to certain resolutions and is in progress on another, the Chairman reports "that the committee have come to certain resolutions and that they also report progress and ask leave to sit again".

PROCEDURE ON CONSIDERATION OF REPORT OF RESOLUTIONS

On the Order of the Day being read for the consideration of the Report of a Committee of the Whole House, the House proceeds to take it into consideration without any question being put (S.O. No. 18). The old procedure on consideration of Report has been considerably shortened by modern practice. The question for the first reading has been dropped. Each resolution is considered in turn. The reading by the Clerk of the House of a resolution is taken to be the second reading. Unless a motion is made to postpone the resolution, the question put is: "That this House doth agree with the committee in the said resolution." Amendments may be moved in the interval between the second reading of a resolution and the proposing of this question, but not after it has been proposed. A motion for the recommittal of the resolution must also, if moved, be moved in this interval. Upon the question for agreement a debate may take place on the merits of the resolution.

STANDING COMMITTEES

The function of a Standing Committee is to consider and amend Public Bills. It is true that S.O. No. 57 permits the reference to a Standing Committee of 'other business' as well as Bills, and that in 1919 the experiment was tried of referring to a Standing Committee certain portions of the Estimates. But this experiment is not likely to be repeated[1].

The rules governing the committal of Bills to a Standing Committee are laid down by S.O. No. 38. They make the committal to a Standing Committee automatic in the case of all Bills with the exceptions there specified (see p. 209). In practice, Standing Committees do not receive Bills of first-class constitutional importance, nor, on the other hand, small non-contentious Bills, which are generally found to pass more expeditiously through Committee of the Whole House by agreement. These classes of Bills are generally removed from the Standing Committees, to which they would otherwise automatically go, by an Order made in pursuance of S.O. No. 38.

Which Bill shall go to which Standing Committee is a question that is decided by the Speaker (S.O. No. 57 (2)). In distributing Bills the Speaker is bound by the terms of S.O. No. 59 to send all Public Bills relating exclusively to Scotland which are committed to a Standing Committee to the Scottish Standing Committee, and is guided by the fact that on one of the Standing Committees Private Members' Bills have precedence over those of the Government. He may also transfer Bills from one Standing Committee to another. As soon as possible after the committal or transference of a Bill notification is given in *Votes and Proceedings* of the committee to which it is allotted or transferred.

APPOINTMENT AND CONSTITUTION OF STANDING COMMITTEES
(S.Os. Nos. 57, 58 AND 59)

Under S.O. No. 57 not more than five Standing Committees are appointed. They are nominated by the Committee of Selection (see p. 317) and, except the Standing Committee on Scottish Bills, have no names but are distinguished by letters of

[1] See, however, S.O. No. 61 ; see also Appendix IV.

the alphabet. By a sessional order of 1945–46[1], based on the recommendations of the Select Committee on Procedure (H.C. 9 (1945–46)) the number of Standing Committees which may be appointed is unlimited.

Constitution of the Scottish Standing Committee
(S.O. No. 59)

This Standing Committee consists of all the Members sitting for Scottish constituencies, together with not less than ten nor more than fifteen other members nominated in respect of a particular Bill by the Committee of Selection, who, in doing so, are directed "to have regard to the approximation of the balance of parties in the committee to that in the whole House".[2]

Constitution of the Other Standing Committees (S.O. No. 58)

These Standing Committees consist of not less than thirty nor more than fifty[3] Members nominated by the Committee of Selection, who are directed in doing so to have regard to "the composition of the House". When a Bill relating exclusively to Wales and Monmouthshire is committed to a Standing Committee, the committee must be so constituted as to comprise all Members sitting for constituencies in Wales and Monmouthshire. In respect of a particular Bill the Committee have power to nominate not less than ten nor more than thirty-five[3] additional Members to serve on the committee during the consideration of the Bill. The Committee are enjoined in adding these Members to "have regard to their qualifications".

To take a typical example showing how Standing Committees are in practice appointed and nominated. In 1928 two Bills—the Stabilization of Easter Bill and the Slaughter of Animals (Scotland) Bill, both Private Members' Bills—were read on Friday, 17th February. On the following Monday the Speaker's notification appeared in *Votes and Proceedings*, allotting the former Bill to Standing Committee A, and declaring that the latter Bill, being a Bill relating exclusively to Scotland, would be considered by the Standing Committee on Scottish Bills. The next day the Committee of Selection reported to the House the names of the Members nominated to serve on Standing Committees A and B and on the Scottish Standing Committee respectively, also that Standing Committee A had

---

[1] Now a standing order ; see Appendix IV.

[2] For additional powers conferred on this Committee, see Appendix IV.

[3] These numbers are now altered ; see Appendix IV.

R

been nominated as the committee on which Government Bills should *not* have precedence.

All Standing Committees thus consist of a large permanent nucleus together with additional Members who vary with each Bill. In the case of the Scottish Standing Committee the addition of Members is obligatory; in that of the other Standing Committees it is optional, but regularly effected. From 1919 to 1926 a committee when at work on a Bill consisted of not less than fifty and not more than seventy-five members. After 1926 it consisted of not less than forty and not more than eighty-five members. The Scottish Standing Committee remains not less than eighty-four and not more than eighty-nine members. Under a sessional order of 15th November, 1945,[1] modifying in several respects the standing order relating to numbers of Members, each ordinary Standing Committee consists of twenty permanent Members, with up to thirty additional Members.

The duties of the Committee of Selection in making up the lists of the Standing Committees are delicate. In addition to maintaining in each Standing Committee roughly the same balance of party strength as exists in the House, they have to provide for the due representation of different parts of the country, of rural and industrial areas, etc., and have also, without unduly disturbing this balance, to find places for numbers of specially qualified Members when a new Bill is to be taken into consideration. The Committee of Selection also under S.O. No. 58 discharge Members from a Standing Committee for non-attendance or at their own request and nominate other Members in substitution. In this function they have laid down the rule not to entertain applications for changes in the composition of a committee in respect of a Bill upon which consideration has been begun.

CHAIRMEN OF STANDING COMMITTEES (S.O. No. 62)

The Chairman of a Standing Committee is appointed by Mr. Speaker from a body called the Chairmen's Panel whose members act as temporary chairmen of committees of the Whole House (see p. 235). The Chairmen's Panel consists of not less than ten members who are nominated by Mr. Speaker. The Chairman of Ways and Means and the Deputy Chairman are ex-officio members. This body settles points of procedure affecting the powers, etc., of chairmen which are not covered by Standing Orders and reports its resolutions to the House from time to time.

[1] Now a Standing Order ; see Appendix IV.

The Standing Order permits the Chairman of a Standing Committee to be changed from time to time, and he is now regularly appointed in respect of one (or occasionally more) specified Bills.

SITTINGS OF STANDING COMMITTEES

The day and hour of the first meeting of a Standing Committee on any Bill is fixed by the Member who has been appointed Chairman of the Committee in respect of the Bill. By the sessional order of 15th November, 1945, it was ordered that after the first meeting, Standing Committees should sit from half-past ten till one; and another order of the same day enabled the House to be adjourned for part of the evening to facilitate the business of Standing Committees[1]. Since 1919 they have been empowered to sit also while the House is sitting and even (on a day when the House has met) after it has adjourned. When a division is called in the House, the Chairman is required by S.O. No. 57 (6) to suspend proceedings long enough to enable members to vote.

The *Quorum* of a Standing Committee is twenty[1], and until that number is present the committee cannot proceed to business (May, 620). It is the duty of the clerk of the committee to call the attention of the Chairman during a sitting to the absence of a quorum, whereupon the Chairman must suspend proceedings until a quorum is present, or adjourn the committee to a future day (S.O. No. 74). In fairness to other Bills waiting on the list of the committee it has been laid down by a resolution of the Chairmen's Panel that where, on two successive sittings on a particular Bill, the committee has to be adjourned by reason of the absence of a quorum within the first twenty minutes of the time for which it was summoned, that Bill shall be placed at the bottom of the committee's list of Bills waiting consideration, and the committee shall be convened to consider the other Bill or Bills.

Strangers are admitted to a Standing Committee subject to the committee's power to order them to withdraw.

PROCEDURE IN A STANDING COMMITTEE

Procedure in a Standing Committee follows the procedure of a Select Committee unless the House otherwise orders (S.O. No. 57), but, except in respect of the method of taking divisions and as regards the necessity of the presence of a

[1] For alterations to these rules, see Appendix IV.

quorum, procedure has become assimilated as far as possible to that of a Committee of the Whole House. The Chairman of a Standing Committee has powers (not possessed by the Chairman of a Select Committee) in respect of

(*a*) accepting a motion for the closure (with the substitution of 20 for 100 as the number necessary to make the majority for the closure effective).

(*b*) S.O. No. 20 (irrelevance or repetition).

(*c*) S.O. No. 26 (dilatory motion in abuse of the rules of the House).

(*d*) S.O. No. 31 (selection of amendments).

Divisions are taken by the clerk calling the roll of members. The doors of the committee room are locked during a division, and (following the rule adopted by the House in 1906) a member may vote without having heard the question, and need not vote though present when it was put. Members, who have voted by inadvertence, have been allowed to alter their vote before the declaration of the numbers, but have been refused permission to do so after the declaration (May, 621).

Amendments to a Bill in Standing Committee may be given notice of in advance at the Table of the House or in the committee, and are printed in a separate amendment paper and circulated with the *Supplement to the Votes* (see p. 88). Any Member, whether of the committee or not, may give notice of an amendment, but of course only a member of the committee may move it.

Minutes of Proceedings, which are drawn up like the proceedings of a Committee of the Whole House, are printed and circulated the day following a sitting. They contain also the names of Members present, and of those voting on each side in a division. A complete set of these Minutes drawn up for each Bill separately, with certain additional matter but without the lists of Members voting, is printed and kept in the Library.

Verbatim reports of Debates are published daily in the case of Government Bills. In the case of Private Members' Bills, though a shorthand note is taken, no report is published unless the Chairman decides that this is demanded by the public interest.

Rules of Debate in a Standing Committee

Debate is conducted with the same forms and under the same limitations (of relevancy, etc.) as in Committee of the Whole House.

A Standing Committee can consider a clause imposing a

charge on the people or upon public funds, provided the proposed charge has been sanctioned by a resolution of a Committee of the Whole House agreed to by the House. A Bill has been at the Speaker's direction recommitted to a Standing Committee in respect of a clause imposing such a charge to which it had agreed without the necessary resolution (see p. 211 and May, 621).

SELECT COMMITTEES

APPOINTMENT AND ORDER OF REFERENCE

Select Committees are appointed for the purpose—

(1) of considering a Bill.—In this case the Bill itself is the order of reference. The Bill undergoes at the hands of the committee a preliminary committee stage. The committee reports the Bill with or without amendment and it is recommitted to a Committee of the Whole House (see p. 221).

(2) of inquiry.—In the motion appointing the committee the terms of reference are stated as the purpose for which the committee is appointed. The Report of the committee is usually in the form of a continuous state-ment, divided into paragraphs numbered consecutively, but may take the form of a series of resolutions. The order of reference also gives certain powers—in the case of a sessional committee or one whose inquiry is likely to be long, the power to report from time to time—also the power to send for persons, papers and records, etc.

The scope of a Select Committee is confined within the order of reference, which may be extended by a 'permissive' or limited by a 'mandatory' instruction (see p. 213).

NOMINATION

A Select Committee is generally nominated at the same time as it is appointed, but it may be nominated later. Members are generally nominated by the House itself except in the case of committees on Hybrid Bills (see p. 206), the small com-mittees on Private Bills called 'Groups' (see p. 298), and certain committees (see p. 318), which consider Private Bills. Other methods have been adopted; even the ballot has been resorted to in former times (see May, 578).

There is a special procedure for the nomination of a Select Committee whereby a motion may be put down at the commencement of Public Business, on Tuesdays and Wednesdays by a Private Member, and on Mondays and Thursdays as well by the Government, under S.O. No. 12, with the same limitation of debate to a short speech for and against as in the case of a motion for leave to introduce a Public Bill (see p. 161). The motion for nomination may be combined with a motion to empower the committee to send for persons, papers and records and to fix the quorum. Opposition must be confined to the rejection of an individual name, and the substitution of other Members cannot be proposed.

Notice is required by S.O. No. 67 to be given of the names of persons whom it is proposed to nominate to serve on a Select Committee. In the case of a committee on a matter of privilege notice is held not to be needed, and this practice is similarly followed in the case of a committee to draw up reasons for disagreeing to Lords' amendments (see p. 227) (May, 577). By S.O. No. 67 a Member is required to ascertain in advance whether the Members he proposes to nominate for a Select Committee will be willing to give their attendance on the committee.

Numbers.—A Select Committee may not, without leave of the House, consist of more than fifteen members (S.O. No. 66).

SPECIAL POWERS OF A SELECT COMMITTEE

The House in appointing a committee gives it certain special powers if they are necessary for the conduct of the inquiry. These are:—

(1) *The power to send for persons.*—Witnesses before a Select Committee are summoned by an order signed by the Chairman, and must bring all documents required. If a witness refuses to attend or to give evidence, he is reported to the House and treated as guilty of contempt and liable to the punishment attached to a breach of the privileges of the House (see p. 73). A person in prison, whose evidence is required, can be brought in custody upon the Speaker's warrant issued in pursuance of an order of the House. Witnesses may be examined on oath under the Parliamentary Witnesses Oaths Act, 1871, which attaches penalties for perjury. They are protected in respect of the evidence they give by the privileges

of the House and by the provisions of the Witnesses (Public Inquiries) Protection Act, 1892.

(2) *Power to send for papers and records.*—This power is usually given in conjunction with the power to send for persons, and is exercised in the same way. It has, however, been given alone (May, 588, n.). In exercising this power the committee is limited to such papers as the House itself could order as a Return. Any paper which would require to be 'addressed for' by the House (see p. 92), the Chairman may obtain by moving an address in the House or by communicating with the Secretary of State, who will, if he thinks proper, present it to the House as a 'Command' paper (see p. 93).

(3) Power has also been given to a Select Committee to appoint one or more sub-committees and divide its work with them, and also to appoint persons from outside to serve on such sub-committees or to confer with, or take into consultation, persons outside its own body.

SITTINGS

A Select Committee has full control over the day and hour of its sittings except that it cannot without special leave from the House sit on a day which falls after the House has adjourned. On a day on which the House has sat it can sit after the House has adjourned.

Strangers are generally permitted to attend a sitting, though they may be ordered to withdraw at any time, and are invariably excluded while the committee deliberate. The position of Members of the House, not members of the committee, is uncertain. In practice they are excluded like other strangers, but if they claimed to attend as of right it appears that the committee have not power to exclude them except by the awkward process of applying for an order of the House. Secret committees have been appointed from which all persons, not members of the committee, are excluded.

When a committee adjourns, the date of the next sitting should be fixed by the committee itself, unless by general agreement the date is left to be afterwards fixed by the Chairman.

Committees are sometimes given power, for the purpose of holding local investigations, of sitting outside the precincts of the House.

PROCEEDINGS

Proceedings in a Select Committee on a Bill are assimilated to those of a Committee of the Whole House (May, 582). But powers under S.Os. Nos. 31 (Selection of Amendments), 29 and 30 (Closure), 20 (Irrelevance or Repetition) and 26 (Dilatory Motions) are not exercised in a Select Committee.

The first business of a Select Committee is to choose its chairman. This is often arranged beforehand, some member having been designated for the post, and another member (generally the senior in parliamentary standing on the committee) being chosen to propose him. If a contest should arise, the procedure adopted is that employed in the House for the election of the Speaker.

Divisions are taken as has already been described in the case of a Standing Committee (see p. 242). The Chairman only votes when the voices are equal.

Counsel may by special leave of the House be heard in cases where the private interests, conduct, etc., of persons are concerned. Leave to hear counsel is granted on a special report from the committee, or simply on motion in the House.

An oath is administered to witnesses in inquiries of a judicial or special nature. The oath is administered by the Chairman or, more usually, by the clerk to the committee (S.O. No. 101).

A committee cannot proceed without a quorum, and it is the duty of the committee clerk to call the attention of the Chairman to the absence of a quorum, and the duty of the Chairman to suspend proceedings until a quorum is present or to adjourn the committee (S.O. No. 74). The figure at which the quorum is fixed is specified in the order of appointment of the committee, and depends upon the size of the committee, five being the usual figure for a committee of fifteen or upwards. The quorum is sometimes reduced near the end of a session. Where no figure is specified, all members are required to attend (May, 585).

Minutes of evidence.—The evidence of the witnesses examined is taken down in shorthand and printed daily by direction of the House for the use of the committee. A printed copy of his evidence is sent to each witness for revision and return within six days, after which period, if not returned, it is printed in its original form. The limits within which corrections may be made are narrow. Any correction of substance should be made only on re-examination (May, 596). Parties are occasionally permitted to print evidence for their own use from the committee clerk's copy day by day. The publication of any portion of the evidence, of any document presented to the committee, or of the report of the committee, before they are reported to the House, is a breach of privilege (see p. 72). No document received by the clerk of a select committee may be withdrawn or altered without the knowledge and approval of the committee (S.O. No. 69).

Record of Proceedings of Committee

S.Os. Nos. 70 to 73 lay down certain rules, which it is the duty of the Committee clerk to observe in printing the minutes of evidence and proceedings:—

(1) that the name of every member asking a question of a witness under examination must be prefixed to the question;

(2) that the minutes of every sitting must contain the names of members present, and every question divided upon, with the names of the proposer and of members for and against.

Procedure as to Drafting Report

The preparation of a draft report for the consideration of the committee is usually left to the Chairman. It is, however, open to any member of the committee to submit a draft report for consideration and if more than one draft is submitted, the first step is to decide which draft shall be taken into consideration. This is determined on a motion "That the draft report proposed by Mr. A be read a second time paragraph by paragraph", to which an amendment may be moved to leave out "Mr. A" and insert "Mr. B". When it has been decided which draft shall be taken into consideration, the several paragraphs of the draft selected are considered *seriatim*, each paragraph being open to amendment. Paragraphs may be omitted, and new paragraphs may be inserted in the body of the draft or at the end. When the consideration of the draft in detail is finished, the Committee decide whether the draft report, as amended, shall be the report of the committee to the House.

In some cases, instead of a draft report, draft resolutions are submitted for consideration. In this event, the procedure resembles that of a Committee of the Whole House considering resolutions, each proposed resolution being moved as a substantive motion and being open to amendment. If more than one series of resolutions are submitted for consideration, the Committee first decide which set shall be taken into consideration. When the various proposed resolutions have been disposed of, the Chairman is ordered to report the resolutions which have been adopted to the House.

Procedure in Select Committee on a Bill

When the evidence, if any, is concluded, a Select Committee proceeds to consider a Bill according to the same procedure as a Committee of the Whole House. In doing so it has the benefit of the extension of powers given by S.O. No. 40 and of any permissive instruction that may have been given specially to itself. On the other hand, it has to conform to any mandatory instruction so given. The rules of order respecting amendments, etc., are those which govern proceedings in Committee of the Whole House (see p. 216). A Select Committee can consider a money clause, if duly sanctioned by a Resolution.

Presentation of Report

The report of a Select Committee, together with minutes of evidence and an appendix containing documents material to the report, is presented to the House at the conclusion of its labours. The report, being the decision of the *Committee*, may not be accompanied by any "minority report" or memorandum of dissent. A draft report which has been submitted to a committee, but has not been entertained by them, is, however, entered on the minutes of the proceedings of the committee. In the case of a Select Committee on a Bill, the Bill, or the Bill as amended, as the case may be, is the report of the committee.

Besides the report properly so called relating to the subject-matter referred to the committee it is frequently necessary for a committee to make what is termed a 'special' report in reference to some matter incidentally arising relating to the powers, functions or proceedings of the committee. Leave must be obtained to make such a report, unless the committee have power to send for persons, papers and records.

If a committee makes a report to the House its sittings are assumed to have been closed unless it has received power to report from time to time. Where the subject of inquiry is of such a nature that it requires to be, or admits of being, reported upon in parts, the power to report from time to time or to report evidence only is given on appointment or subsequently by the House.

When a committee finds that it has not time to complete its inquiry before the end of the session, it makes a special report to that effect, and usually recommends the reappointment of the committee in the following session. When the committee is reappointed the evidence taken by it in the previous session is formally referred to it by the House.

No formal consideration of the report of a Committee of Inquiry as a rule takes place in the House, the report being merely ordered to 'lie upon the Table'. If necessary, however, a day is appointed for its consideration, and motions may be made, expressing the agreement or disagreement of the House with the report, or founded upon or giving effect to its recommendations.

A Bill reported from a Select Committee is by the practice of the House recommitted to a Committee of the Whole House.

JOINT COMMITTEES

Instances of Joint Committees are recorded in the 17th century, but none is to be found between 1695 and 1864, when the modern use of this method of inquiry began. They are now used regularly on matters, of equal concern to both Houses, which do not raise political issues, such as the revision of certain branches of the law, and such, in particular, as Private Bills which incidentally involve the settlement of some important matter of principle. The first modern Joint Committee—that of 1864—was on the Bills for the London underground railway system.

Joint Committees are constituted as a small Select Committee of each House sitting together. The old rule, which applied to all joint meetings of the two Houses, that the representatives of the Commons should be double those of the Lords, was not applied to Joint Committees when revived in 1864, and they consist of an equal number from each House.

Appointment, etc., of a Joint Committee

The appointment of a Joint Committee proceeds by stages, the House in which the idea originates awaiting the agreement of the other House to each step before it takes the next. These stages may be set out as follows, the originating House being referred to as the first House:—

1. The first House resolves that it is expedient that a committee of both Houses be set up to consider a particular matter, or that a certain Bill or Bills be committed to a committee of both Houses, and sends a message to the other House to that effect. The second House, if it agrees, returns a message of concurrence.

2. The first House thereupon appoints and nominates a Select Committee of a specified number to join with a Select Committee to be appointed by the other House, gives the committee the powers (to send for persons, papers, etc.) that may be required, and sends a message to the second House to that effect requesting it to appoint an equal number of members to join with the committee appointed by the first House. The second House then appoints and nominates its committee, with similar powers, and sends a message that it has done so.

3. The House of Lords (this is the custom, in whichever House the Joint Committee originated) then sends a message to the House of Commons proposing the time and place of meeting of the Joint Committee, and the Commons direct their Committee to meet the Lords' Committee accordingly.

Procedure in a Joint Committee

The Chairman of a Joint Committee is generally a Peer, and the procedure follows that of a Select Committee of the Lords where it differs from that of the Commons. For example, an equality of votes is not decided by the casting vote of the Chair (who, as a Lords' chairman, votes like other members), but is deemed equivalent to a negative vote. Instructions may be moved, but a mandatory instruction cannot be given to a Joint Committee without the concurrence of both Houses.

Report of Joint Committee

The Report is presented to both Houses, by the Chairman to the House to which he belongs, and to the other House by a member deputed by the committee. A Bill is reported to the House in which it originated, and if the Bill originated in the Lords a Commons member of the committee is ordered to report to his House that the Bill has been reported to the Lords.

This latter formality is, however, dispensed with where the Committee, in addition to reporting the Bill, make a Report upon the subject-matter of the Bill. If the Bill is a Commons' Bill, it is recommitted on report to a Committee of the Whole House. If it is a Lords' Bill, when it reaches the Commons it is, after second reading, as a rule committed to a Committee of the Whole House. If the Joint Committee decide against a Bill, they make a special report to both Houses to that effect and report the Bill, without amendment, to the House in which it originated.

SESSIONAL COMMITTEES

A certain number of Select Committees are set up every year at the beginning of the session, either pursuant to Standing Order or by a special Order of the House regularly repeated, for the purpose of supervising certain branches of business. They are called 'Sessional Committees'. The functions of most of these committees are described elsewhere in this book, but it may be convenient here to give a list of them, showing the way in which they are constituted and referring to the passages in other chapters where they are more fully treated.

The committees constituted pursuant to Standing Order are:—

1. *The Public Accounts Committee*, which is nominated by the House under S.O. No. 90 for the examination of the Appropriation Accounts, and consists of fifteen members (see p. 279).

2. *The Committee of Selection*, consisting of eleven members and appointed by the House under S.O. 109. It nominates the Standing Committees and a number of committees for Private Bills, and performs a variety of functions in connexion with private business (see pp. 238, 317).

3. *The Standing Orders Committee*, consisting of the Chairman of Ways and Means, the Deputy Chairman and not less than two members from time to time selected by the Chairman of Ways and Means from a panel appointed by the Committee of Selection (S.O. 103) (see p. 315).

4. *The Committee on Unopposed Bills* (S.O. 132) (see p. 318).

The committees appointed by order of the House are:—

5. *The Estimates Committee*, consisting of thirty-six members, appointed for the examination of the Estimates and the suggestion of economies consistent with their policy. It is

given power to divide itself into two or more sub-committees each having the powers of the undivided committee (see p. 280).

6. *The Committee of Privileges*, now usually consisting of ten members, appointed to inquire into complaints of breach of privilege (see p. 72).

7. *The Public Petitions Committee*, consisting of fifteen members (see p. 143).

8. *The Publications and Debates Reports Committee*, consisting of eleven members, appointed to assist Mr. Speaker in arrangements for the reporting and publishing of Debates, for the form of the Notice Papers, and to inquire into the expenditure on stationery and printing for this House and for the public services generally.

9. *The Kitchen and Refreshment Rooms* (*House of Commons*) *Committee*, consisting of seventeen members appointed by the House "to control the arrangements for the kitchen and refreshment rooms".

10. *The Statutory Instruments Committee*, consisting of eleven members, to consider departmental rules and orders on which proceedings may be taken under any Act (see p. 327).

11. *The Joint Committee on Consolidation Bills*, consisting of twelve members, six from each House, appointed "to consider all Consolidation Bills in the present Session".

CHAPTER VIII

FINANCE IN THE HOUSE OF COMMONS

THE FINANCIAL SYSTEM[1]

THE English financial system depends, in principle, on a division of functions between the Crown and the House of Commons, whereby, while ultimate control is left to the House of Commons, the initiation of policy and the management of details remain with the Crown, acting through its Ministers in the House and through the Treasury outside. In effect, the House of Commons directly, or through the Treasury, controls the modern financial system, and it does so according to principles whose roots lie far back in history. But while the influence of the past is strongly reflected in the procedure of the House, the powers of the Treasury do not come to it directly from their origin in the prerogative, but through Parliament. It has been modernized into the instrument through which the House controls the infinitely vast and infinitely minute machinery of national finance.

In order to explain the mode in which the House of Commons exercises control over the financial system it will be well to state what that system is, at any rate in outline. It is a simple enough system in its conception, but it has a complicated appearance owing to its vast scale, and to the fact that it has had to make more than one compromise with practical convenience.

The most convenient point of departure for a short description of the modern system is the Consolidated Fund. The Consolidated Fund—the reservoir into which all revenue flows and from which all expenditure issues[2]—is now represented by the account kept by the Government at the Bank of England, which is generally called the 'Exchequer Account', or simply the 'Exchequer'. Issues from the Exchequer are made on

---

[1] Reference should be made to Hilton Young, *System of National Finance*, and J. W. Hills and E. A. Fellowes, *Finance of Government*.

[2] With certain labour-saving exceptions (see p. 255).

the authority of Parliament, mainly by the passing of a Consolidated Fund Act. The Treasury, under the control of the House of Commons, and checked by an independent officer, the Comptroller and Auditor-General, responsible to Parliament, makes the actual issues from the Consolidated Fund—a process which, in the case of 'Supply services' (see below), consists in transferring sums from time to time from the Exchequer Account at the Bank of England to the accounts of the various departments with the Paymaster-General, whose department is the Government's cashier. An issue from the Consolidated Fund in respect of such services is thus not a final expenditure, but only the placing of money at the disposal of the departments. Issues are, however, made to approximate as closely as possible to actual expenditure by economy of balances in the hands of the Paymaster-General and the departments, and at the end of the year a very close approximation is effected.

The expenditure of the departments is based on Estimates, prepared by themselves six months or so before the beginning of the financial year, scrutinized by the Treasury, passed by the Cabinet, and presented to the House of Commons—a process which takes four or five months. To these Estimates, which are divided into separate compartments called 'Votes',[1] the actual expenditure is required to conform, Vote by Vote. Money grants are 'appropriated', or applied to each Vote, by statute. Accounts of expenditure have to be kept in the same form as the Estimates. Finally the accounts are audited by the Comptroller and Auditor-General, and his Report is reviewed by the Public Accounts Committee, which in its turn reports to the House of Commons.

The financial year, running from the 1st April to the 31st March,[2] is a closed period. The departments are not allowed to carry over any surplus, due to underspending their Estimates, from one year to another. The Finance Accounts, which are made up immediately after the close of the financial year, are based on payments into, and issues out of, the Exchequer. The Appropriation Accounts, the audit of which is not completed until six months or so after the close of the financial year, are more detailed and record final payments, *i.e.* payments made by the departments to the creditors of the Government.

[1] A Vote of the Civil Estimates covers a complete service—generally the cost of a department, though a large department with miscellaneous duties, like the Home Office, administers several Votes.

[2] At 3 p.m. on each date.

They do not, therefore, agree exactly with the Finance Accounts, but, as stated above, care is taken to see that the difference is as small as possible.

In addition to the expenditure of the public departments, which is voted each year by the House of Commons, and is called expenditure on 'Supply services', there is a considerable amount of expenditure made under the authority of permanent statutes—the charges on account of the National Debt, the Civil List, the Road Fund, etc. These are known as 'Consolidated Fund services', and do not come up for annual review by Parliament.

Revenue consists mainly of the produce of taxation, and to a smaller extent of other receipts, such as the profits of the Post Office, the revenue of Crown lands, repayments in respect of loans to foreign countries, etc. All these receipts are, with minor exceptions made for the sake of practical convenience, paid into the Consolidated Fund. For instance, the great Revenue departments are allowed to deduct from the sums which they transmit daily to the Bank of England the amount needed for their own expenses subject to subsequent adjustment, and most of the spending departments, which receive payments from the public or other departments in the course of their duties, are allowed to retain such payments as appropriations 'in aid' of their votes, the net amount only of which is voted by the House—or, rather, they retain the estimated amount of such payments and surrender the surplus to the Exchequer. Revenue does not, of course, accumulate to any large extent in the Exchequer. In the first place it would be contrary to national economy to abstract large sums from circulation and leave them lying idle for a period. But, as a matter of fact, the rate at which charges mature is normally more rapid than the rate at which the produce of taxation grows. The Consolidated Fund is emptied more quickly than it is filled, and for the greater part of the year it could not meet the calls made upon it but for the borrowing powers given by statute to the Treasury.

METHOD OF CONTROL BY THE HOUSE OF COMMONS

The way in which the House proceeds in controlling this system is the subject of the following pages. It may be worth while to run over it in outline before beginning to deal with it in detail.

The House works on material provided from outside. It

S

votes expenditure on the Estimates, and adjusts the variable margin of taxation—most of which is permanent—so that the estimated expenditure is covered by the estimated revenue. Expenditure and revenue for the current year are brought into a focus in the Chancellor of the Exchequer's budget statement, which deals also with the realized results of the previous year. Upon this material the House sets to work and continues at work for the first four or five months of the year for which it is providing. In theory it ought to have made provision in advance, but in practice this has been found to be impossible. It is this unavoidable belatedness which introduces the chief element of complication into the financial procedure of the House.[1] The imposition of taxation can afford to await the convenience of the House, but provision for expenditure cannot be delayed. It is therefore necessary for the House to make two stages of the process of authorizing expenditure—first, an interim authorization by means of a Consolidated Fund Act, and then a final authorization by means of the Appropriation Act.

The principal object in a normal year of the main Consolidated Fund Act, passed just before the financial year begins, is to provide enough money to carry the departments over until the moment when it is safe to calculate that the Appropriation Act will have passed—and that is some time in August. The Act does this by providing a lump sum, not specifically appropriated vote by vote, but still roughly appropriated—for the purposes on which the money it provides may be spent have been fixed by the House in earlier proceedings, and the sum it provides may not be more than the total (is in practice the exact total) of all the sums voted for these purposes. To this restriction on the way in which the money thus provided may be spent there is one exception. The period up to August is a longish period, and it may happen that during its course the House votes expenditure on some fresh service, but will not in the ordinary course provide money for it until August. If it is desirable to start spending on this service at once, and not too much is required, the Treasury exercises power (under the Public Accounts and Charges Act, 1891, s. 2 (1)) to apply for this purpose money granted by the Consolidated Fund Act, which was passed before this service was voted.

[1] A further complication, resulting from the fact that the session overlaps two financial years, is that an Appropriation Act appropriates portions of the expenditure of two financial years, and that the Estimates of the same financial year are partly voted in two sessions.

We now come to the Appropriation Act, but before dealing with it, perhaps it will be worth while to state what the doctrine of 'appropriation' in practice does and does not mean. 'Appropriation' does not mean marking a separate envelope for each supply vote and placing in it the sum allotted to that vote by an Appropriation Act, with a prohibition against taking money out of an envelope for temporary use on some other purpose. It means that money granted shall be so spent that at any time during the financial year, or at the end of the financial year, (1) no money shall have been spent for any purpose in excess of the amount granted for that purpose by an Act, and (2) no money shall have been spent on any purpose which has not already been authorized by a Resolution of the House of Commons.

The Appropriation Act, then—the second stage in the authorization of expenditure—provides (being also a Consolidated Fund Act) the balance of money required for the services so far authorized, and also appropriates the money granted by it and by the previous Consolidated Fund Act or Acts to the Estimates, vote by vote, *i.e.* it schedules all the votes and enacts that not more than the sum specified shall be spent on each. The Appropriation Act is generally passed in August. During the interval of seven months or more which lies between this date and the end of the financial year the same difficulty may be experienced which occurred in the interval between the passing of the Consolidated Fund Act just before the beginning of the financial year and the passing of the Appropriation Act in August. Some further expenditure in this case on Supplementary Estimates may be voted by the House, and no money will in the ordinary course be provided to cover such expenditure until the passing of a new Consolidated Fund Act just before the end of the financial year. This situation frequently arises in the early months of a new session. How are such Supplementary Estimates financed? The method varies according to circumstances. (1) If the service for which such a Supplementary Estimate has been voted falls within the ambit of any existing vote comprised in the Appropriation Act, it may, with the express approval of the Treasury, and on their responsibility, be financed out of ways and means already appropriated, savings, if necessary, being made on other items of the same vote. (2) If it is a fresh service falling outside existing appropriated votes, it must be financed out of the Civil Contingencies Fund—a fund of a limited[1] amount established for the purpose

---

[1] The amount was greatly increased in 1946.

of temporarily financing unforeseen expenditure. (3) If, as occasionally happens, it is voted after the passing of an *ad hoc* Consolidated Fund Act, the same section of the Public Accounts and Charges Act referred to above may be invoked temporarily to finance it. This is done in the expectation that before the end of the financial year the new money required for such Estimates will have been provided by the main Consolidated Fund Act, and also on condition that the immediate expenditure on such Estimates is not inconveniently large. If it is too large, they will require to be financed, when voted, by an *ad hoc* Consolidated Fund Act (see p. 273).

In either case the money granted will wait for its appropriation until the Appropriation Act of the same session, but of the following financial year. For while expenditure is regulated by the financial year, appropriation is enacted by the session. This is the reason why the provision of money to make good Supplementary Estimates voted after, but in the same session as, the Appropriation Act cannot await the passage of the main Consolidated Fund Act at the close of the financial year. They require to be financed and appropriated by a new Appropriation Act.

Apart from the complication introduced by the necessity, due to practical considerations, of having to authorize expenditure in two main stages, the rules of financial procedure in the House of Commons reduce themselves to arrangements for the orderly consideration of financial business and its convenient distribution over the session in relation to other business, and secondly to the application to every step taken of certain constitutional principles, the most important of which are the exclusive right of the Crown to originate every proposal for the expenditure of money or the imposition of taxation, and the exclusive privilege of the Commons to have the discussion of such proposals taken first in their House and conducted according to forms devised by themselves, and finally their conclusions embodied without amendment in Acts of Parliament.

PLAN OF ARRANGEMENT

In Chapter I of this book the stages by which the financial procedure of the House of Commons attained its modern form are traced. The three main groups into which financial business falls—those leading up, respectively, to the Consolidated Fund (No. 1) Bill, the Appropriation Bill and the Finance Bill—have been distinguished in Chapter III (pp. 119–122), where something is also said about the way in which the opportunities they provide for debate are utilized, and about the relative amount of time devoted to them during the session. The plan upon which this chapter is arranged is to divide financial business into two main sections—I. Expenditure, and II. Taxation—to trace the proceedings on the various kinds of financial business, separately, from their origin in one of the Committees of the Whole House to the passing of the Bills in which they are ultimately embodied, and to bring out the part played in financial business by the Crown and the House of Lords.

Principles of Financial Procedure

The main effect on financial procedure of the principles governing the relations between the Crown and Parliament (see pp. 30–6) and the rules by which the House of Commons regulates its own practice (S.Os. Nos. 78 to 85)[1] may be summarized as follows:—

(1) All financial business is originated by the Crown alone. No private Member may make a motion or move an amendment which has the effect of imposing a new 'charge' or increasing an existing or proposed 'charge' whether "upon the Consolidated Fund" (expenditure) or "upon the people" (taxation). A Minister acting on behalf of the Crown initiates the first stage of every financial proposal. But his powers of amendment are as limited as those of any other Member (see p. 277).

(2) A 'charge' may only originate in the House of Commons and in a Committee of the Whole House (of which the most important are the Committee of Supply and the Committee of Ways and Means).

(3) After being voted in a Committee of the Whole House, the Resolution containing a charge requires to be agreed to by the House itself and is then incorporated in a Bill, which, after going through the regular stages of a Bill in the House of Commons, is sent to the House of Lords and submitted for the Royal Assent.

The enforcement of the rule that the Crown alone initiates charges is secured by the requirement of the recommendation of the Crown for such charges. In respect of the ordinary annual expenditure the recommendation of the Crown is implied in the presentation of Estimates and the reference to

[1] These Standing Orders are applied (with certain exceptions) to Private Bills by S.O. No. 86A of 1948.

them included in the King's Speech. In the case of extra-ordinary expenditure (see pp. 275–6) the recommendation is explicitly signified by a Minister before the charge is considered in committee.

The extent to which these principles affect all the details of financial procedure will become apparent in the following pages.

TABLE OF FINANCIAL BUSINESS

The following Table is intended to serve as an outline of the general course of financial business during a typical session by showing for the principal items of financial business the committees in which they originate and the Bills to which they lead up.

SESSION 1937

Committee	Item of Business	Bill
EXPENDITURE		
Committee of Supply	Excess Votes, 1935–6 Supplementary Estimates, 1936–7 Vote on Account for Civil Services, 1937–8 Navy Estimates, 1937–8 (Main Votes) Army Estimates, 1937–8 (Main Votes) Air Estimates, 1937–8 (Main Votes)	Consolidated Fund (No. 1) Bill[1] (which must receive Royal Assent before 31st March).
	Civil Estimates, 1937–8 Navy Estimates, 1937–8 (Remaining Votes) Army Estimates, 1937–8 (Remaining Votes) Air Estimates, 1937–8 (Remaining Votes)	Consolidated Fund (Appropriation) Bill.
Committee of Ways and Means (spending)	Resolutions 'towards making good' Supply grants	Consolidated Fund and Consolidated Fund (Appropriation) Bills.
(Money) Committee of Whole House	Exceptional Grants (not presented as Estimates) Demands made by Message from the Crown Addresses for expenditure Incidental charges in Bills	Special Bills.
REVENUE		
Committee of Ways and Means (taxing)	Taxing, Protective, etc., Resolutions	Finance Bill.
Committee of Whole House[2]	Revenue, and Other than Taxing, Resolutions	Finance Bill or Special Bill.

[1] This Bill issues a lump sum equivalent to the total of the votes against which it is bracketed in this Table, but their final legislative sanction is given by the Consolidated Fund (Appropriation) Bill (see p. 256).

[2] The modern practice is for all Resolutions providing only for money entering the Exchequer to be moved in Committee of Ways and Means.

I. EXPENDITURE

The Committees of Supply and Ways and Means

The consideration of expenditure is mainly the function of the Committees of Supply and of Ways and Means. The latter committee has another function—that of voting taxation, which will be considered later (pp. 280–4). When it is desired to indicate in which of its capacities this body is being referred to in this chapter the word '(spending)' or '(taxing)' is inserted in brackets after 'Committee of Way and Means'. The Committee of Supply and the Committee of Ways and Means are set up together at the beginning of the session, act hand in hand (so to speak) in sanctioning expenditure, and are closed together when all the Supply required has been granted[1]. The real work is done by the Committee of Supply, which considers and votes the Estimates. The function of the Committee of Ways and Means begins when the moment arrives for gathering together the sums voted by the Committee of Supply over a period and for authorizing the issue of a sum to cover them from the Consolidated Fund. The Committee of Ways and Means then votes a resolution issuing out of the Consolidated Fund a lump sum equal to the total of the sums voted to date by the Committee of Supply, and on this resolution, when agreed to by the House, the Consolidated Fund Bill is founded.

This function of the Committee of Ways and Means has been objected to by critics as unnecessary. No doubt it has become a mere formality. It might be defended on the ground that, as the Committee of Ways and Means puts money into the Consolidated Fund by imposing taxation, it is the proper body to take money out of it. But probably the true explanation of this function is that it is a survival from the days, before consolidated funds or finance bills, when the House of Commons tried to secure the application of money to the purposes for which it was voted by ear-marking particular sources of revenue (see pp. 34–5).

A rough sketch of the stages of Supply is as follows. Some of the stages overlap:—

(1) The setting up of the two Committees.

(2) Presentation of Estimates and their reference to the Committee of Supply.

---

[1] They are now appointed for the duration of the session; see Appendix IV.

(3) Voting in Committee of Supply of sums to be expended.
(4) Voting in Committee of Ways and Means of issue of money to meet expenditure so far authorized in Committee of Supply.
(5) Agreement by the House to Report of Committee of Supply and Report of Committee of Ways and Means.
(6) The introduction on the Ways and Means Report of a Consolidated Fund Bill.

THE COMMITTEE OF SUPPLY

The Committee of Supply is 'set up' immediately after the conclusion of the Debate on the Address in answer to the King's Speech by a Resolution in the following form:—

Resolved, That this House will, *To-morrow*, resolve itself into a Committee to consider of the Supply to be granted to His Majesty.

The Committee of Ways and Means is similarly set up at the same time. All Estimates when presented are referred by order of the House to the Committee of Supply.

In order to keep Supply prominently before the attention of the House an old custom prescribed that these Committees must be put down for Mondays, Wednesdays and Fridays. Under S.O. No. 15[1] these Committees may be put down for any day on which the House shall meet for despatch of business, and it is no longer obligatory that they be put down for particular days. They are, however, usually put down for every day on which Government business has precedence, but this is often merely formal. When it is intended to 'take' supply, the order for the Committee of Supply is made 'effective' by giving notice on the *Order Paper* of the Votes which it is intended to take.

SUPPLY BUSINESS

The business of the Committee of Supply is to consider the Estimates and vote them with or without reductions. These are classified as:—

(1) The Ordinary Annual Estimates.
(2) Supplementary Estimates.
(3) Votes on Account.
(4) Excess Estimates.
(5) Votes of Credit.
(6) Exceptional Grants (when presented as Estimates).

[1] Old S.O. No. 15 was repealed on 28th July, 1948, but its effect continues.

1. *The Ordinary Annual Estimates*

The Ordinary Annual Estimates are presented in four[1] parts or divisions corresponding to the four branches of the public service, the Estimates for the revenue departments being counted as part of the Civil Estimates though printed as a separate volume. All Estimates ought, according to the Resolution of the House of the 19th February, 1821, to be presented before the 15th January when the session begins before Christmas, and within ten days after the setting up of Supply when the session begins after Christmas. But in practice the House is satisfied if each of the four main branches of the Estimates are presented a reasonable time in advance of moving the Speaker out of the Chair on that branch of the Estimates (see p. 267). The form in which the Estimates are presented is controlled in practice by the Treasury, but changes of any importance are not made without the approval of the Estimates Committee (see p. 280), a sessional committee of the House of Commons. Each branch of the Estimates is divided into a number of services or 'Votes', so called because the decision of the Committee has to be taken upon each of them separately. In the Civil Estimates these Votes are grouped into nine 'Classes'. Votes are sub-divided into 'Heads' and into 'Items'.

The Navy Estimates, Army Estimates and Air Estimates are composed of a Vote A for men, and a number of Votes for money, sub-divided as above.

Appropriations-in-aid.—Most of the Departments show in their Estimates sums for 'appropriations-in-aid', which are deducted from the gross estimate, the House only being required to vote the net sums. These represent estimates of certain receipts which accrue to most of the Departments in the course of their duties for services rendered to the public, etc. Such sums were, until 1891, paid direct to the Exchequer. Now, to save unnecessary transfers, they may be used by the Departments which receive them, and the Treasury is given power by the Public Accounts and Charges Act, 1891, to appropriate such receipts 'in aid of' the services which produce them (see p. 255). These sums cannot be reduced in Committee of Supply, nor can the policy of such appropriations-in-aid be discussed.

'Token' Votes.—In the case of certain departments the estimated receipts may be greater than the estimated expenditure. When this is the case, in order to preserve control by the House

[1] Now five ; see Appendix IV.

of Commons, the appropriations-in-aid are calculated so as to show a net expenditure of £100, which is submitted as a 'token' Estimate, and the surplus appropriations-in-aid are surrendered to the Exchequer.

'Token' votes may also be submitted in respect of Supplementary Estimates, when an excess over the net estimated expenditure is more than covered by a surplus over the estimated appropriations-in-aid. For such a surplus cannot be appropriated to the vote without sanction by the House. 'Token' Supplementary Estimates are usually drawn to show a demand for £10.

2. *Supplementary Estimates*

(1) The most usual kind of Supplementary Estimates are those presented at the beginning of each session in respect of the Estimates of the previous session. They are, frankly, due to under-estimating and cannot be entirely avoided, as our financial system requires the Estimates to be drawn up five or six months before the commencement of the financial year to which they apply. The money to cover these Supplementaries is normally issued by the Consolidated Fund Bill, which has to be passed before the end of the financial year, and such money is appropriated by the Appropriation Act passed in the same session but in the following financial year (see pp. 257–8).

(2) The other kind of Supplementary Estimate is sometimes called an 'additional' Estimate, and provides money for some new head of expenditure arising in the course of the same financial year. An Estimate for a 'new' service must be submitted for consideration by the Committee of Supply not later than two days before the Committee is closed (S.O. No. 16) This is held in practice to mean no more than that it must be placed upon the Notice Paper within the prescribed period.[1]

3. *Votes on Account*

A Vote on Account is an instalment granted in advance to the Crown on account of the Supply of the coming year in order to bridge the gap which would otherwise exist between the beginning of the financial year and the passing of the Appropriation Act in August. It is a device necessitated by the difficulty of reconciling the principles of our financial system with the fact that the session normally begins only a couple of months or so before the beginning of the financial year. To get the Estimates voted and the Appropriation Act

[1] This provision is now no longer contained in S.O. No. 16.

passed within this period is impracticable. And to allow the Departments to keep money in hand from the previous session for the purpose of tiding over this period would be a breach of the principle that money can only be spent in the financial year for which it is voted.

A Vote on Account is normally required only for the Civil Services and is presented as a demand for a lump sum with the amounts allotted to each Department stated in a Schedule.

The Navy, Army and Air Force do not normally, except at the end of a major war, require a Vote on Account unless the session is interrupted by a dissolution. They have, with the sanction of the Treasury, the power (given each year by a section of the Appropriation Act) to spend money granted for one vote upon any other vote so long as the total sum voted is not exceeded. A few large votes in each of these Estimates—for pay and wages, etc.—provide for their general needs until the passing of the Appropriation Act.

The Civil Vote on Account, together with the above votes for the Navy, Army and Air Force, are given provisional legislative sanction by the Consolidated Fund Bill, which requires to be passed before the beginning of the financial year (see p. 257).

It is not permissible to include in a Vote on Account services which have not previously received the sanction of Parliament.

The sum now generally demanded by a Vote on Account represents expenditure up to the middle of August. In the event of a dissolution before the Estimates have been voted, besides the probable necessity for further Votes on Account— for the Navy, Army and Air Force as well—all sums granted on account must be appropriated to the services for which they have been granted by an Appropriation Act.

4. Excess Votes

The voting of an Excess Grant is the parliamentary method of condoning the offence against the Appropriation Act of overspending an Estimate.

An Excess Vote is needed in the case of:—

(1) the Civil Estimates, when the expenditure on any single Vote has exceeded the Estimate;

(2) the Navy, Army and Air Force, only when their aggregate Estimates have been exceeded, because they are given power by the Appropriation Act to make good deficiencies by the application of surpluses.

An Excess Grant, separately drawn for each branch of the Estimates, is first submitted to the Public Accounts Committee, and after being passed by the Committee of Supply, if possible, in the year succeeding that in which the excess expenditure occurred, is sanctioned by the Appropriation Act.

5. *Votes of Credit*

Money is demanded by a Vote of Credit when, as during war, only an estimate of the total sum can be formulated, not of the details. The rule that money can only be spent for the service of the year for which it was voted applies equally in the case of a Vote of Credit.

6. *Exceptional Grants (when presented as Estimates)*

These are classified by May (684) as:—

(1) grants required to meet the cost of an imperial undertaking which forms no part of the current service of the year—as, *e.g.* the vote for the purchase of the Suez Canal shares;

(2) demands made by a message from the Crown either for the maintenance of the dignity and well-being of the Crown, or for the reward of men who have rendered public service to the Empire.

These are considered in the Committee of Supply when the demand is presented in the form of an Estimate. They may also be made by a Resolution presented with the King's Recommendation to a Committee of the Whole House. In the former case they are included in the Appropriation Act. In the latter case they obtain legislative sanction by being incorporated in a special Act (see p. 275).

ALLOTTED DAYS AND CONCLUSION OF SUPPLY

The procedure of allotting a limited number of days to the business of Supply and providing for its conclusion within the time so allotted is laid down by S.O. No. 16, which requires to be studied in detail.

The main points are:—

(1) Twenty days[1] before 5th August (two Fridays counting as one day) are allotted to the ordinary Estimates (including Votes on Account but excluding Supplementaries, Votes of Credit, etc.). Not more than three

---

[1] Many of the details contained in this section have been radically altered ; see Appendix IV.

additional days may be allotted. On allotted days Supply must be the first Order.

(2) Allotted days are 'spoilt' if business other than Supply or the consideration of the reports of the Committee of Public Accounts and of the Select Committee on Estimates is taken before 11 o'clock,[1] or if the business of Supply is taken after 11 o'clock unless the House otherwise order on the motion of a Minister moved at the commencement of public business. They are not spoilt by private business under S.O. No. 7 or by a motion for the adjournment of the House under S.O. No. 9 being taken at half-past seven[1], or by 'privilege' proceedings (4th March, 1929).

(3) One allotted day for Committee and one for Report may be allotted to a Vote on Account, and arrangements are made for bringing each of those stages to a conclusion at 11 o'clock.

(4) On the last but one of the allotted days the committee stage of Supply is brought to a conclusion, the Vote under consideration being disposed of at 10 o'clock[1], and then the outstanding Votes, not individually but by classes.

(5) On the last allotted day the Report under consideration at 10 o'clock[1], and then in turn all the outstanding Reports, are disposed of similarly. In order to secure precedence for the Resolution which it is desired to discuss, it is customary to take this Vote first in Committee on the last allotted day but one and to pass the Vote without discussion.

The Committee of Supply was usually 'closed'—*i.e.* the House omitted to order it to sit again—as soon as the proceedings on the last allotted day but one were brought to a conclusion. It could then only be reopened on the initiative of the Crown, usually by the presentation of Estimates. It is now usually kept open after the conclusion of the allotted days till the end of the session.

'GETTING THE SPEAKER OUT OF THE CHAIR'[2]

Under S.O. No. 17 opportunity is given for a debate in the House as a preliminary to going into Committee of Supply for the first time on each of the four branches of the Estimates or on a Vote of Credit.

[1] For altered hours, see Appendix IV.

[2] For an extension of this procedure, see Appendix IV.

Such a debate arises on the Question "That Mr. Speaker do now leave the Chair", to which amendments may be moved relating to the branch of the Estimates to be considered, and it has been found convenient to decide precedence among the amendments offered with this intention by a ballot which takes place in the House the day after the Committee of Supply has been set up or on such later date as the House may determine (see p. 158).

Debate on such an amendment is confined to its subject-matter until it is disposed of. Further, it can only be moved by the Member in whose name it stands. If the amendment is negatived, no further amendment may be moved. If it is withdrawn, the amendment next in order of priority may be moved. If it is agreed to, a motion is made that the House will immediately, or on a future day, resolve itself into Committee of Supply, and this is also done if the House has negatived the question for the Speaker leaving the Chair (May, 692).

Procedure in Committee of Supply

The functions of the Committee of Supply have changed gradually from scrutiny of the details of expenditure to criticism of the policy underlying the Estimates. A committee consisting of the whole House is recognized to be too unwieldy a body to attempt to overhaul or reshape the financial structure in which the Government has embodied its policy. The Committee of Supply finds itself confined by hard facts to giving general indications of its attitude. Thus the sum of £100 by which an amendment may seek to reduce a vote or item, concrete as it seems, now only has a symbolical meaning. It does not necessarily mean that those who vote in its favour hold that too much is being spent on such vote or item, whether by that precise amount or not (as often as not the objection is that too little is being spent), but rather that the whole policy of the Government, as revealed by that vote or item, is open to objection. The amendment merely provides a peg for criticism, and if it is to an item, or smaller portion of a vote, it serves the purpose of narrowing discussion to that point.

The rules with regard to amendments in Committee of Supply are framed so as to facilitate a constant whittling down of the Estimates. The Resolutions of the House of 1858 and 1868 (which will be referred to later) seem to contemplate the possibility of a stream of amendments directed to various

portions of a vote, and give rules for deciding in what order
they are to be taken. These would be appropriate for a body
which really performed financial functions. In the Committee
of Supply the technical difficulties for which they provide
now hardly ever arise. Amendments are not moved in un-
manageable numbers. Often a single amendment is sufficient
to record the uncompromising hostility of the Government's
critics throughout a whole debate.

The Votes, of which the Estimates are composed, are (see
p. 263) moved as resolutions in the form "That a sum not
exceeding £—— be granted to His Majesty to defray the
charge (or, when a Vote on Account has already been passed,
'to complete the sum necessary to defray the charge') which
will come in course of payment for the year ending 31st March,
19—" for a specified service.

On one or two occasions a Question has been proposed to
the Committee, not on the vote as a whole, but on the items
composing it separately.

Supplementary Estimates retain the Class and Vote number
of the votes to which they are supplementary.

Notice is always placed on the Paper of the votes which it
is proposed to consider in the Committee of Supply on a
particular day, and of the order in which it is proposed to
consider them. Though set down by the Government, the
selection of votes and their order is made in practice by
the Opposition, and is independent of the order in which the
Estimates were presented, or the order of the Votes in any
Estimate. Supplementary Estimates for the current year may
be taken after Estimates for the coming year.

Amendments in Committee of Supply

The Committee of Supply is confined to the resolutions
which are put down for its consideration. It must take these
in the order in which they are moved and dispose of each
before going on to the next. It may not move the postponement
of a vote, or the increase of the sum to be granted, or the
alteration of the destination of the grant (which would be a
means of initiating expenditure). But it may permit the withdrawal of a resolution after it has been moved by the Minister
in charge.

The form in which the Question is proposed on an amendment to a Supply resolution is quite different from the usual
method of proposing Questions on amendments. Instead of

proposing to leave out words and substitute others, the Question follows the form of the original resolution, but with reduced figures substituted for the original figures. The object of this departure from the normal practice is to leave room for "the proposal, without limit, of amendments in the same form and of ever-varying amount" (May, p. 697). When an amendment to reduce a vote by a certain amount has been negatived and the vote is again under consideration on a subsequent day an amendment to reduce the vote by the same amount as on the earlier day is not out of order (12th and 21st May, 1930).

Amendments, also, that a particular item or head of a vote be reduced, are moved with the object of limiting debate to the subject-matter of that item or head.

Precedence among Amendments.—The Resolutions of the House of 1858 and 1868 lay down rules for the precedence of Amendments. For the reasons stated above a Chairman is not often called upon to apply these rules. Their effect is, briefly, that:—

(1) amendments to items are taken before amendments to a vote as a whole, and when the Question for reducing the vote as a whole has been proposed, it is not in order to move an amendment to an item;

(2) amendments to items are taken in the order in which the items are printed in the Estimates, and when an item has been disposed of it is not permissible to go back to earlier items;

(3) when several amendments are moved to the same figure, priority is given to the amendment proposing the greatest reduction, then to that proposing the next greatest, and so on.

Relevancy.—The general rule requiring relevancy to the matter contained in the Question proposed from the Chair is observed in Committee of Supply, whether that Question is on a vote or an item, or other subdivision of a vote. In the case, however, of the Navy Estimates, Army Estimates and Air Estimates (which, though divided into a number of votes, yet form as a whole a single and definite subject-matter) this rule is relaxed so far as to allow a general discussion of the whole service upon the first vote proposed to the Committee, *i.e.* on the vote for pay and wages or on the vote for numbers of officers and men. After this vote has been disposed of, debate must be confined to each vote as it is moved (May, 699).

In the case of the Civil Estimates no opportunity is provided
for a debate on the service as a whole in Committee of Supply
and debate is regularly restricted to the matter of the vote
proposed from the Chair. When it is desired to discuss as a whole
a service for which provision is made under several cognate
votes, the practice since 1942 is to define the subject to be discussed in a single Resolution and to set out a token sum for
each of the related votes in the form of a schedule thereto.

In the case of Supplementary Estimates and Excess Votes
debate must be confined to the objects of the vote under
consideration (which may often be very narrow) and may not
be extended to the other items included in the Main Estimate
to which this is subsidiary, or to the policy of the Main Estimate.

For other limitations on the range of debate in Committee
of Supply, see May, 703. Speaking generally, debate must
be confined to administrative matters for which the Government is responsible, and should not attempt to deal with
matters requiring legislation.

At the conclusion of each day's proceedings in Committee
of Supply the Chairman reports to the House that resolutions
have been agreed to, or, if none have been agreed to, reports
'progress'. He also asks leave to sit again, as, otherwise, Supply
would become a 'dropped Order' (see p. 165).[1]

PROCEDURE ON REPORT OF SUPPLY

The procedure in the House on Supply Reports (which is
the same as on Reports from the Committee of Ways and
Means[1] and Committees of the Whole House) may be briefly
described. The stages are the following:—

(1) Each resolution is read separately by the Clerk at the
Table. This is the so-called 'Second Reading' (the first
reading having disappeared from practice).

(2) The interval between this reading and the putting of
the Question "That this House doth agree with the
Committee in the said resolution" is the time for moving
amendments. The only amendment in order is a reduction of the grant. It is moved in the usual form, not in
that peculiar to Committee of Supply, *i.e.* it proposes to
leave out the original sum and insert a reduced sum.
The Question proposed thereupon is that the original
sum stand part of the resolution, and, if this is agreed
to, no other amendment is possible.

[1] The effect of this has been altered; see Appendix IV.

T

(3) After any amendment has been disposed of it is in order to move the postponement or recommittal of the resolution. Both these motions are rare but the latter would be necessary if it was desired to restore in whole or in part a reduction made in committee. If they are not moved, or when they are disposed of, the Question is proposed "That this House doth agree with the committee in the resolution". After this Question has been proposed it is too late to move an amendment for reducing the sum, or to postpone or recommit the resolution, and to this Question itself no amendment is movable.

When the Resolution in respect of Vote A for each of the Defence Services has been agreed to the Army and Air Force (Annual) Bill is ordered to be brought in.

COMMITTEE OF WAYS AND MEANS (SPENDING)

As pointed out above, this function of the Committee of Ways and Means has become a formal link between voting the expenditure of sums in Committee of Supply and the authorization by a Consolidated Fund Bill of the issue of a sum to cover such expenditure from the Consolidated Fund. When the time for this arrives, the Committee of Ways and Means is made 'effective' by notice being given that the voting of a 'sum (or sums)' will be moved. In Committee of Ways and Means accordingly one or more resolutions (the supply of each financial year having a separate resolution) are voted, and on a later day are agreed to by the House on Report. Care is taken that the stages of the Committees of Supply and Ways and Means proceed *pari passu*. The resolution in Committee of Ways and Means is not moved until the Committee stage of the last Supply resolution has been finished, and similarly with the Report stages. The amount granted by a Ways and Means Resolution must not exceed the total of the supply voted since the last Consolidated Fund Act. Upon the Ways and Means resolution, when agreed to by the House, the Consolidated Fund Bill is founded.

CONSOLIDATED FUND BILLS

There are at least two of these every session:—

1. *The Consolidated Fund (No. 1) Bill*

This Bill is passed for the purpose of issuing money to cover expenditure voted by the Committee of Supply and is introduced in time to get the Royal Assent before the beginning of the financial year.

It authorizes the issue of a lump sum which covers expenditure on:—

(a) Excess grants (if any) for the previous financial year;

(b) Supplementary Estimates for the current financial year;

(c) the Civil Vote on Account for the coming financial year; and

(d) the votes for pay and wages, etc., of the Navy, Army and Air Force for the coming financial year.

This Bill contains no directions as to how the money which it issues from the Consolidated Fund is to be spent. The distribution of the sums to the Departments for which they were voted in Supply is, in fact, made by the Treasury under the Exchequer and Audit Departments Act, 1866, and the Public Accounts and Charges Act, 1891 (May, 640) (see p. 256).

A second, or even a third, Consolidated Fund Bill may be necessitated if the passing of the Appropriation Act is delayed beyond the period (four and a half months or so) for which funds have been provided by the first Consolidated Fund Bill.

Sometimes an earlier Consolidated Fund Bill is passed at the very beginning of the session for the purpose of issuing money for a Supplementary Estimate (see p. 258). In this event the Bill which covers the items referred to above becomes the Consolidated Fund (No. 2) Bill.

2. *The Consolidated Fund (Appropriation) Bill* (which is generally called the *Appropriation Bill* and becomes the *Appropriation* Act)

This Bill issues out of the Consolidated Fund the balance of the money required for the service of the year, appropriates to their objects all the sums voted in Committee of Supply during the session, and authorizes the application of Navy, Army and Air Force surpluses in certain votes to cover excess expenditure in other votes. These are all in respect of the current financial year. It also ratifies the application of Navy, Army and Air Force surpluses for the preceding financial year, and it may authorize the issue of money to cover any excess expenditure incurred during a previous financial year.

This Bill is introduced normally on the last of the allotted days immediately after the conclusion of the business of Supply and Ways and Means. An Appropriation Bill appropriating the Supply so far voted must, however, be passed as a preliminary to a dissolution or prorogation of Parliament, even though the business of Supply has not been concluded (see (p. 265). A second Appropriation Bill may be required if the session continues into the autumn and money is urgently needed for Supplementary Estimates (see p. 258).

Procedure on Consolidated Fund Bills

Debate on a Consolidated Fund (or Appropriation) Bill must be confined to the subject-matter of the votes for which it provides money. Its scope extends from practically the whole range of the Supply Services in the case of the end-of-session Appropriation Bill to a single urgent Supplementary Estimate in the case of a Consolidated Fund Bill. It cannot go beyond the supply services or deal with permanent charges on the Consolidated Fund or with matters requiring legislation.

The second and third reading stages of these Bills are recognized opportunities for general debates dealing with some aspect of the policy of the Government which falls within the limits referred to above. The Committee stage has become formal and usually passes without discussion. In the case of most Consolidated Fund Bills, and still more in the case of the Appropriation Bill, the body of the Bill is a financial framework which has been gradually evolved and could not be altered without disturbing the conduct of the national business, while the schedules relating to the appropriation of the sums voted could not be altered without reversing decisions of the House taken upon them when they were reported from the Committee of Supply.

Under S.O. No. 85 Consolidated Fund Bills are (by an exception to the general rule that Bills founded on resolutions of a Committee of the Whole House may not pass through more than one stage on the same day) permitted to be considered in committee, reported and read the third time on the same day.

(Money) Committees of the Whole House

The Committee of Supply deals with all the ordinary expenditure on the public services comprised in the Estimates. These, as stated, when the issue of money has been voted by the Committee of Ways and Means, are included in an Appropriation Bill to obtain legislative sanction.

(Money) Committees of the Whole House deal with new or extraordinary expenditure, and such expenditure, when agreed to by the House, is sanctioned by a special Bill, either itself founded upon the Report of the Committee, or else containing a clause or clauses so founded. If the *main* purpose of a Bill is to incur expenditure, it is introduced upon resolutions moved in Committee of the Whole House and agreed to by the House.[1] If such expenditure is merely *incidental* to a Bill, the Bill itself is not founded on such resolutions, but the clause or clauses containing expenditure (which are printed in italics) cannot be considered in committee on the Bill until a resolution authorizing the expenditure has been considered in Committee of the Whole House and agreed to by the House. Such resolutions require the King's Recommendation.

The expenditure may be (a) a single payment, or (b) a permanent charge on the Consolidated Fund, or (c) a sum which will afterwards appear as a vote in the Estimates (as when a new department is set up).

KINDS OF BUSINESS

The various forms of such expenditure are:—

(1) Exceptional Grants (see p. 266).—The purpose of these is to meet the cost of some novel undertaking which forms no part of the current service of the year. An example given is the £20,000,000 voted to facilitate the abolition of slavery in the colonies (May, 685).

(2) Demands made by Message from the Crown for the maintenance of the dignity and well-being of the Crown, or for rewarding the services of distinguished servants of the Crown.

These demands for grants may be brought before the House as Estimates and voted by the Committee of Supply. For example, the money required for the purchase of the Suez Canal shares was voted in the Committee of Supply. In the case of the payments occasioned by the marriage of the Princess Royal in 1857, the marriage portion was voted in Committee of Supply, and the annuity was voted in a Committee of the Whole House and charged upon the Consolidated Fund (May, 685).

(3) Addresses to the Crown voted in Committee of the Whole House for action involving expenditure with the intimation that "this House will make good the same".— The King's Recommendation is given in his answer to the Address. This is the method adopted when the House desires to erect a monument to a deceased

[1] But see S.O. No. 80 of 1938.

statesman, and also when the " signal mark of the Royal favour" is prayed for on behalf of a retiring Speaker. (In this last case the Address is voted by the House without a previous committee.)

(4) Expenditure in connexion with Bills other than Consolidated Fund Bills.—Such expenditure may, as stated on p. 275, either form the main purpose of a Bill or be merely incidental. If an item of such expenditure is intended to be an annual charge, the Act in which it is included has the effect of authorizing its subsequent inclusion in the Estimates, and full legislative effect is given to it by the Appropriation Act.

Procedure in Voting Extraordinary Grants

The procedure for voting such expenditure in Committee of the Whole House, as laid down by S.Os. Nos. 78 to 83, is as follows:—

(1) The King's recommendation must be given in the House by a Minister of the Crown before the House goes into committee on the motion.

(2) The motion must be first considered in a Committee of the Whole House.

(3) Its consideration must not be 'presently entered upon', but adjourned to another day. This is done by a preliminary motion, called the 'setting-up' motion (to which the King's recommendation is given): "That this House will (on a future day) resolve itself into committee to consider (the proposal for expenditure stated in general terms)". The committee becomes an Order of the Day, and when the House goes into committee the proposed expenditure is brought before it by a further motion framed in a specific form. This is the old traditional procedure under S.O. No. 83.

S.O. No. 84 (1919) provides a more summary method of going into committee, of which advantage has been regularly taken since 1922. Under this the proposal for expenditure is put on the Paper in the form of a specific motion, and on the King's recommendation being signified, the House immediately resolves itself into committee.

The two methods entail consequential differences in the procedure in committee, which will be dealt with later.

SCOPE OF THE PUBLIC MONEY STANDING ORDERS

The application of the 'Public Money' Standing Orders to
Bills involving expenditure is very strict. On the one hand the
failure to observe them where they are applicable renders proceedings on a Bill null and void. On the other hand there are
certain kinds of Bills apparently involving expenditure to
which they are not applicable. For they are only applicable to
new and *direct* charges upon the Exchequer. The test is whether
the Bill actually causes the issue out of the Exchequer of money,
which would not otherwise be issued, or places a liability on
the Exchequer, which would not otherwise accrue. The
Standing Orders have been held not to be applicable if a Bill
only diverts payments from one recipient to another, or disposes
of money provided by another Act, or intercepts the proceeds of
certain taxes and diverts them from the Exchequer to a special
account. But modern practice tends to the view that any such
action involves the initiation of expenditure and therefore comes
within the spirit of the Standing Orders. The annual Public
Works Loans Bills (except in so far as they sanction the remission of debts in respect of advances) escape the operation of
these Standing Orders because, although they place a particular contingent liability on the Exchequer, this is covered by
the general liability imposed by the Local Loans Act, 1887.
Reference should be made to the instances collected by May
(728–30).

EFFECT OF THE KING'S RECOMMENDATION

The King's recommendation is the machinery by which the
initiative in expenditure is reserved to Ministers of the Crown.
It is given to a resolution which is the preliminary stage in the
consideration of expenditure. The right to signify the King's
recommendation is the sole advantage which a Minister of the
Crown has over a Private Member in financial procedure. It
is necessary to emphasize this as it is sometimes thought that
a Minister can propose a new charge or the increase of a charge
at a later stage, for example by an amendment in committee.
This is not so. Once a Minister has signified the Royal recommendation to a resolution he is as much bound by the terms of
the resolution as a Private Member, and could not increase the
charge therein defined except by withdrawing the resolution
and submitting a new resolution with the King's recommendation.

The insistence upon the recommendation of the Crown limits the power of proposing expenditure to Ministers. But Private Members are not altogether without means for bringing such proposals before the House. In the first place they are entitled to move for a Committee of the Whole House to consider an Address to the Crown for action involving expenditure (see p. 275), as the King's recommendation is given at a later stage. They may also bring in Bills involving *incidental* expenditure in the hope that before the committee stage of such a Bill is reached the Government will make the necessary financial provision, or they may move motions advocating expenditure, provided it is not sought thereby to commit the House to more than the expression of an opinion. Similarly, a Report may be presented by a select committee, which recommends the outlay of public money, as such a committee only acts in an advisory capacity.

PROCEDURE IN A (MONEY) COMMITTEE OF THE WHOLE HOUSE

Debate proceeds according to the rules observed in Committee of Supply except that amendments are framed in the ordinary form and not in the form peculiar to Committee of Supply.

The scope of amendment is limited by the terms of the. resolution which has received the King's recommendation Any amendment exceeding the terms of this resolution would amount to the exercise by the House of the initiative in expenditure which is constitutionally reserved to the Crown.

It should be clear that not only any increase in the amount of the charge recommended but any alteration in the objects to which it is directed, even if no additional charge is incurred, implies the exercise of such an initiative and is therefore out of order. The King's recommendation may be figuratively represented as drawing a line round the objects of expenditure set forth, often in great detail, in the recommended resolution. Any changes entirely within, or exclusions from, this circle are in order. But nothing may be brought into it from outside.

When, under S.O. No. 84, the King's recommendation is given to the resolution considered in committee, it is the terms of this resolution itself which limits the scope of amendment. But when, under S.O. No. 83, the King's recommendation is given to the resolution under which the committee is set up, it is the terms of this resolution by which amendment of the resolution moved in committee is governed. Since it was often the case, when the procedure under S.O. No. 83 was employed, that the 'setting-up' resolution was in wider terms than the resolution moved in committee itself, there might be considerable scope for amending the latter resolution. In terms of the simile just employed, the setting-up resolution enclosed the committee resolution as a large circle encloses a smaller, and the smaller circle might be extended in any direction up to, but not beyond, the circumference of the larger circle without infringing the royal monopoly of the initiation of expenditure.

Subsequent Stages

The Reports of resolutions voted by (Money) Committees of the Whole House are considered by the House in the same manner as Reports of the Committee of Supply, and no amendment is in order which is any way extends the charge agreed to by the committee. Upon the resolutions agreed to by the House, with or without amendment, Bills may be ordered.

S.O. No. 83 prescribes intervals between the stages of resolutions moved in Committee of the Whole House, and by an extension of this rule the usage of the House forbids more than a single stage of a Bill founded upon such a resolution to be taken on any one day.

SESSIONAL COMMITTEES WITH FINANCIAL FUNCTIONS

The House of Commons is assisted in its control of expenditure by two select committees.

The Public Accounts Committee.—The duty of this committee, which, pursuant to S.O. No. 90, is appointed every session, is, by examination of the Appropriation Accounts and a re-check of the appropriation audit, to make sure that no sums have been expended on purposes other than, or in excess of, those for which they were granted by the House. They also report on any Excess Vote (see p. 265) which may have been presented, and, in the case of the Navy, Army and Air Estimates, on the application of surpluses on certain votes to cover deficiencies on other votes (see p. 265). And, finally, they make recommendations from time to time for the purpose of improving the form and method of the national accounts.

The Member selected for the important position of Chairman of the Public Accounts Committee is by a convention of long standing a member of the Opposition and, if there is one available, an ex-holder of the office of Financial Secretary to the

Treasury. The Minister serving in that capacity is also regularly a member of the Committee. The Committee maintain close relations with the Treasury and with the Comptroller and Auditor-General, whose reports serve as a basis for their inquiries.

The Estimates Committee has been regularly appointed by order of the House every session since 1912, with the exception of 1915–20 and 1939–45. Its order of reference is 'to suggest the form in which the Estimates shall be presented for examination, and to report what, if any, economies, consistent with the policy implied in those Estimates, may be effected therein'. Among the reforms due to this Committee is the reclassification of the Estimates which took effect in 1927. The work of the committee upon the Estimates does not begin until they have been presented to the House, when their form is to all intents and purposes final, and proposals have been made to submit them to the committee at an earlier stage and also to bring the *policy* of the Estimates within its purview. But it is difficult to see how such an extension of its powers could be reconciled with the doctrine of ministerial responsibility, and it is necessary to go back, beyond the establishment of the cabinet system, to the reign of William III, to find a precedent for this course (see Todd, i. 206, where, however, the editor takes a rather different view).

II. TAXATION

The House of Commons deals annually with a comparatively small portion of taxation. The greater part of the taxes is permanent, having been imposed by legislation in the past. A smaller portion is imposed for a limited period, and only comes before the House when that period is about to expire. Two taxes, the Income Tax and the Tea Duty, used to be imposed, and came up for review annually. Recently the Tea Duty has ceased to be annually imposed.

These and any other taxes dictated by the needs of the revenue are initiated in Committee of Ways and Means, and upon the resolutions of the Committee, when agreed to by the House, the Finance Bill is founded. The principle that taxation requires the sanction of the Crown applies not only to the imposition but also to the increase of taxation, and to any variation in its incidence. All such proposals can only be initiated in Committee of Ways and Means and by a Minister acting on behalf of the Crown. The proposals which must be so initiated include proposals:—

(1) to impose a new tax;
(2) to continue an expiring tax;
(3) to increase a permanent tax;
(4) to continue a temporary (and expiring) addition to a permanent tax; and
(5) to pay any sums into the Exchequer (if such payments are incidental to a scheme imposing expenditure they may be included in the resolution by which the scheme is initiated in a Committee of the Whole House).

A proposal to reduce or repeal taxation does not necessarily require a resolution in Committee of Ways and Means, although the repeal of the Paper Duties in 1861, the reduction of the Sugar Duty in 1924, and also certain exemptions from Purchase Tax in 1945-46, originated thus.

Although it was previously the rule that alterations in the fiscal system, which are not made with the object of increasing the revenue, should originate in Committee of the Whole House upon the King's recommendation (May, 750), the recent practice is for all taxation, whether for revenue or for any other fiscal purpose, to originate in Committee of Ways and Means.

PROCEDURE IN COMMITTEE OF WAYS AND MEANS (TAXING)

The scope of amendment in Committee of Ways and Means is limited as in other financial committees by the principle which reserves the right to initiate charges to the Crown. An increase in the rate of a tax proposed by a resolution submitted to the Committee of Ways and Means, or the extension of its incidence, is accordingly out of order. This principle is not, however, expressed by the machinery of signifying the King's Recommendation to a resolution proposing a tax. But such a resolution, when proposed from the Chair, is taken as imposing limitations upon amendment analogous to those imposed, in the case of expenditure, by a resolution recommended by the King. As notice is not required (though it is usually given when possible) of a resolution imposing a tax, there is nothing to prevent a Minister modifying the terms, even by way of increasing the charge, of a resolution appearing upon the Notice Paper so long as he does so before the question upon it is proposed from the Chair.

When the Budget Resolutions are to be moved the Committee of Ways and Means is made 'effective' (see p. 262), notice being given, not of the Budget Resolutions themselves, but merely that the financial statement is to be made. After the conclusion of the Chancellor's statement, the Question is proposed from the Chair on the first of the Budget Resolutions.

Debate on these resolutions is governed by two conditions which differentiate it from other debates in committee.

1. The Chancellor's statement, although technically based on the first resolution (usually a customs duty), is by a custom of long standing allowed to take the form of a general survey of the whole field of national finance, and is followed by a debate equally wide.

2. In the interests of the revenue it is necessary to pass the resolutions which effect changes in taxation or the renewal of expiring taxes the same day as they are moved. For since 1913 under the Provisional Collection of Taxes Act (and previously by practice) a Resolution comes into, and continues in, force as soon as it has been voted by the Committee of Ways and Means, or from the date on which it is expressed to come into force, provided that:—

(1) it is agreed to by the House within ten sitting days;

(2) the Bill confirming it is read a second time within twenty sitting days after it has been agreed to by the House; and

(3) this Bill receives the Royal Assent within four months after the Resolution has been voted by the Committee of Ways and Means.

(4) The Resolution does not impose a new tax.

The fact that an Income Tax Resolution comes into effect on the 6th April necessitates the Finance Bill receiving the Royal Assent not later than the 5th August. And in order to ensure, under s. 1 of the Parliament Act, 1911, that the Bill receives the Royal Assent by that date it must be passed by the Commons not later than the 4th July.

It is now the practice[1] to pass all resolutions the first day, except the last resolution (which is generally that entitled 'Amendment of Law'), and to use this resolution as a peg on which to carry on the general debate on the succeeding days.

It must be noted that the adoption of this procedure practically excludes the possibility of moving any amendments at all at the Committee stage.

The imposition of several duties of a similar kind, or the

[1] Now prescribed by S.O. No. 86 (1) ; see Appendix IV.

renewal of a number of existing taxes, may be effected by a single resolution, but not the imposition of a number of new duties on different commodities (May, 751).

PROCEDURE UPON REPORT OF WAYS AND MEANS RESOLUTIONS

Debate at this stage[1] must be relevant to the resolution under consideration, no opportunity for a general discussion being afforded.

As in the case of the consideration of Reports of Supply and of Committee of the Whole House, the interval between the reading of a resolution and the Question "That this House doth agree with the Committee", etc., is the time for moving an amendment to the resolution (see pp. 271–2).

An amendment[1] proposing to increase a charge on the people is, of course, out of order at this stage as in committee. In certain circumstances, however, it may be in order to move an amendment increasing the rate or extending the incidence of a tax voted in committee. This is not really an exception to the rules, for it can only arise where the resolution proposes to reduce the rate of a permanent tax. By amending the resolution so as to restore the existing rate of the tax no increased burden is imposed on the taxpayers above what they already bear. Accordingly, when, in 1924, a Ways and Means resolution reducing the Sugar Duty was considered on Report, an amendment was permitted which aimed at restoring the existing rate for certain kinds of sugar. Similarly, amendments are in order which diminish the amount of a proposed reduction of taxation, or postpone the day when it is to take effect. They may increase an existing drawback, or diminish or increase a proposed drawback. In fact, any amendment may be proposed which has not the effect of increasing *existing* taxation (provided, of course, that it does not incidentally impose a charge upon the Consolidated Fund).

When all the Budget Resolutions have been agreed to on Report by the House, the Finance Bill is ordered to be brought in upon these resolutions. Sometimes, as in 1927, resolutions of a Committee of the Whole House have also to be agreed to by the House as a preliminary to the introduction of the Finance Bill. As in the case of the Consolidated Fund and Appropriation Bills, the fact that the House of Commons collaborates in their introduction in a special way is marked

[1] Amendment and debate at this stage are now excluded (S.O. No. 86 (2)); see Appendix IV.

by the inclusion among the 'backers' of the Finance Bill of the name of the Chairman of Ways and Means.

THE FINANCE BILL

The most important rule of order with regard to a Finance Bill is that all its provisions must be covered by the resolutions upon which it is founded. That is to say, the clauses imposing, renewing or increasing taxation must do so at rates not exceeding those contained in the corresponding Ways and Means resolutions as agreed to by the House. The other clauses, probably far more numerous, which embody the necessary administrative regulations, and also (as a rule) any clauses which reduce or repeal taxation, are covered by the single resolution 'Amendment of Law', which is generally drawn so widely as to cover national debt, customs, and inland revenue. This resolution has much to answer for, as it equally covers all the numerous amendments which are moved to the Finance Bill every session for the purpose of repealing or reducing existing taxation, not included in the Bill.

It is an old rule of the House that the provisions of the Finance Bill must relate to the finance of the current year. Accordingly the inclusion, or insertion by amendment, in a Finance Bill of provision for taxation which is not to take effect in the current year, or of machinery connected with such provision, is out of order. In 1931 and in the autumn of 1945, when it was proposed to include provisions of this kind in the Finance Bill, a resolution was passed before the introduction of the Bill recognizing the practice of the House but nevertheless authorizing such provision to be included.

In applying the rule, which forbids the imposition or increase of taxation, to amendments moved in committee on the Finance Bill, certain (at first sight) apparent exceptions may be noted:—

(1) If the Bill contains exemptions which were not in the resolutions, or in any way reduces the charge imposed by a resolution either in respect of the rate or of the period for which it is imposed, amendments restoring rate, incidence or period up to the level of the resolution are in order.

(2) If the Bill reduces existing taxation (and such reduction was not voted in committee and agreed to by the House as part of a resolution the total effect of which was to increase a tax), an amendment is in order which increases

the proposed rate up to the existing level of taxation. Such an amendment would also be in order on the Report stage of the Bill.

It should be remembered that the Report stage of the Ways and Means resolutions and the various stages of the Finance Bill are exempted from the Eleven o'Clock Rule.

No more than one of any of these stages may be taken on the same day.

All Bills authorising expenditure and taxation, which have been introduced upon resolutions of the Committee of Ways and Means, are returned, after being agreed to by the Lords, to the custody of the Clerk of the House and are handed by him to the Speaker at the Bar of the House of Lords, to receive the Royal Assent.

HOUSE OF LORDS AND FINANCE

The restrictions on the power of the House of Lords in matters of finance depend partly on their (tacit) acceptance of the privileges claimed by the Commons and partly on the Parliament Act, 1911.

1. RESTRICTIONS ON LORDS THROUGH COMMONS' PRIVILEGE
(see pp. 32–3)

The Lords cannot initiate or amend Bills or provisions in Bills dealing with public expenditure or revenue, or dealing with local rates. In the last matter privilege is thus wider than the class of matters which need the King's recommendation and originate in a Committee of the Whole House.

The Lords are constitutionally entitled to reject any such Bill, although, as explained later (p. 287) the effect of such rejection is, in the case of Bills certified as Money Bills under the Parliament Act, rendered inoperative. The Lords may omit from a Bill, which they are otherwise entitled to amend, provisions creating a charge upon the people, provided that such provisions are separable from the rest of the Bill and that they are omitted as a whole. Such omission is held to be equivalent to the rejection by the Lords of a whole Bill which they are not entitled to amend.

Privilege is waived:—

(1) if the infringement of privilege is not material;

(2) in the case of local rates, if the effect on local rates is incidental, and especially if the amendment is designed

to carry out the intentions of the Commons (May, 773). In view of the difficulty of separating the rating from the other provisions, a rigid insistence on privilege might have the effect of practically excluding the Lords from the consideration of such Bills.

Privilege insisted upon

In the case of Lords' amendments infringing privilege the Commons, in giving reasons for disagreeing (see p. 227), state the nature of the infringement, and that they do not consider it necessary to offer any further reason, hoping the reason given may be deemed sufficient. If the Lords insist upon the amendment, the Commons, as a rule, order that the Lords' amendments be laid aside or that their consideration be deferred for six months.

Relaxation of privilege by Standing Order

(1) *Fines and fees.*—In pursuance of S.O. No. 55 the Commons do not insist on "their ancient and undoubted privileges" in the case of fines, the object of which is to secure the execution of an Act, and of fees not made payable into the treasury or exchequer. The Lords may both initiate and amend Bills having such objects.

(2) *Local rates in Private Bills.*—Under S.O. 191 (Private) the Commons do not insist on their privileges in the case of Private, or Provisional Order, Bills sent down from the Lords dealing with rates assessed and levied by local authorities.

Devices for permitting Lords to make Privileged Provisions in a Bill without infringing Privilege

A Lords' Bill, containing privileged provisions, when introduced or through amendment, is sent down to the Commons without these provisions (they have been struck out on third reading) and is received and printed by the Commons with these provisions underlined and in brackets and a note that they were left out by the Lords to avoid questions of privilege (May, 768). In committee the insertion is made by an amendment proposed, usually without notice, by the Member in charge of the Bill. Privilege is thus saved because the insertion of such provisions is technically not made by the Lords, but by the Commons at the suggestion of the Lords.

This method is only available for Bills originating in the Lords, but other devices for suggesting the desires of the Lords with regard to the amendment of Commons' Bills have been used in the past, and are recorded by May (p. 775).

2. Procedure under the Parliament Act, 1911

As the procedure to be followed under the Parliament Act is explicitly laid down by the Act itself, it will be unnecessary to do more than cite the relevant section with the addition of a couple of notes.

(1) If a Money Bill, having been passed by the House of Commons, and sent up to the House of Lords at least one month before the end of the session, is not passed by the House of Lords without amendment within one month after it is so sent up to that House, the Bill shall, unless the House of Commons direct to the contrary, be presented to His Majesty and become an Act of Parliament on the Royal Assent being signified, notwithstanding that the House of Lords have not consented to the Bill.

(2) A Money Bill means a Public Bill which, in the opinion of the Speaker of the House of Commons, contains only provisions dealing with all or any of the following subjects, namely, the imposition, repeal, remission, alteration or regulation of taxation; the imposition for the payment of debt or other financial purposes of charges on the Consolidated Fund, or on money provided by Parliament, or the variation or repeal of any such charges; supply; the appropriation, receipt, custody, issue or audit of accounts of public money; the raising or guarantee of any loan or the repayment thereof; or subordinate matters incidental to those subjects or any of them. In this subsection the expressions 'taxation', 'public money', and 'loan' respectively do not include any taxation, money or loan raised by local authorities or bodies for local purposes.

(3) There shall be endorsed on every Money Bill when it is sent up to the House of Lords and when it is presented to His Majesty for assent the certificate of the Speaker of the House of Commons, signed by him, that it is a Money Bill. Before giving his certificate, the Speaker shall consult, if practicable, two members to be appointed from the Chairmen's Panel at the beginning of each session by the Committee of Selection (1 and 2 Geo. V, c. 13, s. 1).

U

Notes to Parliament Act Provisions

(1) The Commons are not debarred from considering amendments made by the Lords to a Bill which has been certified by the Speaker as a Money Bill (May, 779).

(2) The definition is nearly the same as that of Bills required by the practice of the House to originate in Committee of the Whole House, but

(a) it is *narrower*, because not only Bills which *only* contain the provisions enumerated, but also those which *mainly* contain them, are required to originate in Committee of the Whole House.[1] Thus the Finance Bill, 1911, and at least six others, have failed to receive the Speaker's certificate as containing other provisions besides those enumerated. To avoid this result the finance of 1913 and 1914 was distributed into two Bills—one the Finance Bill, containing only the provisions enumerated and receiving the Speaker's certificate, and the other the Revenue Bill, which contained other provisions.

(b) it is *wider*, because it is possible for a Bill which satisfies the definition of the Parliament Act not *effectively* to impose a charge, and therefore not to be required to originate in Committee of the Whole House (see p. 277).

---

[1] Or would be but for S.O. No. 80.

CHAPTER IX

PRIVATE LEGISLATION

NOTE.—References to Standing Orders in this chapter are to Standing Orders [Private Business] except where otherwise expressly stated.

No account of the functions and activities of Parliament would be complete without some description of Private Legislation, but in a subject so full of complicated and technical detail it is not possible to do more than give a very brief outline of the history of such legislation in the past and to sketch—in somewhat greater detail—the procedure by which it is conducted at the present time.

Before proceeding on this course, however, it would be desirable to give some definition of what is meant by Private Legislation and to state by what means it is conducted through Parliament.

Private Legislation is legislation of a special kind for conferring particular powers or benefits on any person or body of persons (including local authorities and private corporations) as opposed to Public or general Legislation which is for or on behalf of the general community. In Parliament, Private Legislation falls into several categories which may be enumerated as follows:—

Private Bills.

Bills for confirming Provisional Orders.

Bills for confirming Provisional Orders under the Private Legislation Procedure (Scotland) Act, 1936.

Special Procedure Orders under the Act of 1945, see Appendix V.

Special Orders.

Finally, some account will be given of various Committees and officers who deal with Private Business.

For proceedings in the House in connexion with Private Legislation (known as 'Private Business') see pp. 140–2.

BRIEF HISTORY

In the earliest parliamentary times in this country, just as no clear distinction was drawn between the legislative and judicial functions of Parliament, so no clear line of demarcation existed between private measures and measures of public policy. Petitions for redress of grievances were dealt with alike by Parliament and by the Law Courts, and in the same way measures granting redress of the grievances of a particular individual often contained enactments of a general or public character applying to all the people in the land. This confusion was not speedily cleared up, but in the reign of Henry IV petitions were granted that bore some resemblance to Private Acts, and the distinction became clearer when legislation by Bill and Statute grew up about the reign of Henry VI. It was not, however, until 1798 that the distinction between 'Public General Acts' and 'Local and Personal Acts' was introduced into the Statute Book. This created a clear division between Public and Private Bills, whereas before that date no Bills could be distinguished definitely as private except certain Bills of a 'personal' nature. Since 1868 Public Acts of a local character have been printed among the local Acts, but there is now no difficulty in distinguishing between the two. Formerly, too, a large number of Private Acts were never printed, but now, with the exception of a few purely personal Acts, they are all printed.

It may also be of interest briefly to trace the chief subjects of Private Bill Legislation. While nearly all the earlier measures that bore some resemblance to Private Bills were measures granting the redress of grievances, peculiar powers were sought, and sometimes granted, giving individuals rights and privileges above the general law of the land, from about the time of Henry IV. Private measures, however, largely fall into the personal class until a comparatively recent period in our history. Such measures were for the regulating of estates, for naturalization, for the reversal of attainders and similar subjects.

Though the first Inclosure Act was passed in 1606–7, it was not until the 18th century that a large volume of Private Bills seeking powers to permit inclosures began. About 1760 the era of canal-making set in, and in 1801 the first pure Railway Bill was passed; twenty years later the Stockton and Darlington Act became law, and about 1840 came the great mass of railway bill legislation.

In modern times, though there is still railway legislation, Private Bills consist chiefly of measures seeking police and sanitary powers for our great cities or the extension of their boundaries, and for supplying water, gas and electricity to our people, whether by the municipalities or by companies set up by Statute for the purpose.

Finally, it may be said that Private Bill Legislation is definitely on the down grade. The heyday of Private Bill Legislation was in the period of the great railway activities round about 1840. At that time Private Acts were not only very numerous but also very voluminous. Some six or seven hundred such Acts were passed through the House in a single session, many of them containing several hundred clauses. At the present time less than fifty such Acts are passed in a session, and their size is very much diminished.

The reasons for this are many and varied, but the chief ones may be briefly mentioned:—

In our restricted country most of the railways are now built, the canals made, and the land enclosed, and, though new discoveries such as electricity lead to fresh activity, the majority of our recent inventions, *e.g.* the aeroplane and wireless, having little territorial basis, have less need for private legislation. The most important cause of the decline in Private Bill Legislation is, however, the passing of general Acts removing the need for much special legislation, and enabling that which is still required to be much less voluminous.

The Private Bill itself, moreover, is being gradually superseded by the system of Provisional Orders, the institution of Special Orders, and the prospective development of Special Procedure Orders. It has been almost entirely supplanted in *Scotland* by the Provisional Order system as set up by the Private Legislation Procedure (Scotland) Act, 1899, amended in 1933, and now regulated by the Consolidating Act of 1936. These systems, though all part of Private Legislation and as such dealt with in this chapter, are all aimed at accelerating and cheapening procedure by Private Bill, and being so recent, may be said to have little real history.

PRIVATE BILLS

A Private Bill has been defined as "a Bill for the particular interest or benefit of any person or persons", and as such can be sharply distinguished from measures of public policy, and is treated by the House in an entirely different way. In practice, however, it is by no means easy to distinguish between Public and Private Bills in certain cases, and Public Bills have been objected to on the ground that they affected particular private interests, while Private Bills in the same way have been debarred from proceeding on the grounds that their scope was so wide that they affected public policy. (For cases of this see May, p. 826 *et seq.*)

The first point to notice is that every Private Bill is founded upon a Petition solicited by the parties themselves who are interested in promoting it; secondly, that, unlike Public Bills, every stage of a Private Bill prior to and after presentation is elaborately regulated by the Standing Orders of the House. These Standing Orders are known as 'Standing Orders [Private Business]'.

Private Bills to which Standing Orders apply are now treated as one class, but different deposits are required according to the type of Bill, and compliance with the relevant Standing Orders (4 to 68) must be proved, except where the Chairman of Ways and Means has certified that the Bill relates to personal affairs of an individual (S.O. 3 ; May, 843–44).

Every Private Bill, then, is founded upon a petition signed by the suitors for the Bill, which is, together with all other documents relating to Private Bills, presented to the House by being deposited in the Committee and Private Bill Office. The suitors for the Bill are commonly known as the 'Promoters of the Bill', but the actual conduct of a Bill through the House is, in practice, almost invariably carried out by Parliamentary Agents who are known as 'The Agents for the Bill' or 'The Agents for the Promoters'.

In the same way opposition to Private Bills is founded upon Petitions and normally conducted by Parliamentary Agents except such opposition as comes from Members in the House itself.

Fees are charged to promoters and opponents of Private Bills, a table of such fees being appended to Standing Orders. These fees are retained appropriations in aid of the House of Commons Vote.

It should be noted that—as in the case of a Public Bill—if any proceeding on a Private Bill is postponed for three or six months such postponement is equivalent to a rejection of the Bill and that no new Bill for the same object may be introduced until the next Session of Parliament. Further, that any provisions which create a charge on the Consolidated Fund or on the public revenue or[1] the revenues of India, or—the most usual case in connexion with Private Bills—which involve the payment of a Stamp Duty, must be sanctioned by a Resolution

---

[1] Now no longer applicable.

of a Committee of the Whole House (see p. 259). The only difference in procedure from that on a Public Bill is that the proceedings are taken at the time of Private Business and under Standing Order No. 83 (Public) and sometimes an Instruction is given to the Committee on the Bill to make provision accordingly.

Further points that should be noted here are that two stages of a Private Bill may not, except by order of the House, be taken on the same day and that all Private Bills are placed under the peculiar care and supervision of the Chairman of Ways and Means.

PRELIMINARIES TO PRESENTATION

It may be convenient to summarize in tabular form the chief preliminaries, and their dates, to the presentation of a Private Bill. It should be understood that this table does not apply to personal Bills introduced into the House of Lords, late Bills introduced by leave of the House, and certain other exceptional Bills:—

Proceeding	Latest date for Proceeding
Deposit of Plans	20th November
Deposit of Petitions for Bills	27th November
Estimates of Expense ... ... ⎫ Declaration under S.O. 43 ... ⎬ Estimate of Expenditure under S.O. 45 ⎭	4th December
Deposit of Working Class Statement ...	11th December
Memorials relating to Petitions... ...	17th December
Examiners begin to sit	18th December
Division of Bills between the two Houses	8th January
Petitions against Bills originating in the House of Commons	30th January

The sessional work in connexion with Private Bill legislation begins on 20th November, which is the last day for plans in connexion with certain Bills to be deposited. On or before 27th November Petitions for Private Bills engrossed on vellum are deposited together with a printed copy of the Bill. On the following day a list known as the *General List of Petitions* is published, with the Bills numbered in the order of their deposit, although a certain latitude is allowed in changing these numbers. After this, certain other statements and declarations required by Standing Orders are deposited.

When the time has expired for depositing documents and complying with other preliminary conditions, parties interested are enabled to judge whether the Standing Orders have been complied with. If they consider that the Promoters have neglected to comply with any of these Standing Orders, they may prepare what are known as *Memorials* addressed to the Examiners of Petitions for Private Bills complaining of such non-compliance. These Memorials are deposited on or before 17th December.

On or about 18th December the Examiners (see p. 314) begin their examination of the petitions, to see whether Standing Orders 4–68, which govern the preliminaries to Presentation of a Bill, have been complied with.

On or before 8th January, the Chairman of Ways and Means or Mr. Speaker's Counsel, in conference with the Lords' Chairman of Committees or his Counsel, determines in which House each Private Bill shall originate.

On or before 30th January, petitions against Bills originating in the House of Commons are deposited. These may be "Petitions praying to be heard", in which case they are referred ultimately to the Committee on the Bill; or "Petitions not praying to be heard", in which case they are a protest against the Bill but entail no further action.

House of Commons Bills: Stages before Committee
Presentation and First Reading

Where the Examiner has reported to the House that he has endorsed the petition for a Private Bill "Standing Orders complied with", the Bill is presented by being laid upon the Table of the House not earlier than the first day in February upon which the House sits nor later than one clear day after that date, or after the date of the Examiner's Report, whichever is the later. Provision is made by Standing Orders for cases when the House is not sitting.

Where the Examiner has reported to the House that he has endorsed the Petition "Standing Orders not complied with", the report is referred to the Select Committee on Standing Orders (see p. 315) and subsequent proceedings depend on the action taken by that Committee.

Prior to the day fixed for Presentation a printed copy of the Bill is deposited at the Committee and Private Bill Office, and this, together with a list of all Private Bills being presented at the same time, is laid upon the Table of the House the following day. The Presentation and First Reading of a Private Bill is a purely formal stage. The Bill is presented, deemed to have been read the first time and ordered to be read a second time. It is recorded as having been so read in the Votes the following morning.

Second Reading

Between the First Reading and the day first appointed for the Second Reading of a Private Bill there may be not less than three clear days nor more than seven. The Agent for the Bill is required by Standing Orders to give notice in writing, in the Committee and Private Bill Office, of the day proposed for the Second Reading and for all other stages of the Bill. The amount of notice required is regulated by Standing Orders and varies for different stages.

After Second Reading certain Bills relating to companies are referred to the Examiners, before whom compliance with Standing Orders 62–68 has to be proved. These Orders, which are known as 'The Wharncliffe Orders', after Lord Wharncliffe, who was responsible for their introduction, compel companies to obtain the consent of their proprietors, members and directors—under certain conditions—to the Bill that is before Parliament.

All other Bills stand committed.

The Second Reading of a Private Bill is still a comparatively important stage in its existence. It is used by opponents of all kinds to block its further progress, though this can only be done by the agency of Members—unlike opposition in the Committee stage. As compared with Public Bills, however, the tendency is more and more to leave the actual decision to the Private Bill Committee and to use the Second Reading either as a means of delaying the progress of the Bill or to air grievances, as on the once frequently recurring Bills of the great railway companies in particular and other public utility companies in general. Many of the railway grievances bore little relation to the Bill[1] under consideration and it might be said that the annual Bills of the companies were discussed on Second Reading much as if they were public estimates for the railway services.

---

[1] General Powers Bills covered every aspect of railway service. If, however, the Bill dealt with limited objects, debate must be relevant to those objects. (H.C. Deb. (1943-4) 402, c. 1176-7.) The nationalisation of railways has altered the application of this principle. But it still holds. (H.C. Deb. (1948-49) 461, c. 1765-6).

It happens sometimes that there are real issues of principle involved and in that case a Second Reading debate takes place and is decided in exactly the same way as on a Public Bill. The issue is often raised that the Bill attempts to do something which is beyond the scope of a Private Bill and which should only be introduced as a public measure. For instance, such issues as municipal trading, compulsory notification of certain diseases and extensions of municipal boundaries, have all been raised on Private Bills. In some cases the subject has been of such importance that the Government of the day, instead of giving general or partial approval or disapproval—a matter of frequent occurrence—have gone so far as to demand the support of their Members on one side or the other and have enforced this demand by putting on their Whips.[1]

Instructions and Resolutions

Instructions are moved in the House after the Second Reading of a Bill for the direction of the Committee on the Bill. They may be either mandatory or permissive. Mandatory instructions leave the Committee no option in the exercise of their functions with regard to the particular matter that is the subject of the instruction. Permissive instructions confer on Committees powers of inquiry or legislation on matters relevant to the subject-matter of the Bill which might not otherwise be brought to their attention or which do not come within the ordinary scope of their inquiry. No instruction may be proposed which in Mr. Speaker's opinion, requires or authorizes a Committee to amend a Bill in such a way that, if proposed by the Promoters, a petition for additional provision (see p. 307) would have been necessary. (For further information see May, 905 et seq.)

In the same way, any resolutions passed by the Select Committee on Standing Orders are dealt with by the Committee on the Bill.

Committal of Bills

After Second Reading all Private Bills (other than those referred to the Examiners) are committed and unless referred

---

[1] Thus the Government Whips were put on against the Channel Tunnel Bill in 1887, 1888 and 1890; in the case of the Edinburgh Corporation Bill—which sought for powers for the compulsory treatment of venereal diseases—in 1928, the Government, though not actually putting on their Whips, expressed strong disapproval of such a proposal in a Private Bill; while in the debate on the Railways (Road Transport) Bills in 1928, they declared themselves to be strongly in favour of the proposals contained therein.

to a specially constituted Committee stand referred to the Committee of Selection (see p. 317).

Bills referred to the Examiners after Second Reading are not committed until (*a*) the Examiners have reported (i) that any Standing Orders not previously inquired into are not applicable; (ii) that any such Standing Orders as may be applicable have been complied with; or, (*b*) if the Standing Orders have not been complied with; the Select Committee on Standing Orders have resolved that such Standing Orders should be dispensed with, and the House has agreed with the Committee in such Resolution.

It is laid down that there shall be six clear days between the committal of every opposed Private Bill and the sitting of the Committee thereupon, with the exception of certain 'certified' Personal Bills for which the interval is three clear days (*cf.* p. 306).

COMMITTEE STAGE

The Committee Stage of a Private Bill is by far the most important stage of its career through the House. Here, if the Bill be opposed, the real battle is waged, not between the Bill and the House or between parties in the House, but between the promoters and the opponents of the measure, with the House—in the form of a Private Bill Committee—acting as referee. The House of Commons can here be seen still retaining its ancient judicial function side by side with its more ordinary legislative function.

A Private Bill Committee is far more like a court of law than a Committee of the House. Promoters and opponents are represented by Counsel, evidence from witnesses is heard on oath, and the proceedings are in many important particulars very similar to those in the Law Courts. In place, however, of a judge and jury is found a Chairman and three Members of the House of Commons not locally or personally interested in the Bills before them but giving their decisions in accordance with the weight of evidence, the Standing Orders of the House and the public interest in general. They not only give their decisions but also have them embodied in legislative form. In other words, they either find the preamble not proved and so reject the Bill, or find the preamble proved and allow the Bill to proceed with or without amendment, reporting their decisions in every case to the House.

That the House views Private Bill Committees in rather a

different light from other committees, and so stresses the judicial side of their functions, is indicated by the fact that the attendance of all the Members of such committees is required except in case of sickness or by order of the House. The absence of any Member is reported to the House in certain circumstances and the member has frequently been ordered to attend. Furthermore, by Standing Order No. 22 (5) (Public) it is laid down that suspension from the service of the House does not exempt a member from service on a committee on a Private Bill to which he may have been appointed before his suspension. This is the sole duty required or permitted of a suspended Member.

It will be clear from this that the attendance of Members on Private Bill Committees is very important, not only because of the judicial nature of their functions but also because the inquiry may be delayed and the parties may be put to considerable inconvenience and expense.

In committee, then, the fate of the vast majority of Private Bills is decided, and to this stage attention should primarily be directed in studying the passage of Private Bills through the House.

Private Bill Committees

Unopposed Private Bills are dealt with by the Committee on Unopposed Bills (see p. 318).

Opposed Private Bills are formed into groups by the Committee of Selection, who also nominate a committee consisting of a Chairman and three Members to consider each group. These committees are known as Private Bill Committees, and may be termed 'ordinary' Private Bill Committees. Each Session these groups of Bills are distinguished by a letter of the alphabet. The first sitting of the committee and the Bill or Bills to be taken on the first day is laid down by the Committee of Selection, four clear days' notice being given.

Members' Declarations

Before a Private Bill Committee can proceed to business the Chairman and each member must have signed a declaration in which he declares that he is not locally or personally interested in any of the Bills forming a group of opposed Private Bills.

Quorum and Voting

Three is the quorum of a Private Bill Committee, but all members are required to attend. Each member, including the

Chairman, has a vote, and whenever the voices are equal the Chairman has a second or casting vote.

Arrangement of Business and Sittings

After having dealt with business in the order prescribed by the Committee of Selection, the committee are free to arrange the remaining business, but they are required to give two clear days' notice of the appointment of a day for the first consideration of any Bill. It may be explained here that Bills that are not to be taken into consideration on any particular day appear in the list marked with an asterisk or star, and are known as 'Starred' Bills. 'Unstarred' Bills, on the other hand, may be taken into consideration; promoters and opponents, however, have to be in attendance with the Counsel and witnesses, whether they are taken into consideration or not, and so are subjected to expense. It is important, therefore, for the business to be arranged as exactly as possible. For the same reason committees usually sit from day to day on days when the House sits, the usual hours being from eleven until four o'clock, with an interval for lunch. If the committee adjourn over any day on which the House sits, a Report must be made to the House stating the reasons for such adjournment.

If all the petitions against a Bill are withdrawn, the Bill is referred back to the Committee of Selection, provided that no evidence on behalf of the promoters has been given.

Proceedings in Committee

No petitioner is entitled to be heard before the Committee unless he has taken out a *Certificate of Appearance* in the Committee and Private Bill Office and handed it to the Clerk to the Committee. These certificates state the names of the petitioners desiring to appear, together with their Counsel (if any) and Agents, and whether they desire to appear against the preamble, against Clauses, or any particular part of the Bill. Appearances are also important in connexion with fees.

Petitions against alterations in a Bill are sometimes presented, but it is not usual for the Committee to hear such petitions unless they themselves or the promoters should be disposed to accept the alterations. The *locus standi* of petitioners against alterations is decided by the committee on the Bill and not by the Court of Referees (see p. 316). *Petitions in favour* of a Bill involve no right of appearance before a committee.

A copy of a Private Bill as originally presented to the House, together with any amendments, new clauses, or additional provisions, as proposed to be submitted to the Committee by the promoters, is known as the *filled-up Bill*, and is laid before the Committee at their first meeting.

Although, for reasons of space, it is obviously impossible to give anything like a complete description of the proceedings in committee or the great number of points that may arise in connexion therewith, a brief account of the proceedings before a Private Bill Committee, as they normally occur, may be of value.

At the beginning of the proceedings on a Bill the preamble is taken as read the first time. After the Appearances have been read, Counsel for the Bill opens his case and calls witnesses in support of the preamble. The witnesses are sworn by the Chairman or—more usually—the Committee Clerk, and are subject to cross-examination by Counsel representing the petitioners against the Bill.[1]

On the conclusion of the promoters' case, the several Counsel for the petitioners address the Committee and call witnesses, or they may adduce their evidence first and then address the Committee. Witnesses for the petitioners are liable to cross-examination by Counsel for the Bill.

When the case for the petitioners is concluded, Counsel for the Bill replies upon the whole case, but if no evidence has been called or document put in by the opponents there is no right of reply. If a petitioner puts in a document or even, without putting it in, cross-examines the witnesses for the promoters upon it, this generally entitles the promoters to a reply restricted, in some cases, to the particular document quoted.

The Committee-room is then cleared and the Committee deliberate. The preamble is taken as read a second time and the question that the preamble is proved is put by the Chairman.

If the preamble is not proved, the Committee call in the parties and announce their decision; their only remaining business being to report the Bill to the House. A Report of 'Preamble not proved' is, of course, fatal to the Bill, unless, as very rarely happens, the Bill be recommitted and a different decision arrived at.

If, however, the preamble is proved with or without conditions imposed by the Committee, parties are called in and

[1] At this point, the Committee may find the preamble not proved.

informed by the Chairman of the decision of the Committee. Clauses are then considered and amended, rejected or agreed to, as the case may be. Sometimes Counsel are heard and witnesses called.

Finally the Chairman, together with the Agent and Committee Clerk, goes through a copy of the Bill known as 'the Committee Bill' which contains the amendments made in committee. Where any matters have to be specially reported upon to the House, a draft Report is submitted to the Committee and considered by them. This Report is then agreed to and the Bill ordered to be reported to the House.

Such is the usual course of a Private Bill through committee. There remain a few points which it is necessary to mention.

(a) Any *Reports by Government Departments* on a Bill stand referred to the Committee on that Bill. They must be dealt with by Counsel in his opening statement. Representatives of the departments concerned are sometimes present but are not heard unless summoned by the Committee to speak as to the practice and policy of their departments or to explain the report. Public departments can claim no right to be heard except upon petition and, if so heard, their representatives are subject to cross-examination.

(b) In certain cases, Private Bill Committees are bound by Standing Orders to report or to *report specially* on certain subjects. Among the more important points may be mentioned:—

(1) If required by the House or Select Committee on Standing Orders the Committee must state how they have dealt with any Instruction or Resolution.

(2) An appendix is added showing how any reports from Government departments have been dealt with. If the Committee disagree with the recommendations, they must state their reasons.

(3) Any alteration in the Preamble, together with the reasons for making it, must be stated.

(4) In the case of Bills promoted by local authorities all loans and certain other matters must be reported specially upon, and in no case may a period of more than sixty years be allowed for repayment of any loan.

(5) Certain other kinds of Bills must have special matter inserted in their reports, more especially Railway and Tramway Bills.

(For further information reference should be made to Standing Orders.)

(c) If the Committee wish to inform the House of any matter incidentally arising relating to the powers, functions or proceedings of the Committee or of any matters other than those upon which they are required by Standing Orders to report, they must obtain leave from the House to make a *Special Report*.

(d) The *Minutes of Evidence* are printed at the expense of the Promoters of the Bill for the use of members of the Committee and others.

(e) Under the Parliamentary Costs Act, 1865, Committees may award *costs* to promoters or petitioners in certain circumstances. Special mention of such awards must be made by the Committee in their reports. Awards of costs, which in recent years have been very rare, must be unanimous.

STAGES AFTER COMMITTEE
Recommittal of Private Bills

Sometimes Private Bills, after having been reported by a committee, are recommitted by the House. The order for recommittal is often accompanied by an instruction to the committee on the recommitted Bill. Unless the House otherwise directs, a recommitted Bill stands referred to the Committee of Selection; usually, however, such a Bill is referred by the House specifically to the former committee. In a few cases Private Bills have been recommitted to a Committee of the Whole House or to a specially constituted committee.

A Bill may be recommitted either generally or partially and the recommittal motion is usually proposed on consideration in the case of an amended Bill and on third reading in the case of a Bill that has not been amended. A motion to recommit a Bill of which the preamble is declared not to have been proved or which has been reported "Parties do not proceed" may be proposed at any time after the Bill has been reported to the House.

The procedure of the committee on a recommitted Bill

follows, with minor deviations, that of an ordinary Private Bill Committee.

Consideration of Bill and Amendments on Consideration

All Private Bills that have been reported from committees are ordered to lie upon the Table of the House if they have been amended, but, if unamended, are ordered to be read the third time. Three clear days must elapse between the Report and the consideration of a Bill ordered to lie upon the Table, and three clear days before such consideration printed copies of the Bill, as amended, must be deposited in the Vote Office for the use of Members.

Amendments on Consideration may be proposed:—

(a) By the promoters—who must obtain the approval of the Chairman of Ways and Means and the Counsel to Mr. Speaker to such amendments and must, if the Chairman of Ways and Means considers such printing expedient, print the amendments at their own expense.

(b) By Members—who hand in any such amendments at the Table of the House in the usual way or to the Committee and Private Bill Office.

Private Bills that are put down for consideration in the House appear in Private Business under the heading 'Consideration of Bills ordered to lie upon the Table'. The Consideration stage of a Private Bill is largely a revision stage, but it cannot be said to be of nearly such importance in this respect as the same stage of a Public Bill. The House reviews the Bill as reported from the Committee and an opportunity is given to the promoters and to Members of the House to propose amendments. Amendments on consideration by the Promoters of a House of Commons Bill are comparatively rare, as an opportunity for revision will occur in the House of Lords. For Members, however, except those who have actually served on the committee on the Bill, this is the first and only stage for proposing amendments of substance to a Private Bill. Such amendments are restricted by the practice of the House regarding charges upon the people (see p. 259) and by Standing Order No. 51 (Public) which applies to Private Bills and provides that no amendment may be proposed which could not have been proposed in committee without an instruction from the House.

Members may also move to postpone the consideration of

the Bill or to recommit the Bill. In most cases, however, the consideration stage of a Private Bill, like all its other stages except committee stage, goes through without opposition or debate.

When a Bill has been considered by the House, it is ordered to be read the third time.

Third Reading

Notice[1] for the Third Reading of a Private Bill may not be given until the day after that on which the Bill was ordered by the House to be read the third time.

The Third Reading stage of a Private Bill is very similar to that of a Public Bill in principle. The House finally approves of the entire Bill with all the alterations made since Second Reading.

Only verbal Amendments may be made on Third Reading, and if they are proposed by the promoters, they must, if he considers such printing expedient, be printed and receive the approval of the Chairman of Ways and Means or the Counsel to Mr. Speaker.

Certain Bills affecting Crown property or the property of the Duchies of Lancaster and Cornwall require the consent of the King. If there is a Prince of Wales his consent instead of the King's is required on behalf of the Duchy of Cornwall. It is at this stage that such consents are usually signified. When the Third Reading of such a Bill is to be taken in the House, the consent must be signified by a Privy Councillor before the Bill can be read the third time (see p. 323).

A Private Bill may, if necessary, be recommitted at this stage, but this is very unusual. Normally the Bill is passed and sent up to the Lords in a message in the same way as a Public Bill.

Lords' Amendments

When a Private Bill has been amended in the Lords, it is sent back to the Commons with the amendments attached. No notice[1] for the consideration of such amendments may be given until the day after that on which the Bill is returned from the Lords.

Amendments proposed to be made to the Lords' Amendments go through the same process as amendments on consideration (see p. 303).

---

[1] One clear day's notice is required.

Shortly before the summer adjournment, an order is sometimes made by the House—on the motion of the Chairman of Ways and Means—suspending the Standing Orders relating to the consideration of Lords' Amendments, and ordering them, with certain exceptions, to be considered on the day after they have been received from the Lords.

In the rare cases when the House has resolved to disagree with any of the Lords' Amendments, the procedure is similar to that in the case of a Public Bill.

Royal Assent

When a Private Bill has been finally agreed to by both Houses, it receives the Royal Assent in the usual way and becomes an Act of Parliament (see p. 229). It is declared to be a Public Act[1] and is judicially noticed as such though printed in a separate volume of the Statutes and given a chapter number in Roman numerals.

HOUSE OF LORDS' BILLS

Private Bills that are brought from the House of Lords to the House of Commons may be of three kinds:—

(1) Bills which, though founded on petition to the Commons, have originated in the Lords according to the decision of the Chairman of Ways and Means and the Lord Chairman of Committees.

(2) Late Bills introduced into the Lords.

(3) Bills certified as Personal Bills, *i.e.* Estate, Naturalization, Restitution and Name Bills, which in practice originate in the Lords.

Private Bills that have been brought from the Lords pass through the same stages and follow the same procedure in general as Bills originating in the Commons. Certain differences must, however, be now described.

Bills brought from the Lords are read the first time on the day that they are received and, unless they are Name Bills, are referred to the Examiners.

Memorials may only be deposited if the Bill is a Personal Bill or a Late Bill, as all other Bills have already been examined prior to their introduction in the House of Lords.

Petitions against any Lords' Bill must be deposited not later than ten clear days after the First Reading of the Bill.

[1] Interpretation Act, 1889, ss. 9 and 39.

The day first appointed for the Second Reading must not be later than seven clear days after the report of the Examiners, or of the Select Committee on Standing Orders, has been presented to the House.

There must be an interval of three clear days between the committal and the committee on every opposed 'certified' Bill of the category relating to personal affairs of an individual (see p. 292); in all other cases of opposed Bills the usual interval of six clear days must elapse.

After the Third Reading, the Bill is returned to the Lords with a copy of any amendments made in its passage through the House of Commons, in much the same way as a Public Bill. If the Lords do not agree to any amendments made by the Commons, the procedure again follows that of a Public Bill. Instances of this, however, are very uncommon.

LATE BILLS, LATE DEPOSITS, AND WITHDRAWALS

Some reference must be made to certain cases of the following:—

(1) Late Bills and deposits.

(2) Withdrawals of Bills and documents.

(1) *Late Bills and Deposits*

Late Bills are Bills for which a petition has not been deposited on or before the 27th November. As they are of various kinds and the procedure on them differs to some extent, they can only be briefly mentioned here.

(*a*) They may arise from the fact that parties, who have not deposited a petition at the correct time, desire to introduce a Private Bill during the current session.

(*b*) Sometimes the House gives leave for a Late Bill to be introduced in lieu of a Bill withdrawn by order of the House.

(*c*) The annual Money Bill of the London County Council is specially provided for in Standing Orders 220 and 221.

The further procedure upon such Bills and the opposition to them together with the deposit of late documents in connexion with them is normal except for periods and times of stages and deposits which are laid down in Standing Orders.

One form of late deposit must, however, be specially mentioned here. If the promoters of a Bill wish to insert additional provisions such as could not be inserted by way of ordinary amendment, they may deposit a *Petition for Additional Provision(s)*. Such petitions, which must be endorsed by the Chairman of Ways and Means, together with a printed copy of the proposed new clauses, may be deposited at any time before a Bill is reported from a committee. The petitions stand referred to the Examiners, and as they always involve a non-compliance, are subsequently referred to the Standing Orders Committee, who give leave to the Committee on the Bill, if they think fit, to insert the provisions or withhold such leave.

(2) *Withdrawal of Bills and Documents*

The Promoters of a Private Bill may at any time give notice of their intention not to proceed with their Bill. If, however, the Bill has been put down in the House for any stage by order of the House, it can only be withdrawn by a further order of the House. Under the direction of the Chairman of Ways and Means the order for that particular stage is read and discharged, and the Bill is then withdrawn. It should be noted that, if the promoters of a Private Bill refuse to proceed and if no further parties undertake its support, the Bill is dead, however sensible the House may be of its value.

Petitions or Memorials may be withdrawn at any time by the parties, who must fill up a requisition for the withdrawal of their petition or memorial in the Committee and Private Bill Office.

Suspension of Bills at Prorogation or Dissolution

A Dissolution of Parliament sometimes occurs before the Private Business before the House has been disposed of, and in this case it is usual for both Houses to make Orders suspending further proceedings on Private and Provisional Order Bills in order to enable the promoters to proceed with the same Bills in the next session. Such Orders are general; but special Orders are also sometimes made late in a session by the House in which the Bill is being considered and then communicated to the other House, where similar Orders are made.

In order that they may not lapse when Parliament is prorogued or dissolved, all Suspension Orders are made Standing Orders of the House.

In the following Session Suspended Bills, unless the House otherwise orders, go through—*pro forma*—those stages which they have already completed, and are taken up precisely at the point to which they had previously attained.

BILLS FOR CONFIRMING PROVISIONAL ORDERS

During the latter half of the 19th century there sprang into being what is known as 'the Provisional Order System.' The chief objects of this system were to simplify, shorten and cheapen procedure by Private Bill. Under a great variety of Acts—passed mostly between 1870 and 1900—most Government departments are empowered to issue Provisional Orders which in their scope and object are practically Private Bills. The Orders are usually issued by the department on the application of the parties concerned. Thus the Government department is 'the Promoter' and the parties 'the Applicants'. In certain cases, however, departments may issue Orders on their own initiative. In the ordinary way the Government department brings in a Bill declaring the expediency of confirming the Orders which are scheduled to it, the Bill being known as a Provisional Order Confirmation Bill and the Orders themselves as Provisional Orders.

It is not possible here to enumerate all the Acts under which Provisional Orders may be issued (this information may be found in the current "Index to the Statutes"—see also May, pp. 976 *et seq.*), but a brief account will be given of the method by which the confirming Bills are dealt with in the House of Commons.

PROCEDURE

It may be stated here that an important feature in the issue of Provisional Orders is the preliminary local inquiry conducted by the department concerned. The procedure, however, varies in many cases and can only be studied by reference to the enabling Act; moreover, it is departmental in nature and need not be noticed further here.

In certain cases it is expressly prescribed that the confirming Bill shall proceed as a Public Bill; with these exceptions the procedure is as described below:—

Presentation to Committal

Bills for confirming Provisional Orders are introduced as Public Bills by the Minister concerned, but at the time of Private Business, and, after First Reading, are referred to the

Examiners. No notices are given of the various stages and no intervals are required to elapse; the various proceedings, except before the Examiners or in committee, being taken from day to day, unless the Bill is opposed in the House or for some other good reason.

Before the Examiners, compliance with Standing Orders 212 and 213, which relate to the deposit of certain documents and the acquisition of land, is required to be proved (S.O. 214). In the case of a Bill brought from the Lords certain other compliances are required. When the Examiners have reported that no Standing Orders are applicable, or that the Standing Orders applicable have been complied with, or the Standing Orders Committee have reported that Standing Orders should be dispensed with, the Bill is ordered to be read a second time on the following day. If, however, the Standing Orders Committee report that Standing Orders ought not to be dispensed with and the House takes no further action in the matter, the Bill is dead.

After Second Reading, every Provisional Order Bill is committed and, unless expressly referred to a Joint or specially constituted Committee, stands referred to the Committee of Selection.

Committee Stage

The Committee stage of Provisional Order Bills is subject to the Standing Orders regulating the proceedings on Private Bills so far as they are applicable. Fees are invariably remitted to the Promoters, but the applicants are liable to certain fees, and also opponents who appear before any Committee. Petitions against a Provisional Order Bill originating in the Commons must be deposited not later than seven clear days after notice has been given of the day on which the Bill will be examined; while in the case of Bills brought from the Lords they must be presented not later than ten clear days after First Reading.

Proceedings in Committee

Provisional Order Bills are dealt with in Committee either by ordinary Private Bill Committees or by the Committee on Unopposed Bills according to whether they are opposed or unopposed. The great majority of them are, however, unopposed.

When any Order contained in any such Bill is opposed, the Committee may divide the Bill into two Bills, dealing with the opposed or unopposed Orders respectively, and report them separately to the House.

If there is more than one Order, the consideration of the preamble of the Bill is postponed until each Order has been separately considered. The Question put by the Chairman is, "That the —— Order be confirmed", instead of "That the preamble is proved", as in the case of a Private Bill. Opposed Orders are considered before unopposed Orders.

If an Order is not confirmed, the title is amended by striking out the name of the Order in question.

The Committee may amend a Provisional Order if the amendment is of such a nature that it would have been within the powers of the Department by which the Order was made to incorporate it in the Order as issued. Such amendments are made in the scheduled Order and a consequential amendment, to indicate that the Order has been amended, is made in the confirming Bill. But no new matter should be introduced into the scheduled Order which would be inconsistent with or go beyond the notices required by the Act under which the Order is issued. It has also been held undesirable that new matter of this kind should be introduced into the confirming Bill. Furthermore it is not now the practice to entertain an amendment to the confirming Bill which goes beyond the scope of the powers conferred by the Act under which the Order is made.

In a few cases costs may be awarded by a majority of the committee instead of unanimously, as is required in the majority of cases of Provisional Order Bills and of all Private Bills.

After Report, a Provisional Order Bill is ordered to be considered, as amended—or if not amended, to be read the third time—on the following day, and thereafter pursues its course as an ordinary Public Bill though at the time of Private Business.

BILLS FOR CONFIRMING PROVISIONAL ORDERS UNDER THE PRIVATE LEGISLATION PROCEDURE (SCOTLAND) ACT, 1936

Private Legislation in Scotland is almost entirely conducted under the Private Legislation Procedure (Scotland) Act, 1936, which consolidated the Acts of 1899 and 1933 and which gives the Secretary of State for Scotland very wide powers of issuing Provisional Orders. The Act does not apply to the power of issuing Provisional Orders possessed by any Government

Department or the Electricity Commissioners under any Act passed before the 29th July, 1933, or to Estate Bills, but Bills for confirming Orders issued by the Secretary of State for Scotland under any Act passed before the 10th August, 1899, are brought under the procedure of Section 9 of the Private Legislation (Procedure) Act when passing through Parliament (see p. 312).

Proceedings under the Act are regulated by 'General Orders' made by the Chairman of Committees of the House of Lords and the Chairman of Ways and Means acting jointly with the Secretary of State and laid before Parliament. These Orders in the main follow closely the Standing Orders of the House relating to Private Business.

All documents relating to Scottish Provisional Orders are deposited at the Scottish Office. Petitions for the issue of Orders are deposited on or before the 27th November or 27th March—two opportunities being thus provided. Copies of the draft Orders must be deposited in the Committee and Private Bill Office, and a list of such Orders is published on each occasion.

The Chairmen of the two Houses, who are empowered by the Act to determine all questions of practice and procedure, report to the Secretary of State on each draft Order and a copy is laid before Parliament. The draft Orders are referred, by arrangement, to the Examiners, and they report to the Secretary of State and the Chairmen; any question of dispensing with General Orders being decided by the Chairmen.

When the Chairmen have reported that a Draft Order may proceed, the Secretary of State considers the Order, and if there is opposition or he considers it necessary, directs that an inquiry should be held. The inquiry is held in Scotland by Commissioners (chosen partly from a Parliamentary Panel of not more than 25 members appointed by the House of Commons and nominated by the Committee of Selection in each session), who recommend what action should be taken on the Orders submitted to them, and the Secretary of State takes action accordingly.

If there is no inquiry or the Commissioners have reported that the Order should be issued, the Secretary of State makes the Order as prayed with such modifications as appear to be necessary having regard to the recommendations of the Chairmen, of Public Departments and, when an inquiry has been held, of the Commissioners.

Any modified Order is again referred to the Examiners and a copy deposited in the Committee and Private Bill Office. As soon as may be the confirming Bill is introduced, and proceeded with according to whether or not an inquiry has been held.

Procedure under Section 7 of the Act

A Bill to confirm any Order upon which no inquiry has been held is introduced and ordered to be proceeded with under Section 7 of the Act. Such a Bill is deemed to have passed all stages up to and including Committee, and is ordered to be considered, as a rule, upon the following day. The Bill is subsequently proceeded with in the same way as an ordinary Provisional Order Bill.

Procedure under Section 9 of the Act

A Bill to confirm any Order upon which an inquiry has been held follows a somewhat different procedure, which is laid down in Section 9 of the Act. Such a Bill is introduced and read the first time and ordered to be read a second time, but an opportunity is then given for the presentation of a petition against the Order. If within seven days after the introduction a petition against any Order contained in the Bill is presented, any member may move to refer the Bill to a Joint Committee— such motion being made after Second Reading. If the motion is carried, the Bill is referred to a Joint Committee of six members, three from each House, the Commons members being nominated by the Committee of Selection. Parties are heard by Counsel and agents in the usual way, the committee being given power to determine any question of *locus standi* and, by a majority, to award costs. After the report of the Joint Committee, the Bill follows the usual course.

If there is no petition against a Scottish Provisional Order, there is no opportunity of referring the Bill to a committee in either House. When no such petition is presented or the motion for a Joint Committee is either not made or not carried, the Bill is deemed to have passed committee stage—being ordered to be considered after Second Reading. The consideration and Third Reading stages follow the usual course.

A Bill to confirm any Order upon which an inquiry has been held, when brought from the Lords is read the first and second time without the interval for the presentation of a petition, is deemed to have passed committee stage and subsequently follows the usual course.

Bills to confirm Provisional Orders under the Private Legislation Procedure (Scotland) Act are seldom opposed, and they almost invariably pass through all their stages in the House with great rapidity.

Substituted Bills

If the Chairmen report that the provisions of any draft Order relate to matters outside Scotland to such an extent, or raise questions of public policy of such novelty and importance that they ought to be dealt with by Private Bill and not by Provisional Order, the Secretary of State must refuse to issue a Provisional Order. The applicants may proceed, however, by way of a Private Bill known as a 'Substituted Bill'.

The Petitions for and against the original Draft Order are held to apply to the Substituted Bill, and are transmitted by the Scottish Office to the Committee and Private Bill Office. Compliance with certain other conditions must be proved before the Examiners, and then the Bill proceeds as an ordinary Private Bill, the Chairmen deciding in which House it shall originate.

Parliamentary powers in Scotland and elsewhere

If representation is made to the Secretary of State by any public authority or persons that they desire to obtain Parliamentary powers to be operative in Scotland and elsewhere and by means of one enactment for the uniform regulation of the affairs of an undertaking, the Secretary of State and the Chairmen may allow these powers to be sought by means of a Private Bill instead of by a Private Bill and a Provisional Order and in this case the Private Legislation Procedure (Scotland) Act no longer applies to any such powers.

SPECIAL PROCEDURE ORDERS, see Appendix V.

SPECIAL ORDERS

As Private Bills have been to some extent superseded by Provisional Orders, so the Provisional Order system has, in certain cases, itself been superseded by the system of Special Orders, apart from the Special Procedure Order system.

Under Section 10 of the Gas Regulation Act, 1920, as extended by Section 7 of the Gas Undertakings Act, 1929, and under Section 26 of the Electricity (Supply) Act, 1919, the Ministry of Fuel and Power are empowered under certain circumstances to issue to local authorities or other applicants draft Special Orders relating to gas and to electricity respectively. Special Orders do not become operative until they have been laid in draft before both Houses of Parliament and until both Houses by resolution have approved the draft either with or without modifications or additions.

The resolutions approving draft Special Orders appear on the Order Paper among the Orders of the Day and are approved or discussed at the time of Public Business. As a rule the resolutions are agreed to after eleven o'clock[1] (see p. 166) without discussion or opposition. Sometimes slight modifications in the draft Special Orders are made at this time.

In several cases the Special Orders have been opposed and the Resolution has been amended so as to refer the Order to a select committee. Opponents were given leave to deposit Statements of Objection—in the earlier cases at the Department concerned but later in the Committee and Private Bill Office—upon which they were entitled to appear before the Committee. The committee were ordered to proceed with the Order as if it were a Provisional Order Bill under Standing Order 217. The Chairman was appointed by the Committee of Selection in two cases and in the later cases fees have been charged to applicants and opponents.

The Special Order system is still somewhat fluid so far as procedure is concerned. An entirely different procedure has been laid down by the House of Lords for that House, and it is perhaps still rather early to speculate on how the system will develop or in what way it will achieve a more final form.

COMMITTEES AND OFFICERS FOR PRIVATE BUSINESS

THE EXAMINERS

The Examiners consist of one or more officers of the House of Commons who are known officially as the Examiners of Petitions for Private Bills and are appointed by the Speaker. In practice there are two Examiners, one appointed by the Speaker and the other by the House of Lords, who act impartially for, and report to, the two Houses. Before them are proved all facts relating to compliance or non-compliance with the Standing Orders. The Examiners have been given the same

[1] For altered hours, see Appendix IV.

powers by both Houses and report to both Houses on Bills or other matters which at the time may only be within the cognisance of one House. The object of this is to save time and to prevent expense to the parties which might result from conflicting decisions in the two Houses separately.

The Examiners deal, in the same way, with Provisional Order Bills and, by an arrangement with the Scottish Office, with Bills for confirming Provisional Orders under the Private Legislation Procedure (Scotland) Act; in this last case compliance with General Orders issued by the Scottish Office is proved.

The Examiner appointed by the House of Commons also acts as Taxing Master for that House and is responsible for the taxation of the costs incurred in the promotion of, and opposition to, Private Bills on the application of parties or the Minister of Health.

About the 18th December the Examiners begin their work for the session, when they severally examine the petitions for Private Bills which have been deposited on the 27th November. Opposition to Petitions before the Examiners is founded upon a 'Memorial' which complains of non-compliance with Standing Orders (see p. 294). On the day appointed for the examination of a petition, the memorialist enters an appearance upon his memorial in the Committee and Private Bill Office. Unless this appearance is handed in, the memorialist has no right to be heard. The Examiner then hears the case for and against, and certifies on each petition whether the Standing Orders have or have not been complied with. Memorials are, nowadays, rather rare and proceedings before the Examiners tend to become brief and informal, consisting chiefly of the reading of affidavits.

The Examiners continue their work throughout the Session, reporting on the various matters referred to them from time to time. They report their decisions to the House, and may also make Special Reports. All reports of non-compliance or special reports are referred to the Standing Orders Committee.

The Standing Orders Committee

The Standing Orders Committee is a sessional committee entirely connected with Private Business consisting of the Chairman of Ways and Means (who is *ex officio* chairman), the Deputy Chairman, and not less than two Members selected by the Chairman from a panel appointed by the Committee of

Selection at the beginning of each session. The quorum of the committee is three and they have the assistance of the Counsel to Mr. Speaker.

To this committee are referred:—

(1) All reports of the Examiners stating that Standing Orders have not been complied with.

(2) All special reports made by the Examiners.

(3) All petitions for leave to dispense with Standing Orders.

The duty of the committee in cases (1) and (3) above is to decide whether Standing Orders ought or ought not to be dispensed with, and—if to be dispensed with—under what (if any) conditions. In case (2) the findings of the Examiner on any question of fact are binding on the committee whose duty is to decide how the Standing Orders are to be construed and whether, on the facts as found by the Examiner, the Standing Orders have or have not been complied with and, in the latter case, whether they should be dispensed with.

The Committee are given special power to report on cases referred to them in respect of Private Bills originating in the Lords and not before the House of Commons.

The proceedings of the Committee are comparatively informal. According to the usual practice, written statements are prepared on the one side by the Agent for the Bill, and on the other by the Agents for the memorialists (if any) who had appeared before the Examiners and, in the case of Petitions, by the Agent for the petitioners and the Agents for the opponents (if any). Sometimes the parties are heard, but speeches are, as a rule, limited to one on each side.

The Committee report their decision to the House, and it should be noted that if they report that Standing Orders ought to be dispensed with the House agrees with their Resolution, whereas if they report that Standing Orders ought not to be dispensed with the House merely orders the Resolution to lie upon the Table. This latter procedure is to enable the question to be reopened, but this has seldom been done. If no action is taken there can be no further proceedings on the Petition or Bill.

(For further information see May, 852 *et seq.*)

COURT OF REFEREES

The Court of Referees consists of the Chairman of Ways and Means, the Deputy Chairman, the Counsel to Mr. Speaker, and not less than seven members appointed by the Speaker for such periods as he thinks fit. The Referees may form one or more Courts consisting of at least three members.

The practice and procedure of the Referees are prescribed by rules framed by the Chairman of Ways and Means and laid on the Table of the House. Their duty is to decide on the *locus standi* of petitioners where such *locus standi* has been challenged and to report whether they should be heard and under what (if any) conditions or whether they should not be heard.

The procedure of the Court is very similar to that of a Private Bill Committee. Appearances are taken out, but only one Counsel may be heard on each side unless specially authorized by the Referees. Evidence is seldom given and witnesses, if called, are not sworn. The decisions of the Court are governed to some extent by Standing Orders but more largely by cases and precedents. (For which see May, 874 *et seq.*)

COMMITTEE OF SELECTION

The Committee of Selection is a sessional committee consisting of eleven members, of whom three constitute a quorum. Though nominated at the time of Private Business, the Committee are concerned both with Public and with Private Business. To them, in their latter capacity, are referred all Private and Provisional Order Bills, other than Bills referred to specially constituted Committees or Provisional Orders under the Private Legislation Procedure (Scotland) Act.

The powers and duties of the Committee may be summarized briefly as follows:—

(1) To refer unopposed Bills to the Committee on Unopposed Bills;

(2) to form opposed Bills into groups and to refer them to Private Bill Committees;

(3) to appoint and nominate all Private Bill Committees consisting of a Chairman and three members not locally or otherwise interested in the Bills, to fix the time for holding the first sitting of every such Committee and to name the Bill or Bills to be considered on the first day;

(4) to obtain declarations from all members of Private Bill Committees that they are not locally or personally interested in any of the Bills before them;

(5) to discharge members from such Committees and substitute other members for them;

(6) to appoint members to the panel for the Standing Orders Committee and for the Committee on Unopposed Bills and to nominate members of the panel under the Private Legislation Procedure (Scotland) Act, 1936, and of such other select or joint committees as they may be ordered to by the House.

It should be noted that the Committee of Selection may not treat any Bill as an opposed Bill unless, within the time specified in Standing Orders, a petition in which the petitioners pray to be heard has been presented against it; or unless the Chairman of Ways and Means has reported to the House that any unopposed Private Bill ought to be treated as opposed (see S.O. 85).

(For the work of the Committee of Selection in relation to Public Business, see pp. 239-40.

For further information concerning Private Business, see May, 857 *et seq.*)

COMMITTEE ON UNOPPOSED BILLS

The Committee on Unopposed Bills is composed of five members, namely, the Chairman of Ways and Means (who is *ex officio* chairman), the Deputy Chairman and three members selected from time to time by the Chairman from a panel appointed by the Committee of Selection at the beginning of each session. This committee consider and report upon all Bills referred to them by the Committee of Selection, whether unopposed Private or Provisional Order Bills. The Committee have the assistance of the Counsel to Mr. Speaker, and the quorum is three.

The proceedings of the committee are necessarily more brief and informal than those of an ordinary Private Bill committee. There being no opposition, parties are usually represented by their solicitor or agent. The main duty of the committee is, in reality, to see that the Standing Orders of the House have been complied with and that public rights have not been unduly infringed.

SELECT COMMITTEE ON A PRIVATE BILL

Private and Provisional Order Bills are sometimes referred to specially constituted Committees which are usually nominated partly by the House and partly by the Committee of Selection. These cases are somewhat rare, but it may be of interest to mention some of the differences in procedure between a Select Committee on a Private Bill and an ordinary Private Bill Committee:—

(1) The quorum is usually fixed by the House, in which case members are not bound to attend nor is their absence reported to the House. If no quorum is fixed, all members must attend.

(2) The Chairman is chosen by the Committee and can only vote when there is an equality of voices.

(3) The members sign no declarations.

(4) The Committee may adjourn over a day on which the House sits without reporting the fact to the House.

(5) The Committee have power to send for persons, papers and records, and do not have to obtain leave to make a Special Report.

(6) The House usually makes an Order—on appointing the Committee—that all petitions against the Bill presented a certain number of clear days before the meeting of the Committee, or before a certain date, be referred to the Committee and that the petitioners be heard by themselves, their Counsel or Agents against the Bill, and Counsel heard in support of the Bill. This Order overrides all the ordinary rules regarding petitions.

In other respects, the procedure follows closely that of an ordinary Private Bill Committee.

JOINT COMMITTEE ON A PRIVATE BILL

Joint Committees are sometimes set up on the initiative of one House or the other to deal with Private Bills—the Committee being proposed by the House in which the Bill originates. The communications between the two Houses follow the usual course with the exception that they take place at the time of Private Business.

Private Bills are referred to Joint Committees for various reasons; but it may be said that as a rule a Bill, or group of Bills, so referred contains some important point of principle which it is considered advisable for both Houses to decide upon together. Of recent years, Bills dealing with questions such as water charges, docks and harbours, and the right of railway companies to run road and air transport have been dealt with by Joint Committees.

Y

The main difference between a Private Bill referred to a Joint Committee and to an ordinary Private Bill Committee should be noticed at the outset, namely, that the Committee stage in the second House is usually dispensed with.

A distinction, therefore, must be drawn between Commons' Bills and Lords' Bills; the former—if referred to a Joint Committee—go through their normal course; the latter, however, when they subsequently reach the House of Commons, go through the usual stages up to and including Second Reading, but at that point Standing Orders are usually suspended—on a motion proposed by the Chairman of Ways and Means—and the Committee stage, and sometimes also the Report stage, is dispensed with and the Bill proceeds at once to the Third Reading stage.

Bills are sometimes referred to Joint Committees already set up, and in 1928, and again in 1929, a Joint Committee was appointed to which were to be referred all Private Bills containing consolidating enactments only.

In the order setting up their half of the Committee, the Commons either nominate the members themselves or—more usually—order the Committee of Selection so to do.

Proceedings in Committee

A Joint Committee, from the point of view of the House of Commons, is simply a Select Committee on a Private Bill appointed to join with a Select Committee of the House of Lords, and as such shows some of the same differences from an ordinary Private Bill Committee. (See Select Committee on a Private Bill.)

Certain further differences may be summarized as follows:—

(1) The Chairman is usually—but not always—a member of the House of Lords.

(2) The procedure of the Committee—in whichever House the Bills originate—follows the practice of the House of Lords (see p. 250).

(3) Fees are payable to the House of Commons only if the Bill originates in that House.

(4) The Standing Orders which require certain matters to be reported upon in certain cases by Committees on Private Bills in the House of Commons are held not to apply to Joint Committees.

When the consideration of a Bill is concluded, the Bill, if originating in the House of Commons, is reported to that House by a Commons' Member of the Committee deputed for that purpose. If, however, the Bill originated in the House of Lords, it is reported to that House, and a Commons' Member of the Committee is directed to make a report to that effect to his House except in cases where the Committee make a Special Report, when it is considered unnecessary to give any such direction as the Special Report is presented to both Houses and serves sufficiently to inform the House of Commons of the proceedings of the Joint Committee.

FORMAL COMMUNICATIONS BETWEEN THE CROWN AND THE HOUSE OF COMMONS

It will be convenient to bring together and set out briefly the various occasions and methods of formal communications between the Crown and the House of Commons, scattered references to which are contained in several chapters of this book. The occasions of direct communication between the Crown and the two Houses assembled together in Parliament for the purpose of the delivery of the King's Speech or the giving of the Royal Assent to Bills are not here in question. They are fully dealt with elsewhere.

Occasional Messages from the Crown

Written messages under the sign-manual are brought from the Crown by a Member of the House who is a Minister of the Crown. The bearer of the message appears at the Bar, informs the Speaker that he has a message to the House from the King signed with his own hand, and on being so desired by the Speaker brings it to the Chair, when it is read at length by the Speaker, all the Members being uncovered.

These messages, relating as they do to important public events may be considered as additions to the King's Speech (May, 781).

A message under the royal sign-manual is generally acknowledged by an Address, ordered to be presented by Privy Councillors or members of the Royal Household. To messages respecting pecuniary aid the voting of a sum of money, not of an Address in answer, is the customary acknowledgment.

Occasional messages are sometimes communicated to the House verbally (C.J. 1911, 75).

Messages from the Crown Incidental to other Business

The Royal Pleasure.—This phrase covers communications dealing with certain recurring business of the House of Commons, *e.g.* the election of the Speaker, the announcement of a prorogation, and the summons of the House for this and other purposes to the House of Peers. The bearer of the summons on such occasions is Black Rod—more fully, the Gentleman Usher of the Black Rod—an officer who performs similar duties in the House of Lords to those of the Serjeant at Arms in the Commons. His entrance interrupts business in the House of Commons and forms a House, when it has been suspended, *e.g.*, for lack of a quorum. If the House is in committee, the Speaker resumes the Chair before Black Rod is admitted.

The *King's Recommendation*, which is required, by an important rule of the constitution, to be given to motions involving public expenditure, is signified by a Minister of the Crown (see p. 259).

The King's Consent (to be distinguished from the Royal Assent to Bills) is given by a Privy Councillor to Bills (and occasionally amendments) affecting local and personal interests which concern the royal prerogative, the hereditary revenue or personal property or interests of the Crown or Duchy of Cornwall (May, 783). If the Prince of Wales is of age, his consent, not the King's, is signified in respect of the Duchy of Cornwall. The King's Consent cannot be communicated in committee, is generally given at the third reading, and its omission, when it is required, renders the proceedings on the passage of a Bill null and void. Similar to the King's Consent is the form of communication from the Crown "placing its interest at the disposal of Parliament", which is required in the case of Public Bills specially affecting the rights of the Crown, its patronage or prerogative (Todd, ii. 60), and should be given before the committee stage (Church Temporalities (Ireland) Bill, 1833). In 1868 the Queen placed her interest at the disposal of Parliament for the purpose of a Bill in reply to an Address of the House of Commons (May, 786).

Addresses to the Crown

The presentation of an Address is the method by which either House communicates with the Sovereign, and is reserved for that purpose, communications (of congratulation or condolence) with members of the Royal Family being effected by messages. An Address may deal with any matter connected with the government or welfare of the country. It is generally presented by a Privy Councillor or member of the Royal Household, but may be presented by the whole House headed by the Speaker (C.J. 1918, 250, C.J. 1934–35, 191, May, 789).

His Majesty's answer to an Address is reported to the House either:—

(1) by the Speaker in the case of an Address presented by the whole House, or

(2) when the Address was presented in the ordinary way, by a member of the Royal Household (who is also a member of the House), who appears at the Bar in levée dress immediately after prayers, and on being called by the Speaker reads His Majesty's answer, and then brings it to the Table, advancing and retiring with the formalities customary on such occasions.

An Address is the recognized way of obtaining papers from the department of a Secretary of State, etc. (see p. 92). An Address for this purpose is not formally presented, and is answered merely by the presentation of the paper desired.

APPENDIX II
STATUTES, STATUTORY INSTRUMENTS AND MEASURES

A. STATUTES

STATUTE' and 'Act' are now ordinarily used as equivalent terms, the former having, perhaps, a more collective, and the latter a more individual, reference. But the Statute Book includes (in its early part) statutes which were not made with the concurrence of the Commons and are therefore not Acts of Parliament, and on the other hand it now excludes all Acts of a local and personal character.

For the text of what may be called the Statute Book the following should be consulted:

For the period 1235–1713, the *Statutes of the Realm*, officially published under the supervision of the Record Commissioners 1810–22, in nine folio volumes.

From 1713–85, the *Statutes at Large*, Ruffhead's edition, edited by Runnington (these volumes, though unofficial, were printed from the King's Printer's copies, but omit statutes of minor or transitory importance).

From 1786–97, the *Public Acts, i.e.* all Acts with the exception of Private Acts (see below).

From 1798, onwards, the *Public General Acts.*

The classification of Acts (which rests on the classification of Bills) was varied in the last century. From 1798 to 1868 they were issued in two series: (1) Public General Acts and (2) Local and Private Acts (*i.e.* all Acts which had been introduced as Public and Private Bills respectively). After 1868, Public Acts of a local character (*i.e.* principally those introduced as Provisional Order Bills) were removed from the series of *Public General Acts* and placed in that of *Local and Personal Acts.* In the last few years Measures passed by the National Assembly of the Church of England have been included in the volumes of Public General Acts.

A volume of *Public General Acts* for any recent year contains:—

I. A Table for the titles of the Public General Acts.

II. A Table of the titles of the Church Assembly Measures.

Copies of all the Acts followed by all the Measures of a session, arranged in the order in which they received the Royal Assent.

III. A Table showing the effect of the legislation of the session in repealing or amending previous Acts.

IV. An Index to the Acts and Measures.

The Revised Statutes.—The object of the various editions of the *Revised Statutes* has been to give only the statutes in force freed from the mass of repealed and superseded enactments. They are founded on the results of Statute Law Revision Acts, and have been prepared under the supervision of the Statute Law Committee appointed in 1868. By virtue of the Interpretation Act, references in post-1889 statutes are references *prima facie* to the *Revised Statutes*.

There have been two editions of the *Revised Statutes*:—
(1) to 1878 in 18 volumes;
(2) to 1886 in 16 volumes (carried down to 1920 by the issue of eight supplementary volumes).

These editions reduce the bulk of the Statute Book by about five-sixths.

An *Index to the Statutes* is published in two volumes annually under the supervision of the Statute Law Committee. The first volume contains a Chronological Table of all the statutes, showing total and partial repeals. The second volume is an index to laws in force, framed in accordance with instructions prepared by Lord Thring in 1876. It is a classification of statute law into subjects arranged in groups and subdivisions with the references given to the appropriate statutes.

B. STATUTORY INSTRUMENTS[1]

This term includes the greater part, but not all, of the subsidiary law-making entrusted to the executive by statute. As about one in two Acts every session makes use of the machinery for delegating power to issue rules and orders for the purpose of supplementing its own provisions, it is not surprising that these rules and orders are increasing rapidly or that the annual volumes in which they are printed are two or three times as bulky as the annual volumes of the statutes.[2] These volumes appear in an annual series of *Statutory Instruments* edited from 1890 until 1922 by Mr. A. Pulling, until 1942 by Sir Cecil Carr, and now by Mr. A. de J. Carey. A list of the official publications relating to statutory rules and orders is given in Carr's *Delegated Legislation*, p. 61. The more comprehensive term 'statutory instruments' was substituted by the Statutory Instruments Act, 1946, to cover all documents of a legislative character issuing from departments.

What is included?

The documents which come under this head are defined by the Act of 1946 (replacing the Rules Publication Act, 1893) and the Regulations made by the Treasury, with the concurrence of the Lord Chancellor and the Speaker, under the Act of 1893. They include the orders, rules, regulations or other subordinate legislation resulting

---

[1] Reference should be made to *Delegated Legislation*, by C. T. Carr, 1921, from which the following notes are mostly taken.

[2] See the figures given by the Prime Minister (*Deb.*, 4th March, 1929, c. 25).

from the exercise of a power conferred by statute on His Majesty in Council or a Minister of the Crown. They exclude, of course, bye-laws of local authorities or railway companies. But they also exclude Orders in Council or other instruments made by virtue of the prerogative, *e.g.* letters patent granting constitutions to Crown Colonies. (These are printed as an appendix to the annual volumes of *Statutory Instruments*.)

What do they do?

The ways in which delegated legislation affects the Statute Book are classified under three heads (Carr, c. ii).

1. Direct amendment,—such as the power to adapt previous Acts given by section 311 (5) of the Government of India Act, 1935.

2. Creation of legislative machinery,—

(1) power to fix the 'appointed day' for the coming into force of an Act—a convenient method of procedure in the case of Acts introducing constitutional or administrative changes;

(2) power to extend the application of an Act,—(*a*) to other subjects (*e.g.* to apply the Petroleum (Consolidation) Act, 1928, to substances other than petroleum), or (*b*) geographically;

(3) power to apply groups of Acts: *e.g.* the Air Force (Constitution) Act, 1917, by sect. 13 authorized the application by order in council to the Air Force of any statute relating to the Army—more than 100 have been so applied.

3. Supplementary legislation,—*e.g.* the power frequently given to a department to carry out the generally stated purposes of an Act by detailed rules.

How are they limited and safeguarded?

1. The purposes for which the rules may be made ought always to be clearly defined in the parent statute. The question whether any rules are *ultra vires* is then a question for the courts. Thus the validity of rules made under the Defence of the Realm Act, 1914, was more than once successfully contested.

2. The consultation of interests affected is made obligatory

(1) by providing departments with advisory committees.

(2) by provisions in particular enabling statutes, such as section 62 of the Education (Scotland) Act, 1945, which requires the Secretary of State to send a copy of his draft regulations to every education authority and to have regard to the views received in reply.

3. Publicity is ensured by means of the printing and placing on sale of the rules, numbered in an annual series in the order in which they reach the King's Printer, and their inclusion in the annual volumes of *Statutory Instruments*.)

4. An opportunity may be given for the intervention of Parlia-

ment by a direction in the parent Act requiring rules or orders to 'lie upon the Table' of each House for a specified period either before or after they are made. For the procedure in the House of Commons in respect of rules so lying, see p. 167.

5. Since session 1943-4, a sessional select committee on *Statutory Rules and Orders* has been appointed to scrutinize all subordinate legislation which is laid before the House and which either requires an affirmative, or is exposed to annulment on a negative, resolution. The Committee's terms of reference exclude any consideration of policy or merits and confine its function to that of drawing the attention of the House to instruments which impose a charge on public revenues or confer immunity from challenge in the courts or which exhibit an " unusual or unexpected " use of a statutory power or purport to have retrospective effect without specific authority in the parent statute. The Committee is also authorized to report any case of delay in presentation or publication. In effect the reports wave a red light to which the House may or may not pay attention. The Committee has also from time to time made special reports on general tendencies in delegated legislation; one of these led to the passing of the Statutory Instruments Act, 1946.

C. MEASURES

Measures passed under the Church of England Assembly (Powers) Act, 1919, are a species of delegated legislation occupying a position midway between statutes and statutory instruments. Like the latter, they are the children of an Act. Like the former, they require the approval of Parliament and the assent of the Crown, and they are included in the yearly volumes of *Public General Acts*.

The procedure on them is as follows:—After they have duly passed the Church Assembly they are presented to both Houses of Parliament, where, before action is taken upon them, they must first be reported upon by the Ecclesiastical Committee. The Ecclesiastical Committee consists of 15 Peers, nominated by the Lord Chancellor, and 15 Members of the House of Commons, nominated by the Speaker, and is appointed at the beginning and for the duration of a Parliament. It may act through 12 of its members and sit when Parliament is not sitting. The report of the Committee deals with the nature and legal effect of the measure and with its expediency, especially with regard to the constitutional rights of all His Majesty's subjects. When the report and a text of the measure are in its possession, each House may order the measure to be submitted for the Royal Assent. The two Houses act concurrently, and the approval of both is, of course, necessary.

Measures, under the "enabling" Act of 1919, may relate to any matter concerning the Church of England. Sometimes (as in the case of the New Parishes Measure, 1943) they make copious repeals of statutes.

Appendix III

I. SESSIONAL TIME TABLE

Showing the Distribution of the Various Classes of Business, 1919 to 1926

Four main classes of business		1919	1920	1921	1922	1923	1924	1924–5	1926	Average
1.	Private Members' Bills	9	13	7	8	10½	15½	14	13	11
	Private Members' Motions	3	3½	2½	2	5½	7½	9	6½	5
	(total)	12	16½	9½	10	16	23	23	19½	16
2. *Incidental Business*	Opposed Private Business ...	—	4	1½	2	1½	2	3	2½	2
	Adjournment of House Motion, S.O. No. 9	½	5	1½	½	1	½	—	—	1
	Vote of Censure Motion ...	—	—	—	—	1	1	3	1	½
	Opposition Motion in Government time	—	—	—	1	3	3	2	½	1
	Private Member's Motion in Government time	2	4½	3½	2	—	1	½	2	2
	Government Adjournment Motion	1½	2½	4½	1½	—	2	—	—	1½
	Miscellaneous (includes matters of Privilege and Procedure)	2	—	1	—	—	—	—	—	½
	(total)	6	16	12	7	6½	9½	8½	6	8½
3. *Routine and Finance*	Address	4	4	5	6	6	5	7	5	5
	Adjournment (Holidays) ...	3	1½	2½	3	3	2½	2½	3	2½
	Supply Main Estimates ...	26	21½	25	25½	23½	23½	24	24	24
	Supply Supplementary Estimates	4	9½	12	13½	4½	8½	7½	10½	9
	Consolidated Fund Bills ...	6	4½	5½	4	4	4½	4	4½	4½
	Finance Bill (including Budget Debate and Resolutions)	9½	14½	9½	14	12½	9	14½	16	12
	Miscellaneous (*e.g.* Army and Air Force (Annual) Bill)	—	½	½	—	—	—	½	—	—
	(total)	52½	56	60	66	53½	53	60	63	57
4. *Government Programme*	Government Bills (including Money Resolutions)	83½	75	52½	25½	35½	38½	52	49½	51
	Government Motions ...	3	2½	7	3½	1½	—	1½	12	4
	(total)	86½	77½	59½	29	37	38½	53½	61½	55
	Total sittings (effective*)	157	166	141	112	113	124	145	150	137

* Excludes days when House meets but transacts no business, on occasion of :—New Parliament; demise of Crown; prorogation, or death of statesman.

II. SESSIONAL TIME TABLE

Showing the Distribution of the Various Classes of Business, 1928–9 to 1935–6

Four main classes of business		1928–9	1929–30	1930–31	1931–2	1932–3	1933–4	1934–5	1935–6	Average
1.	Private Members' Bills		19	17		16	14		11	9½
	Private Members' Motions		13	5½		9	9		8½	5½
	Total	None	32	22½	None	25	23	None	19½	15
2. *Incidental Business*	Opposed Private Business ...	1	1½	1½	1	2½	½	2	3	1½
	Adjournment of House Motion, S.O. No. 9	—	—	—	—	—	—	—	½	—
	Vote of Censure Motion ...	—	—	3	5	3	—	2	3	2
	Opposition Motion in Government time	—	3½	1	6	1	2	1	1	2
	Private Member's Motion in Government time	—	—	—	1	—	—	—	—	—
	Government Adjournment Motion	—	2½	3	—	3	1	3	2	2
	Miscellaneous (includes matters of Privilege and Procedure)	—	—	—	—	—	1	—	—	—
	Total	1	7½	8½	13	9½	4½	8	9½	7½
3. *Routine and Finance*	Address	7	7	6	5	5	5	7	7	6
	Adjournment (Holidays) ...	1	4	3½	4	4	4	4	4	3½
	Supply Main Estimates ...	16½	23½	24	26	24½	24½	23	23	23½
	Supply Supplementary Estimates	9	9½	7	2	3	1½	5	3	5½
	Consolidated Fund Bills ...	3	4½	4	4	3½	3	3½	4	3½
	Finance Bill (including Budget Debate and Resolutions)	7	21	30½	14	14½	11	10	11½	15
	Miscellaneous (*e.g.* Army and Air Force (Annual) Bill)	½	½	½	½	1	½	1	2	½
	Total	44	70	75½	55½	55½	49½	53½	54½	57
4. *Government Programme*	Government Bills (including Money Resolutions)	52	73	74½	72½	46½	73½	79	36½	63½
	Government Motions ...	2	2	5½	10	5½	4½	9½	10	6
	Total	54	75	80	82½	52	78	88½	46½	69½
	Total Sittings (effective*)	99	184½	186½	151	142	155	150	130	149

* Excludes days when House meets but transacts no business, on occasion of:—New Parliament; demise of Crown; prorogation, or death of statesman.

APPENDIX IV

ALTERATIONS TO PROCEDURE SINCE 1939

THE exigencies of the war years 1939 to 1945, and the subsequent marked increase in the volume of legislation, led to a number of alterations in the procedure described in the previous chapters. Although many of these changes were introduced in the first instance by sessional orders, they were for the most part incorporated in the Standing Orders by a series of amendments and additions made on 4th November, 1947. The effects of these and other amendments upon procedure are summarised below.

Alterations in hours of sitting

A time-table of business differing from that incorporated in the text has been made permanent by amendments to S.O.s Nos. 1, 2, 4, 7, 8, 16 and 28. The following table shows the modified hours, which must be substituted for all references to time throughout the book.

Hour mentioned in book	Nature of Subject	Hour to be substituted
2.45 p.m.	Meeting of the House	2.30 p.m.
3 p.m.	End of Unopposed Business	2.45 p.m.
3.45 p.m.	End of Questions	3.30 p.m.
7.30 p.m.	Adjournment Motions under S.O. No. 9 and Opposed Private Business	7 p.m.
8.15 to 9.15 p.m.	Period during which House may not be counted	7.30 to 8.30 p.m.
9.30 p.m.	End of Opposed Private Business not already under consideration	9 p.m.
10 p.m.	Closure of Supply on specified allotted days	9.30 p.m.
11 p.m.	Interruption of business	10 p.m.
11.30 p.m.	Adjournment of House	See below

Modifications in rules relating to Sittings of the House

S.O. No. 1 (7) now provides that the Government may move, with or without notice, the exemption of specified business from the provisions of that Standing Order (see p. 135), either for an indefinite or for a specified period after the hour appointed for the interruption of business. Such a motion can only be moved at the commencement of public business. If an adjournment motion is accepted under S.O. No. 9, the business superseded by that motion is now automatically exempted for a period as long as the time taken in discussing the adjournment motion (S.O. No. 9 (2)). This applies even to business of supply (S.O. No. 16 (2)).

The Speaker's power to adjourn the House without question put (see p. 133) is now effective not at a specified hour of the clock but at half-an-hour precisely after the proposing (at or after ten o'clock) of a motion for the adjournment of the House (S.O. No. 1 (10)). If a motion for the adjournment has, through an early disposal of public business, been proposed before ten, it lapses at that hour, and a new adjournment motion, valid for a further half-hour, is then proposed (S.O. No. 1 (2)). In this way the opportunity of a full half-hour's adjournment debate is guaranteed every day, and is so eagerly sought after by private Members that securing precedence upon it is determined by a weekly ballot. An amendment to S.O. No. 2 removes the previous distinction between Fridays and other days with regard to exempted business and to the procedure for adjournment, except for the difference in the moment of interruption (ten o'clock on weekdays and four on Fridays); and a further assimilation of Friday procedure to that of weekdays is made by the provision on Friday of an hour (1.15 to 2.15 p.m.) during which the House may not be counted (S.O. No. 28 (2)).

Alterations in rules relating to Notices

S.O. No. 39 (1) now provides that whenever the House is adjourned for more than one day, notices of amendments, new clauses and new schedules proposed to public bills (but not notices of motions) may be received up to 4.30 p.m. on weekdays in the same way and subject to the same rules of notice as if the House were sitting. Similar provision is made for Questions by S.O. No. 8 (6), which also permits the expediting of oral questions handed in during the days immediately preceding the return of the House in conformity with the facilities provided by para. (4) of the same Standing Order. S.O. No. 39 (2) further provides that amendments to a public bill may be accepted for insertion in the notice paper before the bill has been read a second time.

Business Committee

A Business Committee consisting of the members of the Chairmen's Panel and up to five other members nominated by the Speaker is required by S.O. No. 41 to divide into specified parts any bill in respect of which the House has made an allocation of time order covering the committee stage (if the Bill is committed to a Committee of the whole House) or the report stage, and to allot to each part an appropriate number of days. Any recommendations of the Committee must be agreed to or negatived by the House forthwith when they are reported. The Committee is also empowered to recommend the detailed division of a bill which is not the subject of an allocation of time order, provided that the general agreement of the House to this procedure has been signified by a Minister.

Modifications in Rules relating to Standing Committees

(1) The former limitation of standing committees to the maximum number of five is now removed, and the quorum of each committee has been reduced from twenty to fifteen (S.O. No. 57 (1)). A change has also been made in the numerical proportion between the " permanent " members of a committee and the " specialists " added to it for particular bills (see pp. 239-40), the new numbers being twenty and not more than thirty respectively (S.O. No. 58).

(2) After its first meeting a standing committee now normally meets at 10.30 a.m. unless it otherwise resolves (S.O. No. 63 (1)); but it may not sit between 1 p.m. and 3.30 p.m. unless either (a) the chairman permits it to sit till 1.15 in order to conclude the proceedings on a bill, or (b) proceedings following a motion for closure are in progress at 1.0, in which case all the consequential questions must be decided before the committee adjourns (S.O. No. 63 (2)).

(3) Functions akin to those compulsorily performed by the Business Committee on behalf of the House (see above) are performed for a standing committee by a business sub-committee consisting of the chairman of the standing committee and seven other members (S.O. No. 64). Such a sub-committee cannot, however, function voluntarily as can the Business Committee under the terms of S.O. No. 41 (2).

(4) All the Law Officers are now permitted to take part in the deliberations of any standing committee; but they may not vote, move motions or amendments, or be counted in the quorum of any committee of which they are not members (S.O. No. 65).

(5) S.O. No. 62 (4) provides that the chairman of a standing committee may at any time request any member of the committee to act as a temporary chairman for a period of not more than a quarter of an hour; but such temporary chairmen may not exercise any of the powers of the chairman under S.O. No. 57 (5).

(6) Should the pressure of business demand it, the House may

be adjourned for the whole day or until seven of the clock to facilitate the business of standing committees (S.O. No. 10).

(7) The functions of the Scottish Standing Committee have been expanded by two Standing Orders passed on 28th April 1948. S.O. No. 60 provides that the second reading of a bill certified by the Speaker as relating exclusively to Scotland may, on the motion of a Minister, be referred to the Scottish Standing Committee; and S.O. No. 61 allots up to six days in a session for the discussion by the committee of all or any of the Scottish estimates. In each case the functions of the committee are deliberative only, the bill being subsequently (and not necessarily formally) read a second time by the House, and the estimates again standing referred to the Committee of Supply.

Restriction of debate on Question for clause to stand part of Bill

If during the committee stage of a bill the chairman of a committee of the whole House is of the opinion that the whole principle of a clause has been adequately discussed in the course of debate on the amendments proposed thereto, he may, after the disposal of the last selected amendment to that clause, put forthwith the question that the clause stand part of the bill (S.O. No. 45).

Supply

The number of days in a session allotted to the business of Supply has been increased from 20 to 26 (S.O. No. 16 (1)). This nominal increase of Opposition time is in fact a gain to the Government, owing to the simultaneous extension of the definition of " business of supply " (S.O. No. 16 (3)) to cover (a) the (hitherto four) days spent in moving the Speaker out of the Chair (see p. 268) and (b) the discussion of Supplementary Estimates. In order to ensure that the latter are disposed of before the end of the financial year, an additional supplementary " guillotine " has been devised on the lines of the main July guillotine (see p. 267), its two stages taking place not earlier than the seventh and eighth allotted days respectively, and in both cases before the 31st March.

A modification has also been made in the procedure for moving the Speaker out of the Chair. This procedure, formerly used only on first going into Committee of Supply on each of the four main branches of the Estimates, is now available (on a Government motion) for use on any Supply day (S.O. No. 17 (1)), and it is further provided that incidental reference to legislative action is in order whenever such a motion, or an amendment thereto, is being debated (S.O. No. 17(2)). Since the passing of this Standing Order, the Government has by agreement always moved such a motion on each of the four occasions on which it would previously have been moved under Standing Order, although no longer explicitly bound to do so; but this agreement has not been extended to cover the first debate on the estimate of the newly created Ministry of Defence, although this has been made a separate branch of the Estimates. The use of this procedure has been further assisted by an amendment made on 28th July 1948 to S.O. No. 15, whereby the appointment of the Committees of Supply and Ways and Means has been made effective for the duration of the session, thus ensuring that neither Committee can ever become a " dropped order " (see pp. 165 and 271).

Ways and Means

Besides the alteration just mentioned, two further modifications have been made in the procedure relating to Ways and Means. In the first place, S.O. No. 86 (1) now makes compulsory the existing practice (see p. 282) of putting immediately after the Budget statement the questions on all resolutions except the last; and the reports of resolutions from the Committee of Ways and Means relating to charges upon the people are now no longer debatable (S.O. No. 86 (2)), although they may be divided upon.

Money Committees

Resolutions of Money Committees set up under S.O. No. 84 may now, with the general agreement of the House, be reported and considered by the House forthwith.

Statutory Instruments

In order to facilitate the operation of the Statutory Instruments Act, 1946, it is now provided (S.O.s Nos. 109 and 110) that Statutory Instruments as well as Command Papers may be laid during an adjournment or recess by delivery to the Votes and Proceedings Office (not, as formerly in the case of Command Papers (see p. 93), to the Library). Doubts as to the legal validity of S.O. No. 110 were allayed by the passing of the Laying of Documents before Parliament (Interpretation) Act, 1948. The Speaker is enjoined by S.O. No. 111 to lay before the House any notification received in accordance with S. 4 (1) of the Statutory Instruments Act, 1946.

APPENDIX V

SPECIAL PROCEDURE ORDERS

UNDER the Statutory Orders (Special Procedure) Act, 1945, which came into effect on 1st June, 1946, a new procedure has been enacted to give statutory effect to departmental orders more quickly and cheaply than by the system of provisional order confirmation described on p. 308.

The Special Procedure Orders under this Act have nothing to do with the instruments of delegated legislation which were known as Statutory Rules and Orders and are now known as Statutory Instruments (see Appendix II). They are to be distinguished also, of course, from the so-called Special Orders which require a mere affirmative resolution of both Houses (see p. 313).

The Act of 1945 was foreshadowed in the White Paper on a National Water Policy in April 1944. The immediate object of the Act is to give effect to such orders as the Minister of Health may make under the Water Act (for instance, for the amalgamation of two water undertakings) or for the orders made by the Minister of Town and Country Planning for acquisition of land or those made by the Local Government Boundary Commissioners. It is obviously contemplated that this new "special parliamentary procedure" shall be applied to orders made under future Acts. It was specifically applied in 1946 by the Trunk Roads Act and New Towns Act to certain orders made thereunder.

The principle underlying the Act is that these orders will be giving effect to decisions of national policy—for example on water supply—but they may also " affect private rights." Broadly speaking, in so far as the Orders are challenged as a matter of national policy, the issue will be decided on the floor of the House; in so far as private rights are affected, something like the present Private Bill procedure will be available.

For this purpose the Act requires the new Special Procedure Orders to be presented to Parliament for a period during which objection can be taken by a petition. All necessary preliminaries of giving notice to persons affected or holding local inquiries will first have been taken.

If there is no kind of objection to the order, it will become law at the end of the prescribed periods. If there is a petition, the petition will stand referred to the Chairman of Committees in the Lords and

Z

to the Chairman of Ways and Means in the Commons. The two Chairmen have to be satisfied that any petition complies with the Act and Standing Orders and that it is not frivolous; they then have to classify it as either a petition of general objection (in effect seeking to negative the main purpose of the Order) or a petition for amendment.

Within fourteen days after the Chairmen report upon a petition, the House can kill the order by passing a resolution for its annulment, though this will not prevent a fresh order being submitted to Parliament. On the motion for annulment, the House can remit the petition (if it is one of general objection) to a Joint Committee of the two Houses. If no resolution for annulment is passed, the next stage depends on whether the petition is one of general objection or one for amendment. If the petition is one of general objection, it is disposed of by the House unless the House refers it to a Joint Committee. If it is a petition for amendment, it goes automatically to a Joint Committee.

The Joint Committee can report the Order with or without amendment; they may report that the Order be not approved. If reported with amendments, the Minister concerned, should he find himself unable to accept the amendments, may either withdraw the Order or bring it forward in the form of a Bill.

One advantage of the new special procedure is the speed with which an unopposed order will become law. Among other features it will be noted that the Chairmen and the Joint Committee are concerned with the petition, not with the order, and that the petition is submitted by the opponents, not by the promoters, of the proposals.

The Act of 1945 contemplated Standing Orders being made for a variety of purposes—the machinery of petitioning, the business before the two Chairmen, the constitution and proceedings of a Joint Committee, and so on, and these Standing Orders were agreed to by the Commons in 1946.

INDEX

'Accounts and Papers', 92, 93.

Accounts, Appropriation and Finance, 254.

Acts of Parliament, App. II.

Address to Crown, 64, App. I; for Public Money, 275; for Return, 92, 323; in answer to King's Speech, 108.

Adjournment of debate, Motion for, in House, 172 ; in Standing Committee, 242.

    of House, at end of sitting, 132 ; on Friday, 134 ; in absence of quorum, 138 ; in case of grave disorder, 136, 198; on eve of holiday, 106, 119; over next sitting day, 136.

    Motion for, 111, 133, 136, 172; under S.O. No. 8, to discuss 'definite matter of urgent public importance', 111, 117, 152.

    of Select or Standing Committee, see Sittings, of Select or Standing Committee.

    of Standing Committee, 241, 242.

Affirmation, 103.

Allocation of time ('guillotine'), Motion for, 128, 135.

Allotted days (Supply), 119, 266.

Alterations to Procedure since 1939, App. IV.

Amendment of Bills, historical, 23–4.

Amendments to Bills and Motions, 173; selection of, 75, 187, 215.

    in Committee, Private Bills, 301 ; Provisional Order Bills, 310 ; Public Bills, 216.

    on Consideration, Private Bills, 303 ; Public Bills, 223.

    on Third Reading, Private Bills, 304; Public Bills, 224.

    requiring notice, 173 ; requiring seconder, 173.

    to Amendments, 176.

    in Committee of Supply, 269 ; on going into Committee of Supply, 268.

    see also Lords' Amendments.

Ancient Usage, 1, 15.

Anticipation, 178.

Appropriation Accounts, 254.

    Bill, 257, 273.

    of Supply grants, 30, 32, 34, 254, 257.

Appropriation of money granted, 34–35.

Appropriations in aid, 255, 263.

Ballot, for Amendments on going into Committee of Supply, 158, 267 ; for Bills and Notices of Motions, 157.

Bills, basis of legislation, 10–12 ; definition of, 109 ; history of procedure on, 22–25 ; see also Appropriation Bill, Consolidated Fund Bill, 'Hybrid ' Bill, 'Money' Bill, Private Bill, Provisional Order Bill, and Public Bill.

Blanks and italics in Bills, 218, 286.

'Blue Paper', 86.

Breach of privilege, 70; proceedings upon complaint of, 72, 118; time for taking, 159, 161.

'Budget' Resolutions and statement, 112, 281–2.

Business of the House, arrangement of, historical, 37; for Session, 109.
        for Sitting, 139.
        interruption of, 132 ; exempted from interruption,
            134, 166 ; if unopposed, 132.
        Motions dealing with, 128, 135, 160.
Business of the House, Private, 140–1, 165.
        Public, 162 ; 'at the commencement of Public', 159.
Casting vote, of Speaker in House, 17, 75, 182 ; of Chairman, in Committee
   of Whole House, 78, 183, 235; in Private Bill Committee, 299; in
  Select Committee, 246; in Standing Committee, 235.
Censure upon Government, Motion for vote of, 110, 113, 117.
Chairman of Committee of Whole House, 78, 235; and maintenance of
        order, 197; and Report of Progress or of Resolutions, 236;
        temporary, 79.
    of Private Bill Committee, 298 ; of Select Committee, 246 ; of
        Standing Committee, 240.
    of Ways and Means, 78; and closure, 184; and Opposed Private
        Business, 113, 116, 142, 165; and selection of Amendments,
        187 ; and supervision of Private Bills, 293.
Chairmen's Panel, 240.
Charges upon the people or the Public Revenue, 199, 259.
Chiltern Hundreds, 62, 67.
Citing documents not before House, 195.
Civil List, 31.
Clerk, of the Crown, 67, 69, 100, 103 ; of the House, 79.
Clerks at the Table, 80; and Notices of Motions, 158; and Questions to
    Ministers, 146.
Closure of debate, 184 ; in Standing Committee, 242.
Command Papers, 93, 96.
Committal of Bills, historical, 25 ; of Private Bills, 296 ; of Public Bills, in
        general, 209 ; pro forma, 219.
    for contempt, 73.
Committee and Private Bill Office, 80.
COMMITTEES, historical, 25, 43; in general, 232; initiating 'Money
        Bills', 199, 275; on Private Bills, 297; on Provisional
        Order Bills, 309 ; on Public Bills, 210, 215 ; on
        Public matters, 243.
        Instructions to, on Private Bills, 296, 301; on Public
        Bills, 213, 215, 243, 248.
  I. Committee of Whole House, historical, 25–29 ; in general, 233 ;
                Chairman of, 78, 235; Order of
                the Day for, 164, 235; pro-
                cedure in, 236; Report of
                Progress or of Resolution from,
                236.
                Bills committed to, 209–215; re-
                committed to, 223, 224, 249,
                251, 302.
                (Money) 199, 274, 276, 278.
                Supply, 33 ; allotted days in, 266 ;
                business of, 262; closing of, 267;
                Estimates and, 111, 120, 125,
                263; procedure in, 268; Report
                of, 271; setting up of, 234, 262.
                Ways and Means, 33, 261, 272; pro-
                cedure in, 281; Report of, 271,
                283; setting up of, 234, 262;
                spending and, 33, 261; taxation
                and, 33, 111, 281.

COMMITTEES:—(*Continued*)

II. Standing Committee, historical, 28, 39–40 ; in general, 212, 238–241 ; on Public Bills, 89, 209–221, 238, 239.

III. Select Committee, historical, 26; in general, 233, 243; on Private Bills, 318; on Procedure, 39; on Public Bills, 209, 213, 215, 221, 248; nomination of, under S.O. No. 10, 161; sessional, 251.

IV. Joint Committee, generally, 249 ; on Private Bills, 249, 319 ; on Public Bills, 221, 249, 252.

V. Committee on Private Bill, 298 ; on Provisional Order Bill, 309.

VI. Committee on reasons for disagreeing to Lords' amendments, 227.

Commons, House of, *see* House of Commons.

Comptroller and Auditor General, 82, 254 ; and Public Accounts Committee, 280.

Conferences between Houses, 225.

Consideration of Bill reported from a Committee, Private Bill, 303 ; Public Bill ('Report' stage), 221.

of Lords' Amendments, to Private Bill, 304 ; to Public Bill, 225.

Consolidated Fund, 34, 253.

Bills, 121, 273, 256, 261; and excess grant, 265, 273; and Vote on Account, 264, 273; procedure on, 274; services, 255.

Consolidation Bills, Joint Committee on, 252.

Control of finance, *see* FINANCE.

of time, 37, 112, 128.

Counting the House, 137 ; in Committee of Whole House, 138.

Credit, Vote of, 266.

Crown, and finance, 30, 36, 253.

and House of Commons, 9–10, 36; communications between, 10, 64, 323; message from, and interruption of proceedings in House, 137, 323; privileges of House, 63.

and Parliament, prorogation, 104; summoning and dissolution, 99.

demise of, and Parliament, 99, 106.

see also King, King's Consent, King's Recommendation, King's Speech *and* Royal Assent.

Debate, 15, 20; conduct and rules of, 15–17, 168, 188, 193; in Standing Committee, 242; publication of Reports of, 66, 71, 97.

adjournment of, 132, 172 ; resumption of, 163.

Motions for adjournment of, in House, 172 ; in Standing Committee, 242.

Deposit of documents, Private Legislation, 293.

Deputy Chairman, 79.

Speaker, 77.

'Dilatory' Motions, in House or Committee of Whole House, 172 ; in Standing Committee, 242.

Disagreements between Houses, 227.

Disorder in debate, 193.

Disqualifications from membership, 57.

Dissolution of Parliament, 99 ; and suspension, of Private Bills, 307 ; of Public Bills, 127.

Division, of House, ancient practice, 18–19 ; and absence of quorum, 137 ; errors in, 181 ; point of order raised during, 181–182 ; procedure in, 178 ; division lists, 89 ; unnecessarily claimed, 181 ; *see also* Casting vote, *and* Closure of debate.

of Private Bills between Houses, 294.

of Select Committee, 246 ; of Standing Committee, 242.

Documents, citing in debate, 195.

'Dummy' Bill, 204.

Election, of Member, 57, 67–68; writ for, 67–68, 100, 140.
    of Speaker, 100.

'Eleven o'clock rule', 132 ; business exempted from, by special order, 135, 160; by Standing Order, 134, 166–167, 285.

Emergency Powers Act, and meeting of Parliament, 106.

Estate Bill, 305.

Estimates, historical, 31, 33 ; in general, 254 ; presentation of, 95, 262 ; procedure in discussion of, 111, 119; various forms of, 263.
    Main, 119.
    Supplementary, 111, 121, 264.

Estimates Committee, 251, 280.

Evidence, before Private Bill Committee, 301–2; before Select Committee, 246–7.

Examiners of Petitions for Private Bills, and Private Bills, 294–5, 314; and Public Bills, 205–6.

Excess Vote, 265 ; and Public Accounts Committee, 279.

Exchequer, 253.

Exempted business, 134.

Explanation, personal, 158.

Expulsion of Member, 70.

Fees payable, upon 'Hybrid' Bill, upon Private Bill, 292 ; upon Provisional Order Bill, 309 ; upon Special Order, 314.
    and privilege, 286.

FINANCE :—
    Appropriation Accounts, 254.
        Bill, 257, 273.
        of Supply grants, 30, 34, 254, 257.
    appropriations in aid, 255, 263.
    'Budget', 111, 281.
    Committee of Supply, 33, 261 ; allotted days in, 266 ; business of, 262; closing of, 267; Estimates and, 111, 120, 125, 263; procedure in, 268–71; Report of, 271; setting up of, 234, 262–3.
        of Ways and Means, 33, 261, 272; procedure in, 281; Report of, 283; setting up of, 234, 262–3; spending and, 33, 261; taxation and, 111, 280.
        of Whole House (Money), 274, 278.
    Consolidated Fund, 34, 253.
        Bills, 121, 256, 261, 272; procedure on, 274; services, 255.
    Control of finance, 111, 253, 255, 258; history of, 30–36.
    Estimates, see that title.
    Expenditure, 254, 261, 274.
    Finance Accounts, 254.
        Bill, 122, 284; procedure on, 111, 284.
    House of Lords and finance, 32, 285.
    Initiation of expenditure, 36, 159, 259, 277.
    Preliminary resolutions, 33.
    Revenue, 31, 255, 280.
    Standing Orders and finance, 36, 277.
    Taxation, 30, 33, 111, 280; procedure in imposing, 281.
    Vote on Account, 264, 266.
    see also Estimates Committee, Parliament Act (1911), and Public Accounts Committee.

First Reading, of Bill before consideration of King's Speech, 108.
        of Private Bill, 294 ; of Provisional Order Bill, 308 ; of Public Bill, 23, 202–4.

Friday Sittings, 140.
Front Bench, 84.
               Motions, 110, 168.
Government, and expenditure, 36–7, 108, 259; and legislation, 37; and time
    of House, 37, 112, 114, 128, 328.
'Grand' Committee, 28.
Grants, exceptional, 266, 275, 276.
'Guillotine' Motion, 128, 135.
'Hansard', 97.
House of Commons, and Crown, 7, 9, 26, 322; assent to legislation by, 12;
               Chamber of, 83; control of finance by, 6, 30, 34,
               253, 255, 259, 285; control of time of, 112; dis-
               qualifications from membership of, 58; officers of,
               78; privileges of, 63, 102; sittings of, 106, 131;
               see also Members of House of Commons.
       Papers, 86.
House of Lords, and finance, 31–2, 285, 287; legislative function of, 13.
       Bills originating in, Private Bill, 305; Public Bill, 203.
       see also Lords' Amendments.
Houses of Lords and Commons, official communication between, 224, 227.
       Parliament, 82 ; see also Parliament.
'Hybrid' Bill, 205, 206.
Indorsement of Bill passed by one House, 229.
Instruction to Committee, on Private Bill, 296, 301 ; on Public Bill, 213,
    215, 243, 248; difference between 'mandatory' and 'permissive', 213.
Interruption of business, at eleven o'clock, 132, 236; at four o'clock on
               Fridays, 133–4; at half-past seven o'clock,
               166.
           and closure, 186–7.
Introduction, of Public Bill, 160, 202–204.
       of new Member, 152.
Joint Committee, see COMMITTEES :—IV.
Journal of the House, 80, 87, 91.
Journal Office, 80.
King, The, access to, a privilege of the House of Commons, 63–4, 74; see
    also Crown and Royal Assent.
King's Consent, 304–5, 323.
       Recommendation to motions involving public expenditure, 277, 323;
          how signified, 259, 260; to exceptional grants, 265–6, 278; to
          expenditure following Address to Crown, 275–6.
       Speech, 107.
'Kitchen' Committee, 252.
Law officers, opinions, 195.
Legislation, Private, see Chap. IX.
       Public, 10; and Government, 37.
Library, 81; Papers in, 93–5.
Local rates, charges upon, 223, 286.
Locus Standi, 299.
Lords, House of, see House of Lords.
Lords' Amendments, to Private Bill, 304; to Public Bill, 159, 225.
Mace, 54, 74 ff, 81, 85 n.
Measures relating to Church of England, 167.
Members of House of Commons:—
    absence, Motions for leave of, 155.
    access to King, 64.
    arrest, freedom from, 64.
    disqualifications from membership, 57.
    election of, 67; disputed, 69; for more than one constituency, 67.
    equality of, 17.

Members of the House of Commons:—(*Continued***)**
    expulsion of, 70.
    juries, service on, 65.
    'naming' of, 197.
    new, introduction of, 152.
    Parliamentary Bar, and, 71.
            Papers, and, 94–5.
    payment of, 62, 81.
    pecuniary or personal interest of, in Bills, etc., 183, 298.
    personal explanation by, 158, 183.
    privileges of, 63; breach of, 70, 72–3.
    resignation of seat, 62.
    speech, freedom of, 66.
    suspension of, 70, 197.
    swearing of, 103, 152.
    vacation of seat, 61.
    withdrawal of, by order of Speaker, 197.
Memorials, 294, 315.
Messages between Houses, 224; from Crown, 137, 323.
Ministers of Crown, Questions to, 145; restriction on number in Commons, 60; statements of policy by, 159.
Minutes, of evidence, before Private Bill Committee, 302; before Select Committee, 246.
    of proceedings of Standing Committee, 89, 242.
'Money' Bill, 199, 202, 275; and Parliament Act (1911), 287.
    Committee of Whole House, 274, 278.
Motions, classification of, 110, 111, 168, 171; history of, 21–22; oral notices of, 155.
    procedure on, 168;
    complaining of breach of privilege, 72, 118, 159, 161.
    dealing with business, 128–9, 160.
    for adjournment of debate ('dilatory'), 172, 242.
    for adjournment of House, 111, 118, 133, 172.
    for adjournment of House under S.O. No. 8, 111, 117, 152.
    for allocation of time ('guillotine'), 129–130, 135.
    for leave of absence of Member, 155.
    for leave to bring in Bill, 161, 202.
    for unopposed Return, 144.
    for vote of censure upon Government, 110, 113, 117.
    for writ for election of new Member, 67, 140.
    seconder to, 169, 222.
    substantive, 168.
    that Chairman do leave Chair ('dilatory'), 172, 236.
    to report Progress, 172, 236.
    to set up 'Money' Committee of Whole House, 159, 276.
    withdrawal of, 170.
Name Bill, 305.
'Naming' of Member, 197.
Naturalisation Bill, 305.
Navy, Army and Air Estimates, 263–4.
Northstead, Manor of, 62.
Notice, of Motion, 20, 144, 165; ballot for, 157–8; extent of, 157; relating to Order of Day, 88; terms of, 158.
    of presentation of Public Bill, 204.
    of stages of Private Bill, 295, 304.
Notice Paper, 87.
Oath taken, by Member, 103, 152; by witnesses, 246, 300.
Obstruction, 29, 194–5.
Office of profit and membership of House, 59.

Officers of House of Commons, 78; privileges of, 65, 71.
Opposed Private Business, 113, 116, 142, 165.
Opposition, to Private Bill, 292.
Opposition, time allotted to, 114.
Order Book, 89, 112.
Order in debate, rules of, 16, 188.
Order of House, 21, 170.
Orders of the Day, 88, 162; deferred, 164; discharged, 164; dropped, 165; postponed, 164.
Orders, Statutory, 90, 326; procedure on, 166.
     see also Provisional Orders, Special Orders, Special Procedure Orders and Standing Orders.
Ordinance, nature of, 10.
Parliament, and demise of Crown, 99, 106; and Emergency Powers Act, 106; dissolution of, 99; duration of, 99; meeting of, 99; prorogation of, 100, 104, 126, 307; summoning of, 99, 100.
     Houses of, 82, 85; see also House of Commons and House of Lords.
Parliament Act (1911), and duration of Parliament, 99; and 'Money' Bills, 287; and other Bills, 230–1.
Parliamentary Agents, 292.
     Papers, 86, 92; and freedom of speech, 66; index, 94; publication of, 94.
     procedure, control of House over, 6; definition of, 1; history of development of, 5–40; Select Committees on, 29, 39.
Party system, 41, 84, 114.
Payment of Members, 62, 81.
Pecuniary interest of Members, 183, 298.
Personal Bill, 292, 305.
     explanation by Member, 158.
Petition, procedure by, 10–12; replaced by statute, 12; against alteration in Private Bill, 299; against Private Bill, 294, 299; against Provisional Order Bill, 309, 312; against Substituted Bill, 313; in favour of Private Bill, 299; for additional provision in Private Bill, 307; for Private Bill, 292, 293.
     election, 69.
     Public, 142.
Plans relating to Private Bill, 293.
Preamble, of Private Bill, 300; of Provisional Order Bill, 310; of Public Bill, 200, 219.
Presentation of Papers, 92; of Private Bill, 294; of Provisional Order Bill, 308; of Public Bill, 202.
Press gallery, 85.
'Previous Question', 21, 173.
PRIVATE BILL:—
     certified, 292, 305.
     classes of Bills, 292.
     committal of, 296.
     committee on, 297; see also under COMMITTEES.
     consideration of, 303.
     definition of, 109–110, 291.
     deposits in connexion with, 293.
     division of, between Houses, 294.
     Estate Bill, 305.
     estimate of expense, 293.
     examination of, 294–5, 314.
     fees payable upon, 292.
     first reading of, 295.
     founded upon petition, 292.

PRIVATE BILL:—(*Continued*)
    House of Lords' Bills, 305.
    Instruction to Committee on, 296.
    intervals between stages of, 295, 297, 303–5.
    King's Consent to, 304, 323.
    late Bill, 306.
    Lords' Amendments to, 304.
    memorials, 294, 315.
    Name Bill, 305.
    Naturalisation Bill, 305.
    opposition to, by Members, 142, 295; by parties, 292.
    Personal Bill, 292, 305.
    personal interest of Members in a, 298.
    Petition, against, 294, 299, 306; against alteration in, 299; in favour
        of, 299; for, 292, 293; for additional provision in, 307.
    plans in connexion with, 293.
    preliminaries to presentation of, 293.
    presentation of, 294.
    progress of (periodical list), 90.
    railway Bills, 290, 295.
    recommittal of, 302.
    report of, 301.
    Royal Assent to, 305.
    second reading of, 295.
    suspension of, at prorogation or dissolution, 307.
    taxation of costs of, 315.
    third reading of, 304.
    unopposed, in Committee, 318; in House, 140.
    'Wharncliffe' Standing Orders, 295.
    withdrawal of, 307.
Private Business, notice paper of, 87; time of discussion, 140; if opposed,
    113, 116, 142, 165.
Private Legislation, 289; *see also* PRIVATE BILL, Provisional Order
    (Bill), Special Procedure Order *and* Special Order.
Private Legislation Procedure (Scotland) Act, 310.
Private Members, and finance, 277–8; and time of House, 110, 112, 114, 115.
Private Member's Bill, 110, 115; ballot for, 157; Presentation or introduc-
    tion, 160–1, 202; Standing Committee and, 238; *see*
    also PUBLIC BILL.
    Motion, 110, 115, 156, 166; ballot for, 158.
'Private notice' Question, 147.
Privileges of House of Commons, 63, 102; breach of, 70; Committee of, 72,
    252; proceedings upon complaint of breach of, 118, 158, 161.
    freedom, from arrest, 64; of access to Crown, 64, 74; of speech, 66.
    in respect of finance, 31–2, 285.
Privy Councillors, and Address to Crown, 323; and Motions, 169; and seats
    in Chamber, 84.
Procedure, ceremonial element in, 54; foreign, 45; general principles, 50;
    history of, 41 *et seq.*; Select Committees on, 29, 39.
Progress, Motion to report, 172, 236.
Progress reported from Committee, 220, 236.
Prorogation of Parliament, 100, 104; and suspension, of Private Bills,
    307; of Public Bills, 127.
Provisional Order *and* Provisional Order Bill, 292, 308.
Public Accounts Committee, 251, 279; and Comptroller and Auditor
    General, 82, 254; and Estimates, 263; and Excess Vote, 266.
Publication of debates, 66, 71, 97; of evidence before Select Committee,
    72, 246; of Parliamentary Papers, 94.
Publications and Debates Reports Committee, 98, 252.

PUBLIC BILL:—

    amendments to, on second reading, 207; in committee, 210, 216, on consideration ('Report' stage), 221; on third reading, 224.

    'backers' of, 204, *n.*

    charges contained in, 199, 276.

    clauses of, 200; in Committee, 215; on 'Report' stage, 222.

    committal of, ancient procedure, 22, 24, 25; modern procedure, 209; *pro forma*, 219.

    committee on, 209, 210.

    consideration ('Report' stage) of, 221.

    'dummy' Bill, 204.

    enacting formula, 200.

    examination of, by authorities of House, 205; by Examiners of Petitions for Private Bills, 205.

    first reading of, 23–24, 202.

    form of, 199, 206.

    Government and Private Members' Bills, distinction between, 110.

    history of procedure on, 9, 22.

    House of Lords' Bill, 203.

    'hybrid' Bill, 205.

    indorsement of, 229.

    Instruction to Committee on, 213.

    intervals between stages of, 201.

    introduction of, 160, 202-204; under S.O. No. 64A, 199.

    Lords' Amendments to, 159, 225.

    memorandum (brief or 'breviat') prefaced to, 23, 204.

    'Money' Bill, definition of, 199, 288; stages of, 202, 205, 275, 278, 285.

    money clauses in, 199, 276.

    new clauses of, in Committee, 218; on 'Report' stage, 222.

    origin of, 11.

    originating in Committee of Whole House, 199, 275.

    Parliament Act (1911) and, 230, 287.

    preamble to, 200; in Committee, 219.

    printing of, 91, 204.

    private rights affected by, 205.

    progress of (weekly list), 90.

    recommittal of, 223.

    report of, 220.

    'Report' stage of, 221.

    Royal Assent to, 229.

    schedules to, 201; in Committee, 219; on 'Report' stage, 223.

    second reading of, 205; debate on, 207.

    third reading of, 223.

    titles of, 200, 206; in committee, 219; on 'Report' stage, 223.

Public Bill Office, 80, 204.

Public Business, 'at commencement of', 159; definition of, 109; notice paper of, 87.

Public money, *see* FINANCE.

Public Petitions, 142; Committee on, 144, 252.

Question, part of procedure on Motion, 170; proposal of, 20, 170; putting of, 19–20, 170, 171; 'same question' rule, 176.

Question, Previous, 21, 173.

Questions, to Ministers of Crown, 145; notice paper of, 88, 146; list showing order of, 90; 'private notice', 147; general rules for, 148; 'starred' or oral, 146; 'unstarred' or non-oral, 147; to Private Members, 148.

Quorum, absence of, and adjournment of House, 137; and suspension of sitting, 137; *see also* Counting the House.

Quorum of House, 136–7; of Private Bill Committee, 298; of Select Committee, 246; of Standing Committee, 241.

Railway Bills, 290, 295.

Readings of Bills, origin of, 22; *see also* First Reading, Second Reading *and* Third Reading.

Recommittal, of Private Bill, 303-4; of Public Bill, 221, 223.

Referees, Court of, 316.

Relevancy in debate, 190; in Committee of Supply, 270.

Repetition, rule regarding, 194.

Report, by Government Department on Private Bill, 301.
    of Private Bill, 301; of Public Bill, 220.
    of Resolutions from Committee of Whole House, 237; 'Money', 275, 279; Supply, 271; Ways and Means, 283, 285.
    of Select Committee, 248.

'Report' stage, of Private Bill, 303; of Public Bill, 221.

Resolution, of Committee of Whole House, 236; 'Money', 276, 278; Supply, 269; Ways and Means, 281.
    of House, compared with Order, 170; *see also* Motion.
    of Standing Orders Committee, 296, 315.

Restitution Bill, 305.

Returns, 92, 96; motion for unopposed, 144.
    to writs, 100; disputed, 69.

Revenue, 255; *see also* FINANCE.
    Departments, Estimates of, 263.

Rolls of Parliament, 9.

Royal Assent to Private Bill, 305; to Public Bill, 229.
    under Parliament Act (1911), 230, 287.

Rules, of order in debate, 16, 188.
    of practice, 5, 15, 29.
    Statutory, 90, 166, 325.
    see also Standing Orders.

Saint Stephen's Chapel, 83.

Schedules to Public Bill, 201; in Committee, 219; on 'Report' stage, 223.

Scottish Provisional Orders, 310.
    (Public) Bills, Standing Committee on, 239, 240.

Seat, resignation of, 62; vacation of, 58, 67.
    in Chamber, reservation of, 83–84.

Second Reading, of Private Bill, 295, 306; of Public Bill, 205.

Seconder required, for Amendment, 173; for Motion, 169.

Select Committee, *see under* COMMITTEES.

Selection, of Amendments, *see* Amendments.
    Committee of, 239, 251, 317.

Serjeant-at-Arms, 81, 83, 86; and maintenance of order, 196–8.

Session, opening and close of, 104, 107; periods of, 123; time-table of, 109, App. III.

Sessional Committees, 251.
    Orders, 67, 105.

Sittings, of House, 106, 112, 131; suspension of, 136, 198; time-table of, 131, 139; *see also* Adjournment of House.
    of Private Bill Committee, 299; of Select Committee, 245; of Standing Committee, 241.

Speaker:—
    absence of, 77.
    and absence of quorum, 137.
    and arrangement of business, 16, 37–8, 42.
    and closure of debate, 184.
    and Committee of Supply, 267.
    and Committee of Whole House, 27, 235.
    and Crown, 16, 74, 75.

Speaker:—(*Continued*)

    and division unnecessarily claimed, 181.
    and certificate under Parliament Act, 231, 287.
    and privileges of House, 63, 72, 73.
    and seats in Chamber, 85.
    and selection of Amendments, 187.
    and writs for election of new Members, 67, 74–5.
    casting vote of, 17, 75, 182.
    chaplain to, 81.
    Counsel to, 81.
    duties and powers of, 73.
    election of, 74, 100.
    historical survey of office, 16, 42, 75, 77.
    presides over House, 16, 74.
    retirement of, 102.
    salary of, charged to Consolidated Fund, 79.
    secretary to, 81.
Speaker, Deputy, 77.
Speaker's Counsel, 81.
Special Orders, 291, 313.
Special Procedure Orders, 289, App. V.
Speech, freedom of, 66.
    King's, 7, 107.
    reading of, 188, 190.
    reservation of, 193.
    speaking twice, 192.
    see also Debate.
Standing Committee, *see under* COMMITTEES.
    Orders (Private) 292.
        (Public), 36–7; development of, 5, 38–40; relating to
           finance, 34, 259, 277; system of, 40.
        Committee, 205, 251, 315; Resolutions of, 296, 316.
Stationery Office publications, 95.
Statutes, App. II.
    nature of, 10.
Statutory rules and orders ('instruments'), 90, 166, App. II; Committee on,
    252, 327.
Strangers, in House, 85; in Select Committee, 245; in Standing Com-
    mittee, 241.
'Substituted' Private Bill, 313.
Summoning of Parliament, 99, 100.
Supplement to the Votes, 88.
Supplementary Estimates, 121, 125, 264, 273.
Supply, 9, 30, 31, 202.
    allotted days, 119, 266.
    Committee of, *see under* COMMITTEES:—I. Committee of
        Whole House.
    Estimates, 263; exceptional grants, 266; Excess Vote, 265; Sup-
        plementary Estimates, 264; Vote of Credit, 266; Vote on
        Account, 264; 'supply services', 255.
    progress of, 271.
Suspension, of Bills at prorogation or dissolution, Private, 307; Public, 127.
    of Business at half-past seven o'clock, 165.
    of 'eleven o'clock rule,' 129, 135, 332.
    of Member, 70, 197.
    of Sitting, before consideration of King's Speech, 108, 136; in
        absence of quorum, 137; in case of grave disorder, 198.
Swearing, of Members, 103, 104, 152; of witnesses, 246, 300.

Table of House, 85; and Notices of Motions, 158; and Papers, 93; and Questions to Ministers, 146; and Reports of Private Bills, 303; and Statutory Rules and Orders, 90, 166, 167, 327.

Table Office, 80.

Taxation, 9, 30, 33, 111; procedure in imposing, 280.
of costs of Private Bill, 315.

Tellers in divisions, 180–1.

Temporary Chairmen of Committee of Whole House, 79.
Laws, 201.

'Ten-minutes rule' (S.O. No. 10), 161, 202.

Third Reading, of Private Bill, 304; of Public Bill, 224.

Time, control of, 37–39, 112, 127.
Motion for allocation of ('guillotine'), 129, 135.

Time-table, of Session, 109, App. III; of Sitting, 138, 139.

Treasury, control of Estimates, 253.

Unopposed Private Bill in Committee, 251, 318.
Business in House, 140.
Return, motion for, 144.

Unparliamentary expressions, 194.

'Urgency' Motion for adjournment of House, 111, 117, 152.

Vacation of seat, 58, 60, 62, 67, 69.

'Vote' ('Blue Paper'), 86.

Vote, Excess, 265; and Public Accounts Committee, 279.
of censure upon Government, 110, 113, 117.
of Chairman of Committee, see Casting vote.
of Credit, 266.
of Member pecuniarily interested, 183.
of Speaker, see Casting vote.
on Account, 264, 267.
Supply, see Supply.

Vote Office, 81, 95, 96.

'Votes and Proceedings', 80, 86, 91, 93.
Office, 93.

Voting, see Division.

Waiver of privileges infringed by House of Lords, 286.

Ways and Means, Chairman of, 78; and Opposed Private Business, 113, 116, 142, 165; and supervision of Private Bills, 293.
Committee of, see under COMMITTEES:—I. Committee of Whole House.

Westminster, Palace of, 82.

'Wharncliffe Orders, 295.

'White Paper', 89.

Withdrawal, of Member by direction of Speaker, 197; of Motion, 170; of petition relating to Private Bill, 307; of Private Bill, 307; of Public Bill, 164.

Witness before Select Committee, 246; and freedom from arrest, 65, 72; misconduct of, 72.

Writ for election of Member, at bye-election, 67, 68, 140; during recess, 68; in respect of new Parliament, 100.